Sean O'Connor is a writer, director and producer working in theatre, radio, television and film. He has worked as showrunner on several major TV series including *EastEnders*, *Hollyoaks*, *Footballers' Wives* and *Minder*. He produced Terence Davies' film version of Terence Rattigan's *The Deep Blue Sea*, starring Rachel Weisz and Tom Hiddleston. He was also editor of *The Archers* for BBC Radio 4. For the theatre he adapted Boileau and Narcejac's *Vertigo* and Winston Graham's *Marnie*. His adaptation from Shakespeare, *Juliet and Her Romeo*, marked the re-opening of Bristol Old Vic, directed by Tom Morris, and was published by Oberon. *Handsome Brute*, a study of the 1940s murderer Neville Heath, and *The Fatal Passion of Alma Rattenbury* are both published by Simon & Schuster.

For Rob Haywood

THE HAUNTING
OF BORLEY RECTORY

The Story of a Ghost Story

SEAN O'CONNOR

**SIMON &
SCHUSTER**

London · New York · Sydney · Toronto · New Delhi

First published in Great Britain by Simon & Schuster UK Ltd, 2022
This edition published in Great Britain by Simon & Schuster UK Ltd, 2023

1 3 5 7 9 10 8 6 4 2

Simon & Schuster UK Ltd
1st Floor
222 Gray's Inn Road
London WC1X 8HB

www.simonandschuster.co.uk
www.simonandschuster.com.au
www.simonandschuster.co.in

Simon & Schuster Australia, Sydney
Simon & Schuster India, New Delhi

A CIP catalogue record for this book is available from the British Library

Paperback ISBN: 978-1-4711-9479-5
eBook ISBN: 978-1-4711-9478-8

Typeset in Sabon by M Rules
Printed and Bound in the UK using 100% Renewable
Electricity at CPI Group (UK) Ltd

There is no doubt that much could be said about Borley that will never be published. It concerns the private lives of individuals and is only indirectly concerned with the supernatural.

Joe Burroughs, *The Haunted Rectory*, BBC[1]

We do not understand. We cannot understand. We are too finite to understand. The really big things we cannot grasp as yet.

Thomas Edison[2]

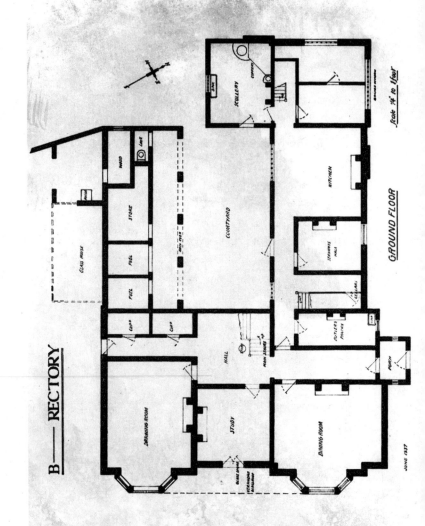

B —— RECTORY

GROUND FLOOR

Scale ¼" to 1 foot

DRAWING ROOM

STUDY

DINING ROOM

HALL

STORE

FUEL

FUEL

Cup'd

Cup'd

GLASS HOUSE

COURTYARD

PANTRY

MAIN STAIRS

SERVANTS HALL

CELLARS

BUTLERS PANTRY

PORCH

KITCHEN

SCULLERY

LARDER

VERANDAH on BALCONY

JUNE 1937

B —— RECTORY

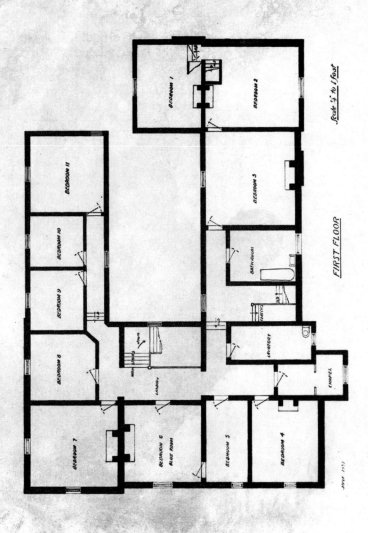

FIRST FLOOR

Scale ⅛ to 1 Foot

JULY 1951

Contents

PART THREE: THE HUNTED

Borley Rectory, 1937

FOREWORD

We all wonder about death, but we don't understand it. Ghost
stories are speculations, little experiments in death. We try it
on for size – it never quite fits. Good, we say, it's nothing to
do with us, this death. But what about that death over there;
what's that one about?

Audrey Niffenegger[1]

The British are less sceptical than they like to believe. Despite
advances in science and technology, since the Second World War
Britain has witnessed an increasing belief in the existence of
ghosts. In 1950, an estimated 10 per cent of the population said
they believed in ghosts, with only 2 per cent claiming to have actually seen one. But by 2014, over a third of Britons said that they
believed in ghosts and 14 per cent said they had seen, felt or heard
one. Thirty-nine per cent believed that a house could be haunted.
This is in contrast to the belief in other supernatural beings such
as witches, fairies and vampires, which has dwindled significantly
since the last century. More British people currently believe in
ghosts than they do in the Devil. Only angels attract similar levels
of belief to ghosts.[2]

Borley Rectory reached the peak of its fame during the interwar
years and its notoriety was a reflection of those anxious times, as the
world recuperated from one international cataclysm and prepared
for the next. It was regarded as the 'most extraordinary and best

documented case of haunting in the annals of psychical research.'[3] Hundreds of witnesses catalogued thousands of incidents over many decades. Every creak of the floorboards, drop in temperature, sinister sound or ghostly sighting seems to have been recorded.

The forbidding and isolated Rectory, situated on a windswept ridge on the northern border of Essex, conformed to the classic image of the spooky rural mansion from Gothic literature such as *The Fall of the House of Usher*, *Jane Eyre* and *The Turn of the Screw*. Fuelled by the media, by the Second World War it had become the most famous real-life haunting of its day, prompting vast numbers to visit the site in order to 'see the ghosts'.[4] Following its publication in 1940, Harry Price's popular bestseller, '*The Most Haunted House in England*'; *Ten Years' Investigation of Borley Rectory*, inspired almost a franchise of books, plays, newspaper features and radio broadcasts. There was even a plan for a Hollywood feature film with a script by the American writer Upton Sinclair.[5]

Though some elements of the Borley story were almost a pastiche of the traditional English ghost narrative – phantom coaches, headless horsemen – the most intense period of activity took place in the midst of a technological revolution in an era of photography, telegrams, telephones, radios and motor cars. This was a vibrantly modern world of extraordinary advances of which the previous generation had only dreamed. Messages could be simply transmitted from one part of the globe to another by electric telegraph, disembodied voices were routinely broadcast from a cabinet in every sitting room in the country, and flickering monochrome images projected onto screens in ornate picture palaces could not only move, but from 1927 could talk as well. The notion of communication by unseen powers was no longer the preserve of science fiction, magic or the supernatural but an everyday reality.

Britain before the First World War was less intimately acquainted with death than any other generation since the Industrial Revolution.[6] From the 1880s onwards, the death rate had fallen to such an extent that, in 1899, an essay in the *Fortnightly Review*, 'The Dying of Death',[7] confidently declared that 'death is disappearing from our thoughts'. The ostentatious funerals and excessive mourning that had characterised the early Victorian period had given way to simpler affairs. By the time Queen Victoria died, in January 1901, Edward VII insisted that the official mourning for his mother should not continue beyond April of that year, lest it affect the English social season.[8] For a nation that had assumed it had tamed death, the Great War came as a terrific shock, being confronted with it on an industrial scale. Sigmund Freud wryly observed at the time that 'death will no longer be denied; we are forced to believe in it. People really die'.[9] At the front, with the remains of many casualties merely mangled body parts, chaplains were unable to give decent burials and clergy at home were ill-equipped to answer the profound questions that such losses prompted in the bereaved: how could an omnipotent God allow such wholesale slaughter? Christianity itself seemed inadequate, unable to comfort a nation riven by grief, leading many in the post-war period to look for comfort beyond the orthodox churches. Attempting to contact the dead became a national pastime and for some, a new religion.

At the beginning of the twentieth century, in his anthology of real-life supernatural tales, Charles G. Harper lamented that 'the era of the "haunted house" [had] long been on the wane':

> There is too much intellectual priggishness prevalent nowadays for the fine old crusted tales of the Moated Grange and its spectral inhabitants to attract more than an amused tolerance, as things only fitted for children.[10]

Many a ghost-ridden mansion had been demolished, and ghosts, sighed Harper, did not 'very appropriately haunt houses less than a hundred years old'. The Irish journalist Elliott O'Donnell similarly despaired of a haunted house he visited near Windsor in 1920, 'sorely out of place among the modern villas that the vandal builder of the twentieth century had erected on all sides of it'.[11] As post-war rural England was increasingly consumed by characterless suburbs, the landscape defaced with motorways, pylons and telegraph poles, a particular vision of English heritage seemed to be in danger, the haunted house itself on the verge of extinction. Even the Society for Psychical Research, the leading paranormal body in Britain, failed to publish any major investigation of hauntings between 1894 and 1923.[12] But at the end of the 1920s, Borley Rectory would reignite the popular fascination with the haunted house, redefining its iconography for the age of the wireless and the tabloid.

Like a golden-age crime novel, the story is set in a lonely country house with a cast of eccentric characters who are examined by a flawed and ambiguous investigator, the celebrated ghost hunter Harry Price. Much of the fascination of the story relates to its setting. A rectory in Jane Austen and Anthony Trollope is a particularly English symbol of order, continuity and faith. What dark forces could threaten such a bastion of probity? 'It is a curious fact,' Price observed, 'that the clergy appear to be more frequent percipients or witnesses of psychic phenomena than men of any other calling.'[13] The testimony of the inhabitants of the house – clergymen and their families – seemed beyond reproach. Though it echoes with the Anglican tone of an M. R. James ghost story, the history of Borley Rectory is suffused with Roman Catholicism, a belief structure hundreds of years old that had been violently cauterised from national culture and consciousness, then dismissed as superstition. But it had defiantly refused to die. The mystery at the heart of Borley Rectory remains elusive. Many key witnesses contradict themselves or change their minds – as does Price, the detective figure tasked with unravelling the clues.

Since the publication of *The Most Haunted House in England*, subsequent examinations of the case have been doggedly partisan – with some dismissing the haunting as an elaborate hoax and others insisting it is one of the greatest examples of verifiable paranormal activity in the history of psychical research. The investigation of the haunting continues to fiercely polarise opinion; there is no consensus. But it remains hugely influential in the study of the paranormal and even more so in fiction, providing the template for

Shirley Jackson's *The Haunting of Hill House*, Richard Matheson's *Hell House* and Stephen King's *The Shining*, as well as influencing the American horror franchise *The Amityville Horror*. Borley holds a particularly intense grip on television audiences in reality formats such as *Most Haunted* – which is indebted to the title of Price's famous book – as well as drama series such as *American Horror Story*, *The Haunting of Hill House* and *The Haunting of Bly Manor*, experiments in camp which aim perhaps to entertain rather than to scare. But to the uncertain, exhausted world between the wars, devastated by grief and startled into an age of mass communication and dizzying technology, to some the story of Borley Rectory seemed to answer the most profound question about the nature of human survival beyond death, and to offer, at last, what religion had failed to do but which science now demanded: proof.

The grave of Reverend Harry Foyster Bull

PROLOGUE

DEATH OF A RECTOR

14 June 1927

The spot's about as unromantic as a cabbage patch. That's why
I think it's genuine. It's about the last place one would pick to
pitch a ghost story. It doesn't look a place for ghosts.

H. E. Pratt[1]

It started with the death of the rector.

On 9 June 1927, 64-year-old Harry Foyster Bull died in his
sleep at Borley Rectory. He had inherited the Rectory from his
father, Henry Dawson Bull, in 1892. Between them, father and
son had shepherded the small Essex parish through sixty-five years
of extraordinary change, from the heyday of the Victorian era
through the turn of the century, to the Great War and its aftermath.
Reverend Bull's death was more than the loss of a parish priest; it
was the end of an era.

The funeral at Borley on the following Tuesday morning was a
large county affair with standing-room only in the small country
church packed with relatives, clergy, local landowners and gentry.
Every family in the district was represented, including the church
warden William Bigg, as well as local dignitaries such as Sir George
and Lady Whitehouse, and Miles Braithwaite, a former mayor of
the nearby town of Sudbury. The plain oak coffin was carried the
short distance across the road from the Rectory to the churchyard,

followed in procession by the Bishop of Chelmsford, Dr Guy Warman, surpliced clergy and the choir. Behind them, dressed in mourning, were Reverend Bull's grieving widow, Ivy, his stepdaughter and his siblings. Placed on the coffin was his rector's stole. In a touching tribute, local schoolchildren lined the pathway as the funeral cortege proceeded towards the church door. Outside and inside the church, magnificent floral tributes were testament to the popularity of the late rector.[2]

Opening with the hymn 'There is a Land of Pure Delight', the service was led by the deceased's cousin Henry Foyster, rector of All Saints Church, Hastings, where the grandfather they shared had also served as rector. The Bishop then gave a short but passionate address. Harry Bull had been educated at Malvern and Exeter College Oxford, where he had been a popular undergraduate, an excellent oarsman, a talented boxer and a kind, loyal friend. He had been ordained in 1886 and held curacies at County Durham and Chippenham before returning home to Borley as curate to his father. He had then served as rector himself for thirty-five years. What struck the Bishop was the extraordinary love the rector had had for Borley, a place to which he had committed his life. Even when visiting him during his last, sad days, the Bishop had found that the one thing that had exercised Reverend Bull's mind was his church and his people: 'He loved Borley with a great love. It was the great passion of his life.'[3]

The service ended with a setting of 'Nunc Dimittis' played on the organ by Ernest Ambrose, who had played at the church since he was a boy: '*Lord, now lettest thou thy servant depart in peace according to thy word.*' At the committal in the churchyard, as the mourners sang 'Abide with Me', the coffin was lowered into a grave lined with evergreens and flowers. Reverend Bull was buried east of the church, just above the graves of his parents, which, dominated by marble crosses, overlooked the Stour Valley.

But among the bereaved that morning, there was anger as well as sorrow. Though the official cause of death had been registered as heart disease and chronic bronchitis, there were some who doubted it. Harry Bull's younger sisters, Freda, Constance and Ethel, suspected that he had been murdered. What's more, the poison that they believed had killed him had been administered by someone who was also mourning at his graveside. In death, the rector would not rest in peace. And life in the tiny rural village of Borley would never be the same again.

PART ONE

THE HAUNTERS

The front of Borley Rectory from the road

CHAPTER ONE

A FIRST-CLASS GHOST STORY

10–12 June 1929

> Who has not either seen or heard of some house, shut up and
> uninhabitable, fallen into decay, and looking dusty and dreary,
> whence, at midnight, strange sounds have been heard to issue –
> the rattling of chains and the groaning of perturbed spirits?
> A house that people have thought it unsafe to pass after dark,
> and which has remained for years without a tenant, and which
> no tenant would occupy, even were he paid to do so? There
> are hundreds of such houses at the present day ... which are
> marked with the mark of fear – places for the timid to avoid,
> and the pious to bless themselves at, and ask protection from,
> as they pass – the abodes of ghosts, and evil spirits.

> Charles Mackay, *Memoirs of Extraordinary Popular Delusions*
> *and the Madness of Crowds* (1841)[1]

Two years after Harry Bull's death, on Monday 10 June 1929,
a story appeared in the *Daily Mirror* concerning some strange
occurrences at the Rectory.[2] The new incumbent and his wife,
the Reverend and Mrs Eric Smith, had been startled by a series of
peculiar happenings that couldn't be rationally explained. Before
they had arrived at the Rectory the previous autumn, they had
heard rumours that it was haunted.[3] According to the newspaper, Reverend Bull had often spoken of a remarkable experience
he'd had one night, walking along the road outside the Rectory.

First he'd heard the clatter of horses' hoofs, then, on looking around, to his horror he saw an old-fashioned coach driven by two headless men.

The Smiths didn't believe in ghosts and dismissed the rumours as local superstition. But as soon as they moved into the Rectory, they began to hear the sound of slow, dragging footsteps across the floor when they knew there was nobody else in the house. Concerned about these sinister noises, Reverend Smith kept vigil in the room where the sounds had occurred and, armed with a hockey stick, waited for them to resume. Once again, he heard the sound of feet treading the bare boards. He lashed out with the hockey stick at the spot where the footsteps seemed to be coming from, sending the stick whistling through the air. But the mysterious footsteps continued across the room.[4]

Then the Smiths' maid, who they had brought with them from London, declared that she had seen a ghostly nun walking in the wood at the rear of the house. Terrified, she handed in her notice after only two days and returned to the city. She was replaced by a local girl who also claimed to have seen a nun leaning over a gate near the house. Just as Reverend Bull had done, she saw an old-fashioned coach on the lawn in the garden. She witnessed the apparition long enough to note the bay colour of the two coach horses.

These sightings seemed to confirm a local legend relating to a monastery that had once stood on the site of the Rectory. It had been the scene of a tragic – and gruesome – romance. A groom at the monastery had fallen in love with a sister at a nearby Catholic convent. They had clandestine meetings in the wood behind the monastery. When they finally arranged to elope together, another groom had a coach waiting in the road outside the wood so that they could make their escape. Here there were variations on the legend. Some locals said that the nun and her lover quarrelled and that he strangled her in the wood; he was then caught and beheaded for his villainy, together with the other groom. Others said that all three were caught by the monks and that both grooms were decapitated. The lovelorn nun was then bricked up in the walls of the monastery, buried alive. This tale of the tragic nun and ghostly coach had, the *Daily Mirror* correspondent observed, all the ingredients of a first-class ghost story. He now awaited further investigation by psychic experts.

The next day, Tuesday 11 June, Alexander Campbell, the editor of the *Mirror*, telephoned the offices of the National Laboratory for Psychical Research asking to speak to the founder and director of the organisation, Harry Price.[5] Price was the most celebrated ghost hunter of the day – a national figure familiar to the general public as well as to journalists, with a body of published work. Campbell was told by Price's secretary that he was 'lunching at a friend's house' but gave him the telephone number where he could be reached. This was actually the number of Edward Saunders & Son in Cannon Street, one of the largest paper suppliers in London, who made paper bags, greaseproof paper and wrappings for tea. For Price led a double life, juggling his enthusiasm for psychical research with his day job as a paper salesman. The editor duly rang the number and was put through to Price. Campbell excitedly explained that a *Mirror* journalist and photographer were at that moment investigating some remarkable occurrences at a rectory in a small village in Essex. He wondered if Price could help in 'unravelling the mystery'. Would he take up the case? Price, who was known for his desire for a good story over all else, was grateful for the tip-off and said he'd make arrangements to visit the Rectory immediately. Having acquainted himself with the *Daily Mirror* reports, he sent a telegram to the Smiths informing them that he would travel to the village by motor car, arriving around noon the next day. By return he received a desperate plea from Reverend Smith: 'Thank God. Come Quickly. Will expect you for lunch.'[6]

Price was an expert in the exposure of fraud. In the *Sunday Sentinel* on Whit Sunday that year, he had contributed a feature laced with scepticism, entitled 'My Adventures with Ghosts in Haunted Houses'. 'A character in a certain ghost story once remarked,' he wrote, '"Rats is ghosts, and ghosts is rats."'[7]

In nine cases out of ten this is true. Houses often acquire a reputation for being haunted when in reality, they contain nothing worse than rats, or an occasional tramp intent on finding shelter. The silence and darkness of night magnify our terrors. In the full light of day, very few 'ghosts' are about. It is in the stillness of the hours before dawn when, in old houses, the timbers warp and creak, that folk imagine unseen visitants. Still, there is always the tenth case. I have no doubt that some houses contain mysterious forces of which at the moment, we know nothing.[8]

Price would not be an easy investigator to convince. Or fool.

On 12 June, the *Daily Mirror* printed a letter from a Mrs Ernest Byford of Parsonage Farm in Newport, Essex, who shared her experiences at the Rectory from 1886:

Much of my youth was spent in Borley and district with my grandparents and it was common talk that the Rectory was haunted. Many people declared that they had seen figures walking at the bottom of the garden. I once worked at the Rectory, forty-three years ago, as an under-nursemaid, but I only stayed for a month, because the place was so weird. The other servants told me my bedroom was haunted, but I took little notice of them because I knew two of the ladies of the house had been sleeping there before me. But when I had been there a fortnight something awakened me in the dead of night. Someone was walking down the passage towards the door of my room and the sound they made suggested that they were wearing slippers. As the head nurse always called me at six o'clock, I thought it must be she, but nobody entered the room, and I suddenly thought of the 'ghost'. The next morning, I asked the other four maids if they had come to my room, but they all said they had not, and tried to laugh me out of it. But I was convinced that somebody or something in slippers had been along that corridor and finally, I became so nervous that I left. My grandparents would never let me pass the building after dark and I would never venture into the garden or the wood at dusk.[9]

Mrs Byford's testimony seemed to confirm that the strange happenings at Borley were more than a silly-season tabloid news story; the Rectory had been the focus of strange happenings for decades.

Price and his secretary, Lucie Kaye, filled the car – a two-seater Fiat – with their ghost hunters' kit. Lucie was twenty-seven, with blonde bobbed hair and fashionable clothes, and was wonderfully self-possessed and capable. At forty-eight, Price was bald and stocky with a penetrating stare. As a sufferer of frequent migraines, the skin around his eyes was almost black, giving him, at times, an alarming appearance.[10] His eyes 'tended, at first, to be suspicious of you, as if he were uncertain whether you were a mocker or believer'.[11] His voice was a mix of received pronunciation and cockney, betraying his south-east London roots, laced with a stutter that he had developed in his schooldays. He had no interest in clothes; the older and more decrepit his hat and suit, the greater was his affection for them. A heavy pipe-smoker, nothing but Balkan Sobranie Mixture from his tobacconist in London would satisfy him.[12] Though at times he could be nervous and irritable, with a 'peculiar genius for being rude to people', Lucie generally found him a charming, considerate boss.[13]

They had packed all that was necessary for a ghost hunt: felt overshoes, steel measuring tape, screw eyes, lead post-office seals, a sealing tool, adhesive tape, electric bells, batteries and switches, a reflex camera, film packs and flashbulbs, a cinematograph camera and film with remote control, a portable telephone, a notebook with red, blue and black pencils, a ball of string, a torch, matches and a candle, a bowl of mercury and a thermometer. They also packed a medical box, which included a bottle of brandy 'in case member of investigating staff or resident is injured or faints'.[14] The pair headed out in the warm weather on the 60-mile drive to Borley.

Essex is the ancient kingdom of the East Saxons, the most southerly of the three counties that form the eastern plain of England. To the north it is bordered by the River Stour, to the east the North Sea, and to the south the Thames; the rivers Lea and Stort form its western boundary.[15] In the late 1920s, despite its proximity to

London, large parts of the county remained inaccessible by rail. The placid calm of Essex was still unspoiled by the rush and bustle of modern life, and it was as resolutely rural as if it had been on the other side of the country. It had a timeless air, as if its villages had existed for ever, having grown naturally out of the surrounding countryside. London was just a stain on the horizon. Before post-war development and the encroachment of the metropolis, the flat landscape, rarely rising more than 300 feet above sea level, was dominated by intensively cultivated farmland. Agriculture defined the area as well as the people who lived there and worked the land, dictating their activities, monopolising their interests and even providing the distinctive flavour of their speech. The regional dialect was as prevalent as it had been in the nineteenth century and many locals routinely used words that hadn't changed since Saxon times: 'Stop your clanjanderin, do!' an Essex grandmother might reprimand her grandchildren. A rainy day might be 'baingy' and an untidy woman 'slummocky'. Grammar was also specific to the locality: 'I ent seen nothen of shee for a long while.'[16] The character of the district was defined by a sense of humour as well as a guardedness in its attitude towards strangers. The further Price and Lucie drove away from London, the closer they approached a distant, ancient England where language, manners and beliefs were still firmly rooted in the past, barely touched by the technology, communications and speed of the twentieth century.

That Wednesday, 12 June, the British public were still reeling from the drama of the recent general election. It had been the first time that Lucie Kaye – as for all women over the age of twenty-one – had been able to cast her vote. Since 1918 only women over thirty and who owned property had been able to do so. The enfranchisement of young women had been key in deciding the fate of the nation at the polls. The *Daily Mirror* had warned that it was women's duty to vote to 'Keep the Socialists Out', the Labour Party being one step, they shivered, from communists.[17] In a special election feature in the *Sunday Pictorial*, 'It's the Man Who Pays', F. Britten Austin had fuelled the paranoia of British men, arguing that 'women are now in a numerical and effective predominance reducing the mere male to serf level. In his dealings with women man now has no rights, but only duties and liabilities while she has no duties or liabilities, but only rights.'[18]

On polling day, women had been eager to vote early, while hundreds of men took advantage of the prolonged heatwave to sunbathe in the parks. The Conservative leader had run a very personal campaign, led by the slogan 'Safety First! Stanley Baldwin – The Man You Can Trust!'[19] But he had failed to secure the trust (or votes) of an electorate enlarged by a generation of young women. Ramsay MacDonald's Labour Party, whose campaign had focused on the economy and unemployment, formed a minority government, making it only Labour's second term in office. As Price and Lucie drove out of London, the new prime minister further rang the changes by announcing the appointment of Susan Lawrence as Minister of Health. She would join her colleague, Margaret Bondfield, who on the previous Friday had taken up the post of Minister of Labour, making her the first woman cabinet member in British history. In Westminster, if not in Essex, times were changing indeed.[20]

Though Borley is in Essex, it is situated close to the north bank of the River Stour, which divides the county from Suffolk. The nearest town and large village, Sudbury and Long Melford, were over the county border in Suffolk, both of which had shops, pubs, banks and railway stations. At the time, Suffolk remained 'shy and unsophisticated ... a country for the individualist, for the explorer and the lover of loneliness'. The peninsular nature of East Anglia – bounded by the sea, estuaries and marshes – had led to a sense of isolation from the rest of England, the local people awed by a sense of threat; for this was old invasion country – first the Romans, then the Danes. When the Viking 'great heathen army' had invaded the low coastline in the ninth century and made its way up the marshy rivers, many Danish legends had been absorbed into local lore, and tales of Odin's black dogs, their jaws dripping with fire, became the 'Black Shuck', a huge ghostly hound that 'prowls along dark lanes and lonesome field footpaths, where, although his howling makes the hearer's blood run cold, his footfalls make no sound'.[21]

There was no region where 'superstition and ancient folklore kept so strong a hold as Essex', where 'a strong belief in the existence of devils prevailed'. Ghosts, apparitions and spirits were thought to haunt the area's flatlands; a woman in white was said to appear among the ruins of Hadleigh Castle; and Anne Boleyn, perhaps England's most ubiquitous ghost, was believed to visit the nursery of Rochford Hall at night. Another celebrity spectre, the highwayman Dick Turpin, was thought to visit the town of Loughton three times a year, galloping down Traps Hill on his mare, Black Bess. Even an oak tree in Great Hawkwell Wood was thought to be haunted by a shrieking boy whose own mother had murdered him; during the night it was said that his voice could be heard calling, 'Oh, mother, mother, don't kill me!'[22]

In the sixteenth and seventeenth centuries, the Puritans, determined to rid the Protestant Church of the Catholic belief in holy water, exorcism and ghosts, took a stranglehold over Essex. This left the God-fearing locals defenceless against the supernatural forces that they stubbornly continued to believe in. Due to its reputation for the presence of evil spirits, Essex became renowned for witchcraft, more witches being executed there than in any other English county. In 1578, two Borley spinsters, Joan Norfolk and Margaret Welles, 'likewise witches and enchantresses', were tried together for bewitching and murdering another villager, John Fyrmyn.[23] In 1645, the notorious witch-hunter Matthew Hopkins of Manningtree appointed himself Witch-Finder General, 'a trade never hitherto taken up in England'.[24] He is believed to have been responsible for the burning or hanging of over 200 'witches' and boasted of executing sixty women in one year alone.[25] Hopkins's restless spirit was reputed to haunt the upper rooms in the Thorn Hotel at Mistley, which once served as the Witch-Finder General's office.[26]

On the journey to the village, Price and Lucie took turns at the wheel, discussing what the trouble at the Rectory might be:

mischievous adolescents, rats, practical jokers; a media stunt, perhaps? But in the case of Borley there was a sceptical journalist from a national newspaper involved. Price felt that there must be something authentic in the story. He and Lucie reached Sudbury about midday, 'full of hope at what they were about to see'.[27]

The town was built by an ancient crossing of the River Stour, surrounded by water meadows and rolling hills. It had been a centre of the wool industry since the medieval period and, bolstered by the arrival of Huguenots fleeing from France, by the eighteenth century it had become famous for the production of silk. Many of Sudbury's historic three-storey timber-framed houses had been built by prosperous cloth merchants, with distinctive large windows on the first floor to light the looms. Market Hill, the town square, was dominated by the flint-built St Peter's Church, overlooking the market place. In front of the church, a statue erected just before the Great War commemorated the painter Thomas Gainsborough, the town's most famous son. Lucie stopped the car to ask for directions to the Rectory. 'Oh,' one of the local men said, 'you mean the most haunted house in England.'[28] They would find Borley 2¼ miles north-west of Sudbury, taking the road to Long Melford and turning left at Rodbridge Corner. The locals pressed to know what Price was planning to do up at the Rectory: 'No good ever come of seeing ghosts,' they warned darkly.[29]

The land rose gently as they continued to drive a mile or so out of Sudbury. Finally, they reached the long, windswept crest of the hill.

They found Borley more a hamlet rather than a village. On the north side of the road the small stone church with a square bell tower was surrounded by a churchyard full of ancient gravestones and memorials. The pathway to the main door was edged by an avenue of topiary yew trees, curiously formal in this most rural of places. The view from the churchyard looking out over the Stour Valley offered a panorama of rural Suffolk. The fields rolled down to the river and then up again to the distant hills, the sweep wide and spacious. In the middle distance a tiny puff of smoke, as a locomotive found its way along the valley, served to emphasise the remoteness of the spot. Even in early summer, chill north-easterly winds swept across the valley, while those directly from the east brought cold, dry air from Scandinavia. These winds scoured the clay fields and sent up eddies of loam dust, the trees distorted into angular shapes by the force of the gusts. West of the church was a sixteenth-century manor house and across the road a farm and a modern, brick-built cottage. The Rectory itself stood opposite the church, hidden from the road by tall, dark elm trees. Otherwise there was nothing: no pub, no shop, no bus stop or telephone box. Borley was completely isolated, the silence broken only by hens clucking in the lane by the farm and rooks cawing in the empty churchyard.

Lucie swerved the car through the open gate into the semi-circular carriage driveway and stopped on the gravel outside the Rectory. Confronted with the house, she and Price were astonished by its overpowering style and scale. For this was not the honey-stoned, pleasingly symmetrical Georgian rectory of fiction, but a vast Victorian monstrosity in red brick. The side wall facing the road housed the main entrance, which formed the base of an imposing turret topped with fancy ironwork. Nothing about the design or materials from which the Rectory was built seemed to suit its rural setting; it was a suburban imposter. To the left of the main entrance, disfiguring the side aspect of the building, was a bricked-up window, like a blinded eye. To the right were the barred windows of the kitchens and servants' quarters. Rather than a country parsonage, the Rectory gave the impression of a barracks or prison.[30]

At the front door Eric Smith and his wife were anxiously waiting for the visitors with Vernon Wall, the *Daily Mirror* journalist, who had been staying in Sudbury since the weekend. As they got out of the car, Price and his secretary were surprised to find that Smith was of mixed race. Lucie assumed the bespectacled rector was 'pure Indian' and thought him stout ('one might even say, very fat').[31] His English wife, Mabel, seemed 'kindly', but 'a very nervy person to say the least'.[32] They were shown through the small porch and into the hall, quickly absorbing the cold, depressing atmosphere of the house, despite the stove that sat in the well of the turned staircase up to the first floor. The elms outside blocked the light, making the interior of the house dark and gloomy, cowing the visitors 'into a feeling of despair'.[33]

The guests were shown into the dining room to the left of the hallway for lunch. Eric Smith took his place at the head of the dining table, facing his wife, with Lucie to his right and Wall to hers, their backs to the bay window that looked across the lawn. Price sat opposite, with a view of the garden, his back to the 'monstrous' multicoloured marble fireplace he enthusiastically noted was decorated with carved monks – a reference, he presumed, to the Rectory's monastic roots. 'Well executed', he felt, 'but sinister.'[34]

A luncheon of cold roast lamb with mint sauce, salad and boiled potatoes was served by the Smiths' maid.[35] Over the meal, the Smiths outlined how they had come to Borley and what had been troubling them since they'd arrived. Listening to their story, Price found them well travelled, hospitable, intelligent and 'utterly sceptical as regards spirits'.[36] Smith's faith in the goodness of God was as steadfast, Lucie intuited, as the Rock of Gibraltar.[37] Their trust in the powers of professional psychical researchers was like 'a hurt child's cry for assistance'.[38] The couple claimed not to be psychic and knew nothing at all about psychical research. Though puzzled at what they had seen and heard, they weren't afraid that anything would actually harm them. Of course, they admitted, their minds had been turned towards the subject of ghosts owing to so much local gossip but, in spite of this, nothing had occurred that they considered *couldn't* be explained.[39] It was, they told Price, mostly mischievous stuff. Silly, meaningless things, frequently destructive and noisy. But sometimes, *frightening*.[40]

Mary Pearson points to where she saw the phantom coach

CHAPTER TWO

THE THIRTEENTH MAN

1 November 1924–12 June 1929

The house, which somehow seemed to have formed itself,
flying together into its own powerful pattern under the hands
of its builders, fitting itself into its own construction of lines
and angles, reared its great head back against the sky without
concession to humanity. It was a house without kindness,
never meant to be lived in, not a fit place for people or for love
or for hope.

Shirley Jackson, *The Haunting of Hill House*[1]

Eric Smith was forty-four, born and educated in Calcutta (now
Kolkata), the son of a Freemason. He was fond of sport, particularly
athletics, in which he had excelled in his youth, and in middle age
he had the robust build of a rugby player. He had graduated from
the University of Calcutta in 1907 before joining the Indian Civil
Service (ICS) as a clerk. A ban on Indians holding higher posts in
government had been abolished in 1883, but in practice the ICS
offered limited career development to non-whites. The fact that the
examinations were held in London effectively barred Indians from
joining the service, except those wealthy enough to afford the fare.
Clerks of mixed race, like Eric Smith, were excluded from executive
roles in the administration of their own country.

As well as the official strictures imposed on them, social

attitudes to Anglo-Indians in India were superior and racist. Anglo-
Indians found themselves in the uncomfortable position of not being
sufficiently 'English' to be welcomed by the ex-patriate community,
nor were they 'Indian' enough to feel fully integrated into the native
population. Though some Anglo-Indians were highly esteemed, they
were devoid of social prestige.

At the age of thirty-nine, Smith had married Mabel Hart,
a shorthand typist, the eldest daughter of a railway clerk from
Isleworth in Middlesex. Though her mother and grandmother were
from a 'Raj' family and had both been born in India, Mabel had
been born in England. Given the small number of British stationed
in Calcutta, the Smiths and the Harts may have been acquainted or
even related.

In this period, 20 per cent of women Mabel's age in Britain
were unmarried, the situation exacerbated by the loss of 740,000
men in the Great War, when a generation of unmarried women
was declared 'surplus' – or, as the *Daily Mail* gleefully reported,
'superfluous'.[2] At forty-one, Mabel had joined the 'fishing fleet'
of unmarried women who sailed from Britain to India in order to
secure husbands. She and Smith married on 1 November 1924.
Shortly afterwards, she had a miscarriage and was subsequently
unable to conceive, sending her into a depression that ultimately
brought an end to their life in India. Her husband applied to take
two years' furlough from the ICS so that they could travel home to
England. As an uncovenanted civil servant he was not eligible for
the £1,000-per-annum pension that senior white civil servants were
due and instead, despite nearly twenty years of service, he would
leave India with no money and no security.[3] A devout Christian, he
decided that if he could take holy orders in England, he would retire
from the ICS and not return to India.

After a three-week voyage, the Smiths docked in London on
23 February 1926. A little vanity, perhaps: Mabel shaved a couple
of years off her age in the passenger list. Eric then trained for
two years at Chichester Theological College, which followed the
Anglo-Catholic tradition determined to reassert the Catholicity of

the church, embracing greater formality in worship, reintroducing vestments, ceremony, devotional images and sacred music. Many evangelical Anglicans felt marginalised by the growth of Anglo-Catholicism and dismissed Anglo-Catholic clergy as 'unwholesome' and 'sentimental',[4] mocking their elaborate liturgy and vestments as effeminate.

Having completed his training, Eric Smith was then keen to take on his own parish with a property included, known as a benefice or 'living'. But despite his university education and clerical training, he was unable to secure a parish of his own in England. It may be that his ethnicity made it difficult for him to secure a living. There were an estimated 7,128 Indians resident in Britain by 1931, in a total population of 44 million. Though there was a tradition of middle-class Indians in the law, academia, politics and business during the interwar period, the years that followed the First World War had seen an increasing tension in race relations throughout Britain. Race riots had taken place in London, Glasgow, Liverpool and Cardiff. With the shipping industry depressed, jobs were scarce, prompting the Coloured Alien Seamen Order of 1925, which classified colonial workers as 'aliens' and referred to the subsequent enforced repatriation of 'Asiatics'. A 'colour bar' was experienced by non-whites of all classes and backgrounds in the 1920s and '30s. Lodging houses, hotels, bars, restaurants and dance halls would routinely refuse the custom of Black or Asian customers. The writer and first Indian president of the Oxford Union, D. F. Karaka, insisted that 'the Colour Bar is something real – something we have felt. It is not merely an obsession of those of us who complain about it.'[5] One publication described the reality of the welcome afforded to members of the imperial family, such as Eric Smith, returning 'home' to Britain:

> British imperialist agents in the colonies, especially the Church of England missionaries ... try their best to paint England as the most democratic country in the world, where all peoples, irrespective of colour or race, are treated as equals. However, every

negro, Indian, Arab or other coloured person who has ever lived
in England knows from actual experience that all this missionary
twaddle is nothing else but a lie.[6]

Since the death of Harry Bull, Borley Rectory had stood shuttered
and empty for over twelve months. The appointment of a new
rector was the responsibility of the Bishop of Chelmsford and
Reverend Bull's family, who formally remained patrons of the
living. A rector (from the Latin for 'ruler') was responsible for the
administrative operation of a parish. The rectory was not only the
house the rector resided in, but part of a package of duties, rights,
land and salary. Reflecting his high status, in the eighteenth and
nineteenth centuries, a rector would generally reside in a grand
property with some land attached, called the glebe.[7] Where a
rector was absent, a vicar (from the Latin *vicarius*, 'substitute')
was appointed to deputise for the rector in his official duties.[8] The
incumbent rector drew income from parish taxes or tithes amount-
ing to 10 per cent of the worth of the produce of parish lands.
A vicar received smaller tithes and his home was a more modest
building, known as a vicarage. By 1928, lay patronages such as the
one at Borley were increasingly rare as bishops sought more control
over appointments in their diocese. After the death of Harry Bull,
his family left the disposition of the living at Borley solely in the
hands of the Bishop, Dr Guy Warman.

Warman was an evangelical Anglican with progressive views,
refusing, for instance, to wear a bishop's mitre. He had co-founded
the Group Brotherhood in 1905, proposing reform within the
Church. He had little patience with those still fraught about the
challenge to Christian belief made by Darwin's theories and he was
pragmatic about the seductive attractions of paganism as congregations immersed themselves in materialism in the wake of the Great
War. He was no admirer either of what he believed to be reaction-
ary Anglo-Catholics.

By the summer of 1928, having failed to secure a new rector
for Borley, Warman was obliged to offer the living to Eric Smith.

The relationship between them was cool from the start, and over the coming months became icy, with Smith's Anglo-Catholicism at odds with Warman's more radical ambitions for his diocese. Smith was not advised by Warman that the living at Borley had been vacant since Harry Bull's death. Nor was he informed that, due to the sinister reputation that the Rectory had acquired, the position had already been refused by twelve other clergy. Eric Smith was the thirteenth candidate for the job.[9]

Having been used to the frantic heat of Calcutta, when they arrived in the village, the sense of isolation that the Smiths were met with came as a shock.[10] On entering the house, they were further dismayed by its condition: the numbing cold; the smell of damp plaster, dust and decay. It had been built at the height of the Victorian period to accommodate a large family, staffed by an army of servants. The Smiths were childless; it would be just the two of them and a couple of cats in the vast mansion of twenty-six rooms. After Harry Bull's death, all the furniture had been auctioned and the building left empty. In the succeeding year it had fallen into a state of disrepair. The exterior walls were strangled by creepers and ivy. The roof was in a deplorable condition, letting in water, which damaged the walls and plasterwork to such an extent that several of the bedrooms weren't habitable. The structural timbers, creaking and shrunken over time, were riddled with deathwatch beetle, which made a tapping sound in order to attract mates, most audible on quiet nights. As this could often be heard during silent vigils kept by the bedside of the dying, the beetle had long been feared as a harbinger of death.

The kitchen and its cupboards were infested with rats and the cellar had been colonised by newts, lizards and toads.[11] As there was no local rubbish collection, an internal courtyard formed by the three wings of the building was full of domestic waste. There were 'enough bottles and tins to stock a village'.[12] With no gas, the only heat was provided by open fires and an inadequate wood-burning stove in the hall. Without electricity, the gloomy interior was barely illuminated by paraffin lamps and candles, which cast shadows in every room and passage. With no mains supply, drinking water was pumped from a well near the kitchen door and rainwater was collected in a soft-water tank for laundry. Water for bathing and cooking had to be pumped from a well in the courtyard, 80 feet deep and covered with a 6-foot metal plate. A heavy iron wheel was used to pump water by hand up to a large cistern under the eaves. But this would sometimes break down, leaving the house with no sanitation at all. The cesspit in the garden was foul and the only bathroom suite – in the room above the porch – was damaged.[13] Though the Smiths reported the state of the Rectory to the Bishop and the Sanitary Inspector, no action was taken.

The situation at Borley wasn't unusual. By 1925, 20 per cent of English rectories were considered unsuitable for modern life because of their size or condition. Consequently, between 1919 and 1939, nearly 2,000 of the 12,000 rectories in England were sold off by the Church, relics of a more prosperous, more confident age.[14] Since 1923, any improvements to a rectory were the responsibility of the incumbent rector, not the Church. The Smiths would be obliged to spend £200 of their own savings on making the house habitable. It was a large property, so the rates were also very high. Even before they moved into the house, they worried if they could afford to live there. But despite their misgivings, both were committed to their mission and looked forward to putting what seemed to be a very neglected parish – and an equally neglected rectory – in order.

The Smiths found that the farms in the district surrounding the Rectory grew predominantly arable crops, cultivated by traditional agricultural processes. Despite an increase in the use of tractors and steam engines since the war for harrowing and ploughing, horses continued to be the heart of British farming. Consequently, there was plenty of work for blacksmiths, who would also supply and repair agricultural implements – scythes, sickles, hay-rakes and pitchforks. Small fields with miles of ancient hedgerows, together with the retained stubble and grain during the winter, sustained a large population of native birds. Conditions for agricultural workers, though, were hard. In 1921, having previously encouraged the establishment of thousands of new smallholdings, the government abandoned wage controls while resuming the importation of cheap foreign food. The short post-war agricultural boom was over and farm prices collapsed. Wages for agricultural workers fell from thirty-seven shillings a week in 1921 to twenty-four shillings three years later. Many new landowners struggled to pay mortgages they had only recently taken on. Some were also staggered to find that they were obliged to pay an additional sum, which, as tenants, had previously been hidden in their rent. This hugely unpopular levy, known as tithe, was an ancient tax, two thirds of which was paid to the Ecclesiastical Commission at Westminster Abbey and amounted to a substantial yearly income – £3,000,000 – for the Church of England.

There was no public transport between Borley and Sudbury,[15] the nearest town, so the diet of rural workers on low incomes had deteriorated as they had limited access to shops that offered goods at more competitive prices. Like 25 per cent of English parishes at the time, there was no piped water supply in the area and very few farms had access to the national grid. Life for the majority of parishioners at Borley was little advanced from that of their Victorian forbears. As the agricultural depression had taken hold, many farms had become impoverished, equipment was left to rust and farm buildings, hedges and ditches became dilapidated.

The summer of 1928 was one of seismic change for the increasingly beleaguered Church of England. The longstanding Archbishop of Canterbury, Randall Davidson, had announced his resignation after a quarter of a century. He had served in the post longer than any archbishop since the Reformation and, in a break with tradition, was the first to retire. He left the Church in conflict with the government and struggling with bitter internal division. In June, he had failed to secure support from the House of Commons for the proposed revisions to the 1662 *Book of Common Prayer*. When the bishops proposed to sanction the use of the revised version without the assent of Parliament, the Bishop of Birmingham, Ernest Barnes, cautioned that such a course of action would be disastrous, leading to the eventual disestablishment of the Church.[16]

In October 1928, the Church Congress at Cheltenham publicly exposed the various divisions and factions that were weakening the Church. The Bishop of Durham, Dr Hensley Henson, fiercely rebuked Anglo-Catholics and insisted that they should be reprimanded if they continued to promote High Church doctrine and ritual instead of the core articles of the Anglican creed. He warned that the economic dislocation caused by the war had left England in a 'state of moral chaos', alarmingly similar to that which had preceded the revolutions in France and Russia.[17] Canon Streeter of Hereford agreed that 'the masses had begun to ask questions'; young people were far more likely to learn about moral and religious questions from writers like George Bernard Shaw or H. G. Wells than they were from the Church.[18] The Church must begin to think, write and preach in the language of the modern world if it was to stand any chance of survival. Always controversial, Ernest Barnes also used the conference as a forum to discuss his beliefs about life after death, which, he felt, had been 'brought into clear relief' by Einstein's 'doctrine' of relativity.[19] As Einstein had demonstrated, if space and time – like body and personality – formed a single complex, mankind 'had no right to postulate that in the world to come part of this complex will be destroyed while the other remains intact.'

As the Church Congress continued to broadcast the Church's crises of identity and purpose, the *Daily Mirror* reported that Sir Arthur Conan Doyle, the novelist and great advocate of spiritualism, suggested, in contrast, that there had been a boom in spiritualist churches since the war, with as many as 550 in Britain, with 200,000 believers. He imagined that in the future every police station would have a clairvoyant in attendance, acting as a sort of psychic detective: 'every offence will be hunted down so that crime will become very difficult, if not impossible'.[20] Doyle anticipated that clairvoyants would be able to tell who actually committed a crime. 'If you give them a portion of a dress of a murdered person,' he said, 'they are frequently able to throw themselves back to the time of a murder and get a kind of intimation of the circumstances of the murder and how it was done.'[21]

The Smiths moved into the Rectory on 2 October 1928, bringing with them a maid from Clacton, who they'd engaged in London.[22] Charles Pilgrim, a steady, reliable old man who lived in the village, was employed to work in the garden.[23] They decided to live in only five of the rooms in the house: the drawing room, dining room, library and two of the bedrooms in the old servants' quarters in the corner of the house – the rest of the rooms, even the principal bedrooms, being uninhabitable. The damaged bathroom suite was thrown away and they fitted a modern bathroom, with a hot-water cylinder and an airing cupboard in one of the bedrooms. Hot water for the kitchen was provided by its stove, a coal-fired system, much like an Aga. But with so many doors and large windows throughout the house, the Smiths soon realised how icy-cold and draughty living there was going to be.

During the first two days, they worked hard putting the house in order, though they were chilled by rumours from the locals that the Rectory garden had once been the site of a plague pit. One afternoon, Mabel was clearing out the cupboards in the library when she came across a pile of rubbish. Among it, she was shocked to find a human skull. In pristine condition with perfect teeth, it seemed to be the skull of a young woman. They had this gruesome find buried in the churchyard across the road. But it left them unsettled, discomforted, uneasy.[24] Mabel also noticed that the door to the cellar that she had previously found locked before they moved in was now open and she was able to look inside. The cellar was piled with empty wine bottles. She came across a small bottle that seemed newer and cleaner than the others. It was labelled 'Poison'.[25]

On the third day of their occupancy, realising that the maid had been working constantly since they had arrived, Mabel suggested that as it was a fine autumn afternoon, the girl might like to take a break and go out for a ride on her bicycle, and perhaps get to know the locality. This she did. But a few minutes later she returned in a state of hysteria, her clothes covered in mud. She had been cycling past the front gate when she saw the figure of a nun. Giving the nun a second glance, she realised she could see right through her. 'I was so frightened,' she told the Smiths, 'that I fell off my bicycle into the ditch.'[26] They smiled and frowned; the girl must have imagined it. But she was insistent; she was quite sure of what she had seen. Despite their protestations, the maid handed in her notice immediately. Coming from India, where servants were plentiful and cheap, the prospect of running the large house without help was daunting. With neither staff nor telephone, the Smiths felt even more isolated.

Over time they began to feel that there was something not right at the Rectory. At night, when they retired to bed, they heard heavy, muffled footsteps passing their bedroom door and they'd find that doors and windows had been opened or closed, with no explanation. One afternoon, Eric Smith was in the house alone when, on walking through the archway from the master bedroom to the landing, he heard sibilant whisperings over his head. At a loss to explain them, he walked slowly across the landing, but the sounds followed. As he passed back under the archway, the whispering stopped abruptly, as though a wireless set had been switched off. He returned across the landing but the sound had gone. Wondering if some of the locals might be playing a trick, one evening he waited by the dark landing armed with a hockey stick, hoping to catch out any hoaxers. As before, the whispering started – as though three people were talking together in hushed voices. Smith quickly dashed onto the landing and hit out left and right with the hockey stick. But there was nobody there. The whispering continued, then suddenly stopped as though the voices had vanished into the wall.[27]

Not wanting to alarm her, Smith didn't mention the strange noises to his wife. Mysterious things continued to happen. The tablecloth laid for breakfast would be found tugged and crooked in the morning, the crockery out of place. The house cats would often seem to be staring intently at something invisible. And late at night, it sounded as though bricks were being hurled with great force at the ceiling in the Smiths' bedroom.[28]

Alone in the house late one evening and hearing the gate being opened, Mabel hoped that nobody was coming to call at such a late hour. Being in so isolated an area, she was nervous of going out to the front door to see who it was, so she took a paraffin lamp and went to look out of one of the windows. As she lifted the lamp, she saw what appeared to be two headlamps and the outline of some sort of vehicle in the drive, perhaps a coach. But there was no sound of a car or other vehicle. Shortly afterwards, when her husband came home, she mentioned what she had seen, but he assured her that the drive was empty.[29]

As was the custom, every afternoon for the first six weeks after their arrival, Mabel received calls from the well-to-do matrons of the parish. These included Lady Whitehouse, who lived nearby at Arthur Hall on the Melford Road. She was also visited by Mrs Payne of Borley Hall, the ancient manor house down by the River Stour, and Mrs Bigg, a farmer's wife who was the Smiths' nearest neighbour, living across the road next to the church, at Borley Place. Curious to meet the new arrivals from India, they found the Smiths' manners alien, their tastes foreign. Anglo-Indians returning to England, George Orwell observed, with their carved teak furniture, brass trays, yellowing photographs of men in sun-helmets and Hindustani vocabulary, created 'a sort of little world of their own ... a kind of cyst.' He felt that it was 'almost impossible, when you get inside these people's houses, to remember that out in the street it's England and the twentieth century. As soon as you set foot inside the front door you're in India in the eighties.'[30] The ladies would stay for exactly fifteen minutes before departing, leaving their card in a metal bowl on the table in the hall. Mabel was greeted with sympathy, if not pity: 'You are brave. I wouldn't stay [here] another day.'[31] With growing unease, the Smiths began to learn the legends associated with the house from the villagers – the forlorn nun, the phantom coach. The well-travelled and well-educated Smiths, however, thought the locals – many of whom were illiterate – were simply steeped in 'country ignorance'.[32]

Eric Smith soon began to realise that stepping into Harry Bull's shoes would not be easy. Borley was a small, tight-knit rural community of only 121 parishioners, who had always enjoyed a good relationship with their rector, who had acted, in effect, as the local squire. The Bulls, their tastes, habits and network of relationships had been integral to the life of the village since the middle of the nineteenth century. Since Harry Bull's death, and his widow's departure from the house, the villagers had been able to behave as they wished, with courting couples and children using the Rectory at their convenience. Many of them didn't want a new clergyman occupying the Rectory. They didn't welcome an Anglo-Catholic rector, with his belief in ritual, the intercession of saints and the Virgin Mary, when they had contentedly followed the Low Church ministry of the Bulls since the 1860s. Not only was Smith Anglo-Catholic, he was a foreigner, and a brown foreigner at that. Having such a different background and experience, Eric Smith struggled to relate to the well-to-do members of the parish or to the increasingly desperate farmworkers trying to make ends meet. As far as the locals were concerned, he was an interloper. At the same time. William Bigg of Borley Place had been churchwarden during Harry Bull's time, dealing with church matters since his death. He resented relinquishing his authority now that the new rector had arrived. This made Smith's church responsibilities difficult. The parish was at the heart of the little rural community, and the rector and his wife were leading figures in it. As well as daily services, he would celebrate christenings, weddings, funerals and the major events in the church calendar. His wife would provide much of the administrative help for parish matters and for local charities, alongside the running of the large and inconvenient house. The Rectory hosted mothers' meetings, choir practice on Friday evenings, Sunday School and parish meetings. It was used, effectively, as a community centre. The locals were used to having regular access to the public rooms of the house, including those on the upper floor, where the lavatory and the schoolroom were situated. But since the arrival of the new rector and his wife, many would refuse to come to meetings at the Rectory, nor would they walk past it after dark.[33]

After the departure of their maid, Mabel Smith contacted an agency that was the main supplier of domestic servants in the region. Following the Great War, servants had become hard to source and difficult to keep. Young women used to the freedom and higher wages in wartime factories were reluctant to return to the conditions, regulations and poor pay of domestic service. Mrs Smith engaged Mary Pearson, a fifteen-year-old girl who came from the nearby village of Belchamp Walter.[34] She was, to the Smiths' relief, a 'sensible, nice girl'.[35] As well as a domestic support to Mrs Smith, with whom she developed a warm relationship, Mary also became witness to the strange happenings at the Rectory.

One night after dark, Mabel was returning to the Rectory from the church, entering the house at the back door, by the scullery. She noticed that there seemed to be a light in the schoolroom on the first floor, and presumed that it must be Mary. When Mrs Smith asked her, Mary insisted that she hadn't been in the schoolroom at all. They went upstairs together, only to find the room in darkness.[36] On another night, around twilight, the Smiths had gone out for the evening, leaving Mary alone in the house. She was understandably nervous, given the rumours she'd heard about the ghosts. She had gone to lock the library door and was looking through the window, across the veranda, when she saw what she took to be a horse and cart crossing the Rectory lawn. Or could it have been a coach?[37]

For much of the time, the Smiths didn't take the strange phenomena at the Rectory seriously. Mabel and Mary would often laugh together about the very idea of ghosts.[38] Mary's boyfriend, 25-year-old Fred Tatum, a local bad lad who'd been convicted for stealing rabbits and did odd jobs around the house and garden, also joined in the fun. He'd often play the fool by walking around with his coat over his head, pretending to be a headless spook.

However, the strange noises and occurrences got worse. They

would find keys from the doors on the floor, 2 or 3 feet away, as though they had been shot from the locks. The house bells, formerly used to summon the servants, would ring around the Rectory incessantly. These were rung by a cord or lever in each room; the bell wires ran through tubes in the walls to a lever in the attic and fed through the rooms on both floors of the house – eighteen bells in all. A board in the kitchen passage indicated in which room the bell had been rung. Now the bells would ring at all hours of the day and night, to such an extent that an exasperated Reverend Smith had many of the wires cut. But still they would ring, without, it seemed, human agency. Puzzled, rather than alarmed, the Smiths decided to consult the surviving siblings of Harry Bull. What could be behind the strange happenings at the Rectory? Might it be locals playing pranks? Or something more sinister?

The unmarried Bull sisters lived together at Chilton Lodge in Great Cornard, just outside Sudbury. Ethel, Freda and Constance had all been born and raised at the Rectory and it had been their home until their brother Harry had married. The sixty-year-old Ethel Bull found the new rector 'quite charming, but an ignoramus in psychic matters'. His wife, whom she did not take to, seemed to her to be 'frightened of shadows'. Miss Bull confirmed to the Smiths that the Rectory was indeed haunted and that, many years before, she had seen the ghostly nun in the garden with her own eyes. What's more, this incident had been witnessed by three of her seven sisters. She confirmed that the window in the dining room at the Rectory had been bricked up by their father because they hadn't wanted to see the nun leaning over the gate outside and staring in at the window when they were eating. She also went on to share some family confidences. All was not as it seemed, so she and her sisters believed, with the death of their brother. They were convinced that their sister-in-law had unduly influenced Harry during his illness. Shortly before his death, he had altered his will, in which he had left his wife a life interest in his estate.[39] His siblings were to receive nothing until Ivy's death. After he died, she and her daughter moved out of the Rectory and the sisters found a bottle half-full of sugar of lead in the cellar.

Also known as lead acetate, the compound served innocent domestic functions, being routinely used in cosmetics and for thinning paints and varnishes – but in high doses it could be fatal. It was this bottle that Mabel Smith had discovered in the cellar on their arrival at the Rectory and which the Bull sisters suspected Ivy had used to poison their brother. A conventional couple, the Smiths found this scenario extremely unnerving. They had taken on an expensive and inconvenient house, which was already plagued by strange phenomena that they couldn't explain. Now it appeared to be the background to an unpleasant inheritance squabble, if not murder.

The severe winter of 1928 was one of the coldest on record. Ice froze the River Thames for the first time in a generation. The country roads around Borley were impassable with snow and Eric Smith went about his parish duties on foot in icy temperatures, leaning into the bitter north-easterly winds. Surrounded by dozens of empty rooms, they found the dilapidated house difficult to heat and impossible to protect from the harsh weather. Mabel Smith, so used to the Indian climate, began to detest the unforgiving cold of the rural English winter.

The weeks leading up to Christmas were increasingly grim. The local *Framlingham Gazette* printed a dour review of a year of 'despair in agriculture, bad trade and an overwhelming amount of unemployment'.[40] Throughout Advent, as they prepared for one of the busiest periods of the Church year, the Smiths felt tormented by ghosts. That year's newspaper advertising campaign for Bovril was a line drawing of an Elizabethan wraith, complete with chains around his wrists, reading a newspaper advertisement proclaiming '*Bovril: the Proved Body Builder.*'[41] At 9.15 p.m. on 22 December, after a programme of carols and Christmas music, the BBC broadcast a talk about ghosts by the historian and writer Gerald Heard.[42] This was followed on Christmas Eve by a reading of E. F. Benson's 'flesh-creeper' *The Confession of Charles Linkworth,* a chillingly modern ghost story. In it, the spirit of an executed murderer, desperate to confess his crimes, makes telephone calls from beyond the grave to the doctor who had conducted his post-mortem.

As well as the tale of foul play regarding Harry Bull's death, Mabel picked up gossip in the village of more tragedy from the Rectory's dark past. It was rumoured that in the previous century, a female servant had given birth to Henry Dawson Bull's child, but the baby had been hidden away.[43] A cook, it was said, had died in mysterious circumstances in the kitchen in the rector's arms. Inspired by these gruesome legends, during the winter evenings, Mabel started to write a story of her own. She already wrote as a hobby – mostly fiction and devotional stories. Her tale was not a ghost story, though, but a murder mystery. Putting her recent experiences and grim surroundings to creative use, Mabel's novel was set in a large, creepy house in an isolated rural village, haunted by legends and superstition; it all began with the discovery of a skull in a cupboard. She was rather pleased with the title, which she thought 'most lurid': *Murder at the Parsonage*.[44]

At the beginning of January, after fewer than six months in the Rectory, Mabel was finding the house not only depressing, but oppressing. Her husband was increasingly concerned that, she being already highly strung, the house itself was draining her of energy, infecting her moods and making her ill. It was becoming impossible for him to carry out his normal parish duties, so concerned was he about her welfare; he 'always worried over [her] and hated to think [she] might get frightened'.[45] Some sort of drastic action was needed.

The Smiths appealed to Dr Warman that the living conditions at the Rectory were intolerable and requested a transfer to another parish. Mabel stressed the fact that, as well as the appalling condition of the property, it was rumoured to be haunted. The Bishop, however, was a formidable character and firm administrator. Harry Bull had lived happily at Borley Rectory for over thirty years without any such fuss about ghosts; the Smiths had been resident there for only a matter of months. Warman felt that the new incumbent and his wife – needy and neurotic in equal measure – were raising an unnecessary 'mare's nest' and dismissed their complaints.

Warman's disdain for Eric Smith was also complicated by his own personal ambitions; he was to take over as Bishop of Manchester early in 1929 and must have had little patience for the Smiths' local difficulties. At the same time, the Ecclesiastical Commission had plans for Borley. On Harry Bull's death, the Church had bought the freehold of the Rectory from the Bull family. But behind closed doors, they had decided that the tiny rural parish was surplus and that it should be united with that of nearby Liston. In the November of 1928, with Warman's approval, the Commission had agreed that the two parishes would be amalgamated the next time a vacancy came up in one of them. The incumbent rector of the two parishes would live at the much more comfortable Liston Rectory, earning a substantially higher salary of £400 a year. Borley Rectory would be sold. This would have been an ideal solution for the Smiths, but it was not suggested to them as a possibility. As far as Warman was concerned, no alternative living would be offered to Eric Smith; it was Borley or nothing. When Warman took up his post in Manchester in January 1929, the Smiths may have hoped that his successor, Henry Wilson, would look on their situation more sympathetically, but he was equally dismissive, if not more so, rejecting their concerns with 'sulphurous sarcasm'.[46]

On Whit Sunday, 19 May, Mabel came across Harry Price's feature in the *Sunday Sentinel* in which he had declared, 'I have no doubt that some houses contain mysterious forces of which at the moment, we know nothing.' Might the Rectory be a 'tenth case' that he wrote of, infected by such mysterious forces? With she and her husband strangers to the village, with few friends and no support forthcoming from the diocese, Mabel decided to write to their daily newspaper, the *Mirror,* for advice. The couple were keen to consult a psychical research organisation to investigate the Rectory. She wanted to prove that there was nothing sinister or supernatural there and to reassure the 'rustics' of the parish that there were no ghosts, only 'silly tales'.[47] At the same time, this strategy would have an additional purpose: an official investigation might also add weight and credibility to their requirement to the new Bishop that they be relocated to another parish. Naively, perhaps, having requested the expertise of a psychical researcher to hunt a ghost, the Smiths had not anticipated the arrival on their doorstep of a journalist hungry for a story.

The Summer House

CHAPTER THREE

Sixteen Hours of Thrills!

12–13 June 1929

It would be difficult to imagine a more ghostly place than Borley. The very atmosphere is uncanny, and as one moves through passages and corridors, one instinctively feels that he is back again in the dead ages. Conversation is suddenly interrupted by a noise or a tapping for which there is no natural explanation and as one treads from one old fashioned room to another, the very flooring seems to echo with sinister sounds.

Midland Advertiser, 21 November 1929[1]

After a pudding of seasonal gooseberry tart,[2] Price and Lucie proceeded to make an assessment of the house and gardens, the site covering 3.7 acres in all. When it was first built, the Rectory had been L-shaped, but some years later another wing had been added. This made the building an almost complete rectangle, with an uncovered brick courtyard, leaving it an awkward-shaped rabbit warren. On the ground floor were a large and lofty drawing room and dining room, each 20 feet by 16 feet and nearly 11 feet high, with a bay window overlooking the garden.[3] Outside, these were spanned by a glass-roofed veranda that was accessed by French windows in the library. Aesthetically, this was the true front of the house, rather than the ugly side aspect that faced the church and the road. Price noted that all the main rooms on the ground floor were fitted with heavy wooden shutters and he wondered why they were needed in such a remote country hamlet where even a wandering tramp must have been a novelty.

The servants' quarters – a kitchen, pantry, scullery, dairy, larder and servants' hall – were accessed through a green baize door to the right of the central staircase in the hall. The bars at the windows had not been installed to keep burglars out, but rather to prevent the maids from slipping out surreptitiously at night. Including the French windows, there were five entrances to the house and a trap door in the courtyard giving access to the cellar. As well as the main stairs, two back-staircases allowed access to the floor above. On the first floor, there were eleven bedrooms, including a master bedroom above the library, known as the 'Blue Room'. A bathroom and separate lavatory completed the rooms on the first floor. Price and Lucie climbed a further staircase to the attics, where they crawled on their hands and knees as they pointed their torches, illuminating the signatures of some of the men who had built the house scrawled on the rafters. They searched every nook and cranny, tested all the doors, locks and windows, measured the walls, cupboards and floors, looking for hiding places or secret entrances. But they found nothing. Everything seemed to be in order. Finally, they explored the cellars, which could also be accessed by the kitchen passage. They extended under the main hall, the major part of the library and a corner of the dining room. Switching on their torches, they found the cellars damp and slimy, divided by partition walls and full of empty wine bottles.[4]

They were relieved to get out into the fresh air of the Rectory garden. The grounds were beautiful, long and narrow, with some fine mature trees – elms and copper beeches. At the bottom of the lawn was an ancient cedar of Lebanon next to a large octagonal summer house that backed onto the road. The Smiths believed this had been built by Henry Dawson Bull in order to watch the ghost as she proceeded down the 'Nun's Walk', which ran down the south side of the lawn, east to west, parallel to the boundary wall.[5]

Halfway down the garden was a stream that divided it into two, with a little ornamental bridge. Just across the stream to the right was a small cemetery with several tiny headstones, memorials to 'Jem', 'Rollo' and 'Sandy'; the resting place for Harry Bull's many deceased cats. Another timber summer house, Gothic in design, was almost hidden by brambles at the extreme east end of the garden.[6]

Over tea, the Smiths outlined the various local legends and rumours that they had been told about the Rectory since they had moved in. They advised Price that Harry Bull's sisters at Chilton Lodge would be able to tell him more. It had been arranged for two of them to meet Price that evening and join them for a seance in the Blue Room. This room was thought to be particularly haunted as both Harry Bull and his father had died in it.

Other than the front door and the French windows in the library, Price and Lucie sealed every door and window in the house, inserting screw eyes into each doorpost and window frame, through which they threaded tape that was then knotted and sealed with lead post-office seals. They then settled in for a night-time vigil. The Smiths and Price's secretary were to record any unusual happenings inside the house, with Lucie stationed in the hall by the front door and the Smiths in the drawing room. Price and Wall were to keep watch in the garden. The journalist would watch the Nun's Walk and Price would observe the back of the house where a light had mysteriously appeared in one of the first-floor windows the night before. By dusk, they were smoking their pipes in the summer house opposite the Nun's Walk, waiting for nightfall.

After about an hour of silence and darkness, Wall suddenly grabbed Price's arm. He had seen something; 'There she is!' he whispered.[7] Before Price could stop him, Wall had dashed across the lawn. But owing to the deep shadows, it wasn't possible for him to discern exactly what he had seen. By the time he had reached the Nun's Walk, the figure or apparition – whatever it was – had vanished. Disappointed, and feeling they had missed their opportunity, the two men strolled towards the house, discussing what Wall had seen. But just as they approached the French windows, there was a terrific crash. A pane of glass from the roof of the veranda smashed at their feet, missing them by inches.

They ran inside and up the stairs, together with Lucie, to inspect the room above the veranda. Pointing their torches in the darkness, they found nothing. While in the Blue Room, Lucie noted two particularly ugly red and white vases on either side of the mantelpiece. They then made their way down the stairs, Lucie leading, with Price at the rear. Suddenly, something flew at considerable speed past Wall's head, again missing him by inches. It continued down the staircase, hitting the iron stove in the hall, shattering on the floor. They raced down the stairs, pointing their torches. At the same time, the Smiths rushed out of the drawing room to see what the commotion was. At the base of the stove were the broken pieces of one of the red and white vases that had stood on the mantel in the bedroom. Feeling guilty for having made disparaging remarks about them moments before, Lucie instinctively apologised to the Smiths.[8] She, Price and Wall sat on the stairs in anticipation of more phenomena. They waited in the darkness, alert to any sound or movement.

Just as Wall was about to ask Price if they had waited long enough, an object suddenly hit his hand. It went tumbling down the stairs followed by what appeared to be some pebbles. They ran up the stairs again, but could find nothing that could have propelled the objects. When they returned to the bottom of the staircase and switched their torches on, among the pebbles at the foot of it they found a mothball. Wall laughed at the idea of a ghost throwing mothballs about, but Price told him that the throwing of stones was very common among spirits. There was even a word for the throwing of stones in the lore of witchcraft and demonology: lithobolia.

Now that night had descended, the house was lit only by lamplight. After the excitement, Eric Smith took one of the oil lamps and showed Lucie and Price to the rooms they would be occupying for the night. In the room Lucie was to sleep in, he had hung various holy pictures and said a prayer for her safe-keeping. He then guided them across the landing and showed them into the Blue Room, which had been prepared for Price. Price looked dubious and murmured aside to Lucie that no one had said any prayers for *him*.⁹

At 9.30 p.m., as arranged, Ethel and Mabel Bull were driven over to the Rectory from Great Cornard and introduced to Price, Lucie and Vernon Wall. Fred Tatum went home and Mary Pearson went to bed. The Smiths, having been asked to keep to their room and leave the house to Price's authority, provided their visitors with a Thermos of coffee and some sandwiches before retiring to bed.¹⁰

Cold and depressing,¹¹ the master bedroom was decorated with a gentian blue wallpaper. The room was simply furnished with a bed, a couple of chairs and an old-fashioned dressing table with a mirror in front of the window. To the right of the door was a fireplace with a table in front of it, and there was a wash basin and jug on a stand by the door. A door in the left-hand wall opened into a small dressing room. The Bull sisters sat in the two chairs and the others on the bed. They left the door open and made sure that the window was shut. All was quiet.

After about twenty minutes they heard a distinct knock from near the window. Hushed and tense, they waited. Then it came again: a clear, definite knocking, like a knuckle on wood or the branch of a tree knocking against a window pane. The noise seemed peculiarly regular, so they got up and investigated the room. But the source of the sound wasn't from the window. It seemed to come from the back of the mirror attached to the dressing table. The knocks continued off and on with each of the party's heads within inches of the mirror. Used to the form of seances, Lucie waited for a hiatus in the knocks and then addressed the spirit: 'If any entity is present here tonight, will it please make itself known? One knock for "yes", twice for "no" and three times for "doubtful"'.¹² She began to ask questions and then they talked to an apparently intelligent entity for about an hour, smoking and chatting 'as if [they] were in the Rectory drawing room instead of the room that is supposed to be haunted'.¹³

Meanwhile, down the passage, the anxious rector and his wife couldn't sleep. Mabel suggested that they should make some tea and take it along to the guests. When they tried to open it, they found that their bedroom doorknob had been tied with cotton thread and a red cross had been drawn on the door. There was chalk over the floor and other paraphernalia to identify ghosts on the landing.[14] Having made the tea in the kitchen, when they arrived at the Blue Room it was in darkness, but they found the visitors in an excited state. The most extraordinary thing had *just* happened: the others had been listening to the knocking at the dressing table when they had suddenly heard a noise on the other side of the room. A cake of soap from the washstand had been thrown against a china jug on the floor. The Smiths laughed at the idea of the jumping soap. Mabel asked if she might turn up the lamps.[15]

As they drank the tea, Price wondered if Mrs Smith had heard knocks in the room before? 'Yes,' she replied, 'I often read or sew in this room and it is the rosebush that knocks against the window.'[16] Now that they were up and awake, Price asked the rector and his wife if they would join them in a seance. Though uncomfortable with the idea, the Smiths agreed in order to please their guests. The lamps were extinguished and they settled down to the sitting in the darkness. After a while, Price proceeded to ask further questions, prompted by the Bull sisters:

Is that Harry Bull?
One knock. (Yes)
Are you happy?
Two knocks. (No)
Do you mind Mr and Mrs Smith being here?
Two knocks. (No)
Is there money trouble?
One knock. (Yes)
Were you killed?
One knock. (Yes)[17]

The sitters were astonished to witness 'Harry Bull' identify his murderer as his own wife. He discussed his unhappy marriage to Ivy and appealed to them for help regarding his will as it was being 'misinterpreted'.[18] The Smiths were extremely concerned at the direction the questioning was taking. What's more, these personal – and libellous – family issues relating to their patrons were being openly discussed in their very presence and with a journalist as a witness. Eric Smith demanded that the seance end immediately and Price duly brought it to a close. The Bull sisters returned to Chilton Lodge, Wall left for London in his car and an exhausted Price and Lucie retired to bed. Back in their bedroom, the rector told his wife that he would never take part in such an unsavoury episode again.[19]

Lucie slept well for a couple of hours but was later woken with a shock. Price was standing at the foot of her bed, a flickering candle throwing fantastic shadows across his face. 'Let's get out of here!' he said.[20] He hadn't slept a wink and had one of his vicious headaches. He begged her to drive him to Sudbury to catch an early train. Unimpressed at being woken, Lucie told him that it was far too early even for the milk train, so he should wait another hour. Now awake, Lucie read for a while, then crept along the landing to find Price in his room – fully dressed and sound asleep on top of the bedclothes. At breakfast with the Smiths, he insisted that absolutely nothing would induce him to undress in 'that room', nor would he spend another night there.[21] Lucie later recalled that it was 'the only time I ever knew the atmosphere of a haunted house get the better of him,'[22] though Price would write much more enthusiastically about the events he'd witnessed at the Rectory that night: 'Never have such phenomena impressed me as they did on this historic night. Sixteen hours of thrills!'[23] Mr and Mrs Smith were disappointed that Price wanted to leave, but he was adamant. He did, however, agree for Lucie to stay on, partly as company for Mabel, who seemed exhausted by months of disturbed and sleepless nights.

Later that morning, Lucie ran Price to Sudbury to catch the train and then drove back to the Rectory, where she spent a quiet, uneventful day chatting with Mrs Smith, who was glad of the novelty of female company. Everything was perfectly quiet and there were no phenomena at all. During their conversation, Mabel wondered at the strange occurrences since Price had arrived. Lucie admitted that he did seem to attract the attention of spirits wherever he went.[24]

During the afternoon, news came that Price's arrival in Borley had badly upset the neighbourhood; some of the locals resented the presence of a ghost hunter in their village.[25] But it was also rumoured that an enterprising coach firm had arranged for an outing to the Rectory that night, advertising the trip, *'Come and see the Borley ghost!'*[26] Neither the Smiths nor Lucie could quite believe it as, for months, no local would willingly pass the Rectory after sundown. Mabel Smith was convinced that everyone had gone crazy and wondered what on earth she and her husband had stumbled into.[27] As a precaution, Eric Smith closed the gates to the Rectory and they waited to see what the evening would bring.

Later that night, sightseers started to arrive at the Rectory on foot. Soon they were joined by coachloads of families – many of them primed with drink – with mouth organs, beer bottles, penny whistles and even accordions.[28] Hundreds of curious visitors swarmed on the lawn in front of the Rectory, trampling over the garden, singing and shouting at the top of their voices, some becoming hysterical. Mary Pearson ran out with the missionary box and asked the revellers to make a donation if they wanted to see the 'Haunted Wood'.[29] As the lairy crowd continued to drink, they became impatient for an appearance from the ghostly nun or the phantom carriage and started throwing empty bottles at the house, smashing the drawing room windows. The terrified Smiths drew all the shutters on the ground floor. Afraid that the drunken mob might wreck the place, Mabel asked Lucie if she would drive to the police station and alert them.[30] Eric Smith told her where she would find the local constable and, taking the lantern, escorted Lucie to her Fiat. Having unlatched the gates, he berated the drunken crowd on the lawn who briefly listened in sullen silence as Lucie drove away.[31]

When she reached his house, the Borley constable wasn't in, so

Lucie carried on to Sudbury Police Station. Once she arrived there, she was informed that Borley was in Essex, not Suffolk, as Sudbury was, so she would need to go to Braintree, fifteen miles away, to ask for help. By the time she got there, she was told by the duty sergeant that an inspector had already been sent to Borley, having heard of the coach parties and the crowds that had been targeting the Rectory. Lucie returned to Borley in the early hours of the morning; the mob had been dispersed, the coaches had gone and the Rectory was quiet. A shaken and exhausted Mrs Smith was still up, awaiting Lucie's return with a pot of coffee.

The next morning, after little sleep, Lucie and the Smiths assessed the damage that the crowds had done. There were bottles and rubbish all over the garden, flowers and shrubs trampled and windows broken in the house. The sightseers had inflicted 'more damage than an army of ghosts would have made in a century of concentrated haunting'.[32] A police constable was stationed outside the front door to keep sightseers away as Lucie helped the anguished rector and his wife clear up the devastated house and garden.

The Smiths were stunned and frightened by the activity of the preceding twenty-four hours. They had written to the *Daily Mirror* with stories of occasional strange noises and lights, spectral coaches and phantom nuns – generic English spooks with perhaps a touch of local mischief. Until June 1929, Borley Rectory had been no different to dozens of old, dark houses throughout England that possessed a local ghost story. But in the course of a single day, the nature of the phenomena had become violent and personal: broken glass, smashed vases, knocking mirrors, mothballs and stones flying through the air – and now, accusations of murder from beyond the grave and coach parties invading the grounds and vandalising the house. A ghost story that had once been a local legend was suddenly now a national talking point in bold, tabloid print. All this drama had only started with the arrival of the press and Harry Price. It seemed that by inviting them into their home, the bewildered Smiths had unwittingly awoken an entirely different variety of spirit: a poltergeist.

Borley Church

CHAPTER FOUR

ANCIENT AND MODERN

1066–1862

> ... history is a pattern
> Of timeless moments. So, while the light fails
> On a winter's afternoon, in a secluded chapel
> History is now and England.

> T. S. Eliot, 'Little Gidding'[1]

The origins of Borley – the village, its church and its rectory – is in many ways the history of England. A manor at *Barlea*, meaning in Anglo-Saxon 'boar's clearing' or 'boar's pasture' is recorded in the Domesday Book. After the Norman Conquest, it was gifted to the sister of William the Conqueror.[2] In the medieval period, a manor was the centre of English rural life – a commercial enterprise whose success depended on all who lived within it working in harmony and obeying the local laws issued by the lord of the manor. The lord dedicated part of his land and income to the construction of a church and rectory, and had the right to appoint the rector. This was an extremely valuable privilege as the sermons of the parish priest were a way for the lord of the manor to exert order and control over his tenants.

The first church on the Borley site had been made of timber, but in 1236 it was replaced by a more substantial building, constructed of flint rubble from local gravel pits. Its interior would have been colourfully decorated with images and statues of the saints. It was common for an image of the Last Judgement to be painted on the western wall of the church, to be seen by parishioners after the service. This 'Doom' painting was a warning to the faithful of what would take place on the Last Day. With famine, epidemics, war and malnutrition, the Middle Ages were dominated by the cruel fragility of life. Beliefs about the afterlife shaped the way people conducted their lives on earth. Those who performed good deeds and avoided sinful behaviour would reach salvation in Paradise. Those who had committed mortal sins were damned and would go straight to Hell, a torture chamber where the smallest pain exceeded the greatest pain on earth and the punishment would fit the crime; the gluttonous fed on toads, the proud bound to wheels of fire. But those who had committed moderately bad or venial sins were sent to a place of purification in order to repent before entering Heaven; this was Purgatory. Ghosts were thought to be the souls of those trapped in Purgatory, unable to rest until they had expiated their sins. The Church taught that the congregation could help them by praying at Mass or by paying for indulgences to shorten their time there.

In 1534, when Pope Clement VII refused to annul Henry VIII's marriage to Catherine of Aragon, the tremors would be felt even in the small, remote parish of Borley. Monasteries were among the wealthiest institutions in the country, between them owning a quarter of all cultivated land. They were also a symbol of Papal power, which challenged that of the King. In order to bring an end to the political power of the Catholic Church, acquiring its great wealth in the process and at the same time legitimising his marriage to Anne Boleyn, Henry declared himself Supreme Head of the Church of England. He severed his relationship with Rome and confiscated its assets. By 1540, of the nearly 900 religious houses in England before this, fifty were being dissolved or demolished every month. In 1546, having taken possession of the Manor of Borley from the monastery at Canterbury, the King granted it to Edward Waldegrave of Sudbury.

The Waldegraves were an important aristocratic family, closely associated with the royal court. Edward Waldegrave was popular and highly regarded in the district for his 'liberality with the poor'.[3] In 1547, he joined the household of Mary Tudor, the King's daughter by Catherine of Aragon, who was, like her mother, a devout Roman Catholic. The period following Henry's death later that year was traumatic as the schism between the new Church of England and the ancient Church of Rome deepened. There was a ruthless attempt to eradicate any trace of traditional Catholic practices by the supporters of Henry's young heir, Edward VI. Mass was abolished, shrines demolished, statues removed, pilgrimages and processions outlawed. There was to be no holy water, no holy bread and no votive candles; colourful vestments, altar dressings and incense were all prohibited. At Borley, the ancient Doom painting was whitewashed and the heavy stone altar was quietly dismantled and secreted in the floor of the church near the chancel step, where it would remain hidden for the next 400 years. Purgatory was now derided as 'a fond thing vainly invented' ('fond' meaning stupid or daft) and abolished. The dead would proceed directly to Heaven or Hell, from which neither could return. Masses for the souls of the departed were dismissed as 'Purgatory pickpurse', a venal Catholic way of exploiting the bereaved. Funerals were simplified and purged of ritual to such an extent that one commentator described the dead 'being thrown into the ground like dogs, and not a word said'. The new Protestant doctrine insisted that each generation could be indifferent to the spiritual fate of its ancestors; the symbiotic relationship between the living and the dead, which had been at the heart of medieval belief, was instantly broken. Ghosts were dismissed as a symptom of degenerate Catholic belief.

Edward Waldegrave was known to be a recusant, remaining loyal to the Pope. In August 1551, he was imprisoned in the Tower of London for permitting Mass in Mary Tudor's household at Copped Hall in Epping. After he fell ill during his incarceration, his wife Frances was allowed to join him in the Tower, and he was later permitted to spend the rest of his sentence at Mary's residence, by her request. Fortunately for Sir Edward, the sickly King Edward died in 1553 at the age of fifteen. Mary ascended the throne and determined to re-establish the Catholic Church in England, burning 280 Protestant dissenters at the stake in the process and thus gaining the epithet 'Bloody' Mary. In country churches like Borley, the old Latin Mass was immediately reinstated. The trusty Waldegrave was knighted for his loyalty. But Mary herself died only five years later and Waldegrave's erratic fortunes changed again as her younger sister Elizabeth took the throne and once again outlawed Catholic practices.[4] A spy reported a Mass that had been held by the Waldegraves at Borley Hall and the presence of 'various Popish books and superstitious ornaments' around the house.[5] Though the Mass was essentially a private gathering, it would have been deemed a political meeting, incurring harsh penalties. On 20 April 1561, Waldegrave and his family were arrested. He was once again sent to the Tower and died of ill health in September that year.

Lady Waldegrave survived her husband by thirty-eight years and they were interred together in an extraordinary stone tomb in the east end of the nave at Borley Church. It was not unusual for Catholic gentry to be buried in Anglican churches, as they were still patrons of the living and were local squires. With devotional images banished, the only decorations permitted in churches were now these gaudy memorials to the ruling elite that could afford to erect them. Overly large and ornate, the Waldegrave tomb continues to dominate the modest interior of the little country church. Effigies of the couple lie next to each other, Waldegrave in his armour, his wife with a squirrel – an emblem of thrift – at her feet. The stone canopy above them is supported by six Corinthian marble columns. On the edge, carved in black marble is a Latin inscription:

Behold, O man, what honours, what descent, what wealth will profit thee, when breath of life shall leave thy frame! Thou seest nothing remain when the structure of man is dissolved. Earth its part reclaims and so doth heaven.[6]

A local legend subsequently grew that, from time to time, the coffins beneath the tomb would move, suggesting unquiet slumbers for this ancient Borley family.

Though the vast majority of medieval churches were dedicated in honour of a patron saint, by 1929, of the 400 churches in Essex, Borley was one of only a handful that was undedicated, known simply as 'Borley Church'. The parish surrounding it was made up of three neighbouring hamlets. One, situated to the east, down in the Stour Valley, was focused around Borley Hall – once the Waldegraves' residence – which was now owned by Robert Payne, a wealthy farmer and local landowner. Hall Lane led west from the hall up the brow of the hill to another hamlet, which comprised the church, the Rectory and another historic manor house, Borley Place, which was also owned by the Paynes and leased to the farmer, William Bigg. Further westward from the church, the road wound to a small settlement of farmhouses and thatched cottages known as Borley Green, where, by 1929, there was a post office, a beer shop and the village pump, the only supply of water to the village. Though the houses were picturesque, the people, mostly agricultural workers, were poor. To the west of the stretch of Hall Lane that connected Borley Hall to the church were 10 acres of pastureland owned by the Waldegraves that provided a small income for the rector, traditionally known as the glebe. It was on the site overlooking these glebelands that the first rectory at Borley had been built.

After the Reformation, the status of the parish priest in England had changed. He was no longer responsible solely for disseminating Church teaching and holding services. He was now an officer of the Church of England, a political as well as a social force. His home was required to combine and represent these functions, and now that priests could marry, the rectory needed to accommodate wives, children and servants. But many rectors held more than one living, and parishes were often abandoned to recently ordained curates. Over time, social and spiritual order in rural parishes, as well as vicarages and rectories, began to decay. The civil war that followed caused further decline. With the patrons of livings in reduced circumstances themselves, and no money for repairs or rebuilding, rectories such as Borley deteriorated. By 1688 the social standing of parish priests had declined to such an extent that they were considered to be just above labourers on the social scale, with half the livings in England below the poverty line of £50 per annum.

The decline of the clergy and of the Church buildings that housed them was recognised in 1703 with the establishment of the Queen Anne's Bounty Act. This sought to augment the livings of most rural clergy. During this period of improvement and rebuilding, a second rectory was built on the site at Borley by the Reverend William Herringham. Herringham assumed the rectory at Borley in 1805, and made it his home with his wife, Anne. By this time, a series of Residence Acts required priests to live in their parishes, rather than pocket an income from letting the rectory and living elsewhere. By the early Victorian period, the status of English clergymen had risen to such an extent that they were 'fitted to mix with the country gentry and nobility. They [were] not peasants with muck only half-scraped off them by seminary training.'[7] A gentleman rector – or 'squarson' (squire-cum-parson) – very much the type familiar from Jane Austen and Trollope, would live a life of cultured leisure, treating his congregation like dependents on his country estate. He would require a residence that reflected his elevated social status. It is at this time that the English country rectory began to evolve as a national symbol, 'a repository for a mystical spirit of England',[8] rooted in the English landscape. It is this image of the honey-coloured parsonage, the heart of civilised morality and order in the community, that resounds throughout nineteenth-century English literature and continues to be an estate agent's dream.

William and Anne Herringham had four sons and three daughters. But the life of the rector and his family was to be dominated by loss with the premature death of all the daughters. Two of the sisters were interred in a vault in the churchyard within sight of the Rectory and all three sisters were remembered inside the church with a marble plaque. On his father's death in 1819, John

P. Herringham assumed the Borley living. Although a life in the Church was in theory open to all, increasingly the richer livings became so desirable that the gentry, who held the right to make these appointments, began to colonise them for their younger sons, who would retain livings until they died and would pass them on to their own sons. The clergy emerged as a distinct caste – dynasties that would remain in place for centuries, with parishes passed down from one generation of the same family to the next. John P. Herringham continued to serve as rector at Borley for forty-three years.

Some two and a half miles from Borley, situated on the banks of the River Stour, stood the village of Pentlow. This was home to the Bulls, a clerical dynasty who had been farmers, squires and parsons in the area for hundreds of years. Reverend John Bull had been the incumbent at the Norman church of St Gregory and St George since 1802. In 1830, his son Edward, at the age of twenty-seven, began working as curate to his father, in the same year that he married Elizabeth Hodson. They had three children: Mary, born in 1831, Henry Dawson Ellis Bull, who followed two years later, and Winifred, who was born in 1834. That year Edward Bull succeeded his father as rector and assumed the living at Pentlow. Like the Herringhams, the Bulls were stricken with grief. Winifred Bull died in 1843 at the age of nine and her mother died of breast cancer the following year. Just before Easter 1848 the widowed Edward Bull temporarily swapped his parish, moving to Sneinton in Nottingham with his two surviving children, Mary and Henry. The family lived at the rectory there with William Brown, who had been curate at St James's Church for two years. A tall and handsome 26-year-old, Brown was immediately smitten with the seventeen-year-old Mary Bull. Though aware of his liking for her, she did nothing to encourage his affections, though he persisted in his suit.

On the morning of 9 November, Brown asked Mary's father whether he might have her hand in marriage. Due to his daughter's youth, Reverend Bull was concerned about the match, but assured Brown that he would discuss it with her. Mary was clear that she had no romantic feelings for Brown and asked her father to inform the lovelorn curate so. That afternoon, having been told by Reverend Bull of his daughter's wishes, Brown was seen walking the streets of Nottingham and entering some shops in a 'very hurried and excited manner'.[9] At four o'clock, he went to the ruins of Nottingham Castle and shot himself in the head, dying instantaneously.[10] The Bull family, the local press observed, were plunged 'into deep affliction by the shocking occurrence' and returned home to Pentlow.[11] But after a dark period for the family dominated by death and loss, there were to be happier times. In 1851, Reverend Bull married again. His second wife, Cornelia, duly fell pregnant, giving birth to a much-wanted son, Felix – Latin for 'happy' or 'lucky'. Finally, having 'won and lived in the affections of her father's flock',[12] Mary Bull married Samuel Yelloly, a doctor's son, at Pentlow on 12 September 1854, 'amid the rejoicings of the elite and the poor of the neighbourhood'.[13]

Meanwhile, the rector's oldest son, Henry Dawson Ellis Bull, had grown into a tall, broad-shouldered young man of unusual physical strength, which he exploited in his career as an enthusiastic amateur boxer at Wadham College, Oxford. He took holy orders, preaching his first sermon at Pentlow on Sunday 6 June 1858, inspired by St Luke: 'Except ye repent, ye shall all likewise perish.'[14] He confided to his diary, 'May God give me the grace both to know and to preach his holy word.'[15] He was curate at Holy Trinity Church, Ely from 1858 to 1860. With his father very much active at Pentlow, he would need to seek a parish of his own. When John P. Herringham died, in December 1861, with no successor to leave it to, the living at Borley had become vacant. The patron, Lady Waldegrave, duly offered it to the 28-year-old curate.

Henry Bull's father had been friendly with the rector of All Saints Church, Hastings, Henry Samuel Foyster, and the two families frequently paid each other visits. Foyster's son George was a contemporary of Henry's and they had taken holy orders at the same time. It was while staying with the Foysters in Hastings that

Henry became acquainted with George's younger sister Caroline, whom he married on 11 February 1862. As well as the daughter of a much-admired priest, Caroline Foyster was popular with the community in Hastings, where she dedicated much of her time to working with schools and the poor of the district, so their elaborate wedding was a local event as well as a family celebration. After a honeymoon in Tunbridge Wells, on 20 February Henry Dawson Ellis Bull finally accepted the living at Borley.

The rectory built by the Herringhams was a two-storey, typically Georgian affair, elegant but modest in size, perhaps built of pale-yellow Suffolk gault brick with a slate roof. But church finances were not unlimited and the rector's income was dependent on tithes, which would fluctuate according to the size of the harvest. As a result, the grandeur of a Georgian rectory's exterior was often not matched by the interior, where rooms were small and conditions cramped. By the time the Bulls married, larger entertaining rooms and bigger kitchens were required in order to host and cater for social events. As well as an income from the rectory of £250, the Bull family owned a good deal of property in the Sudbury district and Caroline Bull had also brought a considerable dowry to her marriage, including property in central London. With an agricultural boom in the mid-nineteenth century, the young Reverend Bull now had ample means to commission another rectory at Borley, which would be fitted with all modern conveniences.

The construction of the new rectory was part of a period of prosperity and expansion for the Church of England, with huge numbers of churches restored and an increase in the intake of clergy. But despite this demonstration of self-confidence, the Church was being undermined by internal division, external pressures and the progress of science. The Victorian 'Age of Doubt' was gathering pace, inspired by advances in technology and new discoveries. The publications of scientists and geologists, particularly Charles Darwin's *On the Origin of Species*, challenged the Church and the authority of the Bible, on which much of Western thought had been based. Matthew

Arnold's 'Sea of Faith'[16] had dried up, leaving the horrifying possibility of a Godless, empty universe. This gave rise to a generation of doubtful believers, such as the novelist W. H. Mallock, who mourned for his contemporaries who felt 'a strange blankness' in their lives: 'there are many about us, though they never confess their pain, and perhaps hardly to themselves like to dwell on it, whose hearts are aching for the God that they no longer can believe in.'[17]

At the same time, the 1851 census had revealed that the vast majority of the English population never attended church and those who did were drawn from the upper and middle classes. Dissenters, Methodists and spiritualists offered an alternative to traditional Anglican belief, while an influx of immigrants following the famine in Ireland had increased the number of Catholics in the country. Anglo-Catholicism also prospered, fracturing the Church internally. The experiences now offered by the two branches of the same faith were markedly different: modest Low Church sermons took place with little ceremony within bare, whitewashed walls, while High Church liturgy promoted the lives of the saints and sacraments in a highly theatrical form of worship that had been ousted by the Reformation. When John Henry Newman finally converted to Catholicism in 1845, followed by many of his Anglo-Catholic, Oxford Movement colleagues, the apparently insidious growth of Catholicism in national life caused alarm. In 1850, Pope Pius IX re-established Catholic parishes and dioceses in Britain. When Cardinal Archbishop Wiseman chose the name of 'Westminster' for his new diocese, it was greeted with dismay, suggesting, as it did, that Rome had ambitions to establish itself at the very heart of British life.

The re-emergence of Catholic influence in Britain had long been a cause of fear and mistrust, and had culminated in widespread rioting in London on 2 June 1780, when 40–60,000 protestors had marched on the Houses of Parliament in response to the repeal of official discrimination against Catholics. The Gordon Riots that followed over the next five days in various sites across the city were finally brought to an end by the army, leading to the death and arrest of hundreds of rioters. In subsequent years, anti-Catholic demonstrations took place across the country. Suffolk, on whose border Borley sat, was a particular focus of anti-Catholic prejudice. In 1862, in Ipswich, anti-Catholic protestors rampaged through the town, attacking Catholic homes and businesses with rocks and iron bars. A convent was set upon by the mob, who smashed the windows with stones throughout the night. In November 1863, further riots broke out in Ipswich after a series of pro-Catholic lectures were given at the Temperance Hall.[18]

From the middle of the eighteenth century, the growing anxiety about the increasing Catholic presence in Britain had found popular expression in Gothic novels, with dark tales of sexually intemperate nuns and sinister monks. A sub-genre of the Gothic novel soon emerged: salacious 'memoirs' set in convents. Sensational tales of the cloisters, such as Julia McNair Wright's *Almost a Nun*, Charlotte Myhill's *How Perversions are Affected or Three Years as a Nun*, and the eponymously authored *Awful Disclosures of Maria Monk or The Hidden Secrets of a Nun's Life in a Convent Exposed,* dramatised Catholic fanaticism, female hysteria, kidnapping, seduction, sexual perversion, torture and escape. The legend of the enamoured nun who broke her vows at Borley, and was punished for doing so, was characteristic of this period, reflecting the anti-Catholic hysteria which prevailed in the parishes in neighbouring Suffolk and in the popular literature of the time.

In 1859, Edward Bull commissioned a memorial to stand in the garden at Pentlow Rectory in honour of his father, John, who had died in 1834. This was a 90-foot-high octagonal brick tower in the Tudor style, designed by John Johnson, an architect from Bury St Edmunds who specialised in ecclesiastical buildings and churches – best remembered today for his collaboration with Alfred Meeson on Alexandra Palace. Some locals sniggered that Reverend Bull's phallic tower celebrated his father's fertility more than it did his memory. Admiring the style and scale of the memorial, Reverend Bull's son Henry decided that Johnson would be a suitable architect to design a new rectory for him at Borley.

In 1861, Johnson was putting the finishing touches to St Matthew's vicarage in Oakley Square in Camden, a High Victorian Gothic extravaganza of yellow London brick.[19] Many elements of the building would be integrated into Johnson's design for the new rectory at Borley, particularly the square stair tower situated to the side of the building, topped with a steep, spire-like pyramidic roof and an ironwork pinnacle. At the beginning of June, Johnson put out a tender to builders in the local press to demolish the old rectory at Borley and build a new one.[20] Thomas Farrow was a builder and surveyor based in Bury St Edmunds. He consulted Johnson's plans at the old rectory and submitted an estimate of £3,000, which was accepted. With Reverend Bull and his wife moving into his father's house at Pentlow for the duration of the build, the Georgian rectory was demolished. In the summer of 1862, a team of bricklayers, stonemasons, carpenters, scaffolders, plasterers and decorators began work on the new building.

Like many of John Johnson's projects, the house was built in the Gothic style and made of materials at odds with its rural surroundings, the grandiose turret completing the slightly alien design. But this style was considered very fashionable in the smarter suburbs of nearby towns such as Ipswich and Halstead. Like many grand Victorian properties, the bombastic style of the new rectory broadcast to the surrounding county the taste, stature and wealth of its owners.

One of the risks of building such a large house on the foundations of a smaller one, particularly on the local clay, which expanded when wet, was subsidence. And while the walls of buildings in the district had previously been laid with a flexible lime mortar that allowed for movement, from the early nineteenth century hard cement was used, which was prone to cracking. At the same time, Thomas Farrow had his joiners fill in any chinks or gaps in the carpentry throughout the building in order to eradicate draughts. The climate in north Essex was chilled by the biting easterly and north-easterly winds, as well as rain- and snowstorms, and there was even the occasional earthquake. The builders laid the floorboards tightly, made the doors with securely tacked panels and the window frames with no allowances for movement. Consequently, the woodwork throughout the house would creak and groan whenever there was a change in temperature, a frequent occurrence in the rectory's position on the ridge above the Stour Valley. So that future generations might acknowledge their work, in the attics Farrow's carpenters scratched their names on the rafters.

On Tuesday 5 August, a group of the builders working on the rectory site decided to go bathing after the hot summer day. Seventeen-year-old John Whyard was a grocer's son who was working on the site as a bricklayer's labourer. Together with several other builders working on the new rectory, including two of the carpenters, John Mathoby and John Barber, Whyard headed down through the glebelands to the riverside nearest the rectory. Mathoby, who was not a strong swimmer, took a stick and measured the water, which seemed deep, so he warned Whyard to take care. The men began to strip and Mathoby jumped into the river. As Whyard entered the water, he struck out and tried to swim. Barber overheard the boy say that he had cramp. Mathoby had already swum across the river and reached the meadow on the other side when he heard one of the other men shouting that Whyard was in trouble. He immediately jumped back into the water, swam towards the boy and seized him by the hair. But Whyard struggled and pulled Mathoby down with him into the unknown depths of the water. The carpenter let go of the boy, then went back again to try to save him, to no avail. Whyard sank as the other men sent for help. With the aid of some creepers, they finally managed to drag the boy's lifeless body from the river. At the inquest in Long Melford three days later, the jury agreed a verdict of accidental drowning. But superstitious locals muttered that the boy's death was a bad omen for the new rector's grand new rectory.[21]

Mrs Henry Dawson Bull (right) and some of her
children at Pentlow Rectory, c. 1880

CHAPTER FIVE

A CLERGYMAN'S SON, A CLERGYMAN'S DAUGHTER

1863–1922

> Here was a block of stone, even as the desert Sphinx, made by
> man for his own purpose – yet she had a personality that was
> hers alone, without the touch of human hand. One family only
> had lived within her walls. One family who had given her life.
> They had been born there, they had loved, they had quarrelled,
> they had suffered, they had died. And out of these emotions she
> had woven a personality for herself, she had become what their
> thoughts and their desires had made her.
>
> Daphne du Maurier, 'The House of Secrets'[1]

In March 1863, Caroline Bull gave birth to her first child at her
father-in-law's home at Pentlow Rectory. The baby boy was named
after his father, also taking his mother's maiden name: Henry
Foyster Bull. To distinguish him from his father, he would always
be known among the family as Harry. Shortly afterwards, the
Bulls moved into the newly completed Borley Rectory. On 17 April
1864, a daughter was born there – named Caroline Sarah after her
mother but known as 'Dodie'. On Friday 20 May, an apocalyptic thunderstorm broke out over south Suffolk and north Essex.
Lightning strikes destroyed farm buildings, haystacks were burned
and livestock killed. In the garden of the newly built rectory, a

tree was shattered by a bolt of lightning, reducing it to a charred, dead stump.[2]

The large, red-brick rectory now stood complete, an affront to the modest, ancient stone church across the road. It was, according to the lawyer William Charles Crocker, 'as ugly as the bad taste of 1863 could make it'.[3] The interiors of the house were decorated to the highest standard of the day with furniture, fabrics and objets d'art from all over the British Empire. Throughout, the floors and doors were finished in a rich, dark varnish. In the drawing room were plush settees and stuffed armchairs with ball-and-claw feet. There were two pianos and numerous card tables, as well as rosewood, burr walnut and ebonised occasional tables. Porcelain from Dresden and Wedgwood filled the cabinets and dressed the mantels. Popular prints and engravings hung on the papered walls as well as gilt-framed family portraits. Ornate marble fireplaces graced the drawing room and library. The fireplace in the dining room had been purchased by John Johnson from the Great Exhibition in 1851 and was decorated with the figures of a monk on either side. The polished mahogany dining table was huge, with four leaves and twelve leather chairs. In the library there was an oak roll-top desk, the walls were fitted with shelving for ecclesiastical works and glazed bookcases were filled with Gothic novels, sensation fiction and middle-brow popular literature. In the bedrooms were brass and iron bedsteads, washstands and cheval mirrors. Oriental, Axminster and Kidderminster rugs covered the floors. An eight-day grandfather clock kept time in the hall. Outside, the grounds were beautifully tended, the manicured and rolled lawn prepared for outdoor sports. A summer house was built halfway down the lawn for refreshments during croquet and tennis parties. Another summer house, Gothic in design, was situated at the far corner of the garden, furthest away from the house. In the early days of the Bull family's residence, Borley Rectory was, one of the servants remembered, a lovely house kept in excellent condition.

For sixteen years Caroline Bull was almost continually pregnant. In both 1866 and 1868 she gave birth twice. She was supported by a succession of nannies, nursemaids and a Swiss governess, Marie Rolt, who would teach all the children, the boys being sent away to school when they were old enough. After the birth of her tenth child, in 1873, there was a hiatus in her pregnancies as the Rectory was expanded to accommodate the growing family. By 1879, Caroline Bull had thirteen children. Harry and Dodie were joined by Freda, Alfred, Basil, Ethel, Mabel, Gerald, Constance, Hubert, Emily, Elsie and Kathleen. In an era when a quarter of children died before the age of five, just one child, Cyril, had died in infancy, in 1877, and was buried in the churchyard across the road.

The new wing, providing extra bedrooms, a schoolroom, storage and a glass house, created the unusual courtyard at the heart of the building. The ground-floor extension comprised an arched walkway built of red brick, flanked by fuel stores, the servants' lavatory and a new well – eighty feet deep and six feet wide, this provided water to the scullery, the pantry and the lavatory. A large bell placed high on the wall near the back door would summon family members to the house from the grounds, the sound bouncing between the walls of the courtyard and reverberating throughout the house. Reverend Bull continued to update the building and in 1879 commissioned a further re-design of the north aspect facing the road from the London architect Samuel Knight. In attempting to make the frontage of the house more pleasingly symmetrical, Knight also intended to enhance its forbidding Gothic appearance. Though these improvements were never completed, it may have been at this time that the dining room window was bricked up. With the coming of the railway in 1860, Hall Lane had become increasingly busy. With the window's low sill, diners were exposed to passers-by in the lane as well as the harsh north wind blowing from the valley.

During the Bulls' time, the Rectory was a thriving self-contained, self-sufficient community, supported by a large staff. In those days, servants were regarded as a status symbol and reflected the higher caste of the family that employed them. Many of the servants at the Rectory lived on the premises. Married staff were accommodated in one of the cottages belonging to the Rectory. The coachman lived with his wife and daughter in the stable block, which was situated just behind it. This included a coach house, loose boxes, harness rooms and living quarters above. The original stable block, attached to the Herringham rectory, had been remodelled to match the main house in modern red brick. There were also two full-time gardeners, who grew fruit and vegetables for the household.

Daily life for the servants was hard, the schedule tight and punishing. The day began and ended by candlelight, with bedtime often midnight or later. There was no time off except to go to church, though by the 1890s employers would give their staff one day off a month – a half-day that would start at 3 p.m., after luncheon had been served and cleared away. There was no gas or electricity, and with twenty fireplaces, two coppers and a kitchen range, the household would burn half a ton of coal a day. Carrying heavy buckets of coal, cleaning and blackleading the grates, laying the fires and keeping them alight was a full-time job for the maids in the winter months. With no labour–saving devices, and the Rectory decorated with ornaments and bric-a-brac to keep dirt-free and polished, soot from the open fires made cleaning the house a laborious task. Transporting hot water from the scullery to all the bedrooms, and then clearing away dirty water and the contents of the chamber pots and hot water bottles in slop buckets, was a relentless and dirty daily chore. It was important for the housemaids to complete their heavier duties early in the morning, before the gentlemen of the household rose, so they did not see the young women at work and feel obliged to offer chivalrous assistance.

All the food at the Rectory was prepared on site, from scratch. Meat and dairy produce was supplied by the farm next door that belonged to the family, as well as another farm they owned at Lavenham. Surplus produce was sold at the market in Sudbury. The cook and the scullery maids were responsible for providing four meals a day every day for the family and servants. The Rectory would also frequently entertain guests such as Mrs Bull's brothers and their families at luncheon or dinner. Family gatherings were large and boisterous, and the challenge for the Rectory kitchen was more like catering than cooking. Leftovers from family meals would be utilised to feed the servants. The entire household was run by Mrs Bull, who would engage directly with senior staff, who in turn would supervise the junior servants.

The lives of the staff were effectively cut off from the family in the domestic offices beyond the green baize door that led to the kitchens. The servants were party to the intimate lives of the family and yet distanced from them; they were distinguished by particular uniforms for various tasks during the day and referred to by their surnames. They used different entrances and staircases throughout the house as well as separate facilities; the inside lavatory on the first floor was used only by the family, while the staff used the servants' lavatory outside. This formalisation of relations between the servants and the Bulls was a practical arrangement so that the staff could get on with their work without the need for civilities. Only the governess and nurse would engage with the family and eat with them, treated on a par with the older daughters. The other servants were seen by the family as little as possible, but were summoned by a modern, mechanical system of servants' bells that had been fitted throughout the house.

House bells were expected in most 'ordinary' homes and regarded as a necessity of modern life. The bells were rung noiselessly by a cord hung in each room or a lever by the fireplace. These were attached to copper wires that ran, through tubes sunk into the plasterwork, to levers mounted in the attic, where they ran to a point vertically above the kitchen. They then all descended to the bell board in the kitchen passage. The size of small handbells, the bells themselves were mounted on a coiled spring and fastened to the bell board. Each bell was individually labelled with the name of the room to which it was wired. These labels could be repainted as the use – or occupant – of the room changed. The bells were of slightly different sizes and rang with different tones, so that the servants could distinguish one bell from another. The highest-toned bell was placed at one end of the board and the deepest at the other, with those in between growing gradually deeper in tone. The bell board was hung on the wall in the passage opposite the servants' hall, where the staff could see which bell had been rung even after it had stopped, as the swinging continued for some time afterwards. Domestic bells had dramatically changed the way that employers communicated with their servants, increasing privacy and convenience for the family as staff no longer needed to be within calling distance but could be summoned from anywhere in the house when needed. This technology further polarised the lives of the family and the staff, with the latter expected to drop what they were doing and answer the summons when called. Though they inhabited the house with the family, the servants haunted the passages and backstairs early in the morning and late at night, unseen and rarely heard.

While the servants' lives revolved around the family, the family's lives revolved around the social life of the parish, the church calendar and the celebrations throughout the year that marked the passing of the seasons. In the winter, Plough Monday, the first Monday after Epiphany, marked the beginning of the new agricultural year. That night at dusk local lads would blacken their faces and turn their coats inside out before dragging an old ploughshare around the local farms demanding 'largesses for the ploughboys'.[4] If the landowner paid well, they would scratch a line across the drive to show he'd been generous. But if the offering was mean, they'd plough up the ground in front of the door so that it was a sea of mud for weeks in the winter rains. Lady Day fell on 25 March, when rents were traditionally due and contracts made. In the spring, there were a host of festivities in Holy Week leading up to Easter. On the afternoon of Easter Saturday, the vestry screen in the church would be decorated by Dodie and her sisters with daffodils, ox-eye daisies, arum lilies, moss and ivy. Scarlet geraniums, violets and laurel would brighten the chancel, and white hyacinths, white azaleas, geraniums and tulips would dress the altar.

The first three weekdays after Ascension Day marked Rogationtide, when Reverend Bull would lead the villagers in procession around the parish, carrying banners and crosses, blessing the fields, crops and livestock. This 'beating of the bounds'[5] fixed the geography and extent of the parish in the minds of the congregation. In the early summer, a range of open-air events – sports, games, morris dancing and village walks – were enjoyed in the week following Whitsun, marking the occasion when the Apostles had been inspired by the Holy Spirit. This, regarded by many as the highlight of the year, had been distinguished with a rare Bank Holiday from 1871. The first Sunday in August was Lammas Day, the festival of the first fruits and the harvest of the corn. The most important season of the year for the local farmers began in September, when the weather could dictate their income for the next twelve months. The last cart of corn to be harvested would be decorated with flowers and ribbons, with women and children riding on top as king or queen of the harvest. A thanksgiving festival was celebrated in the church, which was decorated with fruit, flowers and vegetables donated by the congregation, with wild hops entwined around the columns of the Waldegrave tomb.

In the darkest days of the year, Advent marked the lead-up to Christmas, when the panels of the pulpit and the vestry screen were decorated with holly leaves and berries, the chancel seats with ivy and box. Underneath the stained-glass east window was a festive display of moss and holly. On Christmas Day itself, there were services at 8 a.m. and 11 a.m., with evensong at 3 p.m. Every year, the Bull family hosted a Christmas party for the villagers at the Rectory and Reverend Bull would present seasonal gifts to his parishioners – the ingredients for plum pudding for the women, tobacco for the men, and sweets for the Sunday School children. When it snowed, Harry, Basil, Alfred and Hubert Bull would make a snowman in the Rectory garden, dressing it with one of their father's oldest hats.

The Bulls socialised with the most respected families in the district and hosted a routine of engagements at the Rectory throughout the year: suppers, tea and card parties, amateur theatricals, garden fetes, balls and dances. They were part of a coterie of local middle-class and aristocratic friends and the Bull siblings grew up surrounded by a close network of dozens of other young people. In addition, Mrs Bull's brothers in Hastings each had eight children.

Henry Dawson Bull's younger half-brother, Felix, had assumed the
rectory at Pentlow on the death of their father in 1871 and, having
married in middle age, had subsequently sired four children. In the
summer, when the boys returned from school, Borley Rectory was
filled with youthful energy. Being ardent and active sportsmen, the
men in the family would shoot, hunt, fish, cycle and play football.
Reverend Bull regarded himself as a 'hedge parson' and never wore
a cassock except for Sunday-morning service.[6] He would change
straight into his civilian clothes before noon on Sundays and would
then lie on the drawing room floor, taking pot-shots at rabbits at the
bottom of the garden with his single-shot 'rook and rabbit' rifle.[7] He
was a keen member of the Suffolk and Essex Hunt and kept several
horses in the stables behind the Rectory. Though only the men took
part in the hunt itself, the stag hunt was a key community event,
with the women watching from the lanes as a stag was released
from one of the farms and hunted across local landowners' fields.

As the Bull children grew older, when hosting social events in
the autumn and winter the Rectory would be gaily decorated with
evergreens and flowers, with Chinese lanterns hung in the passages giving an intimate, romantic glow 'intended for spooning'.[8]
Programmes for the evening and dance cards would be handmade
and decorated by the sisters. The study was commandeered as a
reception room, supper was served in the dining room, tea and
coffee in the schoolroom. The drawing room was the heart of every
party, prepared for dancing with painted canvas rugs which would
be washed with cloths soaked in milk and then buffed to a sheen – a
precursor of linoleum. The music was played on the piano, accompanied by a violinist, for guests to dance polkas, quadrilles and
cotillions. They would dance into the night, sometimes until three
or four o'clock in the morning.

Throughout 1885, Dodie Bull kept a diary that recorded the
most mundane events of life at the Rectory – 'We went to church
this morning. Same as every other Sunday'; a maid cuts her thumb
in the kitchen, the cat dies, letters are written and received, trips
are taken in the Brougham, she skates, makes dresses and picks

wild primroses in the woods.[9] The diary is more vivid – and, for the period, risqué – when she records her sexual awakening, her engagement with young men and her anxieties about the prospect of marriage – 'Why wasn't I pretty and fascinating? Damn my ugly face, it won't attract anyone, worse luck.'[10] In her entry describing a party in the winter, she reveals herself to be a passionate, imaginative and forthright young woman, far from the image of the demure rector's daughter. Wearing pale-blue satin finished with coffee-coloured lace and wearing Irish crystals around her neck, she was dressed for seduction:

[Charlie and I] went up the back stairs. There was a candle alight in the window. He asked me to blow it out. I did so. Then he put both his arms round me and kissed me lots of times. Oh, it was so sweet. He squeezed his leg against mine and held me so tight and kissed me on my lips and cheeks. Oh heaven, it was delicious … we went into the nursery and shut the door. He sat down in the armchair and I in another close beside him. He put his arm around my waist, asked me to kiss him. I did so of course. Then he asked me to come and sit on his knee. I pretended to hesitate, but did so. He put his arm around my waist and drew my head down on his shoulder and laid his cheek on mine so our lips touched … Oh, delicious party. How too quickly you were over. My darling I love you awfully much. Charlie, love me a little.[11]

Unlike her brothers, who were expected to go to university, travel and take up a profession, Borley was the limit of Dodie's expectations, with few trips further afield than London or to her cousins in Hastings or Pentlow. With no option of a profession, and voting or property rights denied to her, her future lay as a wife or spinster. 'How old one begins to feel,' wrote the twenty-year-old Dodie, 'what a crop of old maids are growing up.'[12] This sense of frustration at the lack of opportunities open to her blazes from a New Year diary entry:

I wonder will this year be happy, shall I have sorrow or glad-
ness, health or sickness, who can tell? Of the past year I have
little to write, the same humdrum round of daily pleasures
and disappointment, a couple of visits to Uncle's at Hastings,
the same tennis parties and cricket matches in the summer, the
same dances last winter. I am very discontented but I yearn for
something more than the quiet, uneventful life of a small country village. I long to do something wicked even for the sake of
change. I have an intensely wicked heart I fear, not cruel or selfish
or treacherous, but very unprincipled. I like to do what pleases me
without considering the cost or the future. I am extremely fond
of men, that is my fault; it may sound small but it is not. I shall
come to a bad end one day, I fear. Anyone seeing me would take
me for a sufficiently uninteresting little person; but I have more
brains than most girls about here though I do not look smart
and talk and go on so much. I have a strong imagination and a
rather sharp tongue. I can write rather good short stories. I am
nearly twenty-one, and have been out three years. Freda and I
teach Ethel and Mabel since last Christmas and all the boys go
to school, college or elsewhere. Oh that I could travel, oh that
I had wings to soar away from the narrow limits of this slow
little place.[13]

Though the pace of life changed little in Borley, Victorian England
was in the midst of rapid industrialisation that drew rural workers
into towns, dislocating them from families and communities that
had been established over generations. With the broadening of
access to education, literacy improved dramatically, reaching even
the poorest, and a large, hungry reading public quickly emerged.
Technological advances meant that printing and paper were now
much cheaper, and the new rail network made distribution easier.
Dozens of weekly and monthly periodicals, journals and magazines
were launched to satisfy this new readership.

On 19 December 1843, Charles Dickens had published the

first of his seasonal tales, *A Christmas Carol*, which was an enormous – and immediate – popular success. In the years that followed, Dickens continued to write supernatural stories for Christmas and encouraged them to be read aloud as family entertainment in front of the fire on Christmas Eve, a seasonal ritual echoing the ancient oral tradition of tales of demons and sprites in the depth of winter. As the night descended, thick velvet curtains would be drawn tight against the cold outside, the lamps turned low, and families like the Bulls would sit and listen to tales of the uncanny. Such was the popularity of Dickens's yuletide tales, the English ghost story quickly emerged as a distinct and hugely popular genre.

As Dickens was refining the fictional ghost story, in 1848 the novelist Catherine Crowe published *The Night Side of Nature*, a fragmented anthology of – purportedly – true anecdotes, rumours and stories about 'ghosts and ghost seers'.[14] Crowe saw herself as a cataloguer of supernatural phenomena, collecting and curating stories from people she'd met or who'd written to her with their experiences. She claimed them to be evidence that could prove that supernatural forces were real and true. Some of the stories were German and it was Crowe who introduced the word 'poltergeist' into the English language from the German for 'noisy spirit'. Reviewing it in the *Literary Examiner*, Dickens wrote that Crowe's supernatural anthology was 'one of the most extraordinary collections of "ghost stories" that had ever been published'.[15] It was so popular that it went through eighteen editions in six years. For the reader, the stories were entertaining, and that was considered more important than whether they were fact or fiction.

Just before Christmas 1850, a gruesome discovery had been made five miles from Borley in the village of Glemsford. Two skeletons, a male and a female, had been unearthed in a field near Glemsford Bridge. They had been buried in a shallow grave east to west, with two sticks across each of their chests, which implied a Christian burial, though there was no evidence of a coffin. A coin from the reign of Henry III was found in the vicinity. This was thought to represent 'St Peter's fee', which was placed into the hand of the deceased to pay the toll for admission into heaven. Local legend said that the field was once the site of an ancient monastery. Two years after the discovery in Glemsford, William Sparrow Simpson wrote in *Notes and Queries* of a mysterious legend he had been told by his nanny, associated with the nearby village of Acton. The park gates at Acton Place, Simpson wrote, were wont to 'fly open at midnight "withouten hands", and a carriage drawn by four spectral horses, and accompanied by headless grooms and outriders, proceeded with great rapidity from the park to a spot called the "nursery corner"'.[16]

Real-life ghost stories in the district were not all confined to the past. In December 1857, the *Ipswich Journal* had reported the story of a haunting at nearby Liston Rectory. Strange happenings, loud knockings and rappings were heard all over the house, sometimes from the roof, sometimes in the various rooms. Windows were broken and rattled and, at times, the very foundations of the building seemed to shake. The rector's family were much disturbed and called in Police Constable Edwards of Foxearth to investigate. Edwards didn't believe in ghosts or 'the modern vagaries' of spiritualism and felt that the cause of the phenomena must be somebody within the household. His suspicions fell upon a fourteen-year-old servant girl called Deeks. It had been noticed that the sounds generally occurred whenever she went about the house unaccompanied. She would then rush back, exclaiming, 'Did you hear that noise?' One day Edwards surreptitiously followed her as she went about her work. Shortly after she entered an empty room alone, he heard noises from within. Quietly observing Deeks, he noticed the shadow of her arm on the opposite wall moving up and down, corresponding to the noise. Catching her red-handed, he informed the rector. The girl was dismissed and returned to her parents' house. The rappings and noises ceased immediately and the rectory at Liston was quiet once more.[17]

As well as developing a taste for factual and fictional ghosts, Britain in the 1850s had enthusiastically embraced the craze for spiritualism. This had been imported from America by the medium

Maria Hayden, who found a wildly enthusiastic market for her seances, which offered the possibility of contact with dead relatives for considerable sums – a minimum half a guinea for each consultation. Within a few months of her arrival in London, spiritualism spread throughout the country. Over time, British mediums evolved a variety of ways of communicating with the dead, including seances and 'automatic writing', where the medium's hand was directed by the spirits into writing or drawing pictures. Some mediums would offer 'materialisations'. These might be 'apports', where physical objects would appear, or music might be heard. The most dramatic – and most theatrical – were 'full body materialisations', where the medium would first be bound in a 'cabinet' behind a curtain before summoning a ghostly apparition to appear to the horror or delight of the invited circle. So popular was the new craze of spiritualism in parlours and kitchens throughout the country that George Bernard Shaw sneered that Britain had become addicted to 'table–rapping, materialisation, seances, clairvoyance, palmistry, crystal gazing and the like.' One of the attractions of spiritualism, in both Britain and America, was its accessibility. Without priests as middlemen, anybody who wanted to could contact the next world. This had a particular appeal to the socially excluded – the working-class and women like Dodie Bull and her sisters, who had wealth but little autonomy.

Dodie's diary poignantly observes the beginning of change in the family as the older siblings began to reach adulthood. Harry went up to Oxford and, seduced by press reports of the 'last best West', where opportunity was plentiful and land cheap, the nineteen-year-old Basil decided to make his fortune as a farmer in Canada. Dodie dutifully packed for him the night before his departure, unsure of when she would see him again and sensitive perhaps to the adventure that was calling him and denied to her. 'Dear old boy,' wrote Dodie, 'may he have health, strength and prosperity in his new life ... in the far West. God bless him, dear boy.'[18] Having arrived in Manitoba, Basil sent his sister a letter describing some of the extraordinary and exotic sights he had seen on the voyage: icebergs, whales spouting and awe-inspiring cities such as Toronto and Chicago. Increasingly aware of a world that was open to her brothers beyond Borley, Dodie asked her father to place an advertisement on her behalf in the *Morning Post*, which appeared on 9 June. With her knowledge of French and German, she offered her services as a companion to a lady, seeking a position abroad for six months. 'Of course I won't get anything,' she lamented, 'I never do – but it would be luscious to travel for two months or so for nothing.'[19] Dodie was disappointed and never secured this, or any other job.

Before graduating, the young Harry Bull brought a friend from Oxford to stay at the Rectory, on 10 June 1885. Percy Shaw Jeffrey was the same age as Harry and was studying at Queen's College. According to Dodie, he was 'not very tall' with 'fair hair and moustache, very good features, lovely dark gray eyes and long lashes and eyebrows and splendid teeth and sunburnt complexion.'[20] She was clearly taken with him; 'I mean to go in for him,' she wrote. 'Freda had better not thwart me for I mean to have him.'[21] During his stay, the Rectory was a hothouse of adolescent crushes and sibling rivalry, particularly between Dodie and Freda.

Like many young people at the time, Harry and his friend had a shared interest in spiritualism and the paranormal – and this may be why Shaw Jeffrey had been invited to the Rectory for the summer. He was fascinated by 'folklore, witchcraft, the evil eye, charms and amulets and the rest of it'.While a guest of the Bulls, he claimed to experience a series of disconcerting incidents: stones falling about, his boots found on top of the wardrobe. He saw the ghostly coach sweep down the narrow lane beside the Rectory so often that he got used to the noise and would sleep through it. His biggest 'adventure' was when he lost his French dictionary.[22] He had been studying for some days, when the book disappeared. Nobody could tell where it had gone. But one night, shortly after it had gone missing, he was awoken by a loud thump. He lit his candle and found the dictionary, 'a good deal knocked about', on the floor.[23] But his bedroom door was locked. Shaw Jeffrey seemed convinced of supernatural activity, but he may simply have been caught in the midst of a prank between the two sisters competing for his affections.

This was not the first reported strange activity at the Rectory. The young Ethel Bull had seen a man dressed in dark clothes standing by her bed. Afterwards she was sure that she had felt someone sitting on the edge of the bed. This had scared her so much that from that point onwards, she shared the room with her sister Mabel. Once Mabel moved into the bedroom, both sisters began to experience strange phenomena. Every night, between nine and ten, the girls would hear three raps on the door. When they opened it, there was nobody there.

On 4 October 1885 the family was shocked to hear of the sudden death of their neighbour, Mary Ann Coker, who lived across the lane at Borley Place with her brother. She had been found dead in bed, having had a heart attack. Dodie and her sisters were particularly shocked as they had only seen Miss Coker, looking well, the day before. Her death may have been the inspiration for an experiment that Dodie made with 'chair moving' the next evening.[24] Marie Rolt, her former governess, was visiting when Reverend Bull was away, so the two young women began to explore the paranormal. Dodie wrote:

> I made a chair walk all over the room, and answer questions some of wh[ich] were quite right. I asked it the age of a friend of Marie and it said 25, wh[ich] was quite right. It is great fun and I seem to have a great deal of electricity in me as I can make it walk quite fast.[25]

The next August, Shaw Jeffrey returned to the Rectory for the summer holidays. One day, Harry's Uncle Felix, the rector of Pentlow, came to lunch. He told the family that he thought that Pentlow Rectory was troubled by a poltergeist, just as Liston had been. The next day, Harry and Shaw Jeffrey, both fascinated by the idea of ghosts, took the family carriage to Pentlow to investigate.

When they arrived there, Felix Bull was out, but the young men spoke to the cook. She was sure that the strange occurrences in the house were all down to a new housemaid called Mary, who was at the time making the beds upstairs. Harry and Shaw Jeffrey went up to the main bedroom. Mary was at the far end of the large room and the men were in the doorway, near the fireplace. Harry said, 'Well, Mary, cook says you can show us a few tricks. What about it?'[26] Shaw Jeffrey recalled:

The maid said nothing, but a tooth glass came flying across from the washing stand, behind the maid's back, and circled gracefully round, hitting the jamb of the door just above my head. Just afterwards, the fender and fire-irons moved right out across the room with a clatter. The maid never spoke a word. Nor did we.[27]

But though Harry and his sisters were fascinated by the idea of spiritualism and ghosts, their brothers were sceptical. Alfred insisted that he had never seen anything paranormal at Borley. He had slept in the same room that Shaw Jeffrey had occupied and had experienced 'nothing odd'. Basil had always dismissed the notion that the Rectory was haunted as a product of 'feminine imagination' – the 'ghosts' conjured perhaps from local tales, the influence of popular magazines, the fashionable craze for spiritualism and, perhaps, even an expression of his sisters' growing frustrations, being denied the freedoms and opportunities that their brothers enjoyed.

Shaw Jeffrey's stay at Borley coincided with the arrival of a new under-nursemaid, Martha Seaber Wilson. When she joined the Rectory staff, Martha was given a room at the back of the house overlooking the stable yard. One evening, she was having dinner with the other maids in the servants' hall, when the cook told her, 'You know your bedroom is supposed to be haunted?'[28] Another of the maids told the cook, 'Shut up. You will frighten the girl!'[29] She had been there about a fortnight when, in the middle of the night, something woke her. She heard someone coming down the passage to the bedroom door, shuffling, as if they were wearing slippers. She expected it was the head nurse wanting to talk to her. But nobody came in. She remembered what the cook had said about the room being haunted, so put her head under the bedclothes and lay trembling all night. Too nervous to stay, after only a month Martha left the Rectory. It was always, she thought, a weird place. From then on, she would only pass it after dark if she was accompanied by her grandparents. In 1891 she would marry a farmworker, Ernest Byford, and for the rest of her life would swear that she had had a paranormal experience at the Rectory.

By the time Harry Bull returned to Borley to work as a curate, his father's eyesight and coordination had begun to deteriorate. As Reverend Bull became increasingly immobile, his son took on more parish and social responsibilities. Finally the Reverend went blind, and he died in the Blue Room at the Rectory on 2 May 1892 at the age of 59. The cause of death was recorded as *locomotor ataxia*, a neurological condition affecting the spine, which results in blindness and a loss of motor skills – the symptoms of syphilis.

Syphilis was the much-feared, unspoken corruption at the heart of Victorian life. The creeping terror of this disease was not only in its symptoms, but in the stealthy, undetectable nature of its progress. Invisible during the early stages, untreated it spread throughout the body, progressively destroying the skin, the mucous membranes, bones and internal organs – inflicting horrific mutilations on those who suffered from it. Ultimately, a softening of the brain would then lead to insanity. It was particularly prevalent among middle- and upper-class men. The social stigma of the disease meant that the voluntary hospitals remained unsympathetic to sufferers and many resorted to ineffective remedies from chemists and quacks. Ignorance about the nature of the infection led many men to put their faith in superstition, some believing, for instance, circumcision to be a cure. In 1884, a man in Liverpool defended himself against a charge of raping a fourteen-year-old girl, believing that by having sex with a virgin, he would cure himself by passing the disease onto her. 'Quack doctoresses' in a Liverpool brothel were also said to provide such cures, providing disabled children for the purpose.

Syphilis could be transmitted to the next generation and some of the signs of infection passed to children were deafness, saddle-nose – where the bridge of the nose collapses – inflammation of the cornea and Hutchinson's teeth, a malformation of the incisors.

Following Reverend Bull's death, the Rectory and the patronage of the living passed to the main beneficiary, his eldest son, Harry, with an implicit understanding that he would make provision for his sisters, though £100 was left specifically to Dodie. Reverend Bull was buried in the churchyard, touchingly alongside his son Cyril, who had died in infancy. As a memorial to his father, Harry commissioned a stained-glass window that was placed to the south of the nave in the church, celebrating the relationship between the rector and his congregation: '*I am the good shepherd: the good shepherd giveth his life for the sheep.*'

At twenty-nine, Harry Bull was tall and athletic with a heavy moustache. Like his father, he enjoyed outdoor pursuits – shooting, hunting, walking and tennis. In contrast to his father, he seemed to have little interest in women or family life and appeared to be very much a confirmed bachelor. He was especially fond of boxing and would pay the local boys to spar with him. One curious incident took place, when he had been visiting the East End of London. He was set upon by two thugs. Whether this was a street robbery – or even a sexual pick-up gone wrong – is unclear. But he was able to hold his own and knocked the two assailants out cold. He had a dog, Juvenal, and also began to collect cats, between twenty and thirty of them, which he adored, calling each one by name. At the same time, he'd feed countless strays, which he never turned away. Though regarded as eccentric by the locals, he was a popular 'puckish, lovable man'.[30] At his first Christmas as the rector, he hosted a supper of roast beef and plum pudding as well as turning the drawing room into a miniature theatre at New Year, complete with footlights and scenery. The family presented a play, *Why Women Weep*, in which Harry took centre stage as the leading man. His brothers having forged lives away from Borley, the Rectory was now dominated by women: his mother and seven sisters, all unmarried – 'old maids', as Dodie had predicted.[31] Borley Rectory, once vibrant with the energy of a large growing family and their friends, had assumed the air of a convent.

The afternoon of Wednesday 3 July 1895 was 'delightfully fine' for the wedding of Dodie and John Anderson Hayden, a vicar from Dent in Yorkshire.[32] She was the only one of the Bull sisters who would marry. It was a joyous family occasion after the death of her father, as well as an opportunity for a big local celebration. Carpets were laid all the way from the Rectory, across the road and up the pathway to the church porch. Dodie's sisters were bridesmaids and wore pink crepon skirts and corselets with ivory-white chiffon chokes and sleeves. Their hats were brown straw trimmed with white chiffon and pink carnations. The bride wore a dress of ivory-white satin trimmed with orange blossom and chiffon embroidered with silk spots; her veil was of white tulle. Her brothers Alfred, now a teacher in Worcester, and Gerald, a boat fitter in County Durham, were in proud attendance, though there were significant absences. Settled as a rancher in British Columbia, Basil did not make the ceremony, nor did Hubert, who was at the time on bail. He had gone to work on a farm in Yorkshire at the age of twenty-two. Just before the wedding, he had been arrested for raping a twelve-year-old girl, Anna Mary Johnson, the daughter of his employer. Tried at Howden police court, he pleaded guilty, saying, 'I thought there was no harm in it.'[33] He would serve twelve-months' hard labour in Hull Prison, before becoming a commercial traveller and remaining in the north, very much the black sheep of the family. He did manage to send a travelling rug, cream jug and sugar basin as a wedding present.

Mrs Bull's brothers, George and Alfred Foyster, also attended the wedding celebrations, bringing their families from Hastings to stay at the Rectory. George Foyster was accompanied by his eight children, including seventeen-year-old Lionel, who later remembered being entertained with ghost stories by his younger Bull cousins. But after staying at the Rectory, Alfred admitted that he was so unsettled while sleeping in one of the guest bedrooms that he begged his sister never to put him in the same room again 'or I won't ever come back'.[34] He refused to give any explanation.

On the evening of 28 July 1900, Freda and Mabel Bull had just returned to the Rectory from a tennis party. They met their sister Ethel, who was in the Rectory garden, and together they walked around it discussing the day's gossip. It was 9 p.m. and, given that this was before the establishment of British Summer Time in 1916, it was quite dark already, the sun having set just before eight o'clock. The sisters walked towards the house up the pathway next to the summer house. At one moment, Freda and Mabel wondered why Ethel seemed distracted as she wasn't taking any notice of what they were saying. She had stopped, terrified, pointing towards the path opposite, alongside the boundary wall. 'Look, there's a nun walking there,' Ethel said.[35] Turning to look, Freda and Mabel were astonished to realise that they could see the apparition, too. They watched the figure move down the pathway and then they flew up to the house in terror, to be met by Dodie, who was visiting from Yorkshire. On learning what her sisters had just seen, she said, 'Oh, I'm not going to be frightened!' and went towards the figure to meet her.[36] All of a sudden, the figure disappeared. Seized with panic, Dodie raced back to the house. The sisters continued to tell pretty much the same version of this story for the next fifty years. Crucially, the apparition – ghost, hallucination, whatever it was – had been witnessed by four individuals all at the same time.

In 1896, at the age of eighteen, Ernest Ambrose from Long Melford had first been invited to become organist at Borley Church. The sisters were always very happy to talk to him about the ghostly nun they had seen. They pointed out the pathway alongside the garden wall where they had seen her walking. When he asked what they felt about it, they said, 'Oh, we are quite used to it. It doesn't bother us at all.'[37] They were, he felt, very down-to-earth women, not given to exaggeration or emotionalism; nor were they inclined to look for supernatural explanations for what they saw.

But they were convinced that they had seen an apparition on several occasions. They had even seen the nun inside the house – sitting at one of the bedroom windows in the west wing. Later, a young housemaid, who had been at the Rectory only a short time and hadn't heard about the ghosts, told Ambrose that she came home one evening and in the semi-darkness saw a nun or nurse standing at the lower garden gate. She approached the figure, only for it to vanish. The girl was so terrified, she told him, that she fainted. On another occasion, Ambrose was approaching the front door of the Rectory intending to speak to Harry Bull, when he saw a nun about to knock on the door. Thinking, therefore, that the rector already had an appointment, Ambrose went away intending to speak to him another time. The next day, when he saw Reverend Bull, he told him about the incident the previous evening. 'Oh yes,' said the rector, 'it could well have been the ghost nun. She is very active at night.'[38]

In 1909, Dodie's husband died, but rather than return to Borley, she left Yorkshire and established an independent life in the London suburb of Wandsworth, with her sister Mabel for company. In fond and nostalgic tribute to their childhood home, and with no indication of any fear of ghosts, they named their small terraced house 'Borley'. As Mrs Bull grew older, the remaining sisters took on more of her parish duties, as well as running the house. For nearly twenty years, the Bulls lived harmoniously at the Rectory together, and though the world around them was advancing technologically, their lives changed little from when they had grown up there as children. But in 1911, Harry made a shocking announcement: at nearly fifty, he was getting married.

The daughter of an engineer, Ivy Brackenbury was thirty-two years old and had been working as a midwife at the Walnut Tree Hospital in Sudbury when Harry had been a patient there. At the time she married him, Ivy claimed to be a widow. At the age of twenty-one she had married Harold Brackenbury, a civil engineer, at Lincoln Register Office and they'd had a daughter two years later. But the marriage had not been a success. In a pre-digital age, each parish or district kept its own register of births, marriages and deaths. It was impossible for vicars or registrars to check or cross-reference the information people submitted on official documents. Until well after the Second World War, divorce in England was expensive, extremely difficult and carried great social stigma – it was often easier for the partners in a broken marriage, such as the Brackenburys, to separate informally and move to a different part of the country to begin a new life. Though giving incorrect information on official registers was a criminal offence, it was commonplace and prosecutions for bigamy were rare.

Ivy was living at St Ursula's Women's Hostel in central London when she and Harry married on 12 September 1911 at St Alban's, the church next door. Known as 'one of the ecclesiastical curiosities of London',[39] St Alban's practised the Anglo-Catholic tradition. The law at the time was that marriages must take place in the parish church where the bride resided, and not her husband's, hence the ceremony not taking place at Borley. The wedding was witnessed by Harry's brother Alfred and sister Dodie, so, at this point, relations between Harry's siblings and his new wife seemed perfectly civil.

Harry set up home with Ivy, renting Borley Place next to the church from the Payne family. But Ivy's ten-year-old daughter, Constance, 'hated her new step-father like poison'; he was even known to have struck her on more than one occasion.[40] Consequently, she was sent away to a Roman Catholic convent in Surrey. The Rectory was run by Harry's mother and sisters, who continued to work on the administration of the parish. The Bull siblings, the majority of them unmarried, planned to leave their estates to those remaining. Now Harry would need to make provision for his wife and for any future children, as Ivy was still of child-bearing age. On 21 January 1912 his new will outlined that, on his death, Ivy should be paid £100 at once and that all his assets should be sold and converted into money. This was to be used to form a trust, from which the income would be paid to Ivy for the rest of her life or until she should remarry. His siblings would inherit nothing. At the same time, perhaps due to Ivy's Catholic influence, Harry began to wear a stole during services, an Anglo-Catholic practice that was frowned on by traditionally Low Church Anglicans such as the Bulls.

On 13 April 1914, Mrs Bull died at the age of seventy-seven. At the funeral five days later, the coffin was carried from the Rectory and followed in procession by ten of her children, including her shamed son, Hubert. After the funeral, Harry's sisters now took their mother's place supporting him with his parish duties. But after many years in which time had stood still and life had remained the same at Borley, that summer there was traumatic change as the world suddenly collapsed into turmoil.

Before 1914, Britain had long been accustomed to peace, with armed conflicts only on the periphery of national consciousness fought in remote parts of the world such as India, Burma, Crimea, China and South Africa. These campaigns had been fought on behalf of the British Empire by professional armies. Six million British men – most of them conscripts – were now embroiled in the 'carnival of death' on the Western Front; just over 740,000 died. Twenty thousand soldiers were killed on the first day of the Battle of the Somme alone, more than all British losses in the Boer War. 'The list of dead piled up,' remembered Harold Macmillan, 'month by month and year by year, to a frightful sum.'[41] Bereavement became a universal experience affecting just about every household in the country. Borley Rectory was no exception. Basil Bull had become an American citizen in 1909, and when war broke out he was already forty-eight. But in 1916, keen to fight on behalf of the Empire, he had volunteered for the Canadian Expeditionary Force, claiming to be five years younger on his application. At the same time, always keen for adventure, his widowed older sister, Dodie, joined the Red Cross as a nurse and was sent to work at a military hospital at Vichy to care for typhoid patients. She was highly esteemed by the doctors she worked under, remaining at the hospital for four years. Finally becoming ill herself, she was forced to return home, but was decorated for her service. On 1 August 1917, Basil was wounded in Belgium by a high-explosive shell and died later that day. He left his estate to his brother Hubert and his older sister Dodie.

As the war ended, troops returned home by boat and train, unaware that many were carrying a deadly strain of influenza that they'd contracted in northern France. The movement of demobbed soldiers across the planet ensured that this particularly virulent virus became a global pandemic. Young adults between twenty and thirty were particularly susceptible to what became known as Spanish flu, and though most cases saw a three-day fever before recovery, in some patients the progression of the disease was shockingly rapid. More than 500 million people were infected around the world, with an estimated 20–50 million deaths. More people died of the virus than had died as a result of the war. A quarter of the British population was infected and 228,000 died. These casualties, so cruel after the carnage of the war years, only compounded the sense of loss.

There followed an extraordinary outpouring of national grief channelled into public acts of mourning and remembrance. The remains of an anonymous soldier who would embody every family's loss was brought back from France and given the highest honour, a resting place in Westminster Abbey. A festival of remembrance evolved that included a new innovation of a two-minute silence in honour of the war dead. An empty tomb of wood and plaster, designed by Sir Edwin Lutyens, was erected to acknowledge the dead. So acutely did it express the public mood of sorrow that within a fortnight a plan – and a budget – was agreed to make the memorial permanent. The temporary structure was dismantled in January 1920 and a stone replacement erected on the same spot. By the end of the week, an estimated 1 million people had paid their respects and the Cenotaph has stood ever since, the focus of national mourning.

The Cenotaph inspired local war memorials in towns and villages, schools, universities and churches across the kingdom. On Sunday 7 November 1920, a brass memorial tablet was unveiled in Borley Church by the Waldegrave tomb in honour of the seven men from the village who had lost their lives during the war, including

Basil Bull. The service was led by his brother Harry, who had launched the campaign to fund the memorial.

The war over, Ivy Bull proceeded to initiate a strategy that would fracture the already fragile relations between her and her husband's family. Harry and Ivy wanted to take possession of the Rectory with her now eighteen-year-old daughter. Having, not unreasonably, expected that they would spend the rest of their days together in the house that their father had built, Harry's four unmarried sisters were aghast when instructed to find somewhere else to live. As the new mistress of the Rectory, Ivy decorated it as she pleased, furnishing separate rooms for Constance to use in her holidays from school, as her relationship with her stepfather remained toxic. Harry's sisters moved four miles away to Chilton Lodge in Great Cornard, taking with them some of the remaining furniture and family pictures that had not been sold in the auction following the death of their mother. Forced into exile from their childhood home by Harry's wife, his sisters' dislike of her now festered into a bitter and abiding hatred.

In 1922, John Meighen Osborne Harley lived a few miles from Borley, in Cavendish, with his family. At the age of fifteen, he was convalescing from an attack of whooping cough when he was sent to lodge at the Rectory for extra Latin instruction with Harry Bull.[42] The boy was already aware of the stories of the ghosts, and was intrigued rather than frightened, thinking that the spirits might offer an excuse for him to neglect his studies. He would join the rector in long ghost-watching sessions, many of which took place in the large summer house facing the Nun's Walk or in the Gothic summer house at the bottom of the rose garden.

One night, at about two o'clock in the morning, the large bell in the courtyard rang. Harry Bull rushed out from his bedroom in a very distressed state, pulling on his plum-coloured smoking jacket and calling to Osborne Harley, 'Did you hear it? If you did, for goodness sake don't tell anybody.'[43] When Osborne Harley promised to keep the secret, the rector became much calmer. 'Good boy,

I'm sure I can trust you. I don't suppose it will happen again.'[44] On cue, the bell rang even more violently. 'That's strange,' said Bull. 'I've never known it ring twice in quick succession like that before.'[45] When Osborne Harley suggested that perhaps somebody might have rung the bell – Mrs Bull, or one of the servants, perhaps – the rector dismissed him. 'Who on earth would come and ring the courtyard bell like that at this time of night? No, it's the nun, she does some-times.'[46] Osborne Harley lay awake, hoping to hear the bell ring again, but it remained silent.

The next day, nobody mentioned the ringing of the bell. Unlike Reverend Bull, neither his wife, his stepdaughter nor the servants were interested in spiritualism and appeared to take the hauntings and the existence of the nun for granted. Was the bell-ringing caused by rats gnawing at the bell ropes? Or a nocturnal practical joker? Osborne Harley couldn't be sure. But he had no doubt that Harry Bull was happier in the presence of the 'ghosts' than he was in the company of his student. He felt that he bored the rector; the ghosts, on the other hand, stirred him profoundly. One evening, when they had finished their studies, he told the boy that when he died, if he was dissatisfied with the rector who succeeded him he would make his displeasure clear – but not with footsteps or bell-ringing; Harry Bull promised to 'turn into a poltergeist and pelt 'em with mothballs.'[47]

'Mystery of the Walled-up Spook of Borley Rectory'

CHAPTER SIX

Murder at the Parsonage

13 June 1929–14 March 1930

Whereas the ordinary ghost of our story-books is a quiet, inoffensive, noiseless and rather benevolent spirit, with – usually friendly feelings towards the incarnate occupants of any place where it has its abode, the Poltergeist is just the reverse; mischievous, destructive, noisy, cruel, erratic, thievish, demonstrative, purposeless, cunning, unhelpful, malicious, audacious, teasing, ill-disposed, spiteful, ruthless, resourceful, and vampiric. A ghost *haunts*; a Poltergeist *infests*.

Harry Price, *Poltergeist Over England*[1]

On 13 June 1929, the early summer weather continued to be warm in north Essex, improving prospects for the farms surrounding Borley. A drought in the spring indicated a longer hay harvest and farmers looked forward to some rain to nourish their grazing land and cereal crops. Meanwhile, reports about the strange activity at the Rectory continued to appear in the *Daily Mirror*. The sleepy village had suddenly and unexpectedly found itself the 'hub of the universe'.[2]

Now grown up and living in London, John Osborne Harley, reading the reports of Reverend Bull's unquiet spirit in the previous days *Mirror*, had almost dropped his newspaper.[3] For a moment he felt that he was back at the Rectory, helping his tutor feed his cats, sitting beside him in the summer house, waiting, watching and wondering. He wrote to the *Mirror* about his days with Harry Bull:

> I distinctly recall him assuring me that on many occasions he had had personal communications with spirits. In his opinion the only way for a spirit, if ignored, to get in touch with a living person, was by means of manifestation causing some violent physical reaction such as the breaking of glass or the shattering of other and similar material elements. The rector also declared that on his death, if he were discontented, he would adopt this method of communicating with the inhabitants of the rectory.[4]

As he had promised, Osborne Harley felt, Harry Bull had indeed thrown the mothball to express his displeasure with Eric Smith. The late rector had ever been a man of his word.

Not everybody, however, embraced the story of the ghosts at Borley. When Charles Pilgrim, the gardener at the Rectory, was interviewed by the press, he said that he had never seen *anything*, and although there had been a great deal of talk about ghosts at Borley many years ago, he believed that it was really 'only couples sweet-hearting'.[5] Other villagers ridiculed the whole affair. The same happenings had occurred many times over the years at the Rectory; what the Smiths were experiencing was nothing new.

On Friday 14 June, Harry Price returned to Borley and, together with Lucie Kaye, drove to visit the Bull sisters for tea in Great Cornard, which at the time was still a separate settlement outside the town of Sudbury. Chilton Lodge was a solid, ivy-clad Georgian building furnished with heavy antique pieces, portraits and pictures, much of which the sisters had brought with them when they had been exiled from the Rectory in 1920. The visitors from London were entertained in the sitting room by Ethel, Freda and Constance, who they found both charming and cultured.

Though she was not the eldest, the sisters looked to Ethel for guidance and direction; she was at once the spokeswoman, correspondent and archivist of the family. Lucie took notes of the conversation as

Price asked questions and Ethel relayed her story. They had had a very happy childhood at the Rectory and though they often heard noises in the house, they were never afraid of them. One twilight, many years ago, Ethel had seen a man dressed in dark clothes by her bed and felt someone sitting on the side of it, which had frightened her. From this point onwards, Ethel shared a room with one of her sisters and every night, between nine and ten, there would be three raps on the door. They never called 'come in' because they knew there'd be nobody there. This took place over a hundred times. But none of this low-key activity ever worried them.

Ethel went on to tell the story of seeing the nun in the garden in the summer of 1900 with great gusto, the details of which Freda confirmed. Ethel was certain that there had been no appearance of the nun before this time. She recalled that she saw the woman bent over in a flowing black robe such as nuns wear. She didn't see her face, nor whether she wore a rosary or a crucifix.[6] She made no record of the experience at the time, though she had discussed it with members of the family. Ethel confirmed that her brother Harry had seen the phantom coach and that once his retriever, Juvenal, had been terrified, apparently growling at a figure among the fruit trees. Harry, who could only see a pair of legs, had followed with the dog, but the legs disappeared through the gate; though, Miss Bull admitted, it could have been a poacher.[7] Ethel was insistent that during all the time they lived in the house, neither she nor her sisters ever saw or heard of any poltergeist activity. The violent and noisy phenomena of recent months had started only since the Smiths had arrived.

The conversation turned to the seance that had taken place earlier in the week and the apparent manifestation of Harry Bull. The sisters' attitude to the death of their brother was driven by a sense of hurt, injustice and resentment towards their sister-in-law. Ivy's first husband had disappeared before the daughter, Constance, was born. When she met Harry, she was only too glad to secure a home for herself and her child. She took the opportunity such security offered but it led to very unhappy results. At first, Harry had seemed to be happy with Ivy, but once they moved into the Rectory together, they found that they were temperamentally unsuited. Harry, always highly strung himself, found Ivy hysterical and affected, and they began to quarrel violently.[8] His affection soon turned to hatred. His sisters feared that one day he might do Ivy some serious injury – or even kill her. The marriage deteriorated further and Ivy came to hate Harry as heartily as he did her. During his final illness, as a qualified nurse she did attend him, but only very grudgingly. As he reached the end of his life, he often said that he hated being alive and wanted to die. Since his death, Ivy had posed – ostentatiously – as the sorrowful widow. Given that they were very open with Price, a man they had only recently met, presumably the sisters were equally as blatant in broadcasting their feelings about Ivy throughout the village.[9]

Harry had left an estate of £6,643, much more than his father. The main provisions of the will outlined the trust that he had set up for Ivy for the rest of her life or until she should remarry. In that case, the remainder from the trust was to be paid in equal shares to Harry's remaining brothers and sisters. Perhaps most significantly, on Harry's death, the Rectory was sold to the church authorities, his widow retaining possession of a portion of the garden. Though the other siblings had arranged to leave their estates to each other, Harry had effectively left them nothing; not even the roof they were all born under. Meanwhile, having inherited the bulk of her husband's estate, 'that vile woman' had quickly moved away from Borley, setting up home with her daughter in a flat she had bought in Primrose Hill in London. Though she no longer lived at the Rectory to witness it, Ethel Bull was convinced that since his death, the ghost of her brother would walk down the main stairs in his smoking jacket, carrying a book or manuscript – a sermon, or his will perhaps – before going into the library.

Ethel recommended that Price should also visit Mr and Mrs Cooper, who worked for them and lived nearby. Edward Cooper had been employed by the Bulls as groom-gardener and he and his wife had lived in the Rectory Cottage for four years.

Just as they departed from Chilton Lodge, Price asked Ethel if she and her sisters were never at all frightened of what they had seen and heard at the Rectory. Ethel was clear: they had grown up with it and had no fear at all. She did say that nothing would induce her to spend another night at the Rectory now, but this may have had more to do with her feelings towards Ivy than any fears regarding the house.

Price and Lucie drove to the Coopers' snug little house in Broom Street. The Coopers had been married since 1898 and were in their late forties when in 1916 they had moved into the Rectory Cottage with their sixteen-year-old daughter, Lily. Cooper had carried on with his duties at the Rectory until the sisters left the house in March 1920. They were happy to tell their story to Price and insisted that they had never discussed it before. They'd never heard of the Rectory being haunted or any legend connected with it, even when they had lived there.

Mrs Cooper told Price and Lucie that they had been there a little while when her husband asked if she had been hearing any noises in the house. Something like a large dog overhead in the attic. Mrs Cooper suggested that it might be cats or rats, given that they lived above a stable and next to a farm. They investigated the loft, but there was nothing there. But one afternoon, she felt she could hear a rapping overhead, quite loud. It was then she realised that there really were noises and it was not her husband's imagination. Shortly afterwards, he had returned home one evening and asked her if she had ever seen a nun up at the Rectory. She told him that she hadn't. He went on to say that it was dusk and he had been leaving by the garden door of the Rectory when he saw a nun leave the back entrance, heading for the road. He thought she might have been making a collection, but there was something odd about her, so he followed her about six yards behind. But by the time she had reached the road, she had disappeared.

One moonlit evening, Cooper was looking out of the window and saw in the distance what appeared to be an old-fashioned coach, with horses and two headlights. The lights glittered on the harness and the horses, but there was no sound whatever. He called his wife to come and see, but before she got to the window, it had disappeared. Mrs Cooper explained that during the last months they lived at the Rectory Cottage, just after the war, they had even more extraordinary experiences. One June night, they'd been in bed some little time, though it wasn't quite dark, their daughter sleeping in the next room. Cooper wasn't asleep but was lying still when he said, 'There's something in this room.'[10] He thought he had heard a slight movement at the head of the bed. Then he saw a dark figure go around the bed, which he thought might be a dog. Suddenly there was a tremendous crash. It sounded as though someone had dropped a heavy tray of crockery all over the table downstairs. Cooper quickly lit the lamp and looked over the house, expecting to find broken crockery in the kitchen after the crash. But there was nothing. All was silent. Waking their daughter, she said that she hadn't heard a thing. They had left the Rectory Cottage in March 1920 and didn't talk about what had happened there until they read about the haunting in the local paper earlier that week. Having interviewed the Bulls and the Coopers, Price returned to London. He was now convinced that Borley Rectory was 'one of the major problems of psychical research'.[11]

The story of the ghosts and Price's arrival in Borley continued to make an impact on the village. On 20 June, an advertisement appeared in the *Suffolk and Essex Free Press* that expressed the tongue-in-cheek attitude that some of the locals held about Borley's new-found fame; the story of the ghost was a local joke:

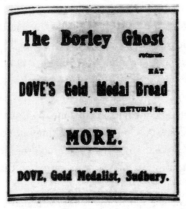

The Borley Ghost returns.

EAT

DOVE'S Gold Medal Bread

and you will RETURN for

MORE.

DOVE, Gold Medalist, Sudbury.

But at the centre of the drama, Eric and Mabel Smith weren't amused. Since the invasion of sightseers following the articles in the *Daily Mirror* and now the local press, life at the Rectory had become unbearable. With the Bishop adamant that Smith would not be offered another parish, they felt they had few options: they must leave. They would stay in temporary accommodation at The Bull in Long Melford and commute to Borley for parish duties until Reverend Smith could find another living. He insisted that they were doing so because of the appalling condition of the building and its expensive upkeep. But the locals nodded knowingly. Mr and Mrs Smith were frightened. It was the ghosts that had haunted them out of Borley Rectory.

On 25 June, hearing that they were vacating the Rectory imminently, Lucie Kaye wrote to Mabel Smith from London, telling her that she and Price were keen to spend 'an enviable night in the haunted room' the following week.[12] They were keen to bring an associate of Price's, Lord Charles Hope, who had a great interest in psychical research. Mabel was only too happy to oblige. The next week, on Friday 5 July, Price, Lucie and Lord Charles motored to Essex.

Thirty-seven-year-old Lord Charles was an Old Etonian, the second son of the 1st Marquess of Linlithgow. A member of the Society for Psychical Research, he was also a Council Member of Price's National Laboratory of Psychical Research and was a regular visitor at their premises in Queensbury Place, South Kensington. He had attended many of Price's seances, financially supporting some of them. Among his varied interests, he also found time to be a champion golfer.

The party checked in at The Bull at Long Melford, where they would all be staying, before driving over to Borley while it was still daylight. The Smiths explained to Lord Charles the activity they'd experienced in the house since they'd arrived. As he was shown around the property, he noted that most of the rooms were empty, the Smiths reduced to living in a corner of the house. Mrs Smith, he observed, seemed particularly nervous and very anxious to move out.

That evening, Price and Lord Charles were sitting in the Blue

Room while Lucie was in the room next to the bathroom. The Smiths were downstairs in the drawing room listening to the wireless as Mary and Fred Tatum chatted in the kitchen. Suddenly the bell for the drawing room rang in the kitchen passage. Mary went to answer it as usual. But when she asked what the Smiths needed, they told her they hadn't rung. Shortly afterwards, the bell rang again. Once more, Mary went to the drawing room, but again she was told that the Smiths hadn't rung. Again and again – four times – the bell for the drawing room rang, but they told Mary that they hadn't called her.

All of a sudden there was a loud clattering at the top of the stairs. Price and Lord Charles ran out onto the landing and were joined by Lucie. Downstairs, almost immediately, Mary and Fred appeared from the kitchen as the Smiths came out of the drawing room. Lying at the top of the stairs, Price and Lord Charles found two small pebbles, smooth and black. The landing window was open, so Price closed it. Mary suggested that they stay together and all go to the Blue Room, which they did, sitting there for about twenty minutes. It was now dark outside.

The visitors decided to hold a vigil in the Blue Room and sat in it with a lamp, while the Smiths remained downstairs in the drawing room listening to the wireless. Fred Tatum was allowed to stay in the kitchen during the evenings to keep Mary company because she was frightened. All of a sudden there was a loud ringing of bells from outside the kitchen. Once again Price, Lucie and Lord Charles ran down the stairs and, reaching the bell board in the kitchen passage, found one of them still ringing. As they were inspecting the bell board, there was another loud crash in the hall.

In the darkness and confusion, they doubled back into the hall, where they met the Smiths, Mary and Fred coming out of the drawing room. There on the hall floor were six or seven keys and a medallion. Picking this up Lucie could see it was decorated with a Latin inscription and what seemed to be the head of a monk. Mabel Smith now seemed very nervous, so they all retired to the drawing room. She was worrying that the aerial for the wireless, which was positioned near the window, had been tampered with. So, they went to look at it. Suddenly a pebble fell on the floor, as if dropped from the ceiling, just like the ones they had found upstairs. Mary was behind Lord Charles, and Price was behind her. It occurred to Lord Charles at the time that the maid wasn't as scared as she might have been of the extraordinary phenomena that had been taking place in the house during the evening. He started to suspect that she, either consciously or unconsciously, was responsible for the phenomena. The Society for Psychical Research had a patriarchal attitude to the working class and was particularly suspicious of servants. When gathering evidence of paranormal phenomena, the society wouldn't record accounts of hauntings from servants, who were thought to be gullible or malicious; the history of the study of psychical phenomena was littered with cases of domestic servants using apparently paranormal phenomena to disguise criminal or licentious behaviour.

Mabel collected the keys from the floor and went to put them in the metal bowl they used for visiting cards on the hall table near the front door. The only one she recognised fitted the dining room door, which she gave to Lord Charles to replace in its lock. After all the activity, Fred went home and the Smiths and Mary retired to bed. Returning to the Blue Room, and now alone with Price and Lucie, Lord Charles outlined his suspicions about the maid. Might *she* be responsible for the phenomena? He hoped that the 'ghost' might do something more now that she was safely tucked up in bed – 'if they want to impress us, let them give us a phenomenon now!'[13] Almost immediately, a bell was heard to ring loudly from the kitchen passage. The three went down the stairs, but when they reached the bell board, this time the bells were still and silent, as if nothing had moved.

Lord Charles suggested that Lucie go and ask Mrs Smith if there were bells anywhere else in the house apart from outside the kitchen. He also suggested that she should give them the keys that they had picked up off the floor so they could see if they fitted any of the other doors in the house. Woken by Lucie, Mabel told her that there were no other bells in the house. She got up and went down the backstairs to show Lucie where she had left the keys.

Lord Charles was just outside the kitchen and Price was in the dark hall at the foot of the stairs when suddenly a key fell on the floor between them. It was the key to the dining room. Lucie was certain that she had seen the key in its lock only a short time before. Suddenly several more keys fell in quick succession out of the darkness. One fell in the hall; another hit the stairs – Lord Charles picked it up and was setting off to try it in the lock of the garden door when another key fell from above, striking the stove in the centre of the hall. Price and Lucie went up the staircase to investigate where the keys might be coming from. In a flash, another key fell and struck the metal bowl on the hall table. Again it was the key to the dining room. As Lord Charles was alone in the hall, he couldn't see how anybody could have thrown it from the top of the stairs.

Mabel retired to bed, telling the ghost hunters to leave any keys in the metal bowl in the hall. Lord Charles then suggested that he, Price and Lucie should inspect the whole house, starting with the first floor. On their tour, they found the bathroom window open, so they shut it. While they were there, Lord Charles noted several squares of linoleum lying on the floor near the bath. He descended the stairs followed by Lucie and Price. Almost immediately he noticed a square of the same linoleum propped up against the middle of one of the steps. They picked it up and compared it with the squares in the bathroom; they were exactly the same. Price suggested that Lord Charles had been last down the stairs, implying that *he* might have placed the linoleum himself, but Lord Charles insisted that wasn't true and Lucie backed him up. Apart from the dining room door, none of the keys seemed to fit any of the locks in the house, so Lord Charles, Price and Lucie placed them in the metal bowl. Then the house was quiet. The activity seemingly over, they left at 2 a.m. and retired to The Bull at Long Melford.

Reflecting on the evening's events, Lord Charles recalled that in the passage outside the bedroom occupied by the Smiths, some of the bell wires were exposed and it might have been possible for someone to ring a bell by pulling one of these wires. Was it conceivable that Mrs Smith herself had produced the phenomena? But why would she need to strengthen the case to leave the Rectory when they had already made plans to do so? As well as Mrs Smith and the maid, he was equally unsure of some other members of the party. He was particularly concerned about the incident of the linoleum on the stairs. He left Borley with a suspicion that Price might have been responsible for at least some of the phenomena that had occurred at the Rectory that night.

On 9 July, Eric Smith wrote to Price enclosing a photo card of the Rectory, perhaps ordered as a memento in preparation for their move:

> It is very strange but we found the table in the 'haunted' room had been hurled over from in front of the fireplace to the washstand in the corner, and lying on its side. Whatever force catapulted this? My wife is very anxious to know what it was that rang all the bells after we retired on Thursday night last? She was only wishing Miss Kaye could have come in and inspected our rooms, only I had gone to bed. She would have found there were no wires anywhere in the back of the house that could pull bells. You see we have been forced into inhabiting what were normally the servants' quarters, the one little bell pull doesn't work at all, and there are no wires connected. Mary's room across the passage has no wires at all. It is very mysterious, isn't it? And we would like to clear up about the bells.
>
> I wonder what the two crashes were that we heard before all of you left? Anyhow it is very kind of all of you to take the trouble that you have, to investigate the horrible phenomena. We are moving (DV)* next week to where no 'spooks' will trouble us, but if they do, we shall not hesitate to let you know. If there is anybody that you know who would care to rent or buy this

---

* *Dio Volente*, God Willing

rectory, do let me know. There would be good commission, I assure you, and the rent would be exceptionally low – I daresay also the sale price.[14]

Though he may not have been aware of it, shortly before they left the Rectory, Mabel had been informed by the maid that there was a place in the pantry where a cluster of bell wires was exposed. By standing on a chair and pulling these wires, bells could be rung in the kitchen passage as if they had been rung in rooms all over the house.

The Smiths had found a house on Westgate Terrace, near Holy Trinity Church in Long Melford. They moved in all their furniture and possessions, leaving the Rectory empty once again. They had endured it for less than a year. Harry Price had arrived at the house on 12 June; little more than a month later, the rector and his wife had abandoned it.

Throughout the summer the Smiths maintained a cordial correspondence with Price. He had promised to write an official report about the phenomena for them and they were very anxious to read it, as this might bolster their argument with the Bishop to secure another living. Smith's persistence in pursuing Price's report is curious, given that they had already left the house. He may have thought it might offer extra colour for the novel that his wife was writing, *Murder at the Parsonage*, or perhaps was thinking ahead – that Price's report might be used for publicity if it were ever published.

They continued to commute to Borley, cleaning the church brasses and arranging the altar flowers on Saturday in preparation for Sunday services. Calling in at the empty Rectory to check the house over, Eric Smith was dismayed to find that much of the glass was broken or cracked; whether by the north-easterly winds, vandals or ghosts couldn't be determined. 'It is dreadful,' he lamented to Price, 'to see the place falling into decay.' At dusk one day, Smith was alone in the empty house, crossing the landing. He was startled by a woman's voice, apparently coming from the centre of the arch, leading towards the old bathroom. It started with a moaning sound, gradually rising in tone and slightly louder than ordinary conversation. It ended with the words, 'Don't, Carlos, don't.'[15] Despite the Smiths' initial scepticism about the haunting, it was clear from their correspondence that they were now convinced that the Rectory was haunted – it had an 'evil atmosphere'. They missed Price's presence. 'Somehow,' Smith wrote, 'we don't feel safe without you.'[16]

After the war, Ernest Ambrose, who had been organist at Borley since he was a young man, had set up a small shop in Hall Street, Long Melford, selling photographic equipment such as cameras and film, but also offering photographic services. After the newspaper reports about the Rectory, an Irish American called into the shop and asked if Ambrose could take some pictures of it, saying that he could charge as much as he liked for the photographs and giving him an address to send them to in New York.[17]

Even though he thought this all sounded too good to be true, the next day Ambrose cycled over to Borley and took six photographs of the house and garden, which had stood vacant since the departure of the Smiths. After considering it, he decided to charge £4 for the photographs – which he considered an exorbitant sum – and sent them to the address he had been given. To his surprise, by return of post he received a cheque for £4 from an American press agency. Six weeks later, he was further stunned to receive a copy of an American newspaper. There, on the front page, was one of his photographs of the Rectory. Superimposed on the image was a drawing of the phantom nun and spectral coach, horses with distended nostrils driven with demonic fury by headless coachmen, under the caption 'Mystery of the Walled-up Spook of Borley Rectory'. He quickly made two copies of the image with his camera on glass plates and developed several prints.

A few hours later, Eric Smith arrived at the shop in a 'towering rage'.[18] He, too, had received a copy of the American newspaper and demanded an explanation. What on earth had Ambrose done? Ambrose explained the story of the American and how much he had been paid for the pictures. A furious Smith asked if he had any more copies of the image? Ambrose admitted he had just copied it onto a glass plate. When he gave it to him, Smith smashed it on the floor and stamped on it, little knowing that Ambrose had kept another copy.

As the autumn turned to another winter at Borley, Eric Smith began to despair of ever finding another parish. All he and his wife wanted was to make a new start and put Borley and its unpleasant memories behind them. They carried on commuting to the village, but the harsh winter weather was making even this a challenge as the country roads were filled with mud, so they were unable to use the car. With no public transport to the village, they had to walk to the church and back every day, taking their food with them and eating it picnic-fashion. They were not looking forward to 1930 and what promised to be a bleak new year. Again they wrote to Price, persisting in the request they had made for a report on the haunting:

> ... we have been ... indulging in some little speculation as to when your report on the Borley case will reach us as kindly promised. You will be perhaps interested to learn that someone had published an illustrated account about Borley in the American papers, because, for the last month, I am being inundated with letters from all over the states – and they still come – asking for further news and so forth. Borley is undoubtedly haunted, though we have tried to dispossess ourselves of the idea. If you could send the report, it would help immeasurably.[19]

On 14 March 1930, Eric Smith wrote to Price informing him that 'funny things' continued to occur at the deserted Rectory.[20] At the time of the full moon, when strange things usually happened, the 'most horrible sounds' were heard in the house. Villagers saw lights at night and found broken glass and lumps of stone ('half a fireplace')[21] deposited on the main staircase. As the 'friends' seemed unable to rest, Smith would not allow his wife to visit the house any more.[22] He assured Price that he and Mrs Smith often talked of the 'thrilling times at Borley' and hoped that he would visit them in Long Melford soon. He enclosed a doctored photograph of the Rectory – which he must have sourced from Eric Ambrose – portraying the ghost of the nun. 'Clever, isn't it?'[23]

Since the sensational publicity that the Rectory had attracted, the Bulls had shut it up once more, despairing of ever finding new tenants. It was put on the market for sale. Despite its reputation, the agents had several enquiries from across Britain but no offer was made. Nobody, it seemed, wanted to buy a haunted house.

Meanwhile, as the story of Borley began to reach an international audience, Price's first article about the Rectory appeared in the *Journal of the American Society for Psychical Research*. He insisted that he was convinced of the authenticity of the phenomena by the 'mass of first hand evidence' extending over a period of forty-five years, including the story of the monastery and the walled-up nun. 'We have not yet had an opportunity of "laying" the ghosts of Borley Rectory,' he wrote. 'On the other hand, the disturbing entities have succeeded in driving out the rector and his wife and the dilapidated mansion is empty once more ... perhaps now the place is empty again the haunting spirits are at rest.'[24]

They would not rest for long.

Harry Price outside his workshop at Arun Bank

CHAPTER SEVEN

CONFESSIONS OF A GHOST HUNTER

17 January 1881–29 September 1930

To work successfully in this field, one has to be absolutely
fearless and independent – with a hide like a rhinoceros.

Harry Price, *Search for Truth*[1]

By the time he arrived at Borley in the summer of 1929, Harry
Price had already redefined, almost single-handedly, the popular
conception of the fairly new science of psychical research in Britain.
He had also cemented the image of what a ghost hunter did – the
'scientific' devices and tests – as well as what a ghost hunter looked
like: tweeds and a pipe during the haunt, a boffin-style white coat
while investigating evidence in the laboratory. He was able to build
this public role by engaging with the new tabloid press, who were
hungry for spooky tales and quirky stories aimed at the popular
audience, particularly women.

To read his autobiography, *Search for Truth*, Price's life and
career has an air of inevitability about it – visiting a haunted
house in Shropshire in his youth (he claimed), set him off on
his journey into psychical research; 'the typical stone-throwing,
window-rattling, and door-slamming "ghost" made a great impression on my adolescent and receptive mind and from then onwards

I decided to become an investigator.' Price and Borley Rectory, it would seem, were destined for each other.[2]

Despite frequently suggesting that he had come from a well-to-do family, Price had a modest, if aspirational background. He was born on 17 January 1881 to Edward Ditching Price, a 47-year-old grocer from Shropshire, and twenty-year-old Emma Meech, the daughter of a newspaper reporter. His grandfather a journalist, his father a salesman, the telling of popular stories – and selling them – was very much in Price's blood. While living in the district around Theobalds Road in central London, Price's father started work as a travelling salesman for Edward Saunders & Son, one of the biggest paper manufacturers in London. As Edward Price prospered, the family moved to Walpole Street off New Cross Road in Deptford. On 26 February 1882, their young son was christened Harry – not 'Henry', which would cause him frequent confusion in his schooldays:

> Headmaster: What is your name?
> Young Price: Harry Price, sir.
> Headmaster: (*marking entry in register*) Henry Price.
> Young Price: No, *Harry* Price, sir.
> Headmaster: Yes, yes, boy, but you were Christened Henry.
> Young Price: No, sir, I was Christened Harry.
> Headmaster: Well, you ought *not* to have been![3]

After several years, the Prices' finances improved and they were able to buy 'Cloverley', a flat-fronted, four-storey house in St Donatts Road, New Cross. This, one of the larger properties in the street, with a coach house attached, was a step up for the Prices. A father ambitious for his son, Edward Price subscribed to the *Encyclopaedia Britannica* and Harry would take a volume up to bed with him and read one or two articles from it every night.

The young Price was fascinated by the glamour of performance and theatre. The 1880s and '90s were the high point of British music hall and south-east London was home to some of the most important venues in the city. The New Cross Empire, a vast 2,000-seat palace of varieties, was situated virtually on the Prices' doorstep. Magic acts, ventriloquists, hypnotists and illusionists were hugely popular and entranced the young Price to such an extent that he pestered his father to buy him Professor Hoffman's *Modern Magic,* a primer that exposed the secrets of parlour magic and illusions. The fact that he was curious to know how the tricks were played at such an early age, was, he later argued, proof 'of that inherent scepticism coupled with the critical faculty, with which my existence has been cursed'.[4] A little boy tugging at Santa's beard, Price's curiosity was compelled by the mechanics behind the magic, the sleight of hand that conjured the illusion.

At school Price met a girl called Constance Knight who lived locally in the more superior neighbourhood of Brockley. She was from a comfortable background, her mother a former servant and her father a hairdresser who had been left a sizeable inheritance by his father and had invested it wisely. Constance was a selfless, unworldly girl. Though a social class above and temperamentally contrary to Price, they became firm friends, then sweethearts.

Attending Haberdashers' Aske's Hatcham Boys School from the age of eleven – very much a suburban grammar school – Price began to contribute articles on coin collecting and archaeology to *The Askean*, the school magazine. Though interested in writing, he was not a distinguished scholar and left school at fifteen, ill-suited to further education. His father secured him part-time work at Edward Saunders as a travelling salesman and in the evening he studied photography, chemistry and mechanical engineering at nearby Goldsmiths College with a view to becoming a mechanical engineer. Throughout his life he retained a boyish love of anything that worked mechanically or electrically, and though he would never become an engineer, the sciences he studied at Goldsmiths would be invaluable in his future work in psychical research. Soon he started to make public demonstrations of the new technologies of the era – photography and the gramophone.

It was while studying at college in 1900 that his father

commissioned a portrait – surely requested by Price himself – by his son's school friend, John Dumayne. The oil painting, in the manner of John Singer Sargent, is the profile of a good-looking young man – almost a dandy – with strong features, upswept dark hair, a cigarette, just lit, dangling from sensitive lips. It is a statement of the man that Price intended to be, but more revealing, perhaps, of the vain and egotistical young man that he had already become.

Still seduced by the theatre, while working and studying, Price filled his leisure time writing and performing his own plays. He also practised conjuring and attended spiritualist meetings and seances. He read – and bought – every book on spiritualism, conjuring and psychical research that he could find. This love of books and the building of his esoteric library was to continue throughout his life. He would also visit the fairgrounds and marketplaces of turn-of-the-century London, vibrant with life and colour – Petticoat Lane, East Street, Walworth and Deptford. Here he would spend many evenings watching 'illusionists, hypnotists, conjurers, thought-readers, fortune-tellers, "monstrosities", fire-eaters, fakirs, quacks and mountebanks.'[5]

At the age of twenty-one, Price left England for the first time to visit the Foire aux Pains d'épices in Paris, known as the 'Gingerbread Fair', an annual exhibition of sideshows that presented strongmen, conjurors and contortionists as well as 'men who swallowed live frogs, goldfish and brass watches'.[6] Hypnotised subjects undressed and made love to each other or ate Spanish onions thinking they were peaches. On further visits to the Continent, Price would frequent the more freakish Parisian fairs, where he saw shows such as Mademoiselle Fifine, a practically naked 200lb woman who appeared to be completely bloodless and insensible to pain. The audience were invited to stick pins into her flesh for half a franc. With thousands of pins stuck into her body, she looked, Price recalled, like 'a good-looking hedgehog'.[7] At another fair he saw a young woman called Olga, 'the girl with the cast iron skin',[8] who, but for a loincloth, lay naked in a glass coffin, reclining on a bed of 200 broken wine bottles. More and more, the grammar-school boy from New Cross was drawn to a darker world of the bizarre, the exotic, the unexplained and the inexplicable.

Modern spiritualism had first been imported to Britain from America, where it had spread, virus-like, from humble beginnings. In the spring of 1848, two young sisters from upstate New York, Maggie and Kate Fox, had claimed to be able to communicate with the dead by establishing a series of taps – one knock for 'yes', two for 'no' and three for uncertainty. Managed by their elder sister Leah Fish, the girls became national celebrities, appearing at P. T. Barnum's American Museum in New York City and even performing for the First Lady at the White House. The Fox sisters inspired a whole new movement. Attempts to communicate with the dead became known as seances, from the old French for 'sitting'. These took the country by storm, and by 1853 there were an estimated 30,000 recognised mediums practising in the United States. Despite the sceptics, people saw what they wanted to see, believed what they wanted to believe.

But by the 1880s, spiritualism had been rocked by controversy, scandal and accusations of fraud. Since the heady days of the 1850s, Maggie and Kate Fox had suffered a sad decline. Both were widowed and had become impoverished alcoholics. Meanwhile, their sister Leah, from whom they were both now estranged, had become a successful medium in her own right and was their 'damnable enemy'.[9] In October 1888, tempted by a fee of $1,500, Maggie Fox appeared at the New York Academy of Music to a house packed with spiritualists and the curious press. 'I am here tonight as one of the founders of spiritualism,' she declared, 'to denounce it as an absolute falsehood from beginning to end.'[10] Maggie explained that she and her sister Kate had developed the ability to manipulate the bones in their feet as children resulting in the sound of taps or knocks. A committee of five doctors was called to the stage to check Maggie's testimony. Kate confirmed her sister's denunciation of spiritualism. It was, she declared, 'the greatest humbug of the century'.[11]

In Britain, spiritualism evolved as a popular working-class entertainment but it had also inspired debate among intellectuals who had become disorientated by advances in technology. Science had identified unseen forces such as cathode rays and electromagnetic waves, which teased the possibility of access to a parallel spirit world. The electrical telegraph had transformed world communications, but it had also changed prevailing attitudes to communication with the dead. The imaginative distance from the dots and dashes of Samuel Morse's code in 1837 to communicating with spirits through a system of raps, less than a decade later, was a step rather than a leap. Now God was dead and Science was King. In an effort to counter the gnawing sense of doubt, spiritualism seemed to offer reassurance that life on earth was not the limit of human existence.

One of the legion of the spiritually disorientated was the son of an Anglican clergyman, the Cambridge philosopher Henry Sidgwick. From 1860 onwards, Sidgwick was increasingly drawn to spiritualism as a way of proving immortality. But he determined to do so only by obtaining evidence that could be supported by scientific proof, just as Darwin had done. Even after the first seance he attended, he wrote that, 'I intend to have as absolute proof as possible whether the whole thing be imposture or not.'[12]

In 1874, one of Sidgwick's students at Trinity College, Frederic Myers, suggested that they expand the interests of the Cambridge-based Ghost Club, which they had both joined in 1851, and form a society to rigorously investigate the claims of spiritualists, thought-transference (it was Myers who conjured the word 'telepathy') and other occult phenomena. When the Society for Psychical Research was finally founded, in 1882, with Sidgwick as president, its aim was 'to investigate the large body of debatable phenomena designated by such terms as mesmeric, psychical and spiritualistic' and to approach it 'in the same spirit of exact and unimpassioned enquiry which has enabled Science to solve so many problems.'[13] The creation of the Society for Psychical Research was, as Harry Price would later comment, 'the turning point in the investigation of the abnormal ... as it marked the beginning of organised scientific psychical research.'[14]

By 1883, the society had attracted 150 members. By 1900 this had swelled to nearly a thousand. The membership included aristocrats, leading clergy and cultural figures such as Alfred, Lord Tennyson, Arthur Conan Doyle, John Ruskin, Lewis Carroll and the former prime minister, Gladstone. He felt that psychical research was 'the most important work that [was] being done in the world'.[15] But the Society for Psychical Research was very much an academic, patrician organisation and didn't seek interaction with the public through the popular press. Rather, it held lectures and set up committees to investigate claims of psychical activity. By 1900, the society had disdained the investigation of ghosts and haunted houses, preferring to channel its support – and its finances – towards the study of psychological phenomena such as telepathy, hypnotism and clairvoyance. Despite the energy it had put into its investigations, it had failed to reach any definitive conclusions about the nature of the paranormal, nor had it secured any proof of the continuance of life after death.

In 1902, Price's mother died of ovarian cancer.[16] Price then joined Edward Saunders as a full-time commercial traveller selling paper to the grocery and bakery trades, but he continued to make a name for himself as a writer about coins, much of his work lifted from standard reference books on the subject. At the same time, having joined the Royal Astrological Society and the Numismatic Society, he began to embellish his correspondence with letters after his name: 'Harry Price, MRAS FRNS'. By this time, the ambitious young man had developed a list of precocious life and career goals:

To be a writer and to write for the *Encyclopaedia Britannica*
To appear in *Who's Who*
To collect the largest magical library in existence
To be offered a doctorate, *honoris causa*, of some university
To possess a Rolls-Royce car[17]

Even at this early age, he betrayed an insecurity about his lack of university education and a desperate desire for recognition, rather than achievement.[18]

By 1906, now twenty-five, Price was engaged to his childhood sweetheart, Constance Knight, who, on the death of her father, had inherited property and government bonds. Subsequently, her widowed mother moved out of London to a house in Pulborough in West Sussex, surrounded by fields and situated by St Mary's Church. At the same time, Edward Ditching Price's own health had deteriorated. It was Price who found him dead at home, following a heart attack.

Constance and Harry were married at St Mary's, Pulborough. After a honeymoon in Scarborough, the newlyweds moved in with Mrs Knight at her home, 'Riverside'. But this proved to be an unhappy domestic arrangement. Mary Ann Knight – straight-laced, truculent and critical – did not get on with her new son-in-law, which led to tense family rows. There's a suggestion that Mrs Knight's attitude to Price was affected by the fact that he and Constance had slept together as teenagers, thus wrecking – to her parents' minds – any prospects of their only daughter ever making a good marriage. By obliging her to marry Price, they had effectively shackled her to a far from wealthy man, and while her inheritance was generous, it was not sufficient for her to live on independently for the rest of her life. According to one of his great friends,[19] Price never slept with Constance again and instead embarked on numerous affairs.Though their marriage was long, Price and Constance would never have children. She took no interest in his enthusiasm for psychical research and found the subject distasteful.

The solution to the domestic discord at Riverside was for Price to commission a new four-bedroomed detached house on an adjacent piece of land to his mother-in-law. The plot was situated on the banks of the River Arun, with views across the South Downs. When it was completed, 'Arun Bank' was a comfortable Edwardian home furnished with solid Victorian pieces where Price had both a workshop and a study. Dumayne's portrait of him was hung proudly in the drawing room.

Now settled in Pulborough, Price began to contribute to the local newspapers and embraced the local athletics club, as well as the literary and drama societies. In 1910 he stage-managed and acted in a community production of *The Pilgrim's Progress* in which Constance appeared as Humility and Price himself as Lord Hate-Good. He also took an active role in parish events, striking up a friendship with the rector at nearby St Mary's, Canon Frederick Baggally. Baggally was a keen collector of Roman antiquities and it was through this acquaintanceship that Price began to insinuate himself into the antiquarian scene in West Sussex. Soon he was writing about and lecturing on the history of the district. At the same time, he began to make extremely fortuitous finds – some conveniently right at the end of his garden. He would announce these 'discoveries' in the local press – a bronze statuette of Hercules in a remarkable state of preservation, an Iron Age hatchet head, a piece of bone inscribed with runic figures and a hugely rare inscribed silver ingot from Roman times. He now presented himself as 'the well-known Sussex archaeologist' and *the* expert on local history.

But later that year, Professor E. J. Haverfield, Britain's foremost expert on Roman history, challenged the authenticity of Price's silver ingot. It was a fake copied from one in the Tower of London. His integrity now in doubt, Price's short-lived tenure as the self-appointed expert on Roman Sussex was over.

When war broke out, in August 1914, at thirty-three Price was young enough to serve but deemed unfit for military service due to a 'badly strained heart'. Despite later grand claims in his autobiography to have helped the Royal Flying Corps and to have run a munitions factory for the war effort, in reality he spent a dedicated but unheroic war in an armaments factory in Brighton.[20]

Psychical research all but disappeared during the war, as many mediums were based in Germany and middle-class sponsors were reluctant to invest their money in such uncertain times. But the war did successfully reignite popular belief in the supernatural. Spiritualism, which had waned in popularity in the years before the war, now flourished again – prompted by emotion, Price observed, rather than scientific curiosity. 'A wave of interest in the possibility of an after-life swept the country like a tornado ... based on the fact that tens of thousands of the flower of our manhood were being shot down. Relatives mourned them, but with their grief was the hope – almost the belief – that their sons, though dead, would survive in another world.'[21] Those disappointed by the cold comfort of conventional religion sought solace, once again, in alternative beliefs. Almost immediately, opportunists exploited the trusting gullibility of grieving families, with phoney clairvoyants offering seances and gypsies selling charms to the thousands of shell-shocked troops returning to Britain on leave from the front. Watching down-at-heel mediums trying to sell them charms on the boat-train platforms at Victoria Station was, for Price, 'one of the most pathetic sights I have ever witnessed'.[22]

There was a hungry market for 'spirit photography', where fake mediums would paste images of the deceased onto photographic plates and then take photographs that gave the appearance of the dead in the presence of the living. Photography had always been undertaken by professionals, until 1888, when Kodak launched a camera specifically designed for use by amateurs: 'You press the button. We do the rest.' With the magic of photography now available to anybody, fake mediums saw an opportunity to benefit from the carnage in the trenches by claiming to photograph auras and apparitions of the dead to sell to the bereaved. These practices weren't illegal and the war saw them produced on an industrial level; a 'damnable trading', Price raged, 'on the most scared emotions of the bereaved'.[23]

By the end of the war, as Arthur Conan Doyle observed, spiritualism seemed to address the deep need felt by grief-stricken widows and mothers that was not forthcoming from the Church. The whole question of survival after death, Doyle noted, became invested with a new meaning:

Were all the brave lads dead, who had gone forth buoyantly to fight for their country? If they lived, where were they, and what were they doing? These were the questions that many a mother pondered in her heart. It was really the bereaved mothers of Britain that lifted Spiritualism out of the dust.[24]

Doyle had flirted with spiritualism since the 1880s, but only became convicted in his beliefs after 1916. He lost his eldest son in the war – 'one of the grandest boys in body and soul that a father was ever blessed with.' Kingsley Conan Doyle succumbed to Spanish flu, having been invalided from the front line. This trauma was compounded by the death of Doyle's brother, two brothers-in-law and two nephews – eleven family members in all, lost to disease or combat. Riven by grief, Doyle subsequently attempted to articulate the impact that the war had had on people like himself:

The deaths occurring in almost every family in the land brought a sudden and concentrated interest in life after death. People not only asked me the question, 'If a man die shall he live again?' but they eagerly sought to know if communication was possible with the dear ones they had lost. They sought 'for the touch of a vanished hand, and the sound of a voice that is still'.[25]

From 1918, now fully convinced that 'spiritualism is the religion of the future',[26] Doyle worked tirelessly on behalf of the spiritualist cause, touring all over the country – sometimes to as many as five towns a week – as well as making international tours to Australia, New Zealand, South Africa and northern Europe. With his worldwide fame as the creator of Sherlock Holmes, he became spiritualism's most famous evangelist: 'God has placed me in a very special position,' he said, 'for conveying it to that world which needs it so badly.'[27]

Though Price believed him sincere and lovable, a 'giant in stature',[28] he felt Doyle had the credulous heart of a child.

*

After the war, Price returned to Saunders & Son as sales manager. At nearly forty, it was not the life his ambitious younger self had imagined when browsing through *Who's Who*.

Price's friend Frederick Baggally, the rector at the church opposite Arun Bank, introduced him to his brother, the magician and psychical researcher W. W. Baggally. Encouraged by him, in June 1920 Price became a member of the Society for Psychical Research, which he felt he joined 'at exactly the right time so I could make such a difference'.[29] But his relationship with the society was to be extremely fraught. Harry Price, the showy, ambitious paper salesman without a university degree, was far from a natural fit for the exclusive, academic and patrician society.

At the same time as joining the Society for Psychical Research, Price joined the Magic Circle. Here he was introduced to several members whom he would engage with throughout his career, such as Will Goldston, who was at the heart of the British magic industry. Goldston ran the biggest magic store in London and knew everybody in the field. In 1922 he introduced Price to the American escapologist Harry Houdini, who was embarking on a British tour. The two men had an immediate rapport and shared many interests. Both were fascinated with the study of psychical phenomena and both collected books about magic. They were also bonded by their mutual antipathy towards spiritualism. Houdini was well acquainted with the tricks of music-hall mediums, having been one himself. Though Houdini claimed to be open-minded in the press, Price was aware that he was 'foe to all mediums good and bad'.[30] The history of spiritualism, as far as Price was concerned, was a history of fraud.

At the Magic Circle, Price became acquainted with the writer and anthropologist Eric Dingwall, who had also recently joined the Society for Psychical Research as its research officer. Very much the antithesis of Price, Dingwall was the son of a well-to-do tea planter stationed in Ceylon, had been Cambridge-educated and benefited from a private income. A frosty, combative yet erudite man, he could also exude great charm when he chose to. The society had been trying to interview the celebrated Crewe-based spirit photographer William Hope since before the war and now appointed Dingwall to investigate him. Doubts about the authenticity of Hope's practice had circulated since 1909, when the *Daily Mail* had set up a committee to examine his photographs of spirits, which concluded that they were fake.

Dingwall approached Price to help him investigate Hope and together they planned to prove that he was an exploitative fraud. In preparation for this audacious sting, Price consulted the Imperial Dry Plate Company at Cricklewood, which manufactured photographic plates. They agreed that the best way of establishing fraud was to invisibly mark the plates with the trademark of the company – a rampant lion – and to ask Hope to use them.

At a sitting in Holland Park on 28 February, Price invited Hope to use the plates that he had brought with him. Price watched Hope's movements carefully in the semi-darkness of the room as Hope photographed him. The sitting over, the plates were developed. One showed an image of Price with 'a charming female form over his shoulders', apparently his mother. He thanked Hope and took two of the plates away with him. When these were later developed by another photographer, it was clear that there was no rampant-lion trademark. Somehow Hope had switched the plates.

When the news was published in the Society for Psychical Research's *Journal of the Society for Psychical Research* in May, it caused a furore. Spiritualists, led by Arthur Conan Doyle, claimed that Price and Dingwall had set Hope up. They dismissed the experiment as an attempt by the society to attack their beliefs. Later that year, Doyle responded by publishing a vigorous defence of Hope's work, but Price's exposure of Hope's fraudulent practices was a blow from which spirit photographers would never recover. They and their work passed into oblivion. Also resulting from the Hope debacle was a fractured relationship between Price and Doyle. Doyle, Price believed, was 'thoroughly honest himself and could not imagine his too sympathetic credulity being imposed upon'.[31] From now on relations between them would vary between comradeship and hostility from month to month.

Price and Dingwall proceeded to collaborate on another project, the republication of *Revelations of a Spirit Medium*, a long out-of-print American guide for fake mediums to fool the public. But Dingwall felt that Price lacked the scientific knowledge required by a good psychical researcher, or indeed writer: 'he showed no signs of the ability to present psychical material in a way which appealed not only to the popular press but to the intelligent general reader who wanted to know what was being done in this field'.[32] He believed that Price needed the opportunity to observe some genuine phenomena at close quarters. To that end, in May 1922, he invited him to Munich, where Dr Albert von Schrenck-Notzing was testing a young Austrian medium, Willi Schneider.

Schrenck-Notzing had heard sensational stories about nineteen-year-old Willi's psychic abilities, which had been reported in the local press: telekinesis and materialisation. Having visited the Schneiders' home in Braunau, Austria, he persuaded Schneider's father to permit him to take the boy under his wing and have him trained as a dentist in Munich. After dozens of sittings in Schrenck-Notzing's apartment in Max-Joseph-Strasse, more than a hundred witnesses from all over Europe had testified that the phenomena surrounding the boy was genuine.

Price and Dingwall travelled to Bavaria and attended a series of three seances in Max-Joseph-Strasse. Though tied with ropes, Willi was able to move and touch objects even though he was cut off from them by a gauze screen. An accordion played and the form of a hand seemed to play the keys. A tambourine rattled and 'ecto-plasm' dribbled from the boy's mouth. In a trance, Willi was guided by 'Olga' who claimed to be 'Lola Montez'. This was the stage name of the actress and courtesan Eliza Gilbert, who had been the mistress of the King of Bavaria in the nineteenth century. 'Speaking personally,' Price observed, 'I was very deeply impressed, as it was the first medium through whom I had witnessed phenomena under unimpeachable conditions.'[33] Price's conviction of the genuineness of Schneider's abilities was international news. The American Society for Psychical Research's journal carried a feature entitled

'The Conversion of Harry Price'. Price, the journal claimed, 'was to Great Britain what Houdini is to America – the expert in the case' and he had found 'something genuine at last'.[34]

On his return from Munich, Price set about securing a venue in London where he could test mediums like Willi Schneider under controlled conditions. Writing to the London Spiritualist Alliance at their offices in Queen Square, he proposed the foundation of a laboratory and seance room where the 'miracle-mongers could be tested and the genuine medium encouraged'.[35] But he was to be frustrated. Though the Alliance thought such a laboratory was a good idea, they hadn't sufficient room to offer him.

In December 1922, hoping to exploit the sensation around the exposure of Charles Hope, *Scientific American* magazine offered $2,500 to the first medium to produce a genuine spirit photograph or other evidence that proved that paranormal phenomena were genuine.[36] The lure of the prize money, and the publicity it promised, hugely appealed to Price, who looked to recruit a candidate in earnest.

Early in 1923, he was put in touch with a 21-year-old nursing assistant called Stella Cranshaw, whose family felt that she had 'natural ability' and were keen to have her tested by the London Spiritualist Alliance. On meeting her, Price felt that she was 'perfectly normal, healthy, good-looking and a typical specimen of the modern, well-educated English girl'.[37] But ever since puberty, she had been the focus of curious happenings – strong cool breezes would blow across the room in which she was sitting, objects would jerk themselves out of her way when she approached and knocks would be heard in the room in which she was present, especially on her bedstead. Convinced of her ability and determined to secure the *Scientific American* prize, Price informed Dingwall that he had met a medium of remarkable powers with whom he hoped to have a series of sittings.

At first, Dingwall was excited at the prospect of investigating a new, untested medium – their very own Willi Schneider. But he was astonished when Price informed him that the seances were to be held at the offices of the London Spiritualist Alliance. Relations between the Society for Psychical Research and the spiritualist organisations had become very strained. The Society for Psychical Research believed in the authority of science, whereas the spiritualists advocated faith. With such fundamentally opposed philosophies, any agreement between them was, Price felt, like 'trying to mix oil and water'.[38] Consequently, quickly taking umbrage, Dingwall thought Price's plan was 'a frank betrayal of psychical research'.[39] Price replied that he felt that the 'cold, critical and academic methods' of the Society for Psychical Research might 'deter [Stella] from sitting at all ... they are not suitable for Stella C at this juncture. I have already promised you that when the phenomena are fairly and absolutely established, you shall have ample opportunities of investigating her.'[40]

The sittings began on 22 March 1923, when it was established that Stella's trance personality or 'control' was a dead child known as 'Palma'. During one sitting, a table levitated above the heads of the sitters before falling to pieces – 'reduced to matchwood'.[41] On 12 April Stella visualised the front page of the *Daily Mail* from 19 May – thirty-seven days in the future – that carried the name 'ANDREW SALT' in capital letters. 'Palma' described the page in some detail: a boy was falling and a man bending over him pouring a white powder out of a tin. None of the images made any sense to the other sitters. But on 19 May, the front page of the *Mail* carried a full-page advertisement for Andrews Liver Salt with the image of the boy and his father as Stella had envisaged – '*A tin kept handy always makes for health and happiness in the home!*' Stella's apparent vision of the future seemed to confirm her psychic powers. But Price's handling of the sittings caused the Society for Psychical Research to question both his methods and his ambitions. Was he a serious psychical investigator or just a showman intent on adulation?

The seance room set up for the sittings with Stella was a dark, intimate environment with more than a touch of erotic frisson. The door was locked, the key removed, the lighting carefully arranged and the temperature closely monitored, as if for seduction. Medium and researcher would be physically close as Price touched Stella, taking her pulse and temperature; he would have direct control over her body during the seance. He played her music and burned incense, and 'at every sitting we linked hands and kept contact with our feet'.[42] She might go into an uncontrolled trance and even produce ectoplasm, claimed Price. 'Never was a medium easier to control,' he wrote; 'she did exactly as she was requested, made no comments – in fact, she hardly spoke at all.'[43] Price and Stella enjoyed an intimate and possibly sexual relationship. Certainly he wrote to her, and about her, like a suitor. When he pursued her, she evaded or avoided him, yet remained tantalising. In his writings about her, he then began to add an extra letter to Stella's surname – changing it from 'Cranshaw' to 'Cranshawe' – as if she had been branded by him.[44]

Though one of the sittings had been under the control of his colleague Lord Charles Hope, Eric Dingwall was generally dissatisfied with them. Price hadn't selected experienced observers to attend and was happy for clearly impartial spiritualists to observe. At the same time, he didn't circulate notes after the sittings for the observers to approve. 'How was it possible,' Dingwall blustered, 'that a man of Mr Price's knowledge should not have taken the opportunity of conducting a properly controlled series of experiments instead of the kind of demonstrations that he was holding? If fraudulent, Mr Price himself *must* have been in the fraud.'[45] But by October, whatever relationship Price had with Stella was over.

The 'conversion' of Price that appeared to take place after his visit to Munich now continued, as he began to emerge as a public figure in the wake of the sittings with Stella Cranshawe. He was offered more opportunities to write for the press and in his correspondence with Price, Arthur Conan Doyle often gave him hints about how to improve his style. Gradually his prose began to evolve as more engaging, more confident and more populist. Price established himself not only as a psychical researcher, but as a journalist.

In 1925, Doyle was appointed as president of the London

Spiritualist Alliance and bought the organisation new headquarters at 16 Queensbury Place. Finally, they agreed to fund Price's venture and he was made the honorary director – unsalaried – of the National Laboratory for Psychical Research with the intention of investigating 'in a dispassionate manner, and purely by scientific means, every phase of psychic or alleged psychic phenomena'.[46]

The very existence of the Laboratory was a reproof of and challenge to the Society for Psychical Research, which Price was all too aware of. After years of being sidelined by the society, he felt that he had had no option but to set up his own organisation to rival them. They had come to loathe the populist, showy Price for his defence of spiritualism, his need for publicity and his payments to mediums like Stella Cranshawe, which, they felt, encouraged fraudulent mediums to cheat. He deliberately antagonised the society with both the name of his rival organisation as well as his accompanying journal, which he called the *British Journal of Psychical Research*. This was a defiant challenge to the Society for Psychical Research as the title was confusingly similar to their own journal. The society seethed politely that it was 'regrettable that names should have been chosen for this new association and its publication likely to lead to misunderstandings especially abroad.'[47] But Price's publication was to be bright, attractive and – importantly – accessible, rather than a publication such as the Society for Psychical Research's, whose articles 'bore the reader through their deadly dullness'.[48] Price had the general reader in mind, not the specialist or scientist. Much to the Society for Psychical Research's chagrin, the Laboratory was a success from the start. Two hundred and fifty members paid one guinea each to join and within two years this would increase to 995, almost as large a membership as the Society for Psychical Research, which had been running for over forty years.

The Laboratory was launched at the London Spiritualist Alliance headquarters at Queensbury Place on the evening of Saturday 26 January 1926. At the opening, Price was in his element as he showed forty guests around his new 'psychic laboratory', which comprised the whole of the top floor of the building and consisted of a chemical and physical laboratory, a workshop, office, dark room and seance room. The place was filled with cameras, microscopes, old X-ray apparatus, gadgets of every kind and shelves full of test tubes, beakers, scales and chemicals. Curious crowds surged through the various rooms and many were unable to get in owing to the crush. Price was particularly keen to show the guests his extensive library and its treasures: old posters, handbills, documents, pamphlets and books relating to magic or psychical activities. There were many representatives of the press, dignitaries, celebrities and renowned members of the psychical fraternity.

One of the guests introduced to Price was a young professional model who was attending the opening with her mother. She was beautiful, blonde and fashionably dressed with her hair bobbed, just like Stella Cranshawe. Twenty-four-year-old Lucy Kay was the daughter of a German who had settled in Britain and worked in insurance. He had met his English wife when she was teaching English in Germany. Lucy had attended various private schools before joining a finishing school in Folkestone, where she developed an ambition to be an actress. She went on to train at RADA during a golden period, alongside John Gielgud, Charles Laughton and Edith Evans. She trained for four terms but didn't finish the course, leaving in the spring of 1925, when she started working as a model. When she attended the launch of the Laboratory, she was about to travel to Paris for the spring fashion shows.

As she was admiring the Laboratory, Lucy met a harassed-looking Price and said, 'What a lovely place to work in!'[49] But he had already walked off to greet another guest. Shortly afterwards, while she was admiring the 'unfeminine' tools in Price's workshop, he approached her again, almost crossly, asking, 'Well, why don't *you*? You can see I need help!' He wanted a secretary. Lucy told him that she didn't do shorthand. 'But I don't *want* shorthand,' protested Price. 'Can you type?'[50] Lucy said that she could. She took the job and never made it to Paris.

The opening of the Laboratory caused a wave of excitement in Fleet Street and among an enthusiastic public already seduced

by the promises of the occult through spiritualism. Price's investigations began to form, as Eric Dingwall observed with grudging
praise, 'a new kind of psychic journalism'.[51] He was 'one of the
very few men in England who was acquainted with the problems
of psychical research and with the relationship of conjuring to the
art of the fraudulent medium'.[52] Price's objective was to demystify
the practice of psychical research, to wrest it from the exclusive
Society for Psychical Research and make the study of 'the unknown
and the unaccountable' accessible to the tabloid-reading man in the
street.[53] With the establishment of the Laboratory, Harry Price had
become a public figure – 'Sherlock Holmes – with just the faintest
perceptible dash of Sir Arthur Conan Doyle.'[54] He was the people's
psychical researcher.

No other organisation was now as active in Britain in the field
of the paranormal as Price's Laboratory. He 'outstripped all other
investigators in the variety and sensational quality of his work'.[55]
Mollie Goldney, a midwife who first visited it on holiday from
India in 1926, recalled that 'something or other seemed always to
be going on'.[56] Despite the heart trouble that had worried him since
the war, Price was an indefatigable worker. He had a nervous energy
and attention to detail that would sometimes wear out his new secretary. For most of the week, he continued to work as a commercial
traveller selling paper products, always dressed in a well-cut suit
from Austin Reed or Simpson's.[57] But each Wednesday and Friday,
he would come up by train from Pulborough and be met at Victoria
by Lucy in her car. It was during this daily five-hour commute that
he did most of his reading and much of his writing. He liked this
routine and would only change it for late sittings, resenting any evenings spent away from Arun Bank. Curiously suburban for a ghost
hunter, he liked to get back to his wife, their dogs and the goldfish
he bred in the two ponds he'd made in the garden.

Lucy observed that Price hated untidiness in the office and that
he kept everything in meticulous order. He disliked untidy thinking too, preferring things to be concrete. He wasn't wealthy and a
considerable portion of his income was spent on the books that he

loved – thousands of volumes about psychical and esoteric subjects. He was a man who liked facts and never bought or read fiction. He also liked value for money, but he was never mean and enjoyed the best of everything – both for himself and his guests. There was always a large tin of premium tobacco on his desk, and the cakes and Russian tea that became a staple at the tea table at Queensbury Place were provided by Fortnum & Mason. Socially, Price was shy with strangers, especially women. Casual acquaintanceships left him at a loss, as he had no small talk and always seemed to be in a hurry. Lucy observed that he lived 'as on a volcano, nerves strung and his agile brain always ahead of himself'.[58]

Price was a generous, indulgent employer, loaning Lucy money and tolerating her many absences away from the office – cruises down the Nile, trips to the Mediterranean, Ceylon and America. These holidays, some taken in the interests of her health, were financed by her mother's wealthy family. Her correspondence with Price when she was abroad indicates that she knew him well enough to cheekily ridicule his pomposity: 'My dear Lord and Master, do I dare expect another [letter] when I land?'[59] A pile of letters from Price would be waiting for her wherever her ship docked.

Attractive, imaginative and sexually forthright, Lucy was 'very fond of men'.[60] In 1927, she found herself pregnant from one of her affairs. She had experience of what she called 'womb scraping' but abortion was expensive and illegal, so she left the Laboratory and, to avoid speculation and gossip in London, travelled to Zurich to have the child. A son was born on 24 May 1928, whom she named Jan Kallenbach, giving no indication of his paternity. She returned to London with the child, but had few maternal instincts. She made an application to the National Children Adoption Association, naming Price as her referee.[61] He wrote very supportively on her behalf that 'despite her present predicament, I have always found her to be a moral person'.[62] After the birth of her son, Lucy continued to work for a living, a necessity now as she was no longer subsidised by her mother's family, who expressed their displeasure with her illegitimate child by cutting her off. The baby, whose name was now anglicised to Ian, was adopted by a family in Oxford before being sent to boarding school, where he had little to do with his absent mother. Holidays and birthdays were spent at school and he never received birthday gifts or Christmas presents from her. According to her son, Lucy was 'not a loving person'.[63] With some self-awareness, she admitted as much to Price in one of her letters: 'I do not seem to be able to really love anybody.'[64]

Lucy had been replaced in the office by the eighteen-year-old Ethel Beenham, from Fulham. When Lucy's baby was born, there were rumours about the paternity of the child at Queensbury Place.[65] Price told Miss Beenham that the father of the child was 'the son of Colgate toothpaste'. Lucy never confirmed the paternity of her baby, and though there has been speculation that he might be Price's son, the adult Ian bore no resemblance to the distinctive-looking Price and recent DNA tests concluded that Ian was not Price's child.[66]

In the succeeding years, when Lucy married, had another child and started work elsewhere, the friendship between her and Price would remain very warm. He would prove to be a most loyal friend, helping her out of debt whenever he could afford it, paternally chastising her for the emotional and financial straits she found herself in and always happy to volunteer support or advice. In return, entrusted with his personal and professional secrets, Lucy was staunchly devoted as his secretary and as his friend, leaping vigorously to his defence if ever his integrity was doubted or his professionalism questioned. She admired Price and what he set out to achieve. 'I believe,' she said, 'his was a most courageous attempt to bring to the man in the street the most mystery – and humbug-ridden – subject in the world.'[67] He was, she felt, a difficult man to get to know well. An indication of the strength of their relationship, from 1929 she changed the spelling of her Christian name and her surname, adding an 'e' to the end of both, as Price had done to Stella Cranshaw's name. From now on she was known as 'Lucie Kaye'. Even late in life, she would remain in awe of Price, her eyes lighting up whenever she mentioned his name.[68]

*

In the New Year of 1928, Price was drawn to some unexplained phenomena that had been troubling a family in an unremarkable house on Eland Road, just off Lavender Hill in Battersea. It was a typical, modest, suburban terraced house of two floors, with a front and back garden, in a respectable neighbourhood. The house backed onto a psychiatric home for veterans who had shell shock from their experiences of the trenches during the Great War.

Eighty-six-year-old Henry Robinson was an invalid who had lived at Eland Road for twenty-five years with his son Fred and three daughters, Lilla, Kate and Eleanor, all of whom were school-teachers. Eleanor was a widow with a thirteen-year-old son, Peter. The strange occurrences had started on 29 November 1927. Lumps of coal, soda and pennies began to fall on the conservatory, a glazed lean-to at the rear of the house. The phenomena carried on in December, with small pieces of coal and pennies breaking the glass of the lean-to. Thinking that somebody was obviously throwing things over the garden wall – perhaps from the psychiatric home at the end of the garden – the Robinsons called the police.

When a police constable arrived, the flying objects continued – even hitting the officer on his helmet – but they couldn't find the source of the projectiles. One Monday just before Christmas, at nine o'clock in the morning, there were loud bangs all over the house. The family found old Mr Robinson, who had just woken up, terrified in his bedroom, with one of the windows smashed. He was so frightened, the family decided to remove him from the house. His son Fred called to a man in the street, a Mr Bradbury, to help him move his father. Just as they were taking him out of the bedroom, a heavy chest of drawers crashed to the floor. Suddenly there was a loud bang from another of the bedrooms and one of the sisters screamed downstairs. Another chest of drawers had fallen to the floor.

At the same time, small slips of white paper began to appear on the stairs. If held up to the light, some writing could be made out, as if made by a pin. Some of the messages were mundane, others more threatening. After some unusually loud raps in the house, Fred

Robinson found a slip of paper signed Tom Blood: '*I am having a bad time here. I cannot rest. I was born during the reign of William the Conqueror.*'[69]

Eve Brackenbury, who had been recruited as secretary to Eric Dingwall at the Society for Psychical Research, went to the house to assess the phenomena. She was convinced that everything she had seen had been done by the thirteen-year-old Peter. When she mentioned this to his family, 'the SPR [Society for Psychical Research] came in for a certain amount of abuse,' she wrote, 'but gradually they calmed down'.

When Harry Price first visited the house, in January 1928, he was able to see the devastation wreaked by the phenomena: broken windows and ornaments, and smashed furniture. The frightened and exhausted family seemed to him to be entirely trustworthy, so he promised to call again. This he did, accompanied by a journalist from the *London Evening News*. While they were being shown around the house, an object was thrown onto the floor in the passage to the kitchen. This was a gas lighter which was always kept in the scullery and had been on the stove there when the family had last seen it. 'It was,' Price observed, 'a curious incident and made an excellent stop-press paragraph for the evening papers!'[70]

Suspicion, however, fell on Fred Robinson as the cause of the phenomena and he was taken by the police to St John's Hospital, Battersea in order to assess his mental health. But his absence made no difference to the activity in the house. During the weekend of 21–22 January, chairs had apparently marched down the hall in single file of their own volition and when Eleanor Perkins, the widowed sister, was trying to set the table for dinner on the Saturday, the chairs stacked themselves on top of it. When this happened for the third time she went outside into the street seeking assistance from a policeman. He thought she had stacked the chairs herself. Eleanor's son Peter was now so frightened – refusing to even sit on a chair, in case it should move – that she sent him away, leaving just her and her sisters in the house.

With both the men away and the boy dispatched to the country, the sisters determined to leave the house for a few days. As would be the case at Borley Rectory, the crowds that were drawn to the house were frightening them too. Over the weekend, mounted police had to keep back the mob that all day and night stood in the road and gazed, open-mouthed, at nothing more thrilling than a couple of broken window panes. On Saturday evening some hooligans threatened to break into the house if they were not permitted to 'investigate' the phenomena for themselves.

When Price visited the house on Monday 23 January – again accompanied by a journalist – he was shown into the sitting room to wait before the sisters gave them a tour of the house. After looking round, the group were talking in the kitchen and Price was just preparing to leave when they heard a noise like the fall of a heavy boot or a brush. They looked to see what might have fallen or been dropped, when Price put his hand under a chair in the corner and found, in a shoe, one of a pair of little metal ornaments in the form of cherubs. The sisters were stunned, as the cherubs had sat on the mantelpiece in the sitting room for twenty-five years. If the ornament had really come from the next room, it must have made two right-angled turns and travelled over Price's, the sisters' and the journalist's heads. Price increased the sisters' distress by telling them that, as was usual in these cases, all their furniture would be smashed sooner or later. After he left, they wondered if Price was a medium. Things always seemed to happen when he was around. Lilla felt that they should keep Price out of the house. With the activity in the house so unsettling, the sisters decided to spend the night elsewhere.

When they returned, on Wednesday 25 January, Price had persuaded Eleanor Perkins to allow him to bring a medium to the house. She sat in the kitchen as he showed another journalist the damage in the rest of the property. The medium complained of cold breezes – as she would, with many of the doors and windows broken and the January weather. When Price was upstairs, there was a crash. He called down to Mrs Perkins and asked if she had heard anything – and did she normally keep her kitchen soap on the landing? Climbing the stairs, Price presented her with a cake of soap that she knew she had used in the scullery before he had arrived that morning. She decided that she didn't want him in the house again.

Henry Robinson died in hospital and Fred was allowed home. The phenomena ceased as abruptly as they had started. The house was put up for sale and the remaining members of the family moved out of Eland Road for good. Many members of the Society for Psychical Research were convinced that the Robinsons were responsible for the haunting. In print, Price was more generous to them but, privately, in a letter to the theologian Arnold Lunn, he felt that the inspiration for the 'haunting' at Eland Road was that the family wanted to force their invalid father out of the house so that they could sell it. 'Unfortunately,' he wrote, 'I am only permitted to write *nice* things about people.'[71]

Fifteen months later, in June 1929, Price and Lucie arrived on the doorstep of Borley Rectory, where an equally exhausted family were being plagued by unexplained phenomena and desperate for help.

With relations still strained between them since the exposure of William Hope, Price now fell further foul of Arthur Conan Doyle when he wrote a series of articles for the *Sunday Chronicle* attacking spiritualism. In one of the pieces, he mentioned that Doyle had been fooled into believing that his late mother had materialised during a seance in America with husband and wife mediums Mr and Mrs Thompson. He had emotionally embraced the apparition before realising, with great embarrassment, that he had been tricked by a puppet. On reading Price's piece in the *Chronicle*, a furious Doyle wrote to him asking him never to mention the incident again. At a dinner, he then publicly upbraided Price for his attitude to mediums and spiritualists. Doyle then wrote to Price and tersely reminded him that he – and his laboratory – were the guests of a spiritualist organisation. He thought it intolerable that he should be falsely and clumsily ridiculed by Price and suggested to his solicitor that every means possible should 'be adopted to get rid of Mr Price as a tenant' from Queensbury Place. Price now petulantly dismissed

Doyle's sensitivity as well as his spiritualist beliefs: 'What amazes me is how a man in your position can be so thin-skinned, even your own followers regard most of your doings and sayings as a joke.'[72]

Price, the former sceptic, now embarked on what was to be one of his most celebrated – and lucrative – investigations: the creation of the superstar medium Rudi Schneider, the younger brother of the famous Austrian medium Willi Schneider.

During a sitting at their home in Braunau in 1919, when Willi's powers had started to fade, his spirit guide 'Olga' had failed to produce phenomena. 'She' had then demanded that Willi's eleven-year-old brother should be a medium. Rudi then entered the seance room apparently sleepwalking and began to exhibit the rapid breathing, extreme muscle tension and restlessness that was characteristic of his brother's transformation into 'Olga'. Rudi's mediumistic skills were promoted by Schrenck-Notzing in Munich, where he would demonstrate raps, knocks, levitation, the moving of a coffee table, the ringing of a hand bell, the tying of a handkerchief and the playing of a toy zither. He soon eclipsed the career of his brother, though his achievements were questioned in some quarters as fraudulent.

In February 1929, Schrenck-Notzing, who financially supported Schneider, died. Immediately, Price travelled to Munich to secure the twenty-year-old's services for sittings in London. Price effectively took over Schneider's career and turned him into a media celebrity. By the time he arrived at Liverpool Street, he was greeted by the press as 'the Austrian psychical "superman".'[73] 'Every possible precaution will be taken to detect trickery,' Price promised, 'so that if Schneider passes these tests his international reputation will become still more enhanced.'[74] And, presumably, this would result in Price having an extremely marketable commodity.

In the first series of sittings in Queensbury Place, between 11 and 22 April, Schneider was bound to a chair by a rope within a curtained cabinet 7ft 3 inches wide, 4ft 10 inches long and 8ft high. The sitters sat hand-to-hand and foot-to-foot wearing gloves and socks that were electrically wired. If the circuit was broken, a signal would flash, revealing – apparently – any trickery. 'Olga' demonstrated her usual repertoire to an impressed audience of journalists, psychical researchers and celebrities including Laurence Olivier and Stanley Holloway. Charles Sutton of the *Daily Mail* was particularly impressed by the materialisation of a 'pseudopod', which was like 'a paw with thick fingers and a large thumb'.[75] Price defiantly offered £1,000 to any conjuror who could repeat the phenomena that Rudi produced under similar conditions, but nobody took up the challenge.

Price presented a certificate to Schneider from the National Laboratory of Psychical Research (i.e. himself) declaring that through him had been witnessed 'absolutely genuine phenomena under control conditions never previously imposed on any medium in this or any other country. Rudi leaves England with an absolutely clean sheet as regards any attempt to defraud.'[76]

Schneider returned to London for a series of twenty-one sittings between October 1929 and January 1930, many of them attended by Lord Charles Hope and Mollie Goldney, who had both contributed to the costs of the experiments. But the results were met less favourably. Reverend Digby Kittermaster, a tutor at Harrow School, thought it a pity that though the sitters and Schneider were confined, Price's secretary, Lucie Kaye, was free to walk around the room, which might fuel the arguments of sceptics. This point was picked up by Charles Sutton in the *Daily Mail,* who now claimed to be unconvinced of Schneider's abilities. If he were to see the phenomena a hundred times under any conditions, he sneered, he would not admit that Schneider was legitimate. Eric Dingwall, who had joined Price in declaring Rudi's brother Willi as genuine in Munich, dismissed Rudi's sittings as 'a cavalcade of entertainment'.[77]

Meanwhile, Conan Doyle's health was in decline as he continued to suffer from angina, but he insisted that he was not afraid – 'to a spiritualist death can have no terror'.[78] In January 1930, after decades of squabbling with the Society for Psychical Research about their anti-spiritualist stance, he resigned his membership, dismissing it as a pointless organisation. Ninety other members followed his lead. He had been a member of the society – mostly grumpily – for thirty-six years. On 7 July, Doyle died in bed at home at Windlesham Manor, his house in West Sussex. He was seventy-one. Just before he passed away, he turned to his wife Jean to say, 'You are wonderful.'[79] Lady Doyle subsequently claimed to receive two or three messages a week from her dead husband. In a seance organised by the medium Eileen Garrett, the spirit of Doyle jousted with Price, who was also present. 'Doyle' challenged Price: 'Here I am. Arthur Conan Doyle. Now how am I going to prove it to you?'[80] Doyle's death didn't seem to have dulled his prickly relationship with his old adversary:

Doyle: It was your fault we disagreed.

Price: But we were working really with the same object in view, but in different ways. I am trying to arrive at the truth.

Doyle: I was always wondering what you were working for, to be perfectly candid. I always had my eye on you, and you used to watch me like a cat watching a bird in a cage.[81]

Whether it really was the spirit of Doyle talking to him from beyond the grave, Price was unconvinced.

Dealt a wounding blow by the Great War, by 1930 the golden age of psychical research, if not quite yet over, was in irreversible decline. Doyle's death left the world of psychic science immeasurably poorer. The loss of Price's most fierce and powerful combatant winded him. The two men had embodied and defined the study of the paranormal for a generation, and though they had infuriated each other, they had inspired each other, too. Beneath the bluster and melodrama there was mutual admiration and respect. His primary antagonist now gone, after years of chasing cases, arguing for funding and expensive, time-consuming international tours in the pursuit of furthering the study of psychical phenomena, Price had had enough of working independently. He mooted the idea of a merger with the London Spiritualist Alliance. But they rejected

Price's offer. His dream of a popular, accessible psychical research body to rival and perhaps trump the Society for Psychical Research had reached a dead end. The future of the Laboratory and Price's library – his whole legacy – was far from certain.

At the end of September, Germany, once the international focus of psychical research and the study of the occult, was host to the rise of extremist politics. In Leipzig, the fascist leader announced to cheering crowds that 'another two or three general elections and we shall be in power. Then the sins of 1918 will be punished ... heads will roll in the sand.'[82] It was a different world to the one where Price and Dingwall had innocently travelled to Munich to observe Willi Schneider in Schrenck-Notzing's apartment. The Schneiders' hometown in Austria, Braunau, was no longer renowned as the home of a celebrated medium but the birthplace of Adolf Hitler.

On 29 September, disillusioned and broke, an uncharacteristically subdued Price sat in his office in Queensbury Place, unsure if the Laboratory around him had a future. Even the flights of stairs to the top floor seemed more challenging every morning. The nights were drawing in and winter was on the way.

That day, Price had an unexpected visit from Ethel and Freda Bull, who happened to be in South Kensington on a day trip from Great Cornard. Miss Bull explained that, after trying to run the parish from another district, the exhausted Eric Smith had handed in his resignation to the Bishop. He had preached his final sermon at Borley Church on Easter Sunday, before leaving the area for good to take up the living at a parish in Norfolk. Throughout the summer, Borley Rectory had once again stood empty. The family, who retained the gift of the living, had been unhappy with Guy Warman's choice of Smith as the rector. They'd also been aghast and embarrassed at the resulting media furore following the arrival of the *Daily Mirror*. Press reports in Britain and America about the happenings at the Rectory contained anything from mild distortion to exuberant fantasy. Every weekend had brought people to the village in cars, on cycles and on foot to peep with curious eyes through the hedges and lean over the gates. The newly-appointed bishop, Henry Wilson, had agreed that Smith's tenure had been a disaster and, with his tacit approval, he was happy to leave the next appointment in the family's hands.

In an attempt to put the recent sensational events behind them, the Bulls decided to source a rector much closer to home, offering the living to a member of the family, their first cousin Lionel Foyster, who had been a visitor at the Rectory since childhood. Now a mature and experienced clergyman, he had been living in Canada for twenty years working as a missionary. He seemed the ideal candidate. However, far from stabilising the situation, this appointment had resulted in a dramatic escalation of the phenomena at the Rectory. The focus of this, 'the noisiest, most violent, and most dangerous period in the whole recorded history'[83] of the phenomena at Borley, was the new rector's attractive young wife, Marianne.

PART TWO

THE HAUNTED

Marianne Foyster

CHAPTER EIGHT

THE RECTOR'S WIFE

26 January 1899–22 July 1930

I don't like the word 'haunted.'

Marianne Foyster[1]

Marianne Emily Rebecca Shaw was born on 26 January 1899 in Romiley, near Stockport, a textile town since the beginning of the Industrial Revolution. She was the only daughter of Annie and William Shaw and named after her father's mother, Mary Ann, who had died four years earlier in a lunatic asylum in Macclesfield. Marianne had an older brother, Geoffrey, and together the family lived in a humble terrace of two-up two-down cottages with a single outside lavatory shared with other families. Her father's income was meagre and his employment insecure. He had been unsuccessful as a schoolteacher and equally unsuccessful as a publican, though he had some talent as an amateur musician. To make ends meet, he gave private lessons in bookkeeping, arithmetic and shorthand while his wife gave piano lessons. Money was tight and life was hard.

Lack of work drew Marianne's father to Widnes, where he worked as a chemist, developing potassium cyanide at the chemical factory there. The family lived at the grim address of Coroner's Lane with Annie Shaw's widowed mother, Emily. Widnes at that time was known as a 'the dirtiest, the ugliest and the most depressing town in England'.[2] Keen to escape, when Marianne was two the family moved to 'Sunnyside', a small house in Oughtrington near Lymm in rural Cheshire. After her early experiences in the industrial heartland of the north-west, for the rest of her life Marianne would despise towns and only ever feel at ease in the countryside.

On 19 June 1906, Marianne was baptised at St Peter's, Oughtrington, a Gothic Anglo-Catholic church, by the curate, Lionel Foyster, who had become a friend of the family. Marianne's father played the organ at the church, and he and Reverend Foyster had gathered a small group of locals to play and sing. Lionel had been born into a clerical family who had served as rectors at the parishes of St Clements and All Saints in Hastings for generations. He was the fourth son of George Foyster, who had served as rector at All Saints for forty-two years, but was the only one of his six brothers to follow their father into the Church. He had graduated from Pembroke College, Cambridge in 1900. Having studied at Wells Theological College, known for following Anglo-Catholic doctrine, he worked as curate at Heptonstall in Yorkshire before taking holy orders at Wakefield Cathedral. His father's sister Caroline had spent her childhood at All Saints Rectory and subsequently married Henry Dawson Ellis Bull, the rector of Borley, in 1862. As a boy, Lionel had visited Borley many times and had heard the stories of the ghosts from his young cousins.

In 1904, George Foyster had given up the living of All Saints, returning it to the diocese. When he retired, as patron of the living he was legitimately empowered to pass it to his son. Lionel, who had recently been ordained, would have reasonably expected to be offered the living but, curiously, wasn't. Instead, he was offered a curacy by his sister Adelaide's husband, Edward Wethered, the rector of Oughtrington, far away from Hastings.

When Lionel baptised her, Marianne was seven and he was twenty-eight. She fondly remembered that it was he who gave her the first book that she read, R. M. Ballantyne's 'Boy's Own' story *The World of Ice* – 'the adventures, the dangers, and the vicissitudes' of an Arctic whaling ship, *The Dolphin*.[3] Marianne later remembered herself at this age as an imaginative little girl who took to 'glamorizing situations'.[4] She would 'make up stories that [she] was a princess, all kinds of silly things'.[5] She and her brother attended Lymm Grammar. A fee-paying school, it may have been Lionel who made this possible for the cash-strapped Shaws, his brother-in-law, the rector at St Peter's, being a governor at the school.

In 1907, the Shaw family were on the move again, leaving England altogether this time for a hamlet in County Antrim, a move not just to a new home but an unknown country. Marianne's father may have been drawn to Ireland by relatives, who would have advised him that nearby Belfast offered many opportunities for work. The city was now the largest in the country, having rapidly expanded in the second half of the nineteenth century, built on industries such as shipbuilding, engineering, rope-making, distilling and tobacco.

The Shaws settled in a small rural village called Drumnadreagh, 20 miles from Belfast itself. Their smallholding was one of the largest in the village, with as many as six rooms and four outbuildings for cows, pigs and hens. All the neighbours were Presbyterians as this area of Antrim had deep ties with the Scottish Lowlands. Being both English and Anglican, the Shaws would have been regarded with suspicion, and even hostility, in their new neighbourhood. Once they were settled, their friend Lionel Foyster visited and wrote them Christmas and Easter cards, as well as sending Marianne copies of *Sunshine*, a children's magazine. But in 1910, he announced that he was leaving England and emigrating to Canada as a missionary.

That September he sailed to Bay du Vin in New Brunswick on the east coast of Canada. In his luggage was a cherished family heirloom, a Bible printed in 1537. Situated between Nova Scotia and New England, land in New Brunswick was plentiful and cheap, and there were enthusiastic campaigns in the European press to attract settlers to emigrate there. But in 1909 only 300 people had done so and 2,000 farms stood empty. The forested uplands that characterised the province offered great opportunities for the lumber industry, but it was a Herculean task to clear such land, with crude agricultural implements for cultivation. There was little infrastructure, with few churches or schools. Many of the population were illiterate and some areas of the province were unable to appoint magistrates as not a single inhabitant had the required standard of education. And though summer could be idyllic, winter was hostile, with the area often entirely cut off from the rest of the country by snow and ice. Essentially it was a frontier, a vast undeveloped forest, populated by fishermen and lumbermen with little interest, Foyster was to find, in God.

Lionel served several congregations in his parish, across a large area, often in extreme weather conditions. He was beset by bouts of ill health, leading to periods of absence. On return trips to England, he would stay with his sister in Northamptonshire or in Hastings. But he also continued to visit the Shaws in Ireland, regaling them with 'stories of blizzards coming up out of nowhere – of summer wild raspberries, wild strawberries, and fishing for trout and salmon'.[6] He had a vivid way, the young Marianne felt, 'of portraying people and places, firing [them] with enthusiasm for faraway places'.[7] In contrast, she felt that the poverty she saw in Ireland before the Great War was extreme: 'people lived on potatoes, wheat, flour and herrings – nobody died of hunger, but nobody got fat.'[8]

In 1914, the British Portland Cement company opened a factory at Magheramorne and jobs were suddenly plentiful. Marianne's father found a job as a caustic finisher and her brother, Geoffrey, became an apprentice chemical analyst. When war broke out in August, the company flourished, bolstered by government contracts.

At the age of fifteen, Marianne was introduced to a work colleague of her father, an Englishman called Harold Greenwood who had come to Ireland to find work. Greenwood was twenty-one and the son of a Church of England clergyman who had died in 1909. 'I had never had a beau before,' Marianne remembered. 'He was a talented violinist and he and mother and father started a music group which ended up in a big concert in a local hall. I thought he was beautiful, and was delighted to be the object of his affections.'[9] As a romance between the two developed, Greenwood asked Marianne to marry him. She was fifteen, and though girls as young as twelve could marry before the Age of Marriage Act of 1929, Marianne knew that her parents would not give their consent. Greenwood suggested that they could be married by declaration in Scotland, which was easily accessible by the ferry from Larne to Stranraer. To that end, he persuaded his sister May to invite Marianne to visit for a holiday in Blackpool. Marianne's father objected to the trip, but her mother thought the visit couldn't be more proper as Greenwood's sister was a schoolteacher and was married to a clergyman. Their daughter would be perfectly safe with such fastidious supervision.

Marianne and Greenwood sailed the short distance to Stranraer, where Greenwood had already booked lodgings three weeks previously, as required by Scottish law. They had an 'irregular' marriage on 8 June and then went on to Blackpool to visit Greenwood's sister. They returned to Ireland, keeping the marriage a secret. But in August 1915, Marianne fell pregnant and 'all hell came out of the closet'.[10] The fact that she was carrying an illegitimate child would have brought great shame on the family and her mother went 'raving mad'.[11] When Greenwood admitted that they were married, this only made matters worse. Marianne's father insisted that they had not adhered to the residency laws and there had been no clergy present; therefore the marriage was illegal. A formal church wedding was held at St Anne's Cathedral on 12 November, with Marianne's mother and brother as witnesses. The fact that the ceremony was held at one of Belfast's great cathedrals, rather than discreetly in a local rural church, suggests a certain bravado on her father's behalf, a public show of support for their daughter in the faces of their Presbyterian neighbours. Harold Greenwood continued to work at the concrete plant and bought a cottage in Larne near Marianne's parents. A child, Ian, was born on 19 April 1916. According to Marianne, everybody seemed happy. But it wasn't to last.

Greenwood had informed the Shaws that his only relations were his brother and sister. But now he began to mention his widowed mother, Emily, who was, according to him, rather delicate. After the birth of their child, Mrs Greenwood suddenly appeared from England, like a witch in a fairy story. She made it clear that she hated Ireland, the Irish, the cottage, the scenery, but most of all she hated Marianne. Marianne had a challenging and independent spirit, and during her time in Ireland had developed a zest for life and fun, as well as a distinct Irish brogue. Within three weeks, Mrs Greenwood had Harold like a 'whipped puppy' and the marriage was all but over.[12] She announced that she was returning to England and taking her son with her, Greenwood assuring Marianne that he'd send for her and their child at a later date. Marianne's father asked her if this was what she wanted. Knowing that her molly-coddled husband would always resent her if she was constantly embattled with his mother, she said it wasn't; she wanted to end the marriage. Mr Shaw consulted a lawyer, who drew up a deed of separation. Mrs Greenwood indicated that she would oppose any financial obligations on her son's behalf, but Marianne's father was clear that they neither needed nor wanted her money – or her son. The Greenwoods left for England and Marianne would never see her first husband again.

With Marianne now a single mother and little more than a child herself, her parents brought the child up as her younger brother, a common tradition among Belfast families where an unmarried daughter had an illegitimate child. Convinced that Marianne was too young to look after him, her mother took over the feeding, bathing and changing of the baby.

At this point in the war, the linen industry in Belfast was booming, with full employment for female workers, but rather than work locally on behalf of the war effort, Marianne reverted to her maiden name and took work in a munitions factory in Coventry, a fresh start away from any awkward gossip in Drumnadreagh. But it also meant that she had no part in the upbringing of her own child. She was to mourn the loss of this relationship for the rest of her life. 'I wanted a baby of my own,' she remembered years later. 'I was not allowed to bring up my own child and longed for a little boy.'[13]

*

By 1921, Lionel Foyster had lived in New Brunswick for over a decade; life was hard and lonely, despite the occasional visit from his unmarried sister, Hilda. He wrote to Marianne saying that he was moving to a new parish called Salmonhurst, a small Danish-speaking village. Marianne replied, enclosing a photograph of herself. He responded quickly, writing that she had changed a lot from the sweet child he had christened at Oughtrington all those years ago. Marianne wrote back, 'Thanks a lot, I'm still a sweet person.'14 This amused Lionel and they began a regular correspondence during which he described to her the pine forests and golden maples that surrounded him and wrote of the local immigrants he worked among. In reply, Marianne described the bloody and anxious times they were experiencing in Ireland, particularly in nearby Belfast. Between 1919 and 1921 the Irish Republican Army had been at war with British forces, intent on Irish independence. The country was partitioned in 1921 with the creation of Northern Ireland and the Irish Free State. The period between 1920 and 1922 would prove to be the bloodiest in Belfast's history. One thousand people were killed in sectarian violence and 4,500 IRA supporters were interned.

In the summer of 1922, Marianne received a proposal of marriage from Lionel, offering to pay her passage to Canada. It would be a fresh start for her in a young country full of prospects, away from the local gossip and the increasing violence in Northern Ireland. For himself, as well as offering a new life and security to a young woman who'd had a bruising experience of adulthood so far, he would gain a companion for his solitary life in the colonies and help to share the burden of his parish duties. Concerned about the validity of such an arrangement, Marianne consulted a lawyer, telling him that she had heard that Greenwood had died and she had written to his sister in Blackpool for confirmation, but hadn't received a reply. The lawyer advised that as she'd had no contact with him for over six years, she shouldn't allow this to prevent a marriage to Lionel Foyster: 'If you like what you see,' he told her, 'take a chance on the man.'15

At twenty-three, Marianne was a vivacious, handsome, young woman, five feet tall, of medium build. Her hair was black and her face round with even features – her eyes dark and luminous, her lips thick and sensuous. She was self-confident and optimistic. 'I could have run the whole world single-handed,' she remembered, 'and told the Lord how to run Heaven.'[16] On 5 August 1922, with £30 in her purse, she boarded the Canadian Pacific steamer the *Victorian* on the five-day voyage to Quebec, intent on a new start in the New World as a missionary's wife.

Salmonhurst was a small farming community of 150, mostly Danish, immigrants with a school, shop, church, post office and hotel. The church, St Ansgar's, flew the Danish flag. Services were held in Danish, with men and women segregated in the two aisles as was the Danish custom. As soon as she met them, Marianne was charmed by the local Danes, who were happy, hospitable, hard-working, and full of life and energy. The rectory at Salmonhurst was not too big and had beautiful hardwood floors throughout. Lionel had made a little chapel in one of the rooms and the whole place, though cold with no heating, was comfortable. After staying less than a month, Marianne was convinced that she could make a home in the Rectory and a successful partnership with the Reverend Foyster, despite the fact that he was twice her age. But from the start, this was to be a mutually beneficial arrangement, not a love match.

They married at St Ansgar's on 28 August. Lionel bought Marianne a wedding ring, but it was far too big so she took to wearing it on her middle finger and would often lose it around the house. In the marriage register, she declared herself a spinster. At different times in her life she would claim that her husband had no idea that she had been previously married and had a son, while at others she insisted she had told him everything about her past. Given that she had corresponded with him since Oughtrington, it's unlikely that she wouldn't have mentioned in her letters her marriage, its breakdown or her baby. And it may well have been his understanding of her delicate situation – a single mother deserted at sixteen and living in the judgemental Presbyterian community of Drumnadreagh – that provoked him to propose marriage.

According to Marianne, a cloud loomed over the wedding reception. While the celebrations continued, Dr Allan Smithers, who had married the couple, was shocked to hear Reverend Foyster boast that he had baptised Marianne when she was a child. Although the marriage was valid in the eyes of the law, Smithers believed that this was not so in the eyes of the Church. Foyster had stood as Marianne's spiritual father so he couldn't be her husband; it would be a sort of spiritual incest. Despite Smithers's awkward observation, the couple honeymooned for four days at Long Lake, where they swam and canoed in the summer sun, playing chess together in the evenings; a warm relationship developed between them. Marianne began to use her own pet name for Foyster, Lion. When they returned to the rectory at Salmonhurst, they were touched that the locals had left a meal prepared to welcome them home. As Marianne unpacked, Lionel had a sermon to write and her life as a rector's wife began.

Marianne observed that Lion worked 'like a dog' to serve his parishioners,[17] but he was also a fun-loving man with a great enthusiasm for music and theatre. He wrote new church music as well as developing experimental forms of the Mass and Communion service based on pre-Reformation liturgy. He took great pleasure in drilling the church choirs himself, and he and Marianne shared a passion for singing. As well as his church work, Lionel produced plays and operettas with the locals. He would often tell Marianne that if he hadn't been a clergyman, he would have liked to have been an actor. Even in the next life he hoped to be putting on plays.

Soon Marianne found a role for herself, enthusiastically making the costumes for Lionel's theatricals, a pastime they could both share. Canada offered her opportunities that she would never have had in Europe. She learned to speak Danish, to sew, ski, skate and dance. She even became accomplished at golf and started to smoke cigarettes. Away from the restrictions and conventions of England and Ulster, in the relaxed and unconventional Salmonhurst, encouraged by Lionel, more father figure than husband, Marianne began to mature into an accomplished, curious and intelligent young woman.

The first winter in New Brunswick, however, was a shock. The weather was extremely harsh and Marianne discovered that the conditions at Salmonhurst Rectory were rudimentary. All the water – including that for the chemical toilet – had to be pumped outside in sub-zero temperatures and lugged into the house up a flight of steps and through a porch into the kitchen. But though the temperatures were cold and life physically hard, hearts in Salmonhurst, Marianne remembered, 'were warm'.[18]

After a couple of years, the Foysters took a three-month holiday to Britain, arriving in Liverpool on 18 June 1924. They spent time with Marianne's parents in Northern Ireland and with Lionel's sister in Northamptonshire, as well as visiting his cousins, the Bulls, at Great Cornard and Borley. Harry Bull was now married and living at Borley Rectory with his wife Ivy, who Marianne thought charming. It was clear that though some of Harry's siblings also liked Ivy, others hated her. Meeting them at Chilton Lodge, Marianne found the cousins engaging and eccentric, reminding her very much of characters from Dickens, each with distinctive character traits. Hearing the tales of the haunted rectory during the visit, Marianne found that, though some of the siblings firmly believed that it was haunted, others didn't, or at least professed not to believe. She felt that it was probably just 'a lot of tall stories'.[19]

In September, having 'had a ball' in England,[20] the Foysters returned to Quebec, with Lionel contracting bronchitis on the voyage. They were thrilled when they arrived home, as their parishioners had fitted a furnace in the house. The following summer, while swimming on holiday at Prince Edward Island, Lionel had a mild heart attack. Though it wasn't serious, he was advised to give up the water sports that he had always enjoyed. His health continued to decline the following winter, when he had a sudden onset of arthritis. It was becoming clear that he could no longer carry on working as a missionary. He resigned from Salmonhurst in January

1927 and a month later was inducted into the parish of St Paul's, Sackville.

Sackville was situated on the Isthmus of Chignecto, connecting Nova Scotia with North America. With a population of just over 2,000, it was a much more civilised, social and comfortable posting than their former life among the country people. The church was a Gothic Revival design clad in local New Brunswick timber, just on the edge of the Sackville marshes, approached by sidewalks made of wood. Again, Lionel made over a room in the Rectory as a chapel for his own private prayer. The institution that defined the town was the Methodist Mount Allison University, the first university in the British Empire from which a woman had graduated. Marianne found Sackville quiet, quaint and 'prim in an old world way' and, at first, began to miss the easy freedoms of her life in Salmonhurst.[21]

Lionel Foyster's liberal High Church ministry and his prioritising of the poor in the community over middle-class interests didn't endear him to his new congregation. At the same time, the tight-knit parish was suspicious of Marianne. She was young, attractive and fashionably dressed, a great contrast to the former rector's wife.

At the Rectory, Marianne had a maid, as was the custom for women in her position. Encouraged by Lionel, she decided to continue her education. She joined Mount Allison Ladies College and took courses at the University as well as involving herself in youth work. But her studies were soon interrupted by her own health. She had been suffering from heavy periods for some time and was now diagnosed with polycystic ovaries. She travelled 20 miles to Amherst Hospital, which was just over the border in Nova Scotia. There was no known treatment at the time and though the cysts were successfully removed, for the rest of her life Marianne would continue to suffer from prolonged and heavy periods, fainting fits, high temperatures and nausea. And she would be unable to have any more children.

It was while she was convalescing at Amherst Hospital that Marianne first heard of the town's infamous ghost story. Some fifty years previously, Amherst had been a small town of 3,500 people. At eighteen years old, the 'dark and sullen' Esther Cox[22] was living in a small wooden house on Princess Street, the home of her sister Olive Teed, who lived there with her husband Daniel, a foreman at the Amherst Boot and Shoe Factory. Esther shared a room with her older sister Jean, who also lived with the couple. All were devout Methodists. Esther was courting a young local man, Bob McNeill, a worker at the shoe factory. On 28 August 1878, he drove Esther to some nearby woods in a carriage he had borrowed. While in the woods, it is thought that McNeill threatened her with a pistol and attempted to sexually assault her. The next day he left town and was never heard of again.

Fifteen days later, Esther began to experience strange phenomena in the house at night. Her hair would stand on end, her face would turn blood red and her body would swell inexplicably. She would also experience fits and heard knocking and banging throughout the night. Objects would fly around the house and chairs would be piled up. As much of the phenomena was focused on Esther's bedroom, it was witnessed by her sister Jean. Some locals thought that Esther was possessed by the Devil, others believed the activity in the house to be the result of mesmerism, which was little understood, or that it was to do with the new phenomenon of electricity. Esther herself felt that she had 'electric currents' passing through her body. When a doctor was called, the bedclothes were violently stripped from the bed by an unseen force and scratching noises were heard. Above her bed, chilling words were scratched deep into the plaster of the wall: 'Esther Cox, you are mine to kill.'[23] Subsequent wall-writings – a peculiarity of the haunting – were considered too profane even to print in the newspapers.

Soon many visitors – and journalists – were attracted to the Teeds' house. The story became a sensation and Esther found herself a local celebrity. Seduced by the extraordinary publicity surrounding the case, Walter Hubbell, an actor and theatrical impresario with interests in psychic phenomena, arrived to examine Esther for himself. She told him that the house was possessed by six ghosts, led by one called Bob Nickle. When Hubbell arrived, the phenomena became more violent. Esther was stabbed in the back, an attempt was made to cut her throat with a carving knife, and pins were found stuck into her flesh. After the 'ghost' threatened to burn the house down, lit matches fell from the ceiling and fires broke out around the house. Having observed the activity surrounding the girl – and the fascination with which the public regarded it – Hubbell arranged a commercial tour in which Esther spoke about her experiences. Some publications deplored the notion of a traumatised young woman now turned into a sideshow. The *Presbyterian Witness* protested against 'a proceeding so base and disgusting. If the girl is sick, should her infirmities be exhibited to the public?'[24]

The next year, the undaunted Hubbell followed the tour with a book, *The Haunted House*, claiming to be '*A True Ghost Story*'. Esther's sister Olive, however, claimed that Hubbell had dramatised and embellished the events. After fifteen months, the activity subsided as quickly as it had started and Esther retired to marriage and obscurity. She was reluctant to talk of the phenomena at Amherst as she was 'afraid they would come back'.[25] But what was the truth of what became known as the 'Great Amherst Mystery'? Was the activity supernatural in origin, a case of post-traumatic stress, or some sort of psychosomatic hysteria provoked by the attack by Bob McNeill? In his study of the case, Harry Price noted that the peaks of the phenomena occurred every twenty-eight days, mirroring the menstrual cycle. Esther Cox died poor in 1912. Meanwhile, true or not, Walter Hubbell's book became a bestseller and sold over 55,000 copies. It has never been out of print.

In January 1928, Lionel was fifty, and Marianne noticed that he was starting to slow down. He was also self-conscious of his declining health and took on even more work to prove that he was still up to the job. But he was finding it hard to sleep at night and was often in pain. He began to worry that he might have cancer, which his mother had died from, but he refused to consult a doctor until the pain became unbearable. Finally, he was diagnosed with chronic arthritis, which was starting to deform his joints. He and Marianne decided that he should travel to England for treatment.

Meanwhile, Marianne was juggling parish duties with her college and university courses when she heard the tragic story of a young family in the isolated rural village of Westcock, 8 kilometres from Sackville. Alice Tower was a farmer's wife who had died of a brain tumour that January, leaving her seven young children to the care of her husband, Seward Tower. A month after his wife's death, he fell off a load of marsh hay on his farm and fractured his skull, leaving the children orphans. The youngest child, Barbara, was less than a year old. Wallace, Edna, Fred, Royal and Merton Tower were to be parcelled out among their various aunts and uncles. The Foysters were asked if they would look after the infant sister, Barbara. She was pretty, blonde and Nordic-looking, reminding Lionel of a photograph of his late mother as a child. He and Marianne agreed to take the baby, changing her name to Adelaide, after Lionel's mother.

In October 1929, Lionel was granted three months' leave of absence from New Brunswick's Bishop of Fredericton to be treated at St Luke's in London, a specialist hospital for clergymen. Concerned about her being lonely in his absence, Lionel suggested that Marianne should take an apartment on the coast in the city of St John, and that her son, Ian, should travel from Northern Ireland to keep her company. Ian was now thirteen years old, high-spirited and 'a bit on the rough side'.[26] As Lionel headed over to England, Ian arrived in Canada and settled down to life with his mother. He proved himself an excellent student and won a scholarship to a strict school. But his relationship with Marianne, distant on her behalf, suspicious on his, had been broken. They would never develop a bond as mother and son.

When Lionel reached England, the world was being enveloped in a seismic economic crisis. On 24 October, the New York Stock Exchange on Wall Street was struck by 'wild turmoil'.[27] On 'Black Thursday', as it became known, 12.9 million shares were traded with losses of $30 billion over four days. One of New Brunswick's key industries, fishing, saw catches decrease, wages fall and thousands of men out of work. Many were made homeless, with neither food nor clothing to protect them against the harsh New Brunswick winters. This crisis had a direct effect on Lionel's investments, which impacted on the family's income. When Ian was taken into hospital with a ruptured appendix, and with the added expense of Adelaide, Marianne was now forced to look for work to contribute to the household bills.

When Lionel returned to Canada, on 8 April 1930, Marianne was concerned that his health didn't seem to have improved. If anything, it was worse; he was now lame. On settling back home, he heard that while he had been away, Marianne had been the subject of scurrilous gossip. It was rumoured that she had been having relations with other men, including a young clergyman who frequently stayed at the rectory. On hearing the rumours, Lionel dismissed them, refusing to believe any story to his wife's discredit; he was adamant that the scandalmongers had misinterpreted Marianne's high spirits and open nature. Inspired by his health and the local gossip, he confessed that he couldn't face another winter in New Brunswick. Discussing the various options, the couple felt there was much to keep them in Canada, where they had been very happy. There was the possibility of settling in Northern Ireland, but Lionel felt the Church of Ireland had no authority. While they were considering their future, he received an unexpected invitation from his cousins in Great Cornard. Eric Smith, the rector at Borley, had given up the living. They were looking to recruit a new rector to take over the parish. Would Lionel consider it?

After living for twenty years in rural Canada, Lionel was unwilling to live in a city, so the location of Borley seemed to be an ideal retirement for a sick, ageing man. Unlike the Smiths, they had close family connections with the district. The prospect of establishing a ministry at Borley run on the lines of a Canadian parish, with American ideals of democracy, appealed to Lionel. He painted a seductive picture to Marianne of the life they could have in an English country village, helping the poor and putting on theatrical productions. They could make an idyllic life for themselves and genuinely make a difference to a needy community. With his health in decline and their finances now in free fall, Borley seemed the sensible option, if not the only one.

On 20 June 1930, Lionel was transferred to the diocese of Chelmsford by the Bishop of Fredericton. Having arranged for Ian to complete his schooling in Canada, the Foysters officially adopted Adelaide, who would accompany them to England.

In July, as the Foysters set sail from Quebec, Marianne had mixed feelings. England was dominated by a strict caste system that she and her husband had lived away from for many years; it was, as George Orwell would observe, 'the most class-ridden country under the sun'.[28] In sharp contrast to the freedom and informal friendships they had developed in Canada, England had a 'different code of life'.[29] As the rector and his wife, they would be expected to uphold the responsibilities of Lionel's position and adhere to established social convention. These misgivings aside, Marianne looked forward with confidence to a quiet life in a sleepy village deep in the Essex countryside.

The Hall

CHAPTER NINE

THEY SETTLE IN THE HOUSE

26 July–31 December 1930

'Do you think the dead come back and watch the living?'

Daphne du Maurier, *Rebecca*[1]

The summer of 1930 was the sixteenth anniversary of the outbreak of the Great War. On 3 August, the final memorials were unveiled simultaneously at Loos, Pozières, Vis-en-Artois and Cambrai to the 53,000 officers and men whose bodies had never been recovered from the trenches and had no recognised graves. Thousands of relatives made pilgrimages to France over the bank holiday weekend, including Rudyard Kipling, who spoke a few words at the unveiling at Loos, where his own son had died on the battlefield.

The war continued to cast a dark shadow on British streets, which were haunted by maimed and blind veterans selling matches and laces or begging for coppers. Large numbers of men suffered with violent coughs, the result of gas poisoning. Many more were afflicted with debilitating shell shock. Two and a half million men were sufficiently disabled to receive a pension. This was coldly calculated according to the severity of the injury. The loss of two or more limbs or severe facial disfigurement qualified for the full weekly state pension of 27s 6d. A man who had lost his right arm would receive a 90 per cent pension. The loss of a left arm merited five shillings less a week, the presumption being that most were right-handed.

The British economy also continued to suffer from the impact of the conflict, yet in 1914 Britain had been one of the most prosperous countries in the world. Its core industries of coal, iron, steel, textiles and shipbuilding had accounted for 75 per cent of the country's exports and had employed 25 per cent of the workforce. But though these Victorian industries had prospered in wartime and enjoyed a short post-war boom, by 1920, with the domestic market in decline and many countries imposing tariffs on imports, Britain's exports shrank and the boom had bust. The war had seen Britain victorious, but saddled with enormous debt. It had cost, all told, £11,325 million, including loans to allies, some of which were never repaid. The national debt, which had stood at £640 million in 1914, had risen to £8,000 million by 1925, the majority owed to the United States. Half of Britain's national expenditure went on servicing the debt and 25 per cent of income tax – which reached an unprecedented five shillings in the pound by 1925 – was earmarked for debt payments.

Against this backdrop of economic depression, there was huge excitement about innovations in technology, promising a brighter, more prosperous future. The owner of the *Daily Mail*, Lord Northcliffe, had anticipated the popular and commercial appeal of flight as early as 1906, when he'd engaged a full-time aviation correspondent. The successes and failures of pioneers in flight would generate dramatic and photogenic press stories that would boost newspaper circulation. But Northcliffe was also acutely aware of the political implications of the dominance of the air: 'England is no longer an island. There will be no sleeping behind the wooden walls of old England with the Channel our safety moat. It means the aerial chariots of a foe descending on British soil if war comes.'[2] Air displays and air races such as the Schneider Cup were front-page news, and pilots like Charles Lindbergh and Amy Johnson became international celebrities. In 1924, the first Labour government had appointed Lord Thomson as Secretary of State for Air, who announced a £2.5 million three-year government research, experiment and development airships programme that would be both a source of national pride and a demonstration of imperial power. During the First World War, German Zeppelin airships had been used for reconnaissance, but had also bombed areas of the Norfolk coast; after the war, German engineering had seen one airship travel 138,975 miles without a single fatality. But success in the air had eluded the British. By 1926, Thomson's successor, the Conservative Sir Samuel Hoare, announced the building of two airships, each capable of long-distance travel. The R100 would be built by Vickers as a commercial airship, at Howden in Yorkshire, where Barnes Wallis, the genius behind the 'bouncing bomb' was chief engineer. Her sister ship, the R101, was to be a state-of-the-art airship built by the Air Ministry at the Royal Airship Works in Cardington. At the Lord Mayor's Banquet, Hoare announced that in a few years it would be possible to have a regular airship service between London and Bombay. 'Her greatest task,' he suggested, 'will be the forging of new links of communication between the British Commonwealth of Nations'.[3] The sea route to India currently took seventeen days, but the airships would fly non-stop, each carrying 100 passengers as well as 10 tons of mail and cargo in less than a fortnight.

The plan had been for the R101 to make its symbolic maiden voyage to India in 1927, but with delays in its construction and escalating costs, it was the commercial airship that was ready first. In July 1930, the R100 flew the 3,385 miles from Cardington to Canada, a trip that had, the *Daily Mirror* enthused, 'no equal in the history of aviation'.[4] The objective of the journey was to acquire the data necessary for the development of airships commercially. On 2 August 1930, the R100 moored at Montreal after a flight of seventy-two hours and now held the Atlantic speed record for both airships and aeroplanes. Lord Thomson praised a leap forward in the new generation of British airships. With the British having successfully trumped German engineering, J. P. Crocker of Eastbourne wrote to the *Daily Mail* dismissing the post-war notion that the best of Britain was over:

> A good way of treating a case of national inferiority complex is
> to persuade the patient to repeat at intervals: We first crossed the
> Atlantic by airship. We first crossed the Atlantic by aeroplane.
> At the present time the fastest airship, aeroplane, railway engine,
> motor car and motor boat in the world are all British.

That July there was, too, much anticipation in the press of John
Logie Baird's 'new wireless miracle', which was emerging 'from
the laboratory stage to the stage of public entertainment'.[5] It was
presented in three short daily shows at the London Coliseum. For
the first time, images of individuals talking in a studio in nearby
Long Acre were broadcast simultaneously to the theatre on a screen
6 foot by 3 foot. The live audiences were reassured that there was
'absolutely no deception' by the host, Sydney Moseley.[6] Though the
ghost-like images were 'blurred and flickering',[7] this new innovation – television – was startling, twentieth-century magic. The press,
however, wasn't convinced that the technology was sufficiently
developed; it could have a 'far reaching effect on entertainment,
international communication, on commerce, and on social life.
Whether anyone now alive will see these effects is impossible to say.'

The Foysters arrived in Plymouth on 26 July, before travelling
to Drumnadreagh to visit Marianne's parents. In August they
passed through an unseasonably bleak and wet London, taking the
London and North Eastern Railway service from Liverpool Street to
Sudbury, where they were met at the station by Kathleen Bull in her
car. They had been invited to take tea at Chilton Lodge, where they
spent the afternoon with Kathleen, Ethel, Alfred, Gerald, Constance
and Freda Bull. They introduced the family to Adelaide, who was
now a nervous and excitable child, full of imagination. The Bulls
thought her a pretty little girl with a look of Greta Garbo. They
were grateful to finally have a trusted incumbent in place at Borley,
and Lionel was relieved to have secured a less demanding parish
that would see him safely to retirement. As the Rectory at Borley
was considered too inconvenient, in a poor state of repair and with

a sinister reputation, the Foysters were to use Great Cornard as a base to look for somewhere to live. After tea, they were shown lodgings that the Bulls had arranged for them nearby.

The house they were to stay in was a typically English middle-class villa run by a typically English middle-class landlady and her daughter. It had been selected as it was near St Andrew's Church so that Lionel could attend regularly and acquaint himself with the vicar there, Arthur Sellwood. When they arrived at their lodgings, for the first time in their married life Marianne and Lionel had to share a confined space with no privacy. With Adelaide's crib in the room, there wasn't even enough space for them both to dress at the same time. So, they agreed for Lionel to get up first in the morning and take a bath, while Marianne gave the baby her breakfast in the dining room. Then she would go upstairs to bathe Adelaide and have her own bath. This was very much to the horror of the landlady, who was astounded that the rector's wife would parade around the house in a dressing gown. It is in these first days at Great Cornard that Marianne began to feel 'adverse criticism' of her character.

It was noted that she was considerably younger than her husband; she was thirty-one and he fifty-three. But he was also beset by health and mobility issues, which made the generational contrast between them more pronounced. Marianne's raven-black hair was shingled and she dressed in fashionable clothes that emphasised her slim figure. She was a witty and vivacious conversationalist on a wide variety of subjects and could speak French fluently.[8] Marianne also smoked, but she particularly scandalised the matrons of Great Cornard by wearing lipstick. Though this had become fashionable in Canada and America, it had not yet become so in rural England. The disapproval that Marianne's lipstick ignited in Great Cornard was as much to do with her position as the make-up itself. She was a clergyman's wife. The locals were accustomed to an older and more conventional woman in this position, such as Caroline Bull or Mabel Smith. They had not expected a permed and painted young woman who looked like an actress. Sensitive to the controversy she was causing, Marianne decided to stop using lipstick altogether until Lionel insisted that she should ignore the locals and do as she pleased.

As the summer weather was warm, they didn't want to stay indoors. With nowhere to sit outside their lodgings other than the front garden, where they felt they'd be on public show, they started to take long walks in the neighbourhood. This was considered a sign of supreme discontent (or eccentricity) by the villagers, who stared as the Foysters took their daughter about with them. This in itself was thought very un-English; middle-class children should be supervised by nannies or servants, not their parents. To make matters worse, Marianne insisted on dressing Adelaide in overalls, which was considered perfectly proper in Canada but bemused the villagers, who were more used to seeing children dressed in sailor suits or tweed.

Just as they had done in Canada, the Foysters frequently enjoyed singing, much to the disapproval of the landlady and her daughter. As well as hymns on Sunday, they would sing Danish songs and, encouraged by Lionel, Marianne would play popular songs on the piano. She particularly offended the sensibilities of the local middle class by triumphantly winning at tennis and beating the men at golf. This delighted Lionel but didn't endear Marianne to the community. Their 'greatest fault', it seemed to her, was that they laughed too much.[9]

With unemployment still rising unchecked by the Labour government, and a general suspicion that socialists were no better than communists, the Foysters' liberal, left-wing politics and unconventional behaviour were not approved of by the Conservative locals. At the same time, Lionel's interpretation of Anglican practice was deemed too democratic for the deferential congregation at St Andrew's. While he had ambitions to help the poor in the district, just as he had done in New Brunswick, Great Cornard seemed insistent on keeping them in their place. This un-Christian attitude to the needy in the midst of the agricultural depression made him angry and he'd often lose his temper. His conscience forbidding him to swear even *in extremis*, he'd vent his frustration with the petty class squabbles in the village, exclaiming 'Jam and plaster!' ('Damn and blast'). Marianne would join in with equally exasperated cries of 'Up the rebels and down with church and state and no home rule for Ireland!'[10] These oaths were overheard by the landlady and tales were soon spread around the village about the odd visitors from Canada. Though Lionel was amused by this gossip, Marianne was further concerned; it was no sort of welcome.

The Foysters viewed many farmhouses and manor houses in the district suitable to accommodate a rector and his family, but they were either too expensive, too far away from Borley Church or just 'too ghastly'.[11] Determined not to be discouraged, after viewing several properties they decided that they would settle at Long Melford, just as the Smiths had done. They had already chosen a house when they happened to be visiting Chilton Lodge and were discussing the move with Gerald Bull. He made an alternative suggestion. Borley Rectory was sitting empty – why didn't they live there? It was always 'such fun'. Thinking it locked up and uninhabitable, the Foysters hadn't even considered the Rectory as a potential home.

The following Friday, Lionel's cousin Bernard Foyster, who was the family lawyer and also had a say in the gift of the living, came to stay with the Bulls for the weekend. He also thought it would be good to have relatives living in the Rectory again. The property would only continue to deteriorate if it wasn't occupied. Bernard Foyster took the keys and accompanied Lionel and Marianne to Borley to view the vacant house.

Driving to the Rectory, Marianne noticed that Borley was bypassed by all the leading arterial roads. High on the hill looking down over the Stour Valley, the village felt distant, like an oasis. There was just one road through it, with some of the surrounding cottages over 700 years old. Bernard Foyster opened up the house for them, pushing back the shutters and revealing the empty, echoing rooms. Marianne was surprised how large it seemed, like an empty hotel. But she could see that it would not be too unwieldy to run. There were unlimited cupboards and closets, wide halls,

and plain rooms with no awkward cornices and corners to collect dirt. It had been built when families were large and servants
plentiful, but they could easily shut off some of the rooms in the
winter, which was common practice in North America. The facilities, though basic, could be updated and were nowhere near as
primitive as the conditions that Marianne had contended with in
the harsh Canadian winters. 'If anyone could stick Salmonhurst,'
she said, 'they could certainly stick Borley Rectory'.[12] The house
had been badly neglected by the Smiths, who had left the water
on, leaving the pipes to freeze. It had obviously been used over the
months by the local children to play in and for courting couples to
meet. Outside, there were beautiful oaks and some lovely mature
trees, including a cedar of Lebanon that must have been hundreds
of years old.

Back at Chilton Lodge, the Foysters began to discuss seriously the
idea of moving into the Rectory. Marianne had no qualms about its
reputation. As far as she was concerned, there was nothing uncanny
or ghostly about the place. She attributed the unhappy experiences of
the Smiths to their imagination or locals playing practical jokes. By
all accounts, Mrs Smith was a strange woman and, having been used
to a house run by servants in India, she must have felt vulnerable in
such a large and isolated property that she clearly couldn't manage
on her own. Ethel Bull hadn't liked Mrs Smith, who had some silly
idea about writing a bestselling book, but she had liked the husband
and thought him quite charming. The Bulls chatted amiably about
the history of the hauntings, rather proudly repeating the tale of the
nun the four sisters had seen in 1900 and the coach that Harry Bull
had witnessed in the lane. As she and her husband had no transport,
Marianne laughed that they would dearly love a coach to whisk
them off to Sudbury. She'd noticed that the Bulls themselves had just
such an old-fashioned coach as the one Mrs Smith had described.
This was used very occasionally by the Bulls' Aunt Mary, now Mrs
Yelloly, who had retired to Long Melford after her second marriage.
The Foysters amused themselves imagining it as 'The Headless
Coach' and the groom who drove it as 'The Headless Coachman'.[13]

Talk of the 'haunting' was a good-humoured family joke. Marianne was convinced that all the Rectory needed was some time, some elbow grease and a bit of imagination. With the diocese and Queen Anne's Bounty agreeing to fund the refurbishment of the house, the Foysters decided that they would make Borley Rectory their home. Compared to the rectories in Canada, Marianne felt, it was like 'coming from darkness into light'.[14]

Marianne and Lionel planned to reinstate the Blue Room as the master bedroom once again. He also wanted to turn the disused bathroom in the tower above the porch into a small chapel, as he had done in Canada. They picked a bedroom for Adelaide above the kitchen, near the bathroom. Marianne would have one of the bedrooms redecorated as a private sitting room for herself, away from the formal reception rooms on the ground floor. She also commandeered the old panelled servants' hall next to the kitchen on the ground floor as a sewing room where she could do her darning, mending and needlework. As a local firm of contractors estimated that it would take some months to refurbish the house, fit a new cistern and make it habitable, Kitty Bull, Felix Bull's widow, suggested that they stay with her at Pentlow Rectory while the work was done. Marianne's grandmother, who she had not seen for some years, was now gravely ill, so Lionel thought it would be a good opportunity for Marianne to visit her. Consequently, she and Adelaide left to spend a couple of months in Ireland as he moved to Pentlow and prepared to be inducted into the parish as the rector. While staying there, he scandalised the local gentry by hitching lifts in farm carts to Sudbury; this had been common practice in the wilds of Canada, but was not at all the behaviour expected of an English clergyman.

On Friday 19 September, a 79-year-old doctor, William Teasdale Wilson, was found dead at his home in Hampshire where he lived with his wife and sister-in-law. An enthusiastic spiritualist, he and his sons would often go into trances and stay in that state for some time, and claimed to make contact with 'the more refined and loftier spirits'.[15] A post-mortem revealed that he had died several days before. 'I do not think any man could have lived nearer to the unseen world,' a friend said, 'and I do not regard it as very surprising that those who lived with him did not realise that he had died. They probably thought that he had gone off in a trance and were waiting for him to come round.'[16]

Meanwhile, a desperate farmer's wife spoke to that day's *Daily Herald* about the plans by farmers to further cut casual farmworkers' wages by 3s as well as demanding longer working hours and increasing cottage rents. 'How on earth shall we manage to keep body and soul together I'm sure I don't know.'[17] When reminded that the farmers had suggested that the cost of living had gone down, she laughed. 'I'd like to see them manage on what I have coming in. People seem to think country folk can always get things to eat off the land for nothing. Well, they can't.'

That evening, a service of institution and induction was held at Borley Church to formally welcome Reverend Foyster to the parish. It was led by the Bishop of Chelmsford, who delivered a short address. There was, he said, no diocese like that of Chelmsford, with such contrasting characteristics and needs. Rural parishes like Borley, surrounded by a wide area of farmland and 'with none of the perplexities of the town',[18] had little changed in hundreds of years. But there was a new England on the horizon. The huge parish of Dagenham, built on technology and progress, was 'a city that should never have been built';[19] before long it would serve 120,000 inhabitants, all of them poor. The Bishop encouraged the congregation of Borley to help churches in the overpopulated districts of this brash, modern England. With reference, perhaps, to Eric Smith and the happenings that had characterised his tenure as the rector, the Bishop wanted them all to start afresh; a new chapter in the life of the village was opening and he hoped it would be one of progress. With the induction of a new rector, the church would become the spiritual home of the people of Borley once more. But he expected the congregation to do their bit just as their new rector would do his, and the best way to encourage Reverend Foyster to preach good sermons was to fill his church.

While Marianne was away, Lionel wrote to her regularly. As they had done in Canada, he planned to put on a theatrical production as soon as possible. She contacted a theatre company in Belfast that gave her recommendations for the best plays for village groups to produce. By October, the work on the Rectory was finished earlier than anticipated, so Lionel moved in. Not wanting him to live in the house alone, Marianne cut short her stay in Ireland, and she and Adelaide returned to Borley in the autumn. 'The air was filled with the scents of wood burning,' she remembered, 'and there was that hazy blue sky which speaks of good weather ahead.'[20]

On the last day of British Summer Time, 4 October 1930, after several design teething issues, the R101 finally took off from Cardington on a 2,235 nautical-mile demonstration flight to Egypt and Karachi. Lord Thomson was determined to fly to India and back to London in time for the upcoming Imperial Conference. At 220 metres long, it was the largest flying aircraft ever made and was dubbed the 'Titanic of the Skies'.

That evening, as the airship left its moorings at 6.36 p.m. and cruised towards London, the weather was already poor. By the time it reached Beauvais Ridge in France in the early hours of the next morning, the airship was pitching and rolling at 50 knots through fierce weather conditions. A split in the outer cover caused the ship to drag and then nosedive. At 2.09 a.m. it crashed into woods outside the village of Allonne, which ignited the hydrogen within the body of the ship, engulfing it in flames. Forty-six of the fifty-four passengers and crew died, including Lord Thomson and his valet. Of the eight survivors, two died of their injuries. Like the loss of the *Titanic*, the tragedy shocked the British public. The dream of connecting the various territories of the British Empire via the air was over. An inquiry later found that the airship should never have taken off on its flight to India with such poor preparation and in such bad weather conditions. But the desire to create a headline-grabbing publicity stunt had trumped the safety of the passengers and crew. The bodies of the victims – impossible to identify – were buried at Cardington. The R101's sister ship, the R100, would never fly again.

By the middle of October, the days in Borley were unseasonably sunny and the nights warm. But there were disturbing reports from the Continent. Having secured 18.25 per cent of the vote in the general election in September, at the opening sitting of the Reichstag in Berlin the newly elected National Socialist Party members were to take their places. A mob of what were now called Nazis gathered outside the building. Mainly men of about twenty, many well dressed and evidently middle class, they smashed the windows of famous Jewish-owned stores and tea shops in the vicinity. The police fired over the heads of the rioters and sixty of them were arrested. Inside the Reichstag, the National Socialist Party members entered the chamber in military order, dressed in their forbidden uniform of brown shirt and black necktie, red ribbons with the black swastika on the left arm. This theatrical scene was greeted with laughter by the other parties' members. Though there were intemperate exchanges between the National Socialists and the Communists, with voices and fists raised, the sitting closed without violence. But by the end of the week, with extraordinary speed, Hitler had put forward bills to confiscate Jewish property and proposed a cancellation of the terms of the Treaty of Versailles.

The Foysters moved into the Rectory on 16 October. With Lionel's income diminished following the Depression, they couldn't afford servants, but a daily woman, Annie Pearson, who lived across the road at Place Farm Cottage, came in three or four afternoons a week. She would do most of the scrubbing and harder domestic work. Her niece, Mary, had been employed as a maid by Mr and Mrs Smith and had subsequently moved with them to Sheringham in Norfolk. Since the departure of the Smiths, tenants had moved into the Rectory Cottage – Mr and Mrs Mitchell and their seventeen-year-old son, Dick. They would do odd jobs around the house, pumping water from the well for both the cottage and the Rectory.

On their first night at the Rectory, the big empty rooms were full of packing cases and boxes. With Adelaide upstairs in bed in the room above the kitchen, Marianne and Lionel had great fun looking around the large house and hatching plans for the future. They made a fire in the library and Marianne produced some play scripts that she had bought on her trip to Ireland. Lionel was very enthusiastic about a play called *Maid Marion*. He couldn't decide whether they should start immediately with a Christmas play or leave their first production to the New Year. Marianne advised that they should wait until they were properly settled. Lionel was slightly peeved at her apparent lack of enthusiasm, but his pique soon subsided. With the fire blazing in the grate and the shutters closed against the dark October night, they settled down to play chess and then a game of cards.

At one point during the evening, they heard footsteps upstairs. They took this to be Adelaide getting up to go to the lavatory, as was her wont at night. Shortly afterwards, they heard the footsteps again. Lionel thought it was time for Adelaide to go to sleep so he went into the hall and called up the stairs, 'Get into bed, you'll catch cold!'[21] Again they heard the footsteps overhead. Lionel took a paraffin lamp and went upstairs to Adelaide's bedroom. He found her tucked up in bed. Returning to the library, he told Marianne that it must be rats. That, she observed, was hardly a pleasant thought.

Settling in took some weeks, with the Foysters busy shopping in Sudbury and Long Melford, though they were helped with unpacking by the Mitchells from the Rectory Cottage. One evening, with the house a wilderness of tea chests and still no sofa in the drawing room, Lionel went upstairs to rest. Marianne was in her sewing room, which was next to the kitchen. Shortly after lying down on the bed, Lionel heard her call from the bottom of the stairs:

'Is anything the matter?'

'No, dear. Why should there be?' he replied.

'What were you calling for?'

'I? Calling?'

'Yes, you calling. Why, were you not?'

'I was not aware of it.'

'But I distinctly heard your voice cry, "Marianne!"'

'I neither called nor heard anything.'

'Well, that's funny, because it was just like your voice.'

'Imagination.'

'I don't see how it could have been,' sighed Marianne, returning to the sewing room, 'but call it that if you like.'[22]

They continued to hear footsteps when they were together and also when they were each alone. One afternoon, Marianne was expecting Lionel home for tea when Adelaide heard his footsteps outside in the hall. She ran out of the room calling, 'There's Daddy!' Marianne entered the hall to find it completely empty. Wherever the sounds came from, the little girl could clearly hear them, too; it wasn't simply Marianne's imagination. When Lionel subsequently arrived home and Marianne told him about the incident, he said he would have been a mile away when Adelaide had heard his footsteps. It certainly wasn't rats this time. 'It does seem,' Marianne observed, 'rather a funny house after all.'[23]

As with the Smiths, for the first six weeks the Foysters were visited every afternoon by callers from the parish leaving cards and who would stay for the requisite quarter of an hour. This was the only way in which a social relationship could begin. The etiquette of leaving cards was rigorously upheld. Cards were required to be 3 5/8 inches wide by 2½ inches deep, printed in small copperplate script and free 'from any kind of embellishment'.[24] They could not be sent by post and were only to be left in person with Mrs Pearson, who would answer the door, not Marianne herself. Calls would be made between 3 p.m. and 6 p.m. as morning calls were made only by intimate friends and not acquaintances. There was a litany of regulations as to how these social calls should proceed, with various pitfalls for ladies, like Marianne, who were unused to them:

A hostess betrays that she is not much accustomed to society when she attempts to amuse her visitor by the production of albums, photographs, books, illustrated newspapers, portfolios of drawings, the artistic efforts of the members of the family, and the like: conversation being all that is necessary, without having recourse to pictorial displays.[25]

The Foysters were now confronted with the prejudices of middle-class rural England. The newcomers were scrutinised with varying degrees of suspicion and disdain. It was immediately clear that despite their English backgrounds, their time in Canada had set them apart. Just like the Smiths, their manners, their opinions and their tastes were considered 'so colonial'.[26] When they happily admitted that they had enjoyed their time in Canada, their visitors couldn't countenance it. The congregation was already suspicious of Lionel as he was Anglo-Catholic, but he, stubborn at the best of times and proud of his work in Canada, would not back down if he heard it denigrated. Yes, Canada was different to England, but it was in no way inferior to it. Marianne, however, dutifully tried to play the role of the rector's wife. She was 'delightful, always cheerful and charming and an excellent hostess' who brought a 'touch of lightness and merriment to the rather sombre Rectory.'[27]

But despite her efforts, Marianne wasn't popular with the villagers, who distrusted the fact that their rector, a member of the Bull family, which they had long revered, was married to such a woman. She was Irish at a time when Irish immigrants were regarded with suspicion and, in some quarters, contempt. Documenting these prejudices in his state-of-the-nation assessment of contemporary English life, *English Journey*, J. B. Priestley deplored the Irish for having infected England with 'ignorance and dirt and drunkenness and disease.'[28] Marianne was also suspect because she was charming, good-looking and full of life, with her own opinions. If she said 'hello' to a man and politely asked after him, it was construed as an attempt at seduction. Lionel was naturally friendly, too. He loved children, adopted stray dogs and cats, and kept an open house, with the doors never locked. Marianne felt that the local gentry thought that they were 'too friendly with the wrong kind of people – the lower classes.' According to her, they were deemed to be 'something less than human' – 'perverts, socialists and entirely un-English'.[29]

In contrast to her role as a hands-on clergyman's wife in Canada, with an active parish and her college studies, it soon became clear that there was little for Marianne to do. With her experience of youth work, she had looked forward to teaching the Sunday School, but was frustrated that there weren't enough children for her to teach. A Miss Byford already taught the younger children and Lionel would teach the older ones. Nor were there any mothers' meetings, as the locals had avoided the Rectory during the Smiths' time there. Lionel controlled the family finances and was increasingly tight-fisted; Marianne had no access to money of her own. If she wanted to buy a new dress and Lionel said they couldn't afford it, she'd developed a subterfuge whereby she would buy the material and pretend to make the garment herself. But secretly she would buy the dress she wanted from the shop. Despite her education and intelligence, she had little agency and was absorbed into the cult of domesticity that had emerged in the wake of the war. Her sole responsibility was to run the large and inconvenient house and look after Adelaide. Though Mrs Pearson did the scrubbing, Marianne did the majority of the household tasks, shopping, cooking and baking bread as well as the laundry – a particularly labour-intensive job as the irons had to be heated on the stove. There were few opportunities to relieve the weekly routine of domestic chores and parish duties. With no car and no bus service, even an outing to Sudbury was an event. Her only excursion away from the area was a day in London to meet Lionel's sister Hilda. Marianne soon found her life as a housewife in the isolated village dispiriting and frustrating; the horizons small, the community inhospitable and petty.

During the calling period, the Foysters did little serious work in the parish, deciding to leave this until after the New Year of 1931. This afforded them the time to finish the work on the house. When they had first arrived, they found that the floors and doors were coated with an old-fashioned dark varnish. This had not been updated since the house was first built and gave the interiors a gloomy, ecclesiastical aspect. They decided to strip, wax and varnish the floors and doors the way they had them in Canada. They informed Sir George Whitehouse, who had succeeded William Bigg as church warden, of their plans. He immediately told them they couldn't make any changes to the Rectory without calling a parish meeting for approval. Among a list of restrictions, he and his wife also advised the Foysters that they were forbidden to drive nails into the walls and were not allowed to keep a goat on the lawn. Exhausted by the seemingly endless proscriptions, Lionel was apoplectic with indignation.

Now in his early seventies, Whitehouse was a civil engineer who had made his career overseeing large infrastructure projects on behalf of the Empire and had been knighted for his services in 1902. Before the Great War, he had retired to Arthur Hall, about a mile and a half away from Borley. Marianne found the Whitehouses kind and down to earth and they would become friends, often lunching with them at the Hall on Sundays after morning service. Florence Whitehouse became particularly fond of Lionel, and though he could be a 'trifle bigoted', she thought him a kind and decent man.[30] She was absolutely convinced of his honesty – 'He could not tell a lie,' she said, 'to save his life.'[31] He was, Florence later recalled, clearly extremely fond of his young wife, though she had the impression that Marianne didn't treat him very well and remained suspicious of her.

Having agreed with the parish council that the house could be redecorated, Marianne ordered a paint they had used in Canada, adding a touch of familiarity to their new home. She furnished the Rectory with inexpensive new furniture. With the fresh paint finish, some wooden chests that Marianne had bought and some large ceramic vases, the hall began to take on a medieval flavour. They soon found the main staircase was hard to use, as the stairs were so highly polished – a 'death trap' for Lionel, Marianne felt – so they took to using the backstairs on a daily basis. In order to turn the old bathroom in the tower above the door into a chapel, a local workman made some wooden altar rails and Marianne sent off for specialist paper, colourfully decorated with devotional images. This would give the plain windows the appearance of stained glass. Florence Whitehouse, who visited the house on Sundays and always went upstairs to use the bathroom, disapproved of the chapel. But Sir George thought it acceptable – as long as the Foysters didn't furnish it with any chairs.

Outside, with help from young Dick Mitchell, Marianne began work on the garden. It was warm and bountiful in some areas, where violets and giant campanulas would grow, making the air sweetly spiced on a summer's day and providing a haven for bees. The Nun's Walk, however, was edged with box and yew, and though Marianne repeatedly tried planting all sorts of flowering shrubs, seeds and bulbs to give the area some colour, nothing would grow there.

Lionel would go across to the church every day at seven in the morning and most days Marianne would accompany him. The ancient churchyard was beautiful, with its topiary yew-tree walk. Within it were memorials to the Herringham and Bull families. One grave was even fitted with a mortsafe. In the early nineteenth century, these intimidating iron cages were designed to protect newly buried corpses from resurrection men, or 'body snatchers', from exhuming cadavers and selling them to medical schools for dissection. The locals continued to be buried in the churchyard and wanted their bones to lie with their forefathers, resenting outsiders being buried there. Whenever there was a funeral, old bones would frequently be dug up, rising to the surface of the earth.

While she was in the church itself, Marianne noticed that the building had a peculiar atmosphere, a 'different feeling' to other churches; 'there was definitely in the church,' she felt, 'a knowledge of survival'; a 'certainty of a hereafter'.[32]

There was also a strange atmosphere in the Rectory itself. Certain rooms felt 'unhappy', with unexplained drops in temperature. It could become bitterly cold and guests were unable to sit comfortably in them. Marianne remembered:

There were weird noises that were heard in the house, but there again, in most houses if you lie awake at night there are all kinds of happenings. There were occasions when we frightened each other. We talked about things and we could get ourselves nervous and excited and then even if the house creaked, you imagined things were coming.[33]

There was little privacy in the Rectory, with villagers in and out of the house all day. With the village so isolated and no conveniences in the church, they would use the lavatory in the house. At the same time, Lionel encouraged local tramps, who would be fed at the back door. In cold weather they would warm themselves in the kitchen and sleep in the outbuildings. Because there were so many entrances, much of the time Marianne wasn't aware who was in the house or where they were. One day, she found a mischievous local lad throwing stones on the roof. When she challenged him, he confessed that he had the idea from hearing stories about boys playing pranks on the Smiths when they lived at the Rectory. He admitted he had often thrown stones, but denied he was responsible for any other activity.

One evening Marianne was on the landing, lighting her way with a candle. By the spare room, she saw an old man. At the time, she thought it might be her imagination, or the way her candle cast a shadow. But later she saw him again. This time she was going up the main stairs when she heard a step behind her. The old man was following her. He had stooped shoulders, an aquiline nose and was wearing a distinctive plum-coloured coat or dressing gown with braid on the lapels. She went into the bedroom and by the time she came out of it, he had gone.

One afternoon shortly afterwards, Marianne was weeding the paths in the garden with Adelaide, as Lionel was reading under the cedar of Lebanon. Crossing the garden in broad daylight, she saw the same old man. Many of the locals made a short cut this way from Bound's Meadow, through the Rectory garden, across the churchyard to Belchamp Walter. When Marianne asked her husband if he had noticed the old man go past, he said he hadn't seen anything. There was nobody there.

When she next saw Mrs Pearson, Marianne described what the old man wore and wondered who he might be. As she took in Marianne's description, Mrs Pearson's face turned 'a kind of greenish white'.[34] The figure Marianne had been seeing was Harry Bull.

Marianne had met Harry on their holiday to England in 1924, but the old man she saw didn't look like the happy, well-fed cleric she had been introduced to. However, he did share a resemblance with Harry's brothers Alfred and Gerald. Lionel told Marianne not to mention what she had seen to anybody else. Nonetheless, she discreetly probed Mrs Bigg at Borley Place, who, as a hospital nurse, had visited the Rectory frequently to help Ivy Bull in the last months of her husband's life. Did she know if he had possessed a plum-coloured dressing gown? Mrs Bigg confirmed that Reverend Bull used to wear a plum-coloured smoking jacket and was barely seen out of it in the months before he died. She wondered why Marianne was asking. Had somebody left it lying around? Marianne said nothing.

The longer they lived at the Rectory, the more the Foysters began to experience strange things. Late at night, a smell of cooking would float through the open bedroom window or a delicate smell of perfume – lavender, roses and eau de cologne – would fill their room. They assumed that these smells must have had some paranormal source. However, in 1899, Stafford Allen had opened a factory on the outskirts of Long Melford on the site of an old watermill. They were the largest manufacturer of natural pharmaceuticals and flavourings in the country, growing lavender, liquorice, saffron and peppermint in fields that surrounded the factory for miles. They also imported ginger, pepper and exotic spices, which they used in the preparation of their products. The villagers at Borley were used to the strange scents that would drift up the hill when the wind was blowing from the north, particularly in the evening, when the nightshift cleaned out the vats. But as strangers to the area, neither the Smiths nor the Foysters would have been aware of the logical source of the unusual smells.

Crockery and kitchen utensils began to disappear and would then randomly turn up. A bag of lavender appeared from nowhere on the mantelpiece in Marianne's sewing room and subsequently appeared in Lionel's pocket. In the bathroom one day, the bracelet from her wristwatch was inexplicably detached from the watch and disappeared. Marianne looked everywhere, in the fireplace and on the floor, but there was no sign; it had vanished. Lionel insisted that it must have been the work of what he now referred to as 'the goblins'.

One night, past midnight, Marianne and Lionel were retiring later than usual when she suddenly jumped. There was a ting-a-ling sound: the ringing of a bell. Other than the front and back door-bells, most of the bell wires had been cut by the Smiths. Lionel got out of bed, walked across the dark landing and looked down into the hall. 'Who on earth rang that?' he called. The bell rang again. And again.

The Foysters looked forward to Christmas 1930, the first they would be celebrating in England since before the war. Marianne decorated the church with holly, ivy, moss and seasonal flowers. In front of the altar, plaster figures of the holy family, the shepherds and wise men, were placed in a nativity scene decorated with straw, glitter and cotton wool. At the Rectory, she draped coloured-paper chains across the drawing room. In the hall, tissue-paper honey-comb bells were hung from the ceiling, with Chinese lanterns and bunches of mistletoe pinned above the doors. Sprigs of holly were placed at the top of the pictures and on the mantelpieces. Marianne and Adelaide decorated the Christmas tree in the drawing room, fixing small candles to the branches and hanging baubles of glass and papier mâché. Sparkling lametta gave the appearance of icicles in the light from the fire.

The shops in Long Melford, Sudbury, Bury St Edmunds and Framlingham were full of gifts and seasonal food in preparation for the festivities. For Lionel, Marianne browsed books at F. T. Groom & Son, who stocked Bibles and prayer books. When Lionel asked

Marianne what she would like for Christmas, she pointed out a small china powder bowl in a shop, which she had seen and liked. But by the time Lionel had reached the counter to buy it, it had been sold and there were no more in stock.

In the *Bury Free Press*, in his article 'Christmas, Today and Yesterday', G. H. Brierley bemoaned the 'declining sentiment' that had affected Christmas since the war. 'We live in a world of change,' he wrote, 'of rapid, often of startling change.'[35] The invention and development of the automobile, the aeroplane, wireless telegraphy and the cinematograph had 'done much to lessen the present generation's love for the old'.[36] Even Christmas cards were not so generally bought to send to relatives and friends, at home and abroad, as they had been even a few years before. But, he wrote, 'the new Christmas is still the old Christmas – in spirit. It has not lost its place as the greatest of the year's festivals.'[37]

One evening, Marianne was upstairs in her sitting room smoking as she put the finishing touches to a Christmas present she was making for her husband. Suddenly she heard footsteps on the stairs. Thinking it was Lionel and not wanting him to walk in and spoil the surprise, she stubbed out her cigarette and ran out to meet him. As she reached the landing, on the dark staircase a few feet below her, she saw a figure. It was the old man she had seen before and had now been told was the ghost of Harry Bull. Turning swiftly on her heels, she ran back into her sitting room, quickly shutting the door behind her.

Becoming more concerned about the activity that they were experiencing in the house, the Foysters began to pray for protection from whatever seemed to be plaguing them. With his interest in ecclesiastical liturgy, Lionel used a text from Archbishop Laud's 1637 *Scottish Book of Common Prayer*:

From ghoulies and ghosties
And long-leggedy beasties
And things that go bump in the night,
Good Lord, deliver us![38]

On Christmas Eve, the *Daily Mirror* complained that it had 'not been a cheerful year. It is not (apart from Christmas) a cheerful moment in our history.'[39] As was traditional, a seasonal ghost tale by Dickens, *The Poor Relation's Story*, was broadcast by the BBC at 7 p.m. read by V. C. Clinton-Baddeley. After a carol service, there followed *And Afterwards* ... a 'creepy interlude' with the actor Felix Aylmer and Lady Cynthia Asquith, the famous writer and anthologist of ghost stories. Again, Bovril had placed special seasonal advertisements in the press. This year, a sketch of a man reading ghost stories in front of a roaring fire, a cup of Bovril on the table beside him, an Elizabethan ghost looking jealously at the warming meaty drink with the lines:

'Of ghostly life I've had enough,'
The spectre said with glee,
'This Bovril is the very stuff
To make a man of me!'[40]

By Christmas, Marianne and Lionel had become used to the house, its queer ways and strange noises. Neither of them was afraid, as Lionel had been aware that the Rectory was haunted from the times he'd stayed there as a boy. 'If there was nothing worse than this,' he said, 'there was nothing very terrible, even if some truth did underlie the stories connected with it.'[41] The phenomena were odd but in no way threatening. They were reassured to see that Adelaide seemed completely untroubled by it. At New Year, the house was much quieter than it had been for several weeks. It now seemed to be 'ordinary and well behaved as all good houses should be'.[42] But in the winter of 1931 'matters suddenly started up with a vengeance'[43] with an escalation in violence that the Foysters had 'never even dreamt of or thought possible'.[44]

The Driveway and front Entrance showing the
bricked up window of the Dining Room

CHAPTER TEN

THE EVIL IN THE DARK CLOSET

January–April 1931

> The Overlook faced it as it had for nearly three-quarters of
> a century, its darkened windows now bearded with snow,
> indifferent to the fact that it was now cut off from the world.
> Or possibly it was pleased with the prospect. Inside its shell
> the three of them went about their early evening routine, like
> microbes trapped in the intestine of a monster.
>
> Stephen King, *The Shining*[1]

The farms around Borley had been particularly badly affected by the agricultural depression. Essex and Suffolk were among the principal wheat-growing counties in Britain, but between 1929 and 1931, the gross return from grain crops was cut by 50 per cent. Agriculture was in crisis, with farmers frequently pursued by bailiffs for non-payment of the tithe – two thirds of which was paid to the Church. More and more, the tithe seemed to be an anachronistic and unfair imposition on an already decimated farming industry. The Ecclesiastical Commission at Westminster employed agents to seize property, livestock and crops that would be routinely auctioned off in lieu of tithe debts. Struggling to keep their businesses afloat, many farmers tried to lower their costs by cutting the wages of casual agricultural workers, increasing their hours or making them redundant.

While farmers headed the list of trades in the bankruptcy courts and farmworkers starved, many rural clergy in tithe-rich counties like Essex and Suffolk had incomes of over £1,000 a year bolstered by the local tithe. The position of the country rector was severely compromised by his parishioners' antagonism towards the source of his income. The extensive and expensive refurbishment of Borley Rectory by the new rector and his wife may have seemed at best insensitive to some parishioners, who were enduring extraordinary hardship. By the end of February 1931, 150 protest meetings against the proposed wage cuts had been organised across Suffolk. In London, the charismatic patrician Labour MP Oswald Mosley proposed that a full-scale re-organisation of agriculture was crucial to his manifesto to solve the industrial crisis in Britain.

On the morning of 25 February, Marianne was in the kitchen making breakfast, and had put the kettle on the range to boil water for tea. She prepared the cups and saucers as usual. As the kettle was boiling, she couldn't find the teapot. It wasn't where she usually left it. She looked everywhere – in the cupboards, in the scullery – but it was nowhere to be found. Then Lionel observed that the milk jugs had gone missing. Though they had become used to things disappearing, they were now exasperated by the interruption of their routine. They couldn't even make a cup of tea. Marianne despaired aloud: 'I *do* wish they would bring them back!'[2]

When Lionel returned to the house later that evening, Marianne said she had something to show him and led him into the kitchen: there on the table was a plate with the missing milk jugs. She and Adelaide had been alone in the house all day. The back door was locked and she would have heard anybody coming in. But when she'd gone to the kitchen to make some tea, she'd found the jugs on the table. 'I wish,' she said, 'they would bring back my teapot.' Sure enough, later that day, the teapot had reappeared. 'You had better,' Lionel suggested wryly, 'ask for your bracelet.' Marianne did so, in 'not very complimentary language'.[3]

The next evening, just before 11 p.m., Lionel was in the bathroom getting ready for bed when he suddenly heard Marianne cry out from the bedroom. Rushing across the landing, he found her with her hand up to her face. There was a bloody cut under her left eye. She told him that she had been just outside the bedroom carrying a candle when something hard had come like a bolt from the blue and hit her in the eye. Inspecting the injury, Lionel wondered if it could possibly have been a bat? Marianne was doubtful; she would have known if it was a bat and besides, bats would be hibernating in February. The next morning, Marianne had a black eye. It was impossible to satisfactorily explain it to any callers who might have assumed that Lionel had hit his wife. But he and Marianne could hardly admit that she had been injured by a ghost.

Three days later, they had got into bed and had just put the light out when they heard an object hit the wall and fall onto the bed. Lionel moved his feet under the blankets and the object then dropped to the floor. Suddenly there was a loud bang and something heavy fell on his side of the bed. Quickly turning up the lamp, they found a broken hammer head on the bedclothes and a cotton reel on the floor. Disturbed by the strange activity, they decided to spend the rest of the night with the lamp lit.

The next afternoon, given the increasingly violent activity, Lionel wrote to his sister Hilda for advice as she had an interest in spiritualism. At four o'clock, Marianne brought the tea things into the library, accompanied by Adelaide; there was tea, sandwiches and cake. She placed the tea tray on the table and was just about to sit down when Adelaide pointed to the seat of the chair and screamed, 'Mummy! Needle!' A sharp pin was sticking upwards, ready to prick anybody that sat on it. Lionel extracted it and sat in the chair himself. Marianne then took the chair at Lionel's desk, but she immediately jumped up; there was another pin.[4]

After tea, Lionel carried on with his letter in the library while Marianne returned the tea tray to the kitchen with Adelaide. Shortly afterwards, on her way back to the library to wish her father goodnight, the little girl tripped and fell over in the dark hallway. Hearing the noise, Lionel rushed into the hall to see if she was all right. 'It's dark, Daddy,' Adelaide said. 'Baby couldn't see.' Outside the door were an old lamp and a battered saucepan they'd never seen before and that certainly hadn't been there earlier.

Later that evening a series of domestic items began to mysteriously appear around the house: the long handle of a floor polisher blocked the kitchen passage; a tin of bath salts appeared outside the bathroom door. The intention of these randomly placed objects seemed to be to trip up the family in the dark. Such was their anxiety, Marianne and Lionel were unable to sleep, worrying about what would happen next.

Over the next few days, the phenomena seemed to subside. But on the night of Friday 6 March, Lionel was in the bathroom when he suddenly heard Marianne scream again. Dashing out, he found her on the landing, very distressed. A heavy object had just flown right past her head. She felt as if something had pushed her out of the way of it. Looking on the floor with the paraffin lamp, Lionel found a doorknob. This last attack really upset Marianne. The activity now seemed to be specifically targeting her, which was beginning to affect her nerves. She started to take Luminal, a sedative that was used to treat anxiety and sleep disorders. Writing again to his sister, Lionel did wonder if Marianne might be responsible for the strange happenings and had somehow staged them. But he didn't think her 'clever enough' to have initiated such a huge hoax. 'Besides,' he wrote, 'what on earth could have been her object?'[5] They trusted each other 'too fully to conceive of such a thing'.[6] Marianne was, Lionel suspected, psychic. But might the activity at the Rectory be an expression of something more psychological? Isolated in a remote rural community, and surrounded by locals who resented her, had the reality of Marianne's situation now fully dawned on her? Did she crave attention, recognition or validation? Or was there something genuinely wrong with the house? Hilda advised Lionel that he should make a note of the occasions when it was impossible for Marianne to have been responsible for the phenomena.

Concerned that the incidents were now no longer unsettling, but dangerous, Lionel decided that he needed some professional advice.

But he was very aware from the experiences of the Smiths that if the incidents at the Rectory were made public, all the sympathy they would get would be incredulous laughter behind their backs and the house overrun with sightseers. He needed somebody he could trust.

Next day, Lionel walked to Great Cornard to discuss what had been happening with his colleague, Arthur Sellwood. When he arrived at St Andrew's Rectory, Sellwood could see that Lionel was 'desperately troubled' and asked what the matter was. He had heard the rumours about the house since he'd arrived in the district the year before, but hadn't taken them seriously. He was sympathetic and ready to do anything he could to help. Lionel admitted that he was particularly concerned about the effect that the strange happenings were having on his wife. Her health had been poor since the surgery she'd undergone in Canada and she was still prone to heavy periods. On the other hand, their daughter Adelaide seemed completely oblivious to the activity in the house. All they wanted was a night of uninterrupted sleep, without the worry that something was going to be thrown at them. 'I am afraid,' Lionel admitted, 'my wife cannot stand very much more.'[7] Having considered the matter, Sellwood suggested that Lionel should bless the rooms with holy water from Walsingham, the former priory and pilgrimage site in Norfolk, of which he kept a small amount.

By the medieval period, the shrine, which housed a sacred image of the Virgin, a phial of her milk and two miraculous wells in the priory garden, had rivalled Canterbury as a place of pilgrimage and had become known as 'England's Nazareth'. The Virgin's milk was thought to enhance fertility, and water from the holy wells was used for exorcisms. Since the revival of Roman Catholicism in England in the 1830s, there had been a growing devotion to the Virgin Mary among late-Victorian Catholics, and a statue of her had finally been placed in the parish church at Walsingham in 1922. Promising to let Sellwood know how he got on with it, Lionel took some of the holy water from him and made the long walk back to Borley.

That night, with Marianne still feeling 'absolutely rotten',[8] the couple went through the main rooms and passages of the house, sprinkling the holy water. Marianne led the way with a lamp as Lionel said the prayers. While they were standing near the top of the backstairs, a stone the size of a fist flew past Marianne and struck Lionel on the shoulder. But they were determined to carry on with the blessing. As soon as they had finished, feeling weak, Marianne collapsed at the foot of the stairs, her exhaustion compounded perhaps by the sedative that she was now taking. Lionel settled her in the kitchen before rushing over to Borley Place to get some brandy from Mrs Bigg.

When he returned with it, Marianne told him that since he'd gone, there had been loud noises coming from her sewing room. Sure enough, when Lionel looked inside the room, he found chaos, with books from the shelves thrown all over the floor. Seeing the distress that Marianne was now in, he called at the Rectory Cottage and asked Mrs Mitchell to come and sit with her for the evening, explaining that his wife wasn't well. When he returned to the Rectory with Mrs Mitchell and her husband, he found that all the pictures from the main staircase had been taken down and left lying all over the floor. Adelaide, as ever, was unphased. 'Don't step on pictures!' she warned.

An exasperated Lionel went to the library and wrote to Sellwood outlining what had happened in the wake of the blessing. Things hadn't improved; if anything, they had got worse. Rather than vanquishing the spirits or goblins, they had only succeeded in irritating them. Meanwhile, the two women stayed in the sewing room. Mrs Mitchell commented on the footsteps she could clearly hear overhead. 'How plainly this house does sound,' she said to Marianne. 'You can hear Mr Foyster walking about upstairs.'[9] Knowing that Lionel was at the time working in the library, Marianne was silent.

Over the weekend, the weather turned bitterly cold and a hard frost set in, freezing the pipes. On the morning of Monday 9 March, a plumber came to thaw them out and pack them with straw as insulation. Dick Mitchell was also over at the Rectory, attending to some odd jobs. Marianne was in the sewing room when she heard something bowling along outside in the kitchen passage; going to see what it could be, she found a wooden log on the stone floor. As it was freezing cold outside, she promptly picked it up, put it on the fire in the sewing room and called out to the 'goblins', defiantly, 'Send me some more!'

During the afternoon, when she was leaving the kitchen with Adelaide, Marianne closed the door behind her and had just reached the sewing room door when a stone was thrown at her from the direction of the kitchen – a distance of about three yards – which grazed her hair. Later, Dick Mitchell told her that while he'd been working in the house, somebody had also thrown a stone at him. He presumed it must have been Adelaide. But Marianne insisted that was impossible.

Meanwhile, concerned after reading Lionel's letter, early that afternoon Arthur Sellwood drove over from Great Cornard. He suggested that they search the attics to make sure there were no vagrants hiding up there; Lionel did have a habit of accommodating tramps in the cold weather. But when Sellwood investigated, he found the attics empty; all was quiet. When Sellwood returned to the library, Lionel was relieved when the bells started to ring in the kitchen passage. He explained that the Smiths had cut the bell wires, but still they would ring. 'Extraordinary,' said Sellwood. 'It's the sort of thing one has to see oneself to believe.'[10] Lionel was pleased that Sellwood had witnessed at least some of the phenomena. With the blessing having failed, Sellwood advised Lionel that they must now conduct an exorcism.

The words 'exorcise' and 'exorcism' didn't originally mean 'to cast out', but came from the Latin *exorcizo*, which is itself derived from the Greek *exorikō*, 'to swear an oath'. Swearing an oath in Ancient Greece meant invoking a deity to punish the oath-taker if he failed to keep the oath. So, in Christianity, an exorcism is an invocation to God to compel Satan to do his bidding. Since the Reformation, exorcism had been outlawed by the Anglican Church and, as recently as 1925, the Bishop of Durham had denounced it. But in practice, for the previous three centuries exorcism had only been driven underground in the Church of England, with dissenting clergy ignoring or circumventing the official restrictions.[11]

The very mention of the exorcism that afternoon seemed to heighten the activity in the house for the rest of the day. As Lionel showed him out, Sellwood agreed that he would return on Wednesday morning, when the rite would take place. Suddenly there was a banging noise from the direction of the backstairs. Lionel and Sellwood rushed through the green baize door to see a large stone come to rest on the floor of the kitchen passage. So violently had it been thrown that it had knocked off the plaster on the corner of the wall at the foot of the stairs. It seemed as if something – or somebody – didn't want them in the house.

That night, things began to happen in 'an absolutely wild way'.[12] Lionel was sitting with Adelaide when another stone was thrown. She looked at the ceiling and casually said 'Stones falling', in 'the same sort of voice,' Lionel later recalled, 'that someone might call attention to the fact that it was beginning to rain.'[13] He took her up to bed, confident that she was used to being alone and wasn't at all frightened. Though he and Marianne had both been targeted, the little girl seemed to have no awareness that anything unusual was happening in the house. Once Adelaide was in bed, she wished Lionel goodnight in her usual, happy way. He went down the backstairs to Marianne's sewing room, where it was warm and peaceful; a contrast to the bitter weather outside and the increasingly weird happenings in the house. Marianne had been doing her needlework when presently she went to fetch something from the kitchen. On her way back to the sewing room, she rushed to the door as a heavy piece of iron clattered on the floor behind her.

At about ten o'clock, when they were getting ready for bed, Marianne was back in the kitchen making up the fire. Lionel was going through the door into the scullery when a stone was thrown from the other side of the room that then hit the scullery door, narrowly missing him. He was now very anxious about going to bed and wondered how much more of this they could stand. Should they go over to Borley Place for the night and stay with Mrs Bigg? 'I feel that if I once give way,' Marianne said to him, 'I should never be able to face the house again'. Besides, the Biggs would think they were mad or suffering with their nerves. And if their nearest neighbours felt that about them, they'd never be able to face them again, either. She could stand it – if he could. Lionel agreed. They should stay where they were and stick it out.

But it was hard for them to go to bed on such a cold winter night knowing it was freezing upstairs in the bedroom and that the phenomena was generally at its worst at this time of night. It had been so bad during the day, what might happen when they got to bed? As it was cosy with the fire in the sewing room, Lionel suggested that they spend the night there. 'We don't know what horrors they have waiting for us upstairs.' But Marianne felt they needed sleep and a proper bed. Lionel took the lamp and cautiously went into the kitchen passage, which was gloomy as the light cast dim shadows in the distance.

They reached the backstairs, nervously anticipating some sort of attack, but not knowing from which direction it might come. As things were usually thrown at them from behind, Lionel looked ahead and Marianne in the opposite direction. She stopped and told him to go ahead. '*What enemy might be lurking round these corners,*' thought Lionel, '*or even be nearer to us than that, invisible to mortal eyes?*' They advanced up the stairs together, unsure what they would meet on the dark landing. Finally, they got to the bedroom and they left the light burning until 3 a.m. At 5 a.m., Lionel woke to find Marianne wide awake. She pointed just behind her pillow. 'Look,' she said. 'While we were asleep ...' There was a small pile of five stones. 'I think they just put them there,' said Lionel, 'as much to say, "See what we *could* do if we wanted to."'

On the morning of 11 March, Arthur Sellwood arrived to exorcise the Rectory. He was accompanied by Bernard Smith, a distant cousin of Lionel, and his wife. Smith was the rector at Newton Green, about six miles away, and had brought a censer and some incense. As there was no Anglican rite of exorcism, Sellwood referred to the Catholic ritual from 1614, which was still current in 1930. They went over the building from attic to cellar; every room and passage was fumigated with burning incense and blessed with holy water from the shrine at Walsingham, as the rite of exorcism was performed:

> We exorcise you, every unclean spirit, every Satanic power, every incursion of the infernal adversary, every legion, every diabolical sect and gathering in the name and by the virtue of our Lord Jesus Christ.[14]

Once the rite was completed, though the house was quiet, Lionel could still feel the unsettling presence of evil. Sellwood and Smith left in the afternoon, and Lionel went about his parish business, leaving Marianne alone in the house.

Returning to the Rectory at 6.30 p.m., Lionel was anxious to know if the demonstrations had stopped. But in his absence, Marianne confirmed that there had been more bell-ringing. And again, a stone had been thrown at Dick Mitchell, who had been working in the house. The exorcism had not been successful. The spirits or goblins, or whatever they were, continued to possess the house.

On Friday 13 March, Sellwood visited the Rectory again, accompanied by Alfred Bull, who he'd informed about the activity. Bull was sceptical about the haunting, but was concerned that the Foysters seemed to be enduring similar problems to the unfortunate Smiths, which might result in more unwanted notoriety. In the years he had lived at the Rectory, he had never experienced anything supernatural, so he was keen to see some sort of demonstration. Lionel told him that he would be disappointed as the goblins didn't perform to order. 'I only wish they would,' he said. 'We should make a small fortune.'

During Alfred Bull's visit, there was no activity so he decided to return to Great Cornard. But just as he, Sellwood and Lionel were leaving by the front door, they heard a cry from within the house. It was Marianne. The three men rushed inside to find her at the bottom of the backstairs with a piece of metal in her hand. 'It was this,' she said, holding it up. 'They threw this and it hit me on the head and I can tell you it hurt. It came down the backstairs.' Alfred Bull quickly seized a stick from the hallstand at the bottom of the main staircase, then rushed back, through the green baize door and up the backstairs – there was nothing there.

As well as informing the Bulls, Lionel had been open about the activity at the Rectory with his family, some of whom couldn't understand why they carried on living there. What if Marianne or Adelaide were hurt in some way – or even killed? Lionel felt sure that such violence wouldn't happen. But he did decide to write their experiences in a circular letter that he would distribute among the family in Hastings in order to keep them informed of developments at the Rectory.

The following Sunday, after they'd had tea in the library, Lionel took off his clerical collar and sat down at the typewriter, with Marianne sitting by the fire reading to Adelaide. He began to write a document outlining their experiences to date.

Since I have been asked by members of our family to tell what I know of the so-called Borley ghost, and since I think it is desirable that a record of our experiences should be preserved, I am writing this before the details have gone out of my mind. I should like to say first of all that if I had been told by anyone what I am about to relate, I certainly should not have believed it, unless I had the very highest regard for their general strict adherence to the truth. In fact, I have during these last two weeks or so, wondered more than once if I should not presently wake up and find it all a dream: I regret to say that I have not done so as yet.[15]

All of a sudden, the collar he had taken off flew at the back of his neck. He wondered if Marianne had seen it, but she had been busy reading. Lionel carried on typing. After a few minutes there was a sudden bang from the other side of the room. A walking stick that had previously been standing in the corner was now lying on the floor on the opposite side of the room. 'Someone or other,' said Lionel, pointing to the typewriter, 'doesn't like my doing this.'

The next morning, Marianne found the kitchen table on its back with its legs in the air. The contents of one of the cupboards were scattered around the kitchen and the passage outside. Among the mess, a small red tin travelling trunk had appeared. Curiously, they found a small powder bowl in it. It looked exactly like the one Marianne had wanted for Christmas.

In between sessions of writing his circular letters, Lionel would keep the document between the pages of the New Testament of the sixteenth-century Foyster family Bible. One day he was correcting the copy in the library when Marianne announced that dinner was ready. He took the document into the dining room and left it on the sideboard as he went to wash his hands. When he returned, pages of the document were strewn all over the floor – and half of it had disappeared. He finally finished the first instalment of the history of their experiences in the house on Thursday 23 March. It was clear from what he wrote that he was absolutely convinced of the veracity of the events that were taking place around them. He continued to have complete faith that his wife was in no way responsible. For – if she was – what would that indicate about her mental health? Or the stability of their marriage?

When the Mitchells gave up the tenancy of the Rectory Cottage, the Foysters quickly missed having the help of an energetic young man like Dick to keep up the maintenance of the house and shoulder the physical work required in the garden. At the time, the personals column of *The Times* was printed on the front page and advertised everything from positions in private houses to potential investments, from situations abroad to kittens and second-hand clothes. They were a daily window into hundreds of stories of quiet desperation to read over breakfast:

YOUNG GENTLEMAN home from India, insufficient means, plenty of spare time, wants OCCUPATION: keen horseman, all games; own car.

WILL THE BURGLAR who visited us please return our canteen of cutlery made from 'FIRTH STAINLESS'? He can keep everything else. DISTRACTED HOUSEWIFE.[16]

Lionel took out an advertisement in *The Times* personals for an odd-job man. Just before Easter, he was contacted by an applicant from north London called Francois D'Arles. Lionel corresponded with him and an appointment was duly arranged for an interview.

D'Arles sped into the village on his motorcycle before being met at the front door of the Rectory by Marianne. He was a 37-year-old Canadian; short, dark, thick-set and handsome. Marianne took him into the library to meet her husband, who outlined the requirements of the job. D'Arles told Lionel that he'd worked in the secret service during the war and boasted an impressive military record. With employment scarce, he was eager to take the job at the Rectory, however menial. Lionel explained that as the tenants had recently vacated it, the Rectory Cottage was now also available to rent, if he were to take the job. After the interview, Marianne showed D'Arles around the house and grounds. They found they had much in common, both knowing Canada well and each fluent in French. He admired the work she had done in the garden. She was proud of it, having planted scillas, grape hyacinths, snowdrops, crocuses, stars of Bethlehem, narcissus and jonquils. D'Arles explained that he had experience of working with flowers himself, as his wife's family owned a florist's shop. But she had recently died, leaving him with a young son. Marianne told him that their daughter had also lost both parents before she and her husband had adopted her. She was taken with the virile and attractive young widower and touched by the story of his motherless son. Equally impressed by him, Lionel decided to offer D'Arles the job. But he also wondered to Marianne if he might help them with an issue of their own.

Adelaide had had to embrace some extraordinary changes in her young life. She had lost both her parents and been separated from her siblings. She had been given a new life and a new identity in a different country, in an alien culture, living in a large and lonely property. Though she had been told that she had been adopted, Marianne had not told Adelaide that she had brothers and sisters living in Canada. When her sister Edna wrote to her, she wrote as a 'cousin'. As she grew older, Marianne told Adelaide that Lionel was her adoptive father but that Marianne was also his daughter – they were half-sisters – so Adelaide referred to her as 'Marianne'. She was brought up by the Foysters very strictly, with Lionel instructing her on religious matters from an early age. They had bought her a puppy and a kitten, which they named Romp, to keep her company, but they had begun to worry that the girl's emotional development was suffering as she didn't mix with children of her own age. Lionel suggested that they should ask D'Arles if he would like to bring his son to stay with them for a month as a playmate for Adelaide. They decided not to discuss the reputation of the house with him nor the strange happenings they had experienced. Adelaide had never been targeted, so they had no reason to believe that D'Arles's son would be.

Having arranged a suitable date during the Easter holidays, D'Arles arrived at Borley on his motorcycle with his son in the side-car. They were immediately excited by the opportunities that life at the Rectory seemed to offer: a regular income with accommodation next door, rural surroundings in a stable environment, a playmate of similar age, and a puppy and a kitten to fuss over. Both children would certainly benefit from having a friend who'd also experienced the death of a parent. Francois Junior was a chubby little boy with big blue eyes, brown curls and a beaming smile. As soon as she saw him, Marianne fell in love with him. She had always wanted a little boy.

As the Foysters played host to young Francois over Easter, from Palm Sunday and throughout Holy Week there was 'absolute peace' at the Rectory, with few disturbances. The two children got on famously. Long before the holiday month was over, the Foysters suggested to D'Arles that his son should live at the Rectory permanently. It seemed an ideal arrangement for all, but particularly for Francois D'Arles Senior. In the midst of the Depression, within days of meeting the Foysters, he had a new job, a new home and even secured care for his young son. And within weeks, he was sleeping with the rector's wife.

The Dining Room fireplace

CHAPTER ELEVEN

THINGS THAT GO BUMP IN THE NIGHT

April–June 1931

> Her life was as cold as an attic facing north; and boredom, like
> a silent spider, was weaving its web in the shadows, in every
> corner of her heart.
>
> Gustave Flaubert, *Madame Bovary*[1]

Since her arrival in England, married to a sick man of a different generation, and her life now so changed from the one she had known in Canada, Marianne was isolated and bored at the Rectory. In a village in which she felt alien, with few friends and little to stimulate her, the arrival of a charismatic and seductive widower on her doorstep was perhaps irresistible. It was no romantic love-match, but a purely physical relationship driven by a desperate sexual need on her behalf and casual convenience on his. 'He was a man I never could have any regard for or affection at all,' Marianne admitted. 'I disliked him intensely.' He was, she thought 'a very dictatorial man'.[2] Almost as soon as she had embarked on the affair, she regretted it. She wasn't particularly attracted to him, but with some self-awareness, she recognised that she was 'desperate' for sex and quickly became addicted to him. D'Arles began to spend more and more time at the Rectory, working, eating and sleeping there. Though the Rectory Cottage was only yards away, he and Marianne would have illicit sex in the Rectory, heightening the thrilling sense of danger.

The tragic story that D'Arles had told Marianne was a fabrication. He was neither a widower nor Canadian. He was a con man, womaniser and fantasist. Even his name was fictitious. He was born Frank Charles Pearless in Bermondsey, the son of a family of leather workers. In the early twentieth century, the family had lived for some time in France, working in a shoe shop in the town of Arles, where the young Pearless became fluent in French. It was there that he conjured his pseudonym. Before the outbreak of war, the family returned to England. At the age of twenty-one, he was one of the first to volunteer for military service. He served throughout the duration of the war in the Royal Army Service Corps, seeing action in France and Salonica. He had given a distinguished wartime service and was awarded the 1914 Star, British War Medal and Victory Medal. Shortly after the armistice, on Boxing Day 1918, he married Ada Ewens, the 22-year-old daughter of a fruiterer and florist from Hackney. In 1919, a daughter – Renee Marguerite – was born, followed in 1922 by a son, Leonard. By the mid-1920s, the family were living near Ada's brother in Stoke Newington and D'Arles was earning a living selling flowers outside Abney Park Cemetery. But in 1927, he began an affair with the daughter of a gamekeeper from Worcestershire, Emily Fernie, and in July 1928 she had his child, Douglas – the boy who'd been introduced to the Foysters as Francois Junior. Now estranged from his wife and children who remained in Stoke Newington, D'Arles took lodgings in Tottenham. But his relationship with Emily Fernie didn't last and, unmarried, she abandoned the child to D'Arles's care. By 1931 he was holding down a casual job as well as raising his son as a single parent. The unexpected opportunity at Borley presented by *The Times* appeared to solve many of the issues that D'Arles was facing. Intent on securing the job, rather than reveal that his son was the result of an adulterous affair, he concocted the touching story of his dead wife.

D'Arles first learned about the strange happenings in the house from Lionel. He wasn't troubled by the idea of the ghosts and was, if anything, bemused. Now living at Borley, he could not help but be aware of the gossip around the village. Many of the locals continued to dislike or distrust Marianne. Despite the long-established legend and the experiences of the Smiths well before the Foysters had arrived, some suspected that it was she who was responsible for the strange happenings in the house.

The activity already at play in the Rectory now became a convenient smokescreen to disguise the clandestine relationship between Marianne and D'Arles. Some incidents recorded by Lionel in his notes as paranormal clearly had a much more human origin. One night when D'Arles was sleeping at the Rectory, a loud cry rang throughout the silent house. The next morning, he appeared at breakfast with a black eye. He explained it by saying that in the middle of the night, he had been in bed when he saw a shadowy form in the room. He had jumped out of bed and raised his fists in front of his face like a boxer, ready to fight the apparition. When he went to punch it, his fist went right through it and hit the wall. Then all of a sudden he felt a terrific smack in the face. But it is more likely the black eye he sported the next morning was the result of his intense relationship with Marianne as they 'fought like cats and dogs' and the sex they had was 'violent.'[3] With the increasingly frail Lionel absorbed by his parish work and Marianne in thrall to D'Arles, the younger man began to dominate the household. After Easter, the happenings in the house were generally subdued, though the Foysters began to find scraps of paper lying around the house with Marianne's name written in shaky, childish handwriting, as had happened during the haunting at Eland Road in Battersea. Given that Adelaide was unable to write, they had no idea who – or what – was leaving the notes. Finding an envelope with her name scrawled across it in pencil, Marianne wrote a question: 'What do you want?' She left the envelope where she'd found it. When she returned to it the next day, a new word had appeared on the envelope, answering her question: 'Rest.'

On Saturday 2 May, the weather was chilly. By early evening there was 'an uneasy feeling about the house'. With no fires in the main rooms and the children in bed, Marianne and Lionel retired to the kitchen for supper. Lionel was reading and as Marianne started cooking, they heard distant noises coming from the front of the Rectory. Suddenly there was a sharp bang in the kitchen. An object appeared to be thrown across the room. Lionel saw that Marianne was wiping her face with her handkerchief – she'd had pepper thrown into her eyes. When the meal was ready, they sat down and began to eat. But every two or three minutes, a stone or kitchen implement was thrown around the room. At first they tried to take no notice, until finally a knife hit Lionel on the hand. Dropping her knife and fork and leaning back in her chair, Marianne was exasperated: 'Can't we do something to stop this?' Thinking of the incense that Sellwood had used around the house, she had an idea. 'I tell you what,' she suggested, 'we have some creosote; let's try that.' A distillation of tar from wood, creosote was used like a pesticide to smoke out mites. As they went up the backstairs to the bathroom to get it, a lump of mortar was hurled at Lionel's neck. Then, on the way down the stairs, a spanner flew past his head. Back in the kitchen, they put some hot coals on a shovel and poured the creosote on them, causing a dense, acrid smoke. Starting with the kitchen, they fumigated the whole house. 'Now, goblins,' said Lionel, 'how do you like *this*?' The commotion stopped for the rest of the evening and the Foysters were able to carry on with their meal.

The next afternoon, Lionel had been writing a letter in the library to his sister Hilda about their experiences, but had to stop for evensong. When he returned, the letter had disappeared. Marianne began to fumigate the house again with creosote. Once she had finished, she was approaching the kitchen from the passage when a jam jar narrowly missed her head, hit the door and smashed all over the floor.

The next day, Monday 4 May, George and Florence Whitehouse were visiting the Rectory to meet the rural dean about some church matters. Some weeks previously, Lionel had confided in them about the activity in the house. They had been very sympathetic and, despite the malicious village gossip, were convinced that Marianne had nothing to do with the phenomena at the Rectory, though Lady Whitehouse believed that Marianne was 'mediumistic'.

After the meeting, Marianne took Florence into the kitchen to show her the mess that had appeared there; the contents of the cup-boards had been strewn all over the room. While the women were talking about the cause of the uproar, they were joined by Lionel and Sir George. Lionel updated them on the phenomena from the weekend and how they had fumigated the Rectory. Then the house bells started to ring. 'We are in for a bad time tonight,' Marianne observed wryly. 'It generally starts like that.' The Whitehouses were aware that the Foysters were more troubled by the sceptical attitude of the locals and their suspicions about Marianne than the actual occurrences in the house, so they volunteered to return after dinner to witness any activity.

When they arrived later that evening, at about 9 p.m., the children, Adelaide and Francois, had been sent to bed and the Foysters outlined more of the strange experiences they had endured since they'd moved in. Lionel showed them the scraps of paper asking Marianne for help. The Foysters were anxious that there would be some demonstrations for the Whitehouses to witness. But – initially – there was nothing. The two couples sat and talked, but still nothing happened. Lionel glanced at the clock. It was getting late. They had reconciled them-selves to a disappointing evening, when suddenly Marianne, who had slipped out of the room, rushed in from the hall. There was a fire! The others sniffed the air and there was indeed a smell of burning. And it was coming from the house.

Suspecting the smell was coming from the bedrooms, they took some lamps and the four rushed up the stairs. The smell was defi-nitely stronger. They ran from room to room, opening the doors, trying to find where the smoke was coming from. Finally, they came upon a locked door to one of the unused rooms in the newer wing of the house. Opening the door, they found the room full of smoke and the window shut. It was too suffocating to remain there for more than a few seconds, until they were able to open the window. The smoke soon cleared and they could see that part of the skirting board was on fire. They rushed to fetch a jug of water from the bathroom in the dark, during which Lionel was hit on the back with a stone. Having extinguished the fire, another stone was thrown in the half darkness. A bemused Sir George said, 'I never thought I would ever see anything like this,' pocketing the stone as a memento. Florence then suggested that she and Marianne fumigate the house with some dried lavender stalks she had brought with her, while the men investigated the cause of the fire. The room was never used and certainly nobody had been in it all day. Below the bedroom was the coal cellar and there was no flue near where the fire had occurred. It could only have been started deliberately.

Meanwhile, Marianne and Florence Whitehouse fumigated the house. In the Foysters' bedroom, they walked slowly around the bed only to be pelted by a shower of little stones. The exasperated Marianne decided to make some tea. 'In any time of weariness or weakness,' Lionel later observed, 'in sickness of body or soul, in disconsolateness or discontent, she always found comfort in a cup of tea.'

Florence thought that Marianne looked exhausted by all the activity and that she was not in a fit state to stay at the Rectory. She insisted that Marianne, Lionel and the children must leave at once and come and stay with them at Arthur Hall. Lionel protested that they had committed to sticking it out. Marianne was unsure too. If they left now, they might never have the courage to return. But Florence wouldn't take no for an answer. Marianne must not spend another night in the place. At the very least, they needed a break. The car was hastily packed with the two sleeping children bundled into it, wrapped in blankets. They drove off to Arthur Hall, arriving there, exhausted, at 11.30 p.m.

The Foysters had been driven away from Borley Rectory by whatever possessed it, unsure when they would return. The convenient presence of Sir George and Lady Whitehouse on the first instance of the now pyrotechnic poltergeists ensured that two of the most respected people in the county were now credible witnesses to the phenomena that were taking place in the house.

The next morning was bright and sunny at Arthur Hall. The Foysters were only a little over a mile away from the Rectory, but it felt like they were in a different country. Lady Whitehouse rose early to assure them that the Rectory was still standing and hadn't been reduced to ashes during the night.

The Foysters remained at Arthur Hall until Saturday 9 May. Florence Whitehouse noticed that, during the break from the Rectory, Adelaide began to 'thaw out' and became 'almost a different child'. Noticing the change in the little girl away from the Rectory, she began to worry that she was very dominated by her parents, and Francois, the young boy, seemed very frightened of what had occurred in the house.

When they returned to the Rectory, the phenomena seemed to have stopped. Lionel used the peace to write the second instalment of the events that had taken place, so that he could circulate it among the family, completing it on 11 May.

Meanwhile, Florence Whitehouse wrote to her husband's nephew in London describing the extraordinary events they had witnessed. Leslie Edwin Whitehouse was the son of Sir George's brother, Francis Cowley Whitehouse, who had served as canon to the British Embassy in Istanbul before the Great War; Edwin had been born in the city in 1899. His mother was the daughter of J. W. Whittall, who headed a successful trading empire that exported mohair, hazelnuts, barley, maize oats and seeds, as well as opium. Known affectionately by his Whittall relatives as 'Boy', Edwin had visited the Bulls and the Rectory as a child.

Perhaps influenced by his father's tales of derring-do, Edwin had joined up as soon as war was declared, going into the Royal Navy at the age of sixteen. He served as a midshipman on HMS *Queen Elizabeth* and on HMS *Vengeance*, which took part in the initial bombardment of Turkish fortresses in the Dardanelles. In a brutal campaign and with half the fleet lost, he then served on HMS *Lord Nelson*, which bombarded fortresses, docks and shipping at Gallipoli. For the next eight months, allied forces had been held on the beaches as trench warfare took hold, just as had happened on the Western Front. But the heat, lack of water, bad sanitation and swarms of flies led to an epidemic of dysentery. There were 250,000 British and dominion casualties, of which 46,000 died. By the end of the year, the campaign had been abandoned and 130,000 troops were evacuated from Gallipoli.

Still not twenty, Edwin had been hospitalised in Malta in 1917 and subsequently invalided out of the navy with nerves or shell shock. He then spent time with his family in Switzerland until 1919, when he rejoined the family business in Istanbul. He returned to England in 1924 to promote the Whittall company at the British Empire Exhibition. But by now, his mental health was even more fragile, his shell shock exacerbated by a broken or unreciprocated romance and the news that a cousin had killed herself. This had preyed on his mind, prompting questions about the afterlife. In 1927, he had spent 'an extremely unpleasant night' with a relative at their house near London, which had been 'infested' with poltergeists, with which he had since become fascinated.[4]

His mental health had continued to deteriorate until he'd had a complete nervous breakdown and had been admitted to Bowdon House, a nursing home in Harrow, where he had undergone 'psycho-therapeutical' treatment under Dr Crichton-Miller.[5] But he had quarrelled with his analyst and run away from the nursing home, his treatment incomplete. A damaged and troubled young man, in May, Edwin was living in London and seriously contemplating the priesthood when he received Lady Whitehouse's letter. Fascinated by what she had written, and still unwell, Edwin decided to take a holiday in Sudbury. While investigating the phenomena at Borley, he would stay at Arthur Hall with his uncle and aunt at the same time as preparing for his new vocation. Before leaving for Suffolk, he consulted Father Herbert Thurston, a Jesuit priest and spiritualist. Though highly esteemed, some orthodox Catholics feared Thurston's attitude to the paranormal was too sympathetic to be compatible with his calling. Thurston was impressed by the phenomena outlined in Lady Whitehouse's letter. He advised that Edwin say prayers at the house and bless it with holy water, though he warned that in almost all the recorded cases of poltergeist phenomena, this had had little effect.

*

The April of 1931 had seen unparalleled rainfall in the district and was followed by an equally wet May. At the beginning of June, the Rectory had been quiet for some weeks, apart from the odd stone or missile thrown. But after the arrival of D'Arles and his son, as well as the intervention of the Whitehouses, the phenomena at the Rectory took on an extraordinary new character.

As had occurred in Amherst, the Foysters began to notice marks and scribbles on the walls. Initially there appeared random 'M's and 'U's, loops and letters. Then, in the passage coming from the bathroom, up the two steps to the main landing, a name appeared, scrawled on the left-hand wall around the corner from the door to the lavatory:

Written in pencil, 4 feet 6 inches above the floor, it appeared as if the writer had been writing quickly and had pulled the pencil away just as they were finishing; the 'e' had an upward stroke and the 'i' wasn't dotted. Remembering that an answer had appeared on the envelope they had found some weeks previously, Lionel wrote on the wall underneath in capital letters:

WHAT CAN WE DO?

There was no response.

Some days later, another message appeared further along the bathroom passage, just past the back staircase, on the wall just before the bathroom door, 4 feet 3 inches from the floor:

Later, still further along the passage, more writing was found on the wall, a desperate plea, it seemed, from a soul in torment:

Marianne herself wrote beneath the unintelligible scribble:

I CANNOT UNDERSTAND
TELL ME MORE

Marianne

Something was added, but it still didn't make sense.

On another day, the Foysters had been out of the house when a further wall-writing appeared, this time on the ground floor between the kitchen and the external door to the courtyard, 4 feet 4 inches from the ground:

This was the first message directed towards Marianne to have a distinctly Catholic flavour.

On the afternoon of Saturday 6 June, a series of electrical thunderstorms broke across the countryside. That evening, Edwin Whitehouse visited the Rectory for the first time with his aunt. Marianne found him 'tall after the fashion of the middle-class Englander and pleasant enough at first sight'.[6] Whitehouse was fascinated to hear the story that the Foysters told him and astonished to be shown the writing on the walls. Like his aunt and uncle, he took the Foysters at their word – a great relief, used as they were to the sceptical villagers, who were eager to point the blame at Marianne. 'I do hope,' Edwin said to them, 'that if anything happens at all while I am staying down here you'll let me know. I should love to come and witness it if I might.'[7] They promised that they would.

Though the electrical storms had passed, that night there was an unseasonable chill in the air; the 'intense blackness of the sky was remarkable, yet the stars were shining brilliantly'.[8] An absolute calm set in across the countryside; not a single dog barked. 'The silence,' one local writer recalled, 'was uncanny.'[9]

As well as the strange atmosphere outside, there was a burst of activity in the house, with stones thrown and a chair knocked over in Marianne's sewing room. As she had been troubled by a particularly heavy period that week, a sick room was made up for her in the old schoolroom next to the master bedroom, which was situated above the drawing room. She was to spend the night in one of a pair of folding wooden camp beds.

But in the small hours of Sunday morning, cockerels suddenly started crowing in the darkness; farm dogs started barking feverishly. Stunned locals were woken by their doorbells ringing, beds rocking, crockery rattling or pictures swinging on the walls. Whole houses seemed to sway or shake. Many rushed into the street in their nightclothes and couldn't be persuaded back to their beds, feeling that there must have been some sort of explosion. Lieutenant Colonel Long of Hall Farm, in Fornham Saint Martin, thought his farmhouse 'was going to fall'; it was a 'horrible experience'.[10] Much of the county had been rocked by the biggest earthquake in the East of England since 1884. After the initial tremor of forty-five seconds, the earth continued to vibrate for another twenty minutes.

The next day Marianne told Lionel that she had slept very badly and complained that during the night somebody had been walking about on the landing and knocking at the door. Lionel put the noises down to the puppy, but when he made his way to the landing, he came across a scene of complete upheaval as if the storm outside had blown throughout the house. The contents of the dirty-laundry basket were scattered all over the hallway, stairs and landing – as well as shoes, bedclothes, books and brushes. Having promised Edwin Whitehouse that they'd let him know about any further activity, Lionel sent a boy with a note to Arthur Hall: 'If you want to see things, come at once.'[11] Concerned about Marianne's health, he then went across to Borley Place and asked William Bigg to send for Dr Richie, who lived in Cavendish.

When the front doorbell rang later, Lionel apologised to the doctor for the mess and as he couldn't think of a credible excuse, decided to come clean with him: they had a poltergeist. Richie looked doubtful as he eyed the chaos. Lionel took him up to see the patient and watched, embarrassed, as the doctor picked his way through the mess that littered the stairs. However, whatever doubts the doctor might have had, 'like all well-bred Englishmen, he kept it to himself'.[12] When he reached the sick room, the doctor asked Marianne what had been going on. What was the truth about the poltergeist? He had certainly heard of the Borley ghost, but always thought it was just a local legend.

Marianne may have discussed with him the history of her heavy periods, which had troubled her for years. The chaos on his arrival and the Foysters' discussion of ghosts and poltergeists may have alerted the rational doctor to some nervous or psychological disorder that Marianne might be suffering from. Whatever the case, after treating her, he told Lionel that what she needed was complete rest – an impossibility in a house that seemed to be active at any point of the day or night. Though Dr Richie's departure was accompanied by some stone throwing, Lionel was unsure that the doctor believed the story of the poltergeist at all. What – or who – did he really suspect had caused the uproar in the house? The rector? His wife? Or were the Foysters complicit in some sort of play-acting?

Shortly afterwards the front doorbell went again. It was Edwin Whitehouse, who was immediately astonished by the scene of disorder that confronted him. Within minutes of him standing in the hall, objects seemed to drop from the upper landing. Picking them up, he found they were a watchcase and a small metal bookrest that belonged to the Foysters. Lionel then took Edwin up to see his wife.

Marianne was lying on her back in the camp bed, her hands under the bedclothes, which were drawn up to her neck. She was, Edwin thought, looking pale and anxious. Her voice was weak, so to hear her better he sat on the edge of the bed. Relieved to have somebody to supervise her, Lionel asked if he might go over to the church for a short while. Edwin continued to chat to Marianne. All of a sudden he saw her start, and felt something land lightly in his lap. It was a brass paperknife, about 8 inches long. Marianne said that it belonged to her husband; he kept it in the library downstairs. She had seen it rise from the floor behind Edwin, then revolve in the air before landing in his lap. Marianne's hands had been under the bedclothes all the while. Edwin was at once convinced that this was a paranormal incident and asked if he might recite the rosary and sprinkle the room with holy water. She made no objection and joined in the prayers.

When the front door slammed, Edwin went out onto the landing to check that it was Lionel. All of a sudden he heard a scream. Rushing back to the sick room, he found Marianne on the floor with the mattress, pillows and bedclothes on top of her as if she had been flung out of the bed. Edwin rushed to help her. Was she alright? Marianne said that she was a little startled. All she knew was that she was lying on her side when, without any warning, she had felt the bed being tilted and found herself pushed out by something, which hit her at the same time. With Lionel having joined Edwin by this point, they put Marianne to bed.

When he arrived back at Arthur Hall, at about 3 p.m., Edwin said to Lady Whitehouse, 'Auntie, you must go and rescue those poor people. They are having a ghastly time!'[13] She and Sir George were due at a Parochial Church Council meeting that evening, so she planned to visit the Rectory before the meeting in the vestry started.

Meanwhile, at the Rectory, all was quiet and Marianne had gone to sleep. Lionel crept out of the room to check on the kitchen fire when he heard a cry. Rushing back, he found the distressed Marianne on the floor again, with the mattress on top of her. He felt he couldn't leave her even for five minutes without something happening. But there were the children to look after, meals to organise and his parish business to do. Perhaps he could ask Mrs Pearson to come and help in the house? But Marianne was anxious that she might spread more gossip around the village about the increased activity. Despite the respectability of the witnesses – Sir George and Florence Whitehouse, Arthur Sellwood – the local gossips would surely continue to blame *her*. With few other options, Lionel told the two children to keep Marianne company as he completed his work.

Having already heard about the events of the morning from their nephew, at about 5 p.m. Florence Whitehouse arrived at the Rectory. As soon as she opened the front door, she could hear things falling from the first floor and she found the hall and staircase a scene of chaos as the laundry basket had been emptied again. She discovered Adelaide and Francois crouching at the dining room door. 'We don't like so many fings falling,' they said.[14]

The determined Florence went straight up to Marianne in the sick room. Seeing how weak and ill she looked, Lady Whitehouse insisted that there was no way that Marianne, in her present state of health, could remain in the house a minute longer. After some persuasion, Marianne agreed. Florence left her gloves and parasol on Marianne's bed and went to organise some clothes for her and the children. As she went to leave the room, Marianne called after her, 'Your things are going!'[15] Florence turned back to find that somehow her gloves and parasol had moved to the dressing table. She went downstairs to make Marianne a cup of tea and when she returned, a small glass bottle seemed to start from the middle of the room and fall at her feet. Lionel and Lady Whitehouse then proceeded to get ready to evacuate the house. As they were doing so, they heard a yell from the bedroom – Marianne had been thrown out of bed a *third* time. Florence made her as comfortable as possible and, soon afterwards, Sir George drove the women and children away from the Rectory as Lionel went to the vestry to start the meeting.

The earthquake which seemed to inspire such activity at the Rectory that weekend was the strongest since records had begun, but it also seemed to articulate the troubled times. Reverend Dinsdale Young, a minister at Westminster Central Hall, believed that the earthquake, as outlined in the scriptures, heralded the second coming: 'I do not mean there will be an immediate return of the Lord. I think these earthquakes are an indication that the time is approaching, is nearer to us than we realise.'[16]

For the next nine days, Marianne recuperated at Arthur Hall, keeping Adelaide with her, while Mrs Pearson took care of Francois. Lionel spent some nights with the Whitehouses, but would stay at the Rectory provided D'Arles slept in the house too. One evening, Lionel was getting ready for bed in the Blue Room when he heard a noise. Thinking it must have come from the room above the kitchen, where D'Arles had retired early, he knocked on the door. There was no answer. As Lionel turned the door handle, he felt resistance from the other side. When he finally pushed the door open, he found it was obstructed by an empty pot of paint on the floor.

Whoever was responsible for the pot of paint, it couldn't have been Lionel's wife as she was a mile away at Arthur Hall.

Marianne appeared to make a swift recovery from her illness and every day she walked over from Arthur Hall to the Rectory accompanied by Edwin Whitehouse. She quickly formed a friendship with the sensitive young man, who admitted to her that as well as recovering from a nervous breakdown, he was also nursing a broken heart. He seemed to have a distant relationship with his family, estranged from his father and never speaking about his mother. He

talked constantly, using his conversations with Marianne to anal-
yse his feelings. He chatted enthusiastically about his interest in
spiritualism and obsessively about religion. He seemed particularly
preoccupied with the notion of sin. Marianne, however, insisted
that there was really very little sin in the world, only selfishness and
unkindness. He was, she felt, deeply lonely.

While they were at the Rectory, Edwin suggested that they ask the
Virgin Mary to assist them by making a novena – a series of Catholic
prayers said over nine successive days. These reflected the nine days
between the Ascension of Christ into Heaven and the descent of the
Holy Spirit, when the disciples first committed themselves to prayer.

The final day of the novena that Marianne and Edwin prayed was
16 June. They walked up the main stairs together and began to recite
the last rosary of the prayer cycle on the landing near the chapel.
Being a Tuesday, they meditated on the Sorrowful Mysteries of the
life of Christ: the Agony in the Garden, the Scourging at the Pillar, the
Crowning with Thorns, the Carrying of the Cross, the Crucifixion
and the Death of Christ. About halfway through the prayers, both
Edwin and Marianne became aware of a presence. Though they could
neither see nor hear anything, whatever it was seemed to be behind
Marianne, near the Blue Room. Seeing that she looked perturbed,
Edwin told her not to worry and they continued to recite the rosary.
After they had finished, she went to check the bedroom and Edwin
went to look at the writing on the walls downstairs. After a few minutes, they met on the landing again, but neither of them had seen or
felt anything more. But as Edwin turned to the arch above the central
landing, he was surprised to see some fresh writing. It was 4 feet 8
inches from the floor, on an otherwise clean patch of the wall, opposite where they had been praying. It said: 'Get Light, Mass, Prayers.'

Coming at the end of a novena, where they had been praying for
guidance, Edwin was astonished that their prayers seemed to have
been answered. He suggested to Marianne that they pray again.
This time, they prayed to the Holy Trinity, asking where a Mass
should be offered.

Before they left the Rectory that day, an answer seemed to have appeared to their question. Scrawled beneath the scribbled message on the wall was the word 'Here' – they must hold a Catholic Mass in the Rectory itself.

Edwin was now convinced that the 'mystery' of the Rectory was 'primarily concerned with R[oman] Catholicism'. Due to his presence, the Rectory – and the Foysters – were now increasingly influenced by Catholic prayers, traditions and beliefs. He gave them each a scapula to wear. These were two small rectangular pieces of cloth embroidered with devotional images, connected by leather or fabric strings. One rectangle hung over the chest, the other down the back, the strings running over the shoulders. Scapulas were regarded as 'the badge of the devout Catholic'.[17] Lionel and Marianne wore them pinned to their underwear, and would pin them to their nightclothes when they dressed for bed. Lionel was never badly hurt, so didn't feel that he needed such protection, but wore his scapula in order to please his wife.

Edwin also gave Marianne a relic. Relics had been hugely valuable to the early Church and were used to cure the sick and fend off invasion, plague or famine. Edwin's relic was related to the French Catholic priest St John Vianney, popularly known as the Curé d'Ars (Priest of Ars). In 1819, at the age of thirty-three, like Lionel Foyster, Vianney had been appointed as parish priest to a small rural community, Ars, north of Lyons. Vianney recognised that, following the revolution, the locals had become indifferent to religion. He began to spend up to eighteen hours a day hearing confessions, and by 1855 he was visited by 20,000 pilgrims a year. Significantly for the Foysters, from 1824 to 1858 Vianney had been persecuted by a demon or poltergeist. As well as physical violence, he had experienced shaking beds, crashing noises, abusive speech (in the local dialect), animal noises, overturning furniture and excrement thrown at religious images. Vianney had been convinced that the disturbances were demonic in nature, rather than from within the local community. He died in 1859 and was canonised by Pope Pius XI in 1925. In 1929, he had been made the patron saint of parish priests, so he had a particular relevance to Lionel Foyster. Though Lionel had been sceptical of relics in the past, dismissing them as 'Romish superstition',[18] now having been influenced by Edwin's conviction in the power of Catholicism, he revised his opinion. Edwin asked Father Moran, a Catholic priest in Sudbury, if he would hold Mass in the Rectory. But Moran realised that Edwin was 'not exactly himself' and 'had too much sense for this kind of foolishness and ignored it in a diplomatic way'.[19] The Mass never took place.

The arrival of Francois D'Arles and then Edwin Whitehouse at the Rectory coincided with the most intense period of activity in the house. Both would insist that the haunting was genuine, and not fraudulently produced by either the rector or his wife. Gossip about what was occurring at the Rectory – and the living arrangements there – started to circulate around the village. At the same time, Marianne and Lionel began to receive a series of anonymous poison pen letters from the local people.

It was now apparent to Lionel that Marianne was sleeping with the tenant at the Rectory Cottage. Though the realisation must have been painful, if not unexpected, when he discussed it with her he merely chastised her paternally as 'a naughty girl'. Their marriage had been, after all, a mutually convenient arrangement, providing her with security. But it had also offered Lionel respectability.

As the only one of his brothers to follow their father into the priesthood, Lionel should have inherited the living at All Saints,

Hastings, as a matter of course. But George Foyster had returned the living to the diocese, even though Lionel had been ordained. When Lionel had emigrated to Canada in 1910, English immigrants were particularly despised, which begs the question why he had sacrificed the comforts of life in Hastings and Cheshire for an uncertain future in an unforgiving wilderness on the other side of the world.

In the nineteenth and early twentieth centuries, the Anglo-Catholic movement offered homosexual men the opportunity to adopt a useful and respected role in society while deflecting speculation about their sexuality. Anecdotal evidence suggests that Anglo-Catholic parishes attracted a disproportionate number of single men whose unmarried status was validated by a tradition that valued celibacy. The sensational trial and imprisonment of Oscar Wilde was a recent scandal and one on which the Church of England, all too aware of the many skeletons in its own closet, had remained silent. Any homosexual scandal would have brought an end to Lionel's ministry and shame on his family. Following the public shaming of Wilde, many men curtailed their behaviour and some left the country altogether. If Lionel had been exposed in – or suspected of – some sort of transgressive behaviour, a posting overseas where he was unknown, and marriage to a young woman who would benefit from a good match with a decent man may have tidily solved the problem for both of them. It may well have been understood that he would tolerate Marianne's indiscretions with other men.[20] And perhaps he assured himself that the licence Marianne was taking was acceptable in the context of Dr Smithers's conviction that their marriage had been invalid in the eyes of the Church. He told D'Arles that he should be ashamed of himself, but made no attempt to bring an end to the affair as, for him, Marianne's happiness was paramount. After years in a lonely marriage, the needy and fragile Marianne was trapped between the physical fulfilment that D'Arles offered and his controlling nature. For her, desire 'would come suddenly and sporadically', she admitted, 'with a sort of overwhelming vehemence'.[21] The *ménage à trois* at the Rectory was now routine, with Lionel reading in the library, a complaisant cuckold in his own home, while his wife was pleasured upstairs by their tenant on a camp bed in the spare room.

Harry Price

CHAPTER TWELVE

THE RETURN OF HARRY PRICE

12 August–14 October 1931

What's wrong with this house that makes everybody so
uncomfortable?

Jay Anson, *The Amityville Horror*[1]

Talk of the strange phenomena at the Rectory was now rife throughout the district. Mary Braithwaite was part of a highly respected local
family, her father Francis J. Braithwaite having served as the rector
of All Saints Church in the nearby village of Acton. Miss Braithwaite
lived at Brook House opposite The Bull in Long Melford. She shared
the house with her brother Miles, the town clerk of Sudbury, who
had once served as mayor of the town. Their brother John was a civil
servant based in London. The Braithwaites had known the Rectory
and the Bull family since childhood and were well connected in the
area, counting Sir George and Lady Whitehouse among their friends.

Concerned about the circulating rumours of the Foysters' expe-
riences, and remembering the furore caused by the arrival of the
Daily Mirror and Harry Price during the time of the Smiths, Miles
Braithwaite suggested that they write to the Society for Psychical
Research in London to investigate the phenomena. A friend of Miss
Braithwaite was the sister of William Salter, the honorary secretary and
treasurer of the society. Salter had been called to the bar in 1905 and in
1915 had married the psychologist and psychic Helen Verrall, who had

first ignited his interest in psychical research. He bore a resemblance to 'an extremely intelligent and respectable Aberdeen terrier' and had a rock-like integrity.[2] Some, though, found him domineering and overly conscious of the status of the sometimes self-important Society for Psychical Research. Miss Braithwaite wrote to Salter, outlining her concern at the situation that was unfolding at the Rectory. The village, she wrote, was becoming 'almost like a plague spot'.[3]

Miss Braithwaite informed Salter that during August, her brother John, who had a great interest in psychical research, was to spend some of his summer holiday with his wife and children with her at Long Melford. He knew two 'wonderful men' who could rid the Rectory of its ghosts.

When he arrived in the area for his holiday, Braithwaite visited Lionel and suggested that he bring his friend, Ernest Meads and a medium called Mr Johnson to the Rectory. Lionel was conflicted, feeling uncomfortable that they were being drawn into the practices of spiritualism, but also desperate for some sort of resolution. Braithwaite reassured him that Meads resolved issues by utilising prayer, which seemed to placate the devout rector. A plan was made for a seance to be held at the Rectory on Wednesday 12 August, but they were careful not to make this public knowledge in the village.

Anxious about the idea of engaging in a seance, Lionel started to research the Church's current position on spiritualism. The official stance would remain ambivalent until the mid 1930s, when Church officials felt compelled to engage with the debate as clergy were 'continually finding that numbers of their congregations were drifting towards spiritualism'. It was widely believed by all factions within the Anglican ministry that the growing popularity of spiritualism was a result of the Church's continuing refusal from the Reformation onwards to engage in a discussion about the nature of the afterlife.[4]

At 6 p.m. on 12 August, Braithwaite arrived at the Rectory and introduced Lionel to Meads and Johnson. Johnson was sixty-seven years old, short, stubby and tanned, and wore glasses. He was, apparently, a masseur with 'some medical knowledge'.[5] Braithwaite found him 'very simple minded'.[6]

The party was shown around the Rectory and the places where various phenomena had occurred were pointed out. Braithwaite noted that the house was untidy, with the beds left unmade. After acquainting themselves with the geography of the building, Johnson confirmed that it had a 'haunted atmosphere' before deciding to hold the sitting in the library.[7] He anticipated that the seance would last about half an hour. Lionel agreed to take part but Marianne had chosen not to.

Sitting down around the table, the four men joined hands. Meads began with a prayer and soon Johnson went into a trance. He then proceeded to communicate as various personalities. These were revealed as Meads questioned each of them. There was a Native American guide, then a local girl who claimed to have murdered her child, and a village idiot called Silly Billy. A Harley Street doctor advised Lionel about his arthritis, recommending he avoid potatoes and starchy foods. He also suggested that the rector suffered from depression, a diagnosis with which Lionel agreed. Finally, a drunken ex-publican called Joe Miles was summoned. He didn't appear to realise that he was dead and kept calling for drinks. 'Miles' promised that he would cause no more disturbances at the Rectory; he would go to church and live as any self-respecting ghost ought to. After the departure of Miles, Johnson and Meads were confident of success. 'There you have, I think, the cause of your worries,' Meads said to Lionel and Braithwaite. 'You will, I believe, be troubled no further. If you are, speak nicely and gently to him as I did. Don't threaten, but coax; remind him of his promise and soothe him down. He will soon respond.'[8]

At this point, Lionel left the library and returned shortly after-wards with Marianne. They were then given a five-minute sermon by Johnson in the guise of the Methodist John Wesley and prayers that were delivered by none other than the Catholic convert Cardinal Newman.

After the seance ended, taking their lamps, the Foysters took the party to look at the writing on the walls. As they made their way up the stairs, Lionel argued with Meads about the practice of spiritualism. Marianne agreed that she didn't think it was right. But as they reached the landing, she stopped. Could any of them see the figure that was with them? They couldn't. Marianne thought that it was the spirit of Harry Bull.

Immediately, Johnson encouraged them to pray for the departed rector. Then, her back to the wall, facing Johnson, Marianne went into some sort of fit and suddenly collapsed down the stairs. Thinking it might be her heart, Braithwaite rushed to help and carried her into the bedroom. Once she was lying on the bed, he took her pulse, but it was normal. When she finally came round, she said that she thought that she had been in a trance during which, Agnes, a friend from Canada, had said to her, 'Marianne, dear, I did not wish to hurt you.' Now absolutely convinced that the rector's wife was psychic, Johnson impressed on her the great responsibility that she held: 'Thou hast a door through which more might come to light. Why dost thou keep it closed?'[9] Marianne was clearly upset by the proceedings and the whole party were exhausted, the sitting having lasted four hours. Braithwaite and his visitors finally left at 10 p.m. On the way out of the house, he noticed the two young children sitting in the kitchen in the dark.

Returning to Brook House with Meads and Johnson at about 10.45 p.m., after their 'perfectly terrible experiences' at the Rectory, an unnerved Braithwaite relayed the events of the evening to his siblings.[10] Johnson concluded that Marianne must be a very advanced medium. The spirits were coming specifically to her; it was she who was the author of everything that went on in the house. If she were able to fight her emotions and control her hysteria, everything would stop.

Concerned about Marianne's mental state, John Braithwaite asked his sister to go up to the Rectory to see if she could be of any help. Though she had never met the Foysters before, Miss Braithwaite duly drove up to the Rectory. When she arrived, Lionel seemed very subdued and told her that Marianne and the children were in bed. Seeing that all was well, she drove over to Arthur Hall to tell the Whitehouses what had happened at the seance and asked them to visit the Rectory in the morning to check on the Foysters.

The next day, having visited the Rectory, Florence Whitehouse called at Brook House and reported that she had found Marianne very distressed. John Braithwaite wondered if Marianne might not only be psychic, as Johnson had suggested, but that the source of the phenomena might be psychological? Already in indifferent health, running the Rectory was exhausting her, it being far too big to manage without servants. Her husband was so much older and troubled with health issues himself, making him of little use running the house. Marianne had no children of her own and Florence doubted that she was able to have any; might her infertility – together with all the tales associated with the Rectory – have played on her nerves and affected her mind? John Braithwaite resolved that he must discuss their conclusions with the rector as soon as possible.

Later that day, he called at the Rectory, looking 'very serious and as if he was doing something out of a huge sense of duty'.[11] With great hesitation and diffidence, he felt he must tell Lionel the truth. Perhaps she wasn't aware of what she was doing and had caused it in some sort of trance, but the person who was responsible for the phenomena at the Rectory was his wife. As well as being psychic, she was suffering from hysteria, getting 'into a state where she is unconscious and does not remember'.[12] In this state, she would write on the walls, turn herself out of bed, mislay things, steal Lionel's papers and upset his study.

Lionel listened patiently, but was indignant. There had been evidence of supernatural phenomena at the house for years – well before he and his wife had arrived. There were plenty of occasions – and he could name them – when Marianne could not possibly have been able to produce the phenomena. He couldn't believe that she would cause it consciously or deliberately. What possible purpose would she have? Braithwaite suggested that perhaps Marianne wanted to get away from the house. If she was dissatisfied with the condition of her life at the Rectory, if it were apparently haunted, that would be a good reason to leave it. Lionel insisted that compared to their life in Canada, life at Borley was luxurious. He had absolute belief in his wife's integrity. Thanking Braithwaite for his kindness in raising such a sensitive issue, Lionel firmly showed him the door.

Lionel was frustrated and hurt by Braithwaite's accusation, but when he informed Marianne, she was angry and resentful:

> As if it was not bad enough to have to put up with this, and live with this and be tortured with this, without having it all laid at one's door. As if anyone in their five senses would trail the clean linen, which one had oneself with much labour just washed, over a dirty floor. As if anyone would, even if one could, hurl something at oneself, hit one's own face and give oneself a black eye. As if anyone could, even if one would, throw a thing from a different part of the room to that in which one was at that particular moment located.[13]

Braithwaite and his family then travelled to stay with friends in Malton in Yorkshire for the rest of their holiday. Mary Braithwaite wrote again to William Salter at the Society for Psychical Research, informing him that she didn't want to get mixed up in the affair, but she *did* want to help the Foysters and 'get this intolerable nuisance stopped'. So, she'd asked her brother to send his notes directly to Salter and suggested he visit Borley once she and her brother Miles had returned from their holiday abroad in September. Then he must talk to the Bulls as well as the Foysters – 'it is almost impossible to explain things,' she wrote, 'as everyone has a different version'.[14]

Between June and December 1931, Edwin Whitehouse visited the Rectory thirty times; very much part of the household, he was a regular witness to the events unfolding at the house. He would join the Foysters for lunch or dinner, and afterwards they would play dice and word games together for hours, with Edwin and Lionel discussing the latest poltergeist events and religion – Edwin was becoming more focused on his plans to join the priesthood. During these conversations he tried to convert Lionel to Catholicism.

The increasingly delicate Lionel and the neurotic Edwin became very close friends. They were, according to Marianne, 'exceedingly intimate', with the suggestion of an attraction between the two men.[15] Ironically, Florence Whitehouse was now concerned about the amount of time that Edwin was spending at the Rectory and that Marianne might be encouraging him. When Marianne mentioned this to Edwin he appeared to be delighted, and Lionel thought the whole idea a joke. Marianne was dismissive of the idea that Edwin had any sexual designs on her – he was 'too ascetic' to take an interest in women.[16]

With Edwin, two young children and D'Arles eating and occasionally sleeping in the Rectory, the Foysters now attempted to secure some more help around the house. Given its reputation, they were unsure if they'd be able to find a housekeeper or maid. Even if they did, would they be able to keep her once she learned of the strange happenings in the house? 'You are aware,' Lionel said to Marianne, 'of what an aversion maids have to ghosts?' 'I don't blame them,' she replied, tartly.[17]

Marianne was pleased to find a young woman who came to live in. But after a week, she failed to return from her afternoon off and sent a message saying she was ill. When her friends had heard of her new position, they had primed her with stories about the ghosts. The next day, somebody came to collect her luggage.

Undaunted, Marianne thought that she should try to find a younger, less experienced girl that she could train up herself. Eventually she found a local girl called Katie, who had just turned fourteen. Immediately she and Marianne got on very well. Marianne explained the situation with the strange occurrences, but the girl felt that if Mrs Foyster and Adelaide weren't afraid, then she wasn't either. Every night, she would go to bed and bury her head under the bedclothes, leaving the lamp burning – and would soon be fast asleep.

On the evening of Saturday 26 September there was a total

eclipse of the moon. In days gone by, a Harvest Moon had struck terror in the hearts of many people, thinking it an augur of the end of days. Frightened villagers would seek sanctuary in the church and pray to the avenging God to spare them. But the weekend newspapers were confident that modern readers regarded the eclipse 'in the same light of science rather than in the dusk of mystery'.[18] Marianne and Katie were in the kitchen preparing dinner together when Lionel came in and invited them to come and look at the eclipse from the window of the library. The moon darkened for an hour and twenty-four minutes, stained a deep red. The three looked at the amazing sight before the maid went back to the kitchen. Taking the lid off the saucepan that was boiling the potatoes on the range, she was astonished to find that it was completely empty. Marianne roared with laughter when Katie told her. 'You must have eaten them yourself, Katie!' The girl replied: 'I must have a very big mouth and a very big appetite to eat that whole potful of potatoes in so short a time.'[19] The incident became a family joke. By now the Foysters had become used to the activity in the house and thought that the only thing to do was to put up with it.

However, increasingly concerned about the activity that now surrounded the Rectory once again, Ethel Bull travelled to London to consult Harry Price. He told her that he would very much like to visit the Rectory again and complete his investigations. He would not charge for his services. All he needed was consent from the incumbent rector.

Miss Bull wrote to Lionel, who then discussed the matter with Marianne. She was immediately doubtful and discussed Price's proposed visit with the other Bull sisters. Though Ethel was clearly keen on the idea, another of her sisters confessed to Marianne that she hated Harry Price. Nevertheless, on 1 October, Lionel wrote to Queensbury Place, inviting Price to investigate:

My wife and I are quite willing that you should come down if you care to but we would be glad if you would keep the whole matter as private as possible, since we do not wish for a recurrence of the publicity the whole thing got two years ago ... I have typed out an account of our experiences up to a few weeks ago.[20]

Price replied that he would indeed be keen to visit the Rectory again and would welcome an opportunity to read the document outlining the Foysters' experiences. By return of post, Lionel wrote to Price enclosing his diary of events that had occurred in the house, based on the circular letters he had distributed among his family. On reading it, Price was astonished at the remarkable tale that had been recorded in great detail by the most credible of witnesses. Perhaps sensing an opportunity to exploit the story of an apparently real-life haunting, he became impatient to visit Borley again.

But in the midst of the arrangements for Price to visit the Rectory, the plans already initiated by Mary Braithwaite came to fruition. Accompanied by Sir George Whitehouse, the Society for Psychical Research's William Salter arrived in Borley on 9 October. When they met at the Rectory, Salter talked to Lionel about Braithwaite's belief that all the strange happenings, including the wall-writings, were the work of his wife. What they really needed was a doctor. Lionel was dismissive. But Salter felt the rector had little worldly wisdom and appeared to be entirely dominated by his wife. When discussing the forthcoming visit of Harry Price, disregarding professional ethics, Salter warned Lionel against having the National Laboratory involved in the case. He tried to persuade him to sever links with the 'publicity-mongering' Price altogether in favour of allowing the Society for Psychical Research to investigate. They were, after all, the most established organisation, with the most experience of such matters. But Lionel insisted that Price had been invited to the Rectory and it was too late to prevent it. As a parting shot, Salter warned Lionel that he would regret it.

Having failed to dissuade the Foysters from inviting Price, Salter subsequently tried to persuade Ethel Bull and her sisters to block Price's visit. Ethel made no comment, but thought that Salter had a cheek to ask. The Society for Psychical Research had no right to

sabotage Price's visit, nor to prevent him from investigating a case
with which he was already associated. Salter's attitude towards Price
stemmed from the fraught rivalry between the conservative Society
for Psychical Research and Price's upstart National Laboratory. The
Borley case was shaping up to be one of great interest to psychic
science and to the general public. Both bodies were keen to take the
lead in an investigation that appeared to be of great significance.

His anxiety now inflated to paranoia by Salter's visit, Lionel
took legal advice then wrote to Price making stipulations about
discretion, particularly regarding publicity. He also wanted Price to
return his *Diary of Occurrences*. Price agreed to Lionel's demands
and reassured him that he would write to The Bull at Long Melford,
where he intended to stay, and request that his visit remain absolutely secret.[21] The strange household at Borley Rectory – the rector,
his wife, her lover, her emotionally disturbed friend, the teenage
maid and two motherless children – looked forward with some trepidation to the return of Harry Price, the most famous ghost hunter
in England.

With a sense of déjà vu perhaps, at around 8 p.m. on 13 October
1931, over two years since he had last visited, Price arrived once
again at the austere Borley Rectory. He was accompanied by
two council members of the National Laboratory of Psychical
Research – Mollie Goldney and Clarice Richards – as well as a Miss
May Walker and Mrs Richards's chauffeur, James Ballantyne, a
dour, unexcitable old Scotsman who had driven them from London.

When Marianne answered the door, the visitors were surprised by
how young the rector's wife was – somewhere between twenty and
thirty, they believed; not at all what they had expected. Despite her
husband's concerns about her health, she looked extremely vital and,
as Mollie Goldney remembered, gave 'the impression of a girl whose
interests lay in hockey-playing and so on, rather than a woman suffering from ill health'.[22] Price thought the rector's wife seemed 'bright,
vivacious and intelligent'.[23] Marianne's first impressions of Price
were equally vivid. He was, at first, very charming, but gave her 'the

creeps': 'He had pointed ears, a balding head with a high forehead and eyes which were startling. They were not polite eyes.'[24]

She showed the guests into the library, where the rector was waiting. They found him a delightful, cultured and well-travelled man, though clearly suffering from arthritis. He explained how he and his wife had come to Borley from Canada and what had taken place since they'd arrived. Price apologised for having forgotten to bring with him the manuscript of Lionel's *Diary of Occurrences*.

The guests were shown the many improvements that had been made to the house in terms of convenience, sanitation and decoration since the Smiths had vacated it, but it was soon clear that Price and his party were keen to investigate the house that very night. Consequently, they took their torches and looked around the house, noting the new chapel that had replaced a bathroom. In the children's bedrooms, Price shone his torch at the beds, waking Adelaide, who smiled sweetly before going back to sleep again. In the bedroom next to the Blue Room, they discovered the maid, who had only been with the Foysters for about a fortnight.

Marianne had been ill that day with one of her periods. She was not expecting to play hostess that night so was hypersensitive and anxious. She was charmed by Clarice Richards, but took an immediate dislike to Mollie Goldney, who was clearly suspicious of her. This put Marianne on the defensive. With little delicacy, the former nurse started to ask intimate questions about Marianne's health, the gynaecological problems that frequently troubled her. Mrs Richards intervened: 'I don't think we should discuss Mrs Foyster's health.'[25] Mollie took umbrage and insisted that it *was* pertinent. In order to bring the awkward conversation to a close, Mrs Richards suggested that perhaps they should eat.[26]

Though Marianne had prepared refreshments, Mrs Richards had not wanted to impose on their hosts' good nature and had brought a hamper with food, a bottle of Sauternes and a bottle of Burgundy. They returned to the library and the women set out the sandwiches on a table, like a picnic.

Marianne poured the Burgundy into one of the glasses. Suddenly it turned jet black. At the same time, May Walker, who was serving the Sauternes, said, 'This smells like eau de cologne!' They checked the bottles but they were both normal. Price poured a little ink into a glass of the Burgundy and this was clearly what had affected the wine. Mollie Goldney roared with laughter at what was obviously a conjuring trick. It was well known that Price was an expert magician. But was he the only trickster in the house? Was the rector's wife playing games? Or were the ghosts?

At about 9.30 p.m., still feeling unwell, Marianne fainted. Lionel helped her upstairs and Mollie Goldney assisted, insisting to Lionel that 'there's nothing wrong with her'.[27] When Mollie returned to the library, they decided to examine the house. Just as they were about to leave the room, they heard a crash in the hall. An empty claret bottle had been hurled down the stairs and had smashed on the iron stove, leaving glass all over the floor, just as the red vase had done when Price first visited the house.

Anxious about his wife, Lionel rushed up the stairs, followed by the visitors. They found her in bed – she had, of course, heard the smash downstairs. Going down the backstairs, they proceeded to the kitchen, where Ballantyne, the chauffeur, had been reading the evening paper. He told them that he'd heard the noise in the hall-way and looked up only to see a 'grisly black hand' move slowly up and down between the jamb and the door. It had then disappeared. Non-plussed, he went on reading the news. When they asked Ballantyne if he was afraid, he assured them he wasn't. He knew that it was a haunted house and the black hand was 'just part of the business'. He thought 'it was them ghosts larking about'.[28]

When they returned to the library, the party heard bells ringing and the sound of pebbles falling down the stairs. Suddenly they heard a cry from upstairs. It was Marianne. They rushed up the stairs again to the Blue Room, but the bedroom door was locked. Lionel liked to keep the doors open and the door keys throughout the house had been removed to prevent the children from locking themselves in. From behind the door, Marianne explained that first the door to the dressing room locked itself, and then the door onto the landing did the same – and they had no keys. The light had gone out and she didn't have any matches. She was trapped in the bedroom in complete darkness. Lionel explained to Price that they were used to this sort of activity. He needed to fetch a relic in order to say a prayer.

Once he had the relic of the Curé d'Ars, Lionel asked the visitors if they would like to join in the prayer. They agreed and knelt on the landing, Marianne kneeling on the other side of the door. Lionel said a reliquary prayer aloud, followed by the Lord's Prayer. They had hardly said 'Amen' when they heard a click. The door was unlocked. They found Marianne anxious but unharmed. But the children were now both awake and the young maid was wondering what on earth was happening. Marianne turned to Lionel and said of the guests, 'I can't put up with very much more of this. Do you think you could get them to go?'[29]

As it was nearly one o'clock in the morning, Price and the visitors were driven back to The Bull at Long Melford. They had been so amused by the crudeness of the staged phenomena that they hadn't taken any notes. When they arrived at the inn, the four congregated in Price's room to discuss the events of the evening. Who was responsible? They ruled out the children and the maid and didn't consider the rector. All of the events – the bell-ringing, the thrown objects – had occurred when the rector's wife was out of their sight. But if she *was* responsible, what was her motive? They decided to return to Borley the next morning to discuss the matter with Lionel Foyster 'as gently as possible'.[30]

They arrived at 8 a.m. the next morning. Clarice Richards asked Marianne if she could show her round the house, leaving Price, Mollie Goldney and Lionel on the tennis lawn. Price had some sensitive news to deliver. 'We are all of the opinion,' he said delicately, 'in fact we have not the slightest doubt about it, that this trouble is caused by Mrs Foyster.'[31] Lionel refused to believe it, pointing out that ever since the house was built, the occupants of the Rectory had been accused of faking the ghosts. Shortly afterwards they were joined by Marianne, who was informed by Lionel of the investigators' conclusions. She was furious.

Lionel suggested that Price and his cohort should stay another evening and put Marianne under surveillance. But Price was adamant: there was no doubt in his mind that Marianne was responsible for the phenomena. He wanted to return to London that day. Attempting to calm the situation, Mollie Goldney said she understood that Mrs Foyster may be absolutely sincere in her denial. Such phenomena could sometimes be ignited subconsciously. She could have a power that was particularly attractive to poltergeists. She may not even be aware of the activity that she was provoking. Mollie took Price aside for a private word: in order not to undermine the stability of the Foysters' marriage, it was only fair to them to stay another night and have Marianne observed under strict test conditions. The whole household should spend the night together confined to one room. A reluctant Price asked Marianne if she would submit to such a test. 'Certainly,' she said, defiantly. In the rector's wife, Price had clearly met his match.

May Walker returned to London by train. Then, at 8 p.m. that evening, the remaining investigators arrived at the Rectory. The maid had been sent home and Price set about securing the house – fastening all the doors and windows that would not lock with screw eyes, tapes and seals. Adelaide and Francois were put to bed, the windows in their bedrooms sealed and the children locked in. Price then assembled the Foysters, Clarice Richards, Mollie Goldney and the chauffeur in the kitchen. They sat around the fire and waited.

It was all very quiet and still after the excitement of the previous night. There was no noise, no movement. After about an hour, the Foysters were getting anxious and feeling foolish. Price was restless. Nothing was going to happen. His point was proved and they might as well return to London.

Suddenly Marianne threw herself on her knees and started praying loudly to St Anthony, the patron saint of lost things. She prayed that some phenomena should occur to convince the investigators that she was not responsible for the activity in the house. As she was praying, they heard the ringing of bells from the kitchen passage. Unsure which room the bell had been rung from, Price took his torch and, accompanied by Mollie, inspected upstairs, opening up room after room. When he unlocked Adelaide's room, he turned to Mollie, saying, 'Blast! I had forgotten about the child!'[32] Adelaide was in bed, but awake. Flashing their torches, they saw the remnant of the bell wire that had been cut by the Smiths slowly swinging. The wire had been cut close to the ceiling; Mrs Richards tried to reach it, but couldn't. 'Nobody could reach that,' she said, 'much less a child.'[33] Price said that it couldn't have been Mrs Foyster, so it *must* have been the child. Nobody could have entered the room without disturbing the seals. But could a three-and-a-half-year-old girl have reached so high? And why would a child play such a trick?

With the atmosphere icy and no further phenomena, just after eleven o'clock Price and his party got ready to return to London. As they were leaving, Lionel discreetly took Price aside for a confidential conversation. Unprompted, he told Price a confusion of truth and invention: that Adelaide was Marianne's daughter, but not his. He had married her in order to save her the embarrassment of an illegitimate child. Though, as a clergyman, he was reluctant to hold such a view, he thought that Adelaide might be 'possessed'.[34] Price wondered if it were possible that Marianne might have some hypnotic influence over the child. 'Yes,' Lionel replied, 'it is *possible*.'[35] For Price, the revelations of the eventful evening were disturbing. Anything seemed to be fair game in the strange psychodrama that was playing out at the Rectory between the Foysters – even the drafting-in of a child.

As the visitors were about to depart, the front doorbell rang. It was Francois D'Arles calling in from the Rectory Cottage. As the chauffeur helped the women into the car, Price asked D'Arles what he thought of the activity in the house. 'One thing I do know,' D'Arles told him, 'is that it can be neither Mr nor Mrs Foyster who is responsible. I have heard noises in the night and have got up and looked in at the door of their bedroom which happened to be open and seen them both sound asleep in bed.'[36] The notion of the handyman voyeuristically watching the rector and his wife as they slept didn't appear to seem odd or indelicate to D'Arles, though it must have given Price pause for thought about the curious domestic arrangements at the Rectory. As the car left the drive, a still fuming Marianne shouted after Price: 'Go and never come back!'

Girl demonstrating a planchette

CHAPTER THIRTEEN

THE WORLD'S BEST GHOST STORY

18 November 1931–23 January 1932

> Poltergeist cases, so-called, are those in which bells are rung,
> crockery broken, objects thrown about etc., by (seemingly)
> some invisible entity. It is a compound German word, meaning
> 'noisy spirit.' ... The question is: Do such phenomena ever
> happen in a genuine supernormal manner? Or are they
> invariably due to trickery, illusion and fraud?
>
> Hereward Carrington, *The Story of the Poltergeist*
> *Down the Centuries*[1]

As the Essex autumn turned to winter, Marianne noticed that a change had come over Lionel. Beleaguered with health issues, he was crippled with arthritis and a swollen hand. He'd developed heart palpitations and started to limp. He had no interest in the plays and theatrical productions that had once been his passion. Depressed about his health and dwindling finances, he was anxious about the future of his family. With his wife still a vital young woman, and continuing her relationship with D'Arles, the age difference between them had begun to tell. He adored the children and was delighted that young Francois followed him about everywhere, calling him 'Daddy'. But for much of the day, he would isolate himself in the library, reading. He was conflicted about the men they now shared their lives with. Having welcomed D'Arles and Edwin Whitehouse into the Rectory, he now found himself sidelined in his own home, torn between the various distractions they offered Marianne and their increasingly dominant presence. Having initially enjoyed the company of Whitehouse, Lionel had become irritated with him. Marianne had also begun to find him a 'nuisance'. But they didn't want to offend Sir George and Lady Whitehouse by saying anything, so the uncomfortable situation continued, with the Foysters reluctantly playing host to their unwelcome but persistent guest.

Ironically, the Whitehouses, too, were concerned about Edwin's close friendship with the Foysters. Worried about his fragile mental health, Florence Whitehouse felt that his regular visits to Borley did him 'no good',[2] particularly suspecting Marianne's designs on her nephew. Perhaps in response to local gossip about D'Arles, she thought Marianne was 'man mad'.[3] Sir George and Florence resolved that they must bring an end to Edwin's relationship with the Foysters, for his own good.

On 18 November, Lionel was going up to London to see his dentist so he asked Edwin to spend the evening with Marianne at the Rectory until he returned. Edwin drove over in the late afternoon. Just as he arrived, the bells rang in the kitchen passage. This usually heralded the outbreak of further manifestations. Edwin settled in the kitchen together with Marianne and the children, where they started to make supper. The two lamps were lit as the maid prepared some fish. Marianne was sitting in the small easy chair while Edwin was talking – again – about religion. Outside there was a thunderstorm that frightened Adelaide and unsettled Marianne, who didn't like storms either. Suddenly there was a crash from right underneath Marianne's chair. An empty bottle had smashed on the stone floor beneath it. Katie swept up the glass.

A quarter of an hour later, supper was ready and Edwin was drawing up a chair to the table to eat, when again a bottle smashed on the stone floor. Once more, the maid swept up the broken glass. After they had finished the meal, the three adults were talking, with Marianne smoking, their backs to the fire, facing the barred window onto the courtyard, when suddenly, in the dim lamplight of the kitchen, 'before [their] very eyes',[4] a bottle appeared poised in mid-air within a foot or two of the ceiling. It remained there for a second or two, then crashed onto the floor at the feet of the astonished trio. The threatening thunder continued outside, terrifying Adelaide.

The door that opened onto the staircase leading up to the servants' quarters and the room above the kitchen was ajar. Now they heard a noise that seemed to start from the top of the stairs, as if something was slowly walking down the dark staircase. They waited. The steps began to get quicker. Suddenly a bottle rolled into the room and spun on the kitchen floor. It circled to a stop. Edwin checked the stairs and the servants' rooms above. There was nobody there. All of a sudden, the bells in the kitchen passage started to ring. Then the large bell in the courtyard rang out sharply – but there was no rope attached to ring it. As Adelaide was frightened of the reality of thunder and Francois scared of the possibility of ghosts, Marianne put the children to bed.

Due to heavy fog, Lionel's train home was delayed. At 11 p.m., Marianne told Edwin she was tired and wanted to go to bed. Taking one of the lamps, she went up the main staircase, escorted by him. At the bottom of the stairs, the wick began to flicker as Marianne staggered. Edwin grabbed the lamp, which suddenly went out, leaving them in the dark. Marianne collapsed. Edwin put the lamp down and helped her up the stairs, feeling his way up to the first floor. Just as he had laid her on the landing by one of the bedrooms, he heard a noise from the hall: Lionel had returned home. Edwin explained the events of the evening before driving home, intensely relieved to be out of the 'extraordinary house'.[5]

Edwin's father now considered Borley to be having such a negative effect on his emotionally vulnerable son that he forbade him to visit the Rectory. Fortunately, Edwin was at the same time accepted into the priesthood, an announcement that was met with relief by both the Foysters and the Whitehouses.

The situation at the Rectory seemed to be getting more unpredictable and threatening. One day, after Adelaide's afternoon rest, when she was called downstairs, Marianne noticed that the child had a black eye. 'How did you get that bruise?' she asked. Adelaide looked down shamefacedly for a moment, then she replied: 'A nasty thing gave it to me ... by the curtain in my room.'[6]

She had seen something by the curtains, so had run up for a closer look. Suddenly she received a sharp smack in the face. Adelaide suggested that there were other children, who hid behind the curtains in her bedroom. As she went past them, they would hit her. After months of the Foysters comforting themselves that the children were not affected by the strange phenomena, disturbingly it now seemed to be the children who were being targeted.

Meanwhile, Mabel Smith was settled at Sheringham Rectory in Norfolk with her husband. Since leaving Borley, she had been busy with her writing. She had laid aside *Murder at the Parsonage* in favour of a new book, a short-story collection, *The House of 101 Things*, which she had self-published. The eight tales were religious parables written as if for children. Keen to distribute as many copies as possible, Eric Smith wrote to their former neighbours and acquaintances at Borley, such as the Whitehouses, the Bulls and the Foysters, asking if they would like to buy a copy. Kathleen Bull was delighted to hear from Mr Smith. She had been meaning to write, but hadn't had their new address. She said she'd buy a copy of Mabel's book and sent a postal order for two shillings. While writing, she took the opportunity to update him about the activity at Borley since he and his wife had left. She remained convinced that the phenomena at the Rectory, which she believed to be real, had in some way been instigated by Ivy Bull:

> I feel sure that horrid woman (you know who I mean) did some-thing vile in that house. Do you know anything that would throw any light on the matter? I think it is dreadful going on like this. I feel sure some harm will come to the cousins; the beastly thing is so violent.[7]

Borley Church, Winter

Borley Church, Interior

Aerial view of Borley village

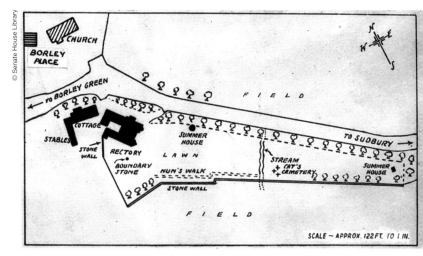

Map of Borley Rectory and grounds

The Drawing Room, 1910

The Dining Room, 1910

Reverend Harry Foyster Bull

Reverend Guy Eric Smith

Mary Pearson

Mabel Smith

Portrait of Harry Price by John Dumayne

Lucie Kaye

Lucie Kaye and Harry Price

Harry Price, Marianne Foyster, Lionel Foyster, Mollie Goldney,
Francois D'Arles Jr, Adelaide Foyster, 14 October 1931

Arthur Hall, 1950s   The Bull, Long Melford, 1950s

Jawbone and fragment of skull
discovered at Borley Rectory,
17 August 1943

The 'Flying Brick' apparently poised in
mid-air against the black background
of the kitchen passage, 5 April 1944

Reverend Clifford Henning and Harry Price bury the
bones of the 'Borley Nun', 29 May 1945

'A lovely house kept in excellent condition', Summer 1910

'The Most Haunted House in England', Winter 1944

Writing to Lionel Foyster, Mr Smith suggested that he give copies of his wife's book as Sunday School prizes at Christmas. He also took the opportunity to commiserate with Lionel, having heard that he and his wife had experienced such trouble at the Rectory. He wondered which room in the house had been the worst for strange activity? Lionel wrote back thanking Smith for his sympathy:

> This is certainly not a pleasant house to live in, and I think we have had an even worse time than you had: but since the diocese and [Queen Anne's Bounty] have spent a lot of money repairing it, we are trying to stick it out. Things have been quieter lately; the worst time we have had so far was in June – just before the anniversary of my cousin, Harry Bull's death. You ask which we have found to be the worst room; it is hard to say since we have had experiences in so many. So far though we have had nothing in the dining or drawing room. Something very peculiar seems to reside in the room over the kitchen, though it has been seen in other parts of the house as well. Besides the rooms, the passages, landing and hall seem all to be pretty bad too. We have also had quite a little trouble from locked doors and things being taken. We have had different people down, but most of them have been rather a hindrance than a help, and have irritated us – at least some have – by suggesting human agency, which we believe to be absolutely impossible.[8]

Lionel also mentioned that the nephew of Sir George and Lady Whitehouse would be staying at the royal family's summer estate in Norfolk, which was only thirty-five miles from them. If he were able to visit the Smiths at Sheringham, he could update them on the news from Borley.

Edwin was to be the guest of Sir Francis ffolkes, the King's Chaplain at Sandringham, where he was to stay before taking holy orders early in the New Year. Perhaps as a parting favour, knowing how exhausted Marianne was by the accusations of faking the phenomena, he had taken it upon himself to assemble supporting testimonies to prove that she was not responsible, that the poltergeist activity was genuine and had occurred at the Rectory well before she'd arrived there.

On 17 December, Edwin was welcomed by the Smiths at Sheringham. They had an agenda in agreeing to the meeting. Given his elevated connections – his uncle and the King's Chaplain – they were eager that he should contact the Bishop of Chelmsford and explain that he, too, had experienced unusual phenomena at Borley Rectory, that the Smiths had *not* exaggerated their experiences there and they had certainly not raised 'a mare's nest' about it, as the Bishop had so dismissively claimed. Edwin shared his own experiences at Borley and they enthusiastically told him theirs. They outlined the details of the seance that Eric Smith had brought to an abrupt end when the spirit of Harry Bull had claimed that he had been murdered. They also showed him various objects that they had kept as mementos of their time at Borley: the china jug that was hit by a piece of soap, the keys that appeared on the night when Lord Charles Hope had visited, a little clock that played tricks no matter how often it was adjusted. They had even brought the curtains from the library with them, which had been left behind from the Bulls' day. What particularly intrigued Edwin was the wooden-backed mirror that had tapped out messages – apparently – from the spirit of Harry Bull. This had continued to make knocking noises when the Smiths had moved to Long Melford. Almost as if the ghosts had followed them there.

Having lost faith in the 'so called psychic research people'[9] – Harry Price and the Society for Psychical Research, both of whom were seemingly determined to blame Marianne for the phenomena at the Rectory – by the new year of 1932, the ailing Lionel Foyster was exhausted and exasperated by the phenomena at the house. Then he received an unexpected letter that was to have an extraordinary effect on the Foysters' lives at the Rectory.

George Warren was a 79-year-old grocer and postmaster at

Marks Tey, a village eight miles from Borley. Warren and his wife, Emily, also headed a group of spiritualist friends who lived across East Anglia that met for seances in the back of the post office they ran in Station Road. He had investigated several cases of haunting and had generally been successful in bringing them to an end. He had heard about the phenomena at the Rectory and in January offered his help if the Foysters would accept it. He assured Lionel that the 'whole trouble could be removed'.[10]

When Lionel discussed it with Marianne, she wasn't keen. She was tired of being accused by psychic investigators – 'It's bad enough to have to put up with it all, without being accused of doing it oneself.'[11] Not wanting to have her upset, Lionel declined Warren's offer. But a few days later, he received another very polite letter from Warren insisting that all he wanted to do was help and might he at least come to the Rectory for a talk? Lionel replied that he would be happy for Warren to visit on the condition that, whatever he might conclude, he must *not* openly accuse his wife of being the cause of the phenomena. If Warren did feel that Marianne was responsible, he must just say that Borley was a case in which he was unable to help. This stipulation agreed, a date and time was arranged.

However, after midnight on 22 January, Warren arrived unexpectedly with his colleague, H. H. Frost, who had been driven to Borley by a Captain Deane of Colchester – another member of the Marks Tey Circle. They told Lionel that the leader of their 'helpers' who were 'on the other side' had warned them that Marianne's spirit protectors could not hold out much longer. The 'helpers' were anxious to 'have the matter cleared up as soon as possible'.[12] Warren outlined his plan to have a sitting in the Blue Room, during which a medium that they were acquainted with, Guy L'Estrange, would go into a trance and the entities would then be visible in his ectoplasm. Finding the Marks Tey Circle kindly and considerate, the Foysters agreed to the seance. The visitors planned to bring L'Estrange to the Rectory the next day, when they would discuss how they would rid the Rectory of the phenomena.

That day, Florence Whitehouse had Adelaide and Francois over for lunch and to stay the night at Arthur Hall. The maid was sent home. At 5 p.m., Warren, Frost and Captain Deane arrived in the early darkness of the January afternoon to have tea with the Foysters and introduce them to Guy L'Estrange. The 32-year-old medium was a cheerful and knowledgeable freelance journalist from Norfolk whose skill as a psychic had been tested by Harry Price at the National Laboratory of Psychical Research in March 1931. He was known for materialising a topless ghost named the Female Dancer, an Islamic spirit guide called Abou ben Mohammed, and the spirit of a springer spaniel called Lady.[13] It may be through Price, who was no longer on speaking terms with the Foysters, that the Marks Tey Circle had heard about the continuing activity at the Rectory.

L'Estrange was immediately struck by the gloomy appearance of the house – 'exactly the sort of place one associates with ghosts'.[14] The atmosphere of the interior was 'heavy and supernormally cold'.[15] In the library, he 'sensed presences'.[16] Over tea, Lionel and Marianne outlined some of their experiences. 'I never believed in ghosts until I came here,' Lionel told L'Estrange, 'and used to laugh at the stories people told about this house. Since then I have discovered that it is anything but a subject for laughter.'[17] Listening to the stories of missiles thrown at them, words scrawled on the walls and physical attacks on Marianne ('It was like a blow from a man's fist, but it was no living man I saw'),[18] L'Estrange advised against Warren's materialisation strategy. It was 'too great a risk'. He suggested they hold an all-night seance in two days' time – 'a sitting like that should be at night; it is so much better.'

As they were talking, there was a sudden crash from the kitchen passage, then another. This was followed by bells ringing. 'I think we are going to have a bad night,' said Lionel, resignedly.[19] He suggested that, as the 'goblins' already seemed to be on the warpath that afternoon, they should hold the seance that very night. After a third crash from the passage, they went out to investigate, finding a pile of broken glass and bottles at the foot of the backstairs. 'Not yet convinced that trickery was out of the question,' L'Estrange and his party carefully examined the house, especially the bell wires.

Lionel and Marianne really took to the Marks Tey group. They were a 'different kind of people' to Harry Price and Mollie Goldney, and not 'bombastic or horrid in any way'. Though they'd been invited to join the seance, Marianne and Lionel chose not to. They had been advised, perhaps by Arthur Sellwood, that spiritualism was wrong. Marianne had been told that she might see the Devil stand beside her, and recalled the biblical story of the Witch of Endor. She was just too frightened to take part. Outside, it began to rain.

Warren and Frost left with Captain Deane to pick up some other members of the group from Marks Tey to take part in the seance, leaving L'Estrange at the Rectory with the Foysters. Bells continued to ring and more old wine bottles were thrown down the stairs, causing a mess in the kitchen passage. After sweeping it up once or twice, Marianne gave up as more and more bottles were added to the debris. 'I am certain these disturbances are caused by devils,' said Lionel.[20] The phenomena got worse and became so loud that Lionel, Marianne and L'Estrange had to shout to hear each other. Lionel suggested that they should pray in the chapel with St John Vianney's relic. They then proceeded with the relic from room to room, making the sign of the cross with it as they went. The phenomena then practically stopped and Lionel left the house on an errand. Alone with Marianne for some time, L'Estrange thought her 'very highly strung'.

At about 10 p.m., a drenched Warren, Frost and Captain Deane arrived with Emily Warren and a Mr Footman. Mrs Warren had brought with her a planchette – a small, heart-shaped wooden board fitted with castors on which each of the sitters would lightly rest their hand. A pencil was fixed vertically into a socket in the board and, as the board moved, it would create 'automatic writing' on a sheet of paper beneath. It was thought that the planchette could move independently and that the 'spirits' could communicate by writing through the pencil. By the late 1880s, elegantly designed 'talking boards' with letters printed on them had supplanted planchettes, which were, by the 1930s, considered out of date.

The Foysters retired to the spare bedroom and soon Lionel was asleep, despite the driving rain outside, leaving the Marks Tey Circle to proceed with the seance in the Blue Room. Marianne heard the visitors going about the house, singing hymns, saying prayers and talking in the library downstairs.

The group then settled in the corner of the Blue Room with their backs to the wall. They kept this position for several hours, noting the extreme cold in the room. The rain outside was now torrential, battering against the windows.

After a while, L'Estrange made contact with his spirit control, 'Zenith', who guided the spirits at Borley into his presence. He asked them to desist in troubling the rector and his family as they were slowly killing them with anxiety. L'Estrange had noted that Lionel and particularly Marianne showed signs of nervous tension throughout the night. In the room, a black shadow appeared to develop against the wall. L'Estrange went across to engage with it. He felt that it was 'intensely evil'.[21] He made the sign of the cross and indicated a veil and rosary with his hands. L'Estrange now took on the spirit of the famous Borley nun. She even gave her name: Evangeline Westcott.

'She' appeared to be very nervous and turned to ask advice from her spirit control. The sitters spoke kindly and gently to her as they asked if she would communicate with them through the planchette. She agreed. The board began to move, expressing the nun's words: 'Virgin! Do forgive me! Oh mother of Jesus, help me.'[22]

L'Estrange, still channelling the spirit of the nun, continued to write with the planchette: 'How long since that living tomb? I did no wrong: my Father Confessor thought me guilty. Ah, the walls! I was thirsty and they gave me empty bottles. Oh, those bottles! I do not know what has happened. Am I now to go to the Judgement throne, the great white throne?' The reference to the empty bottles seemed to indicate a particular cruelty to the punishment of the walled-up nun, suffering death by starvation – that bottles had been tantalisingly proffered, for her to find them all empty, like the vinegar sponge offered to the dying Christ.

Mrs Warren gently intervened: 'No, dear child. Go with the lady who stands behind you and is helping you now,' she said, referring to L'Estrange's spirit control. 'She will take you to a place of rest and beauty. Your terrible sufferings are over. Put them out of your mind. You are now going to progress in your new life and be very, very happy.'[23]

L'Estrange continued to be guided by the nun: 'What will the Father Confessor say? He will not forgive me. Bring me spring flowers.' Mrs Warren brought a bowl of primroses to the table. L'Estrange buried his face in the primroses and smiled. He took some flowers from the bowl and laid them on the table.

At about 4 a.m. the sitters descended to the library, where refreshments were taken before the fire, which had been kept going. They discussed what they had experienced that night. Was there evidence of genuine supernatural activity? Or might a member of the household be responsible? They had been warned by the rector that under no circumstances must they accuse his wife. During this discussion, Marianne came into the library and the visitors quickly changed the subject. It was noticeable to all of them that her manner had been strange all night – at one point she even appeared to be under the influence of something, alcohol perhaps, or even drugs. Finally, the group prayed in three of the rooms and the atmosphere was noticeably quieter. At 5 a.m., the party readied themselves to leave. L'Estrange told the Foysters that he was confident that there would be no more disturbances. He insisted that the house was going to be normal again.

The next morning, the Foysters were startled. Something *had* happened. 'We awoke,' Lionel remembered, 'to a renewed house, a changed house.'[24] Marianne felt it was like 'a new world washed clean'.[25] Katie, the young maid, also noticed the change. Somehow, the rooms felt warmer. The house was – overnight – 'entirely different'.[26]

One evening some days later, the front doorbell rang at the Rectory. Marianne went to see who was calling at such a late hour. She opened the door to find a man she didn't recognise on the doorstep. Thirty-three-year-old Jack Cannell was a journalist and member of the Magician's Club. An amateur conjuror, he had written a popular book about Houdini and was well known for covering ghost stories in the press, including that of the poltergeist at Eland Road in Battersea. In Fleet Street he was popularly known as 'the spook man'.[27] Having followed the story of the haunting closely, Cannell had travelled to Borley by taxi, hoping to spend a night in the Rectory. He'd kitted himself out with various paraphernalia to assess the ghosts or expose the hoaxers: a wooden block to wedge the door open, a special ink to apply to door handles, screws to secure the windows and tin tacks to lay on the floor to defeat intruders. In his pocket he secreted a small pistol.

Lionel recognised Cannell's name from articles he'd read, but insisted that they didn't want any more publicity. Cannell argued that he had never revealed the location of the Rectory in his press stories. Lionel replied, drily, that his employer, the *Daily Sketch* had published a photograph of it. Cannell assured them that it could not have been used by any stranger to locate the house.

The Foysters invited Cannell into the drawing room, where he noted the strong contrast between the rector and his wife – Mr Foyster was tall, solemn and scholarly; his wife lively and shrewd. She, he noticed, did much of the talking, while her husband stood strangely silent.

To Cannell, the rector's wife seemed far from hysterical and gave the impression of an 'alert, self-confident and well-balanced young woman'.[28] Cannell offered to investigate the Rectory. But Lionel shook his head, refusing to permit it. He just wanted to let the whole thing die. 'Things are quiet in this house now,' Lionel said in a low voice, 'and I believe they will remain so.'[29]

Disappointed, Cannell said goodnight and was driven to Sudbury in a taxi. He had several theories: perhaps the phenomena were simply due to a structural defect in the building – many alleged 'hauntings' were due to such natural causes; at the same time, some psychic theorists believed that manifestations were caused by vibrations that resonated in a location where tragedy or violence had occurred; and, of course, it could all be the work of a brilliant hoaxer. A newspaperman always on the hunt for exciting and original copy, Cannell concluded that, whatever their cause, the happenings at Borley Rectory had provided what he considered to be 'the world's best ghost story'.[30]

The Foysters continued to live at the Rectory, with very few instances of strange activity. Now that the ghosts seemed finally to have been banished from Borley, Lionel continued to write about their experiences. It was both a record and an attempt to explain the inexplicable:

When we look back at the old times, it seems like a dream; we can hardly believe ourselves that these things really happened. But material evidence to the fact that they did actually happen remains. Still there is a piece broken off the plaster here, and writings on the walls there. Still one can see the ends of bell wires hanging down, where my predecessor cut them, and I yet have in my cupboards relics of things that were thrown, while upstairs one can view the charred skirting board where the mysterious fire broke out. And sometimes as I walk about the house I think of the smash in the eye my wife received at this spot, of the spanner that went through my hair at that spot, of the lamp chimney shattered by an iron heater at a third place or of the stone that hit me on the shoulder at a fourth. I think of them, but with hardly any more apprehension that such things should happen again than the tourist visiting the scene of the line of trenches on the old battlefields might fear the sudden bursting of a shell over his head.[31]

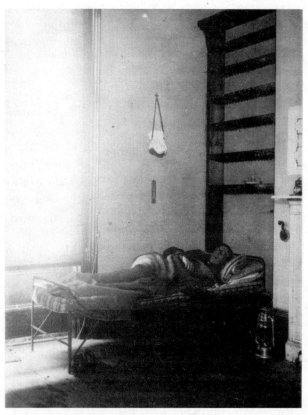

Roger Glanville in the Base Room

CHAPTER FOURTEEN

THE ALLEGED HAUNTING AT B—— RECTORY

26 November 1932–8 October 1937

Haunted House; responsible persons of leisure and
intelligence – intrepid, critical, and unbiased are invited to
join rota of observers in a year's night and day investigation of
alleged haunted house in Home Counties. Printed instructions
supplied. Scientific training or ability to operate simple
instruments an advantage. House situated in lonely hamlet, so
own car is essential.
    Write P.O. Box H 989.

The Times, 25 May 1937

Following his abortive visit to the Rectory in October 1931, Price
had written to his fellow parapsychologist, Professor David F.
Fraser-Harris, to say that, though he thought Borley a 'most amazing case', he was convinced it was fraudulent:

We think that the rector's wife is responsible for the trouble,
though it is possible that her actions may be the result of hysteria.
Although, psychologically, the case is of great value, psychically
speaking there is nothing in it.[1]

Yet he now proposed to address the Laboratory on 6 April with a report of his investigations at Borley in a lantern-slide talk called *The Haunting of B—— Rectory*. The publicity announced that 'Extraordinary happenings have been witnessed at the Rectory, and the present incumbent has kept a diary of some amazing events which occurred during several months of 1931.'[2]

On 26 March Price was surprised to receive a terse note from Lionel Foyster, who had been astounded to hear that Price was not only intending to publicly discuss the phenomena at Borley, which he had been expressly forbidden to do, but was also planning to read from Foyster's private diary. He reminded Price that he had signed a legal document in which he had agreed not to reveal his knowledge of the phenomena at the Rectory and that he would be putting the matter in the hands of his solicitor.[3] As the date of the talk approached, Lord Charles Hope also wrote to Price, requesting that his name should not be mentioned in Price's Borley lecture, either. He insisted that Price make clear that Hope 'was not impressed and thought the phenomena were produced by normal means'.[4] A rivalry, then a schism, began to develop between the two men.

After the success of the first two series of experiments with the Austrian medium Rudi Schneider, Price had been planning a third series for April 1932. But Schneider had annoyed Price by considering a better offer from the Institut Métapsychique in Paris. This 'filthy trick' enraged him; 'If a son of mine did such a thing, I would thrash him within an inch of his life.' Lord Charles felt that Schneider's career should not be dictated by Price and that the boy should be properly tested by the Society for Psychical Research. Consequently, he approached Schneider about taking part in further sittings once Price's experiments had ended. But when Price heard about Lord Charles's proposed tests, he was furious; Lord Charles, William Salter and the rest of the Society for Psychical Research were clearly 'mad with jealousy' at the success – and celebrity – of his Laboratory.

On 28 April, Schneider sat for Price under controlled conditions. As usual, a handkerchief was placed on a table in front of the medium. During a normal sitting, this would be tied during the experiment, apparently by supernatural means. But if it was lifted, a number of cameras would photograph the moment. The experiment began and Price proceeded to control Schneider by holding both his hands. The handkerchief was lifted and a flash went off as the cameras clicked.

Later that day, when Price was developing the pictures in the dark room, he called in his new secretary, Ethel Beenham, who had taken over from Lucie Kaye. In one of the images, Price pointed out that the boy had lifted his arm at exactly the moment that the 'paranormal' movement of the handkerchief was taking place. Schneider had cheated – and Price could prove it. Miss Beenham was immediately concerned that Price would exploit the photograph in his evolving feud with Lord Charles Hope; 'he was terribly spiteful against Lord Charles.' She worried that Price 'was waiting for a chance to hit back at him'.[5]

Unaware of the compromising photograph, Lord Charles organised further sittings with Schneider from October to December 1932, at Tavistock Square. In the spring of 1933, he was about to publish his findings, when, having carefully chosen his moment, Price went public with the Schneider photograph in an exclusive and destructive exposé in the *Sunday Dispatch*. Mollie Goldney, who was absolutely convinced of Schneider's honesty, warned Price that he would never be able to carry out a major investigation with scientific collaborators again, as nobody of any distinction would want to work with him. All the more important members of Price's Laboratory council resigned in protest owing to his behaviour and his attack on Schneider's good faith. The scandal effectively brought an end to the National Laboratory and put Price's career as a psychical researcher in jeopardy. At the same time, since the beginning of the Depression, Price had been struggling financially and had admitted to Lucie Kaye that he was more or less 'living from hand to mouth'.[6] Having alienated potential financiers and collaborators, seemingly unable to bring about an amalgamation between the Laboratory and any other psychical research institution, and his personal integrity now in doubt, what would be Price's next move? He decided to write a bestseller.

In 1933, Price collected his most famous cases in a book aimed at the general reader, rather than the psychical specialist. A demonstration of the scale of his achievement, it was also a riposte to sceptics and critics, as much as an attempt to recover his tarnished reputation. *Leaves from a Psychist's Case-Book* included the stories of the frauds he'd exposed. Price celebrated his founding of the National Laboratory but in doing so, implicitly criticised the Society for Psychical Research for allowing its sympathy for mediums to cloud their critical judgement. Price hoped the book would re-establish his standing – with the general public at least – as the valiant, objective and solitary champion of Truth in a murky industry compromised by fraud. 'One gets the impression,' noted the *Yorkshire Post* review, 'that Mr Harry Price is an honest and sincere man who is really doing his best to apply scientific standards of exactitude to a very difficult subject.'[7]

Price followed up the success of the *Case-Book* with a further volume of his adventures that hinted at greater ambitions than mere entertainment: 'Where shall we go when we die?' he reflected. 'I am afraid there is nothing in this volume that will supply an answer. The answer may be there, but perhaps I cannot read it. For thirty years I have been engaged upon an intensive quest as to what happens after death, and the solution of the eternal problem still eludes me.'[8] *Confessions of a Ghost-Hunter* covered more of Price's engagements with mediums and clairvoyants, as well as his investigations into fire-walking, the Indian Rope Trick and the case of a talking mongoose named Gef on the Isle of Man. There was also a chapter about Rudi Schneider, with a reproduction of the incriminating photograph. The book included an examination of Borley Rectory. This was entitled – with some irony, given Price's feelings about the nature of the phenomena there – 'The Most Haunted House in England', a reference to an infamous Scottish case from the end of the nineteenth century, renowned as 'The Most Haunted House in Scotland'.

Isolated in the Scottish Highlands, Ballechin House was a poorly constructed rural mansion, built in an area prone to earthquakes and subsidence, that had led to an investigation by the Society for Psychical Research. This had inspired a study of the phenomena, *The Alleged Haunting of B—— House*, by the clairvoyant and medium Ada Goodrich Freer. But the investigation – and her book – had been exposed in *The Times* as inept and unscientific. In his memoirs, the psychiatrist Sir James Crichton-Browne derided the Ballechin affair and upbraided the Society for Psychical Research for ever giving it credence. 'The costly and very generously conducted experiment at Ballechin was a fiasco – an illustration of a myth and the magnification and misrepresentation of a few, simple natural phenomena by sensitive minds in quest of the supernatural.'[9] This had not stopped Freer's book becoming a bestseller. The myth of Ballechin had more power – and greater popular appeal – than the truth.

In order to disguise its location and protect the anonymity of the Foysters, throughout *Confessions of a Ghost-Hunter*, Borley Rectory was referred to as K—— Manor. Though he stated that 'there is much good evidence for the haunting of K—— Manor', Price admitted that he had come to the conclusion that 'the supernormal played no part in the "wonders" we had witnessed'.[10] The 'Most Haunted House in England' wasn't haunted at all.

In March 1936, the press disclosed the prodigious plans for German rearmament, particularly in the air, and the belief of a secret alliance between Germany and Japan. In response to the increasingly anxious international situation, a British rearmament scheme was announced on 3 March. 'Britain Awakes' the *Daily Mirror* declared, reporting that millions were to be spent on defence. *The Era* highlighted the negative impact that wireless programming was having on the anxious listener, stating that it was not only the news that was the issue, but 'lugubrious plays' and 'menacing talks' such as the first live broadcast from a haunted house.

On Tuesday 10 March, Harry Price took part in a broadcast

from the twelfth-century Dean Manor in Meopham, Kent, which had been linked to at least one murder and a suicide. There had been reports of footsteps and mysterious tappings; a dog had rushed from the house, mad with fear, and later had to be destroyed. The programme was trailed as a scientific investigation, rather than an attempt at spooky entertainment; it would be 'the first time that a ghost has had the opportunity of manifesting itself at the microphone'.

Equipped with cameras, thermometers and four microphones, at eight o'clock, the BBC settled in – expectantly – for the night, guided by Price and Freddie Grisewood, the BBC's announcer. The first broadcast went out from 8 p.m. until 8.20 p.m., and another at 11.45 p.m. until midnight. The *Radio Times* had warned listeners that they should 'not expect too much' as 'chances are nothing will happen'.[11] After four hours, nothing did, and Price and Grisewood went to bed. *The Times* thought the performance a 'fiasco' and condemned the BBC for attempting it,[12] but for Price, it was good publicity for the forthcoming *Confessions of a Ghost-Hunter*.

In advance of the publication of the book, in a letter to Sir Arnold Lunn, Price confided that he thought that Marianne Foyster had 'wanted to drive her husband away from the Rectory, which is in a very quiet and lonely spot. But I cannot print this explanation: I daren't even hint at it.'[13] Writing to Everard Feilding, a barrister who had been secretary of the Society for Psychical Research for seventeen years, Price shared his excitement about the case and the unique potential of Lionel Foyster's diary. But he needed to bide his time:

This is in confidence. The present incumbent, a Mr Foyster, has seen far more amazing things than ever we did, and has kept a diary of the 'Phenomena'. It makes extraordinary reading. But the last time I visited the place we were convinced that the rector's wife (a young woman of about twenty-five) was just fooling us – for some reason best known to herself. But we had an exciting evening and eventually helped to carry Mrs Foyster up to bed! Of course, we told Foyster we thought his wife was cheating, and that made him very cross. I am afraid I am not now in his good books. But I certainly want to go down again and am waiting for Mr Foyster to move out of the place. Five years ago, the place was literally alive with – something.[14]

Confessions of a Ghost-Hunter was enthusiastically reviewed – 'a scientific book which reads like a thriller!' It was 'not only an important contribution to science but is also an ideal companion for a railway journey'. That summer, it was serialised in ten parts in *The Listener*. In the edition published on 14 August entitled 'The Most Haunted House in England', the last line of the excerpt on Borley, which implied a hoax, was cut.[15] Following the serialisation, Price also removed the line referring to his suspicions about Marianne Foyster from all subsequent editions of *Confessions*, protesting that he didn't want to cause offence to the Foysters. But its omission implied that the greatest ghost hunter of modern times now believed the haunting at Borley to be authentic. Either he had genuinely changed his mind, or he anticipated greater rewards in *appearing* to do so.

Price began to nurse an idea for a book specifically about the haunting at the Rectory. The core of this book would be a scientific examination following the template established by Ada Goodrich Freer in her bestseller about Ballechin House. The setting was perfect for a real-life ghost story – an isolated country mansion plagued by bell-ringing and wall-writing. At the same time, the story was peopled by scrupulous witnesses – clergymen and their families. There was even a contemporary diary to add the frisson of realism – written by a priest. Though he disparaged the majority of hauntings as 'just nonsense',[16] Price was now convinced – at least in public – that the haunting at Borley was authentic and verifiable.

Ada Goodrich Freer had invited dozens of witnesses to spend time at Ballechin and to record their experiences, which she then

reproduced in *The Alleged Haunting of B—— House*. Price now
planned to do exactly the same with Borley.

Enquiring of Ethel Bull about the possibility of renting the
Rectory, he was advised that the Bulls had nothing to do with it
anymore. She understood from her cousin Lionel Foyster that everything was quiet there now. He'd had to give up the living because
of ill health and was now living in Ipswich. She advised Price to
seek permission from Reverend Clifford Henning, who was the new
incumbent at Borley, but she doubted that he would give it. Price
duly wrote to Henning, who replied that he would be glad to let the
Rectory and invited him to lunch. On the morning of Wednesday
19 May 1937, Henning met Price's train from Liverpool Street at
Sudbury Station.[17]

Over lunch, the 48-year-old Henning explained to Price that he
was a clergyman's son. He had been working as a curate in South
Norwood when he'd married his wife Annette, in 1934. After the
birth of their son, Richard, the following May, they had been long-
ing to escape their tiny flat to make a new start in a country parish
with fields around them and expansive rural views which 'deep
down', Henning felt, meant England 'to most people'.[18] When he'd
been offered Borley as his first parish, he'd never heard of it. But
his wife was immediately stunned and unenthusiastic. 'Not Borley,'
she'd said. 'We don't want to start off in a place with a reputation
like *that*.'[19]

When he'd first visited the village, he had been hugely taken by
its idyllic rural setting, but intimidated by the impracticalities of the
vast and ugly rectory. His little son, he worried, would be 'lost in its
immensity'.[20] But the Bishop of Chelmsford had been sympathetic.
When the rector at Liston Church retired, the parishes of Liston and
Borley would be merged and the Hennings could live at the much
more manageable Liston Rectory. The Church authorities would
sell Borley, the proceeds to be invested and the interest added to the
living. The Hennings had accepted the offer of the living and had
arrived at Borley in March 1936. Just before Christmas, they had
moved their furniture from Borley, where it had been in storage,

and settled into Liston Rectory. Borley Rectory had then been put up for sale, but despite some viewings, nobody had wanted to buy it. So Henning was pleased that Price was keen to rent the house. He and his wife were fascinated by psychical research and were keen to encourage Price's investigation. Price wondered what a fair figure would be. They agreed on £30 a year. Henning even offered to pay the rates.

After lunch, Price was driven over to Borley and Henning opened up the house for him. After the warm and cosy rectory at Liston, it was, he recorded, 'like going out of the sunshine into a mausoleum'.[21] Inspecting the empty house, opening up the rooms and cupboards, Price found nothing unusual; it was just as cold and still as it had been on his previous visits. Henning told him that Lionel Arbon, a steam-roller driver, was now the tenant at the Rectory Cottage and held a set of spare keys for the occasional parish meeting in the house. Other than that, the place was locked and visitors rare.

On 25 May, on the front page of that morning's *Times*, Price had taken out an advertisement in the personal columns. He intended to invite dozens of independent observers to stay at the Rectory and document their experiences. He did not want professional psychical researchers (he was particularly firm that they should *not* be spiritualists) but enthusiastic amateurs – 'intelligent, competent and cultured strangers'.[22] Douglas Craggs and several members of the Magic Circle wrote to be considered, but their appeals were rejected. Price was surprised by the volume of enquiries he received – 200 in all – and by the variety of individuals who were keen to take part, from countesses to charwomen. Some were 'Mayfair men' looking for adventure, or girls who thought that ghost hunting might be 'a thrill'.[23] Several mediums applied, as did some journalists on the hunt for a good story. Many expected to be paid, but Price insisted that he did not want 'to *buy* phenomena'.[24] He consigned three quarters of the applications to the wastepaper basket. But he was pleased to receive many replies from 'the "right" sort of people', who appealed to his social snobbery: university graduates, scientists, doctors and military men. 'Just by reading a letter and studying its composition,' he said, he could 'pretty well tell whether the writer was a suitable person'.[25]

On 2 June, Price was driven to Borley in the small saloon car of 27-year-old Ellic Howe. He had left Hertford College, Oxford, in 1930 without a degree, having preferred to wander throughout Europe 'lonely as a youth' refining his Russian, German, French and Italian.[26] He was fascinated by the occult as well as the history of printing, interests that he shared with Price. He would go on to work for the Special Operations Executive during the Second World War, becoming an expert in forging propaganda – the manipulation of the truth.[27] Price and Howe were intent on surveying the house and setting up a research centre where the observers could keep their belongings, write up reports and sleep. They arrived just before noon and nominated the library as their 'Base Room'. It was conveniently located next to the hall where many phenomena had taken place, as well as giving easy access to the garden, with the summer house and Nun's Walk via the French windows. It was also directly beneath the Blue Room, where both Harry Bull and his father had died.

Howe had brought with him a kettle, cutlery, cups, glasses, cleaning materials, a teapot, sugar and condensed milk. In Sudbury they bought a folding metal camp bed, pillows and blankets, a brass paraffin table lamp, a 2-gallon can of paraffin, candles and matches. They placed the camp bed in the library in the right-hand corner, next to the window. Finding a large wooden table and some school benches in the garage, they put these opposite the camp bed, to the right of the door. Having laid out their equipment, they carefully examined every room and cupboard in the house, drawing rings around any moveable objects with coloured chalk as they went. They found nothing unusual, but in the Blue Room they were surprised to find a moth-eaten blue serge ladies' coat hanging on a peg behind the door. Price did not recall the coat from his visit with Henning.

It was now getting dark. Price and Howe went to introduce themselves to 29-year-old Basil Payne and his wife, Edna, who had moved into Borley Place after the Biggs' lease had expired. Basil was the oldest son of Robert and Annie Payne, who owned the property but lived down at Borley Hall. Over tea, they discussed the various occupants of the Rectory and the phenomena that had taken place there. No such activity, the Paynes insisted, had occurred at Borley Place. After tea, Price and Howe went to buy some beer and returned to the house. As Price lay on the camp bed in the Base Room, Howe began to read. It was deathly still and extremely cold.

Suddenly they heard a series of short, sharp taps. 'What was that?' Howe asked. Price jumped out of bed and went to the hall to investigate. There was nothing. Fifteen minutes later they heard two loud thumps, as if somebody had thrown some heavy boots on the floor. Upstairs, a door slammed. They took their torches and investigated the bedrooms, but again found nothing. As it was getting cold and they had neither wood nor coal to build a fire, they decided to return to London. Before leaving, they called at the Rectory Cottage to give instructions to Mr and Mrs Arbon, who had agreed to be caretakers. Winifred Arbon was the daughter of Mrs Pearson, who had worked for the Smiths and who still lived across the road at Place Farm Cottage. Price made it clear that Arbon must not give the keys to any unauthorised people, before returning to London.

When they visited the Rectory again to spend the night on 16 June, Price and Howe patrolled the house as usual. At 8.30 p.m., they drove to Sudbury for dinner. When they returned, in the Blue Room they noticed that a tobacco tin had been moved 3 inches from its chalked outline and a small box was now 7 feet from where they'd left it. Howe 'became scared', so they locked up the house and motored back to London.

Price and Howe now printed an 'Official Observer's Declaration Form' that was to be signed by all participants. They were to provide written reports of their experiences and not permitted to discuss the location of the house or to write or lecture about it. At the same time, Howe produced a confidential guide book. A homage to Ada Goodrich Freer's study of Ballechin House, the booklet was entitled *The Alleged Haunting at B—— Rectory: Instructions for Observers*. It had 'University of London Council for Psychical Investigation' emblazoned on its dark-blue paper cover, giving the appearance of an academic publication. It would be known as the 'Blue Book'.[28]

As well as instructions about their responsibilities as observers ('Spend at least a portion of each day and night [in complete darkness] in the Blue Room'),[29] participants were also offered practical advice about where to eat in Sudbury and the location of the nearest pub. They were offered guidance, too, about what they might expect from their time at the Rectory: bell-ringing, taps, knocks and footsteps. Like the beginning of an M. R. James ghost story, some of the instructions promised much to Price's eager volunteers:

FORMS OR APPARITIONS. If seen, *do not move and on no account approach the figure*. Note exact method of appearance. Observe figure carefully, watch all movements, rate and manner of progression etc. Note duration of appearance, colour, form, size, how dressed, and whether solid or transparent. If carrying a camera with film ready for exposing, quietly 'snap' the figure, but make no sound and do not move. If figure speaks, *do not approach*, but ascertain name, age, sex, origin, cause of visit, if in trouble, and possible alleviation. Inquire if it is a spirit. Ask figure to return, suggesting exact time and place. Do not move until figure disappears. Note exact method of vanishing. If through an open door, quietly follow. If through solid object (such as wall), ascertain if still visible on other side.[30]

Price also warned that 'the greatest effort should be made to ascertain whether such manifestations are due to normal causes, such as rats, small boys, the villagers, the wind, wood shrinking, the Death Watch beetle, farm animals nosing the doors etc., trees brushing against the windows, birds in the chimney-stack or between double walls etc.'[31]

The first potential candidate to make contact with Price was a 52-year-old engineer's agent, Sidney Glanville. A man of great intelligence and integrity, he was the first observer to visit the Rectory and would also prove to be one of the most loyal and most diligent. As a young man he had participated in seances at his parents' house and had been interested in the paranormal ever since. For nearly thirty years he had experimented with automatic writing, and attended spiritualist meetings and seances, having been present at sittings with renowned mediums as well as some famous frauds. His professional work was connected with radiology, mechanical and electrical engineering and measuring instruments of high-speed precision. Glanville wrote a letter of application as soon as he saw Price's advertisement in *The Times*. He outlined his qualifications and suggested that he was 'not in the habit of pre-judging affairs'.[32] His intelligence – so he was told – was 'up to average'.[33] Glanville and his son, Roger, who was twenty-three and had similar interests to his father, returned their declaration forms to Price, booking in three nights at the Rectory: 19 June, and 14 and 28 August.

When they first arrived at the empty rectory, the Glanvilles both agreed that 'if ever there was a house that should be haunted, this was it'. Sidney Glanville asked Price if they might take some photographs and suggested that, as he'd previously been an architect's clerk, he could use his first visit to draw up some ground plans of the house. Though the Glanvilles were not trained psychical researchers, they were expert in the collection and recording of scientific evidence. When Glanville submitted the plans, Price was delighted with them – and the photographs, which he thought magnificent.

Glanville visited the Rectory again on 14 August and recognised the 'dead cold atmosphere that permeated the whole building' as well as its 'intense quietness';[34] 'Once inside the house the only sounds that could be heard were a farm vehicle passing through the lane, the whistle of a train at Long Melford and the screech of owls at night'.[35] On this visit Glanville took tracings and photographs of the wall-writings. He also noticed that the cats' cemetery in the garden had been extensively disturbed. Some of the headstones had been thrown into the undergrowth and an area the size of a small room had been dug up. Lionel Arbon at the Rectory Cottage had no idea who was responsible for disturbing the cats' remains. Glanville and his son then proceeded to excavate the cemetery some more and turned up large bones that they thought might have been those of horses or oxen – but some they couldn't identify.

Sidney Glanville quickly established himself as a committed, reliable and thorough researcher. He then began to consider the history of the building and the experiences of the former residents. This attention to detail seems to have been driven by Glanville himself and not Price, who, though he visited the site from time to time, was very much absent during the investigation. In August, Glanville wrote to Alfred Foyster, Lionel's older brother, asking for information about the history of the phenomena at Borley. Alfred was surprised to receive Glanville's letter as he understood from Lionel that the phenomena had completely stopped. He would write to his brother on Glanville's behalf, but warned that Lionel now found it difficult to write as he was crippled with arthritis and might not want to respond.

But on 31 August, Glanville was delighted to receive a letter from Lionel in Ipswich, who continued to take an interest in Borley. He indicated that the activity during their residence had fallen into two periods. They had moved there in October 1930 and from February 1931 had experienced 'a campaign of frightfulness'[36] until the visit of the Marks Tey Circle, when the Rectory became 'absolutely a different house'.[37] Glanville sent Lionel a list of questions: When was the activity particularly intense? What had stood on the site prior to the Rectory? Was the house thought to be haunted before the arrival of Harry Bull? Did Foyster and his wife feel terror in any particular part of the building? And had he any theory to account for the phenomena?[38]

Lionel told Glanville that he was convinced that in order for the spirits to manifest, there needed to be somebody psychic in the house. His wife Marianne was 'very psychic' and he believed that

Eric Smith must have been, too.[39] He also told him that once the phenomena had subsided in 1932, he had written up a full account of their experiences at the Rectory with the notion of having it published. He offered to send it to Glanville for his candid opinion and for any advice he might have about publishing it. Glanville said he'd be delighted to read it. Lionel duly sent a 180-page typed manuscript entitled *Fifteen Months in a Haunted House*.

Between the beginning of June 1937 and the end of April 1938, sixty-nine observers would sign the declaration form, most of them observing at the Rectory over a weekend. After their visits, the observers would submit their reports to Price. Curiously, for a scientific experiment, there was no logbook kept at the Rectory in order to record the ongoing investigation.

Mark Kerr-Pearse had enthusiastically written to Price to be considered. 'As I possess all the qualifications you mention, I would ask you kindly to consider me as an observer. I am a bachelor, 29 and independent.'[40] After a satisfactory interview with Price on 28 May, he first visited the Rectory on 26 June. He was more than a little relieved to be offered the opportunity to stay at Borley, where he could live for practically nothing. He was out of work, on his 'beam ends'[41] and pretty much living hand to mouth. His expectations high, having read the Blue Book, at first he was disappointed; he had 'no luck and it is most uninteresting'.[42] But after subsequent visits, he became more intrigued by the case and began to make extended stays at the Rectory, ultimately becoming the most frequent observer during the time of Price's investigation. He recorded and numbered every portable object in the house – matchboxes, keys, screws, tins and cups, and noted every pencil mark on the walls. As well as the writings observed during the Foysters' residence, there was various graffiti all over the house. The word 'Borley' was written in the kitchen passage near the green baize door. On the walls by the service stairs was the word 'Edwin'. In the scullery, on the wall to the left of the back door the word 'Adelaide', the figure '4' and the letter 'P' were scribbled. In the Base Room, a game of noughts and crosses was drawn on the wall in yellow chalk, which Kerr-Pearse presumed to be a joke by another observer. Some of the writing appeared to be fresh. The letter 'C' – 9 inches tall – was scrawled between the pantry and the service stairs. In the same passage, 'Ma' appeared twice – perhaps an attempt to write 'Marianne'. Kerr-Pearse also studied one of the earlier messages in the bathroom passage that Marianne Foyster had written beneath. It seemed to him to read, 'Marianne Get Help – well tank bottom me.'[43] He now added a note of his own: 'I STILL CANNOT UNDERSTAND. PLEASE TELL ME MORE.'[44]

Writing to Price, Kerr-Pearse suggested that investigators should consider exploring the well. He himself examined the main well in the courtyard, descending to the first platform, 8 feet down, by means of the supply pipe. But the conditions were slippery and potentially dangerous, so he didn't descend any further. He also investigated a shallow round sump in the cellar, unaware that the 'well tank' was actually situated in the attic. Water was pumped by hand via the wheel pump in the courtyard up into the tank in the eaves in order to provide the house with running water.

Kerr-Pearse would spend many hours in the summer house

observing the Nun's Walk and would often sleep in the camp bed there during warm weather. One night he was disturbed by the unexpected arrival of the Glanvilles, but the next morning they had a long chat and the three men became friends. Kerr-Pearse submitted meticulous reports to Price and was extremely fastidious, complaining when other observers weren't. He also became acquainted with the Hennings and would often lunch or dine with them at Liston. On 16 July, in discussion with their chauffeur, Herbert Mayes, Kerr-Pearse learned that the blue serge ladies' coat that Price had discovered in the Blue Room had definitely not been in the house before Price's tenancy. That night, the Hennings accompanied Kerr-Pearse back to the Rectory to hold an experiment. They hung the coat on the back of the door in the Blue Room, and lit night lights in the chapel and in the kitchen passage. They then went to the Base Room and began a seance. After trying to communicate four times, they heard an extraordinary noise coming from the kitchen, as if something was slowly moving down the passage towards them. When they stood up to investigate, the noise stopped. The night lights continued to burn without a flicker.[45]

On 5 August, Kerr-Pearse was disturbed to find a dead frog in the hall outside the drawing room. It had fluff and dust sticking to its hind legs. He was unsure how it could have got into the house, which had been locked overnight, and wondered, 'Could this be due to Poltergeist activity?'[46] On another night, the Hennings were visiting with their friend Miss Reid – a very level-headed person who did not 'in any way pretend to be psychic'.[47] Outside the Blue Room, Miss Reid said she had pins and needles all over and felt very cold, despite the warm evening. Annette Henning felt her hands and they were icy cold. Several observers would note this 'cold spot' in the house. Sidney Glanville marked the place on the floor with a tiny – almost invisible – pencilled cross. During one weekend at the Rectory, the Glanvilles left a tobacco tin on the drawing room mantelpiece, ringed with chalk. On their next visit, the tobacco tin had been moved and placed exactly on the pencil mark of the cold spot with 'mathematical precision'.[48]

On 21 September, Kerr-Pearse stayed the weekend at the Rectory with his cousin, Rupert Haigh, a 33-year-old barrister and amateur big-game hunter. The weather had turned colder so they had bought a big sack of coal to heat the Base Room. They'd put some coal to burn on the fire and left the heavy sack outside in the hall. At 8.30 p.m. that evening, they were standing on the landing when they heard a rustling noise. Going downstairs, they saw that the bag of coal had been moved about 18 inches. When Haigh and Kerr-Pearse retired to bed for the night, they left the paraffin lamp on; the room also warmed by the fire. At 2.30 a.m. they heard a sharp rap on the window of the Base Room, but Kerr-Pearse thought it 'may have been a moth'.[49]

Though his cousin went straight to sleep, Haigh was in a nervous state and couldn't rest. He had been expecting footsteps, thumps and knocks – even to see something – as outlined in the Blue Book, but as time went on, nothing occurred and he began to feel calmer. But suddenly the air around him seemed to get icy. He felt cold all over his body, his hands became frozen and his hair stood on end. He was rigid with fear. The sensation lasted about twenty seconds before it went away and he felt compelled to wake his cousin. The doors and windows were all closed and the thermometer read 60 degrees Fahrenheit.[50]

Haigh left the next day and subsequently wrote to his cousin from Port Said in Egypt. 'If I did not enjoy my visit to your haunted house, I at least found it most interesting. I entered it with a completely open mind, but left with the firm conviction that it *is* haunted.'[51] He admitted that he may have just experienced nerves and fright, but he believed that what he had experienced was 'not natural'.[52]

Meanwhile, Kerr-Pearse had heard that the BBC was planning a series of radio programmes about haunted houses, so he wrote to the director of talks explaining that he had been living in a haunted house for some considerable time as part of Price's investigation with the London University Psychical Department. He outlined the various phenomena that had been experienced there, including footsteps, strange smells and wall-writing. He indicated that this was the first time that a haunted house had been investigated scientifically. Richard Lambert, the editor of *The Listener*, had taken part in Price's previous broadcast, from Dean Manor, as well as a programme about the 'talking mongoose' case in the Isle of Man, and had co-written a book about it with Price, *The Haunting of Cashen's Gap*.[53] Hearing from Lambert about Kerr-Pearse's approach to the BBC, Price sent him a warning letter, reminding him that taking part in such a broadcast was prohibited under the terms of their arrangement. 'To refresh your memory,' Price wrote archly, 'I am sending you herewith a copy of the Declaration Form. I shall be glad to hear that your offer to the BBC was due to a mis-understanding.'[54] Price's meaning was clear: Borley was *his* story, and nobody else's.

Having read the manuscript of *Fifteen Months in a Haunted House*, on 8 October Sidney Glanville wrote excitedly to Lionel Foyster: 'It is the most astonishing document I have ever read.'[55] Compared to the occasional taps and knocks that he had experienced at the Rectory himself, the phenomena Lionel had described was 'astound-ing'. In order to preserve the anonymity of the Rectory and the identities of those involved, Lionel had used pseudonyms through-out the document. But he was insistent that his manuscript was 'a record of facts' that had been recorded 'just as they happened, no matter how impossible they may appear to be'.[56] Glanville was con-vinced that the phenomena Foyster had recorded were of enormous value to psychic science. But in its present form, he worried that critics would dismiss it as 'not serious enough'.[57] He was too polite to say that it was a fantastic story, poorly told.

Mrs Bull (in black) watches from the veranda with three of her daughters as four of their older sisters play tennis c. 1892

CHAPTER FIFTEEN

THE END OF BORLEY RECTORY

22 September 1937–28 February 1939

So *many* people prefer the 'bunk' to the 'debunk!'

Harry Price, Foreword, *The Mysteries of Versailles*[1]

While his official observers were investigating the Rectory, 150 miles away in Pulborough, Price was engaged in writing what he believed would be his magnum opus. He was keen to follow the development of psychic science up to the present day as Charles Richet had done in his *Thirty Years of Psychical Research*. Price's book was to bring the study up to date as *Fifty Years of Psychical Research* – 'an epitome of all the important developments and experiments which have taken place during the past half-century'.

On 22 September 1937, Price invited Allen Drinkwater, of the publisher Longmans, Green and Co., to lunch to discuss *Fifty Years of Psychical Research* and a projected book about Borley Rectory. Drinkwater was much impressed with the care which Price had taken to investigate the Rectory thoroughly and scientifically, and suggested that he himself would be interested in visiting as an observer. Two days after the lunch, Price reiterated his invitation to Drinkwater to stay at the Rectory. He was convinced that he now had enough material for a book about Borley. 'I believe such a work would create a sensation,' he enthused. 'Nothing like it has been done before.'[2] Following the template established by Ada Goodrich Freer, he saw an opportunity to regain his prestige as 'the people's' psychical researcher and relieve his financial worries by writing the world's best ghost story.

Price subsequently received an enthusiastic letter from Kenneth Potter, Longmans's commissioning editor, expressing great interest in *Fifty Years of Psychical Research*. He was also interested in the Borley book but was unsure what form it was to take. Price and Potter met at Longmans's offices, a meeting also attended by Richard Lambert, the editor of *The Listener*. After their book about the 'talking mongoose', Price and Lambert were planning to collaborate again on the book about Borley. But though Potter commissioned *Fifty Years of Psychical Research*, he was unwilling to commit to the Borley project until Price's investigations were over.

Sidney Glanville now wrote to Mr and Mrs Smith, asking if they might discuss their time at Borley. They were then living at Sevington Rectory near Ashford. Eric Smith replied that they were happy to talk, but would prefer to meet in person rather than talking on the telephone, so Glanville made the trip to Kent. He was greeted very coldly by Eric Smith, until he explained that he was not a journalist but a serious investigator. Smith called his wife and Glanville was invited to stay for lunch. He found the Smiths intelligent and helpful, but not keen to discuss their experiences at the Rectory. They regarded the subject as distasteful and would rather it were left alone. Though they weren't afraid of ghosts or psychic phenomena, Mr Smith insisted that the house had an evil atmosphere; he would absolutely refuse to live there now. But finding Glanville sympathetic, they began to describe in some detail their experiences and the various tales they had heard about Borley.[3]

Their conversation continuing throughout the afternoon, Glanville stayed for tea and dinner, only finally leaving Sevington after midnight. The Smiths told him about the skull that Mabel had found in the library and the bottle of poison she had found in the cellar. They also shared the tale they had been told of a cook who had died in Henry Dawson Bull's arms in the Rectory kitchen. She had apparently given birth to a child – presumably his – but it had disappeared and the matter had been 'hushed up'. They gave their version of the seance that had taken place in the Blue Room during Price's first visit, when Harry Bull's spirit had revealed that he had been murdered. Fully armed with the Smiths' detailed testimony, Glanville left a copy of Price's *Leaves from a Psychist's Case-Book* with them. The day after his visit, the Smiths noticed some unusual tappings in the house, as if the very discussion of Borley had infected the rectory at Sevington.[4]

Mark Kerr-Pearse had been offered a job at the British Consulate in Geneva, so he visited the Rectory for the last time from 23 October to 1 November, during which time he was accompanied by the Glanvilles and their friend Alan Cuthbert, who worked for the Bank of England and was a 'responsible sort of person'.[5] On the first day of his stay, Kerr-Pearse heard a rap in the hallway. A few minutes later, there was a loud creak from the backstairs, 'as of a heavy footstep on a loose board'.[6] Despite the fact that Price was determined that the investigation should be scientific and not involve spiritualism, inspired by Sidney Glanville's visit to the Smiths and the revelation of the cook's death in the kitchen, Kerr-Pearse and Roger Glanville decided to hold a seance.

That night the men sat in the kitchen passage, near to the site of the cook's alleged demise, around a light table that had been specially made for the purpose. Cuthbert sat with his back to the exterior wall, Glanville and Kerr-Pearse opposite. The moment their hands touched it, the table 'felt alive', rocking backwards and forwards.[7] The code was one knock for 'yes', two for 'no' and three for uncertainty. Words would be spelled out as the sitters went through the alphabet, which could be a laborious process. At times the rocking would be slow and deliberate and at others so fast that it was difficult to keep pace with it. Except for a faint glow of moonlight from the kitchen window, they sat in the dark, other than when they needed to write replies, when they'd cover a torch with a handkerchief. All three men felt an icy-cold draught throughout the seance, most noticeable when the table was rocking violently. Kerr-Pearse had the impression that there was a presence behind Cuthbert's right shoulder. Glanville had the feeling that they were being watched. They spoke to various entities during the sitting, sometimes familiar, sometimes unknown to them and occasionally anonymous:

You are Henry Bull?
Yes.
Did something unfortunate happen in the kitchen?
Yes.
Did a servant girl die in your presence there?
Yes.
Did she die a natural death?
No.
Was she poisoned?
No.
Was there a baby?
Yes.[8]

The next day, Sidney Glanville went to the church and consulted the parish register. Among the dead he found an entry: 'Kate Boreham of Sudbury died Easter Day 1888 aged 31'. The same evening, at 6.50 p.m., Sidney and Roger Glanville held a further table-tipping seance in the kitchen with Kerr-Pearse and Cuthbert.

Is it Katie?
Yes.
Were you a maid here?
Yes.
Have you a message?
Yes.
Will you please spell it out?
Light, Mass, [indistinct][9]

The name Kate or Katie had never been mentioned in any of the phenomena at the Rectory until Glanville had consulted the parish register.[10] Later that night, the four men held another seance, this time in the pitch darkness of the landing to the right of the Blue Room door. This time they were contacted by Harry Bull.

Is that Harry Bull?
Yes.
Have you a message for us?
Yes.
Will you spell it out?
Misfor ...
Do you mean 'misfortune'?
Yes.
Will you continue?
A wife.
Do you mean your wife?
Yes.
Did you die in this house?
Yes.
Did you die in the [Blue Room]?
Yes.
Did you die naturally?
No.
Were you poisoned?
Yes.
Were you poisoned by your wife?
Yes.[11]

At 2 a.m. on 25 October, Cuthbert was asleep in the Base Room, with Kerr-Pearse and the Glanvilles sitting in the dark on the landing outside the Blue Room. They all heard heavy muffled footsteps walk across the hall just beneath them. When they went downstairs to investigate, they found nothing, just Cuthbert sound asleep on the camp bed. Leaving him to sleep, Sidney Glanville suggested that they hold another seance on the landing, but this time they should use a planchette that he had brought with him from Streatham. Glanville was aware that Harry Price felt dubious about any information resulting from a planchette sitting. Though there was 'no doubt' that some automatic writing was genuine, some was 'the result of the subconscious activity of the mind and nothing to do with spirits.'

The planchette sittings that night revealed little but repetitive and nonsensical words and phrases. But the Glanvilles took the paper with scrawled messages from the sitting back home to Streatham, where they showed it to Glanville's 27-year-old daughter, Helen. Though she had never used a planchette before, one evening when she was alone in the house, she decided to try it herself. Immediately she had much more success than her father and brother.

Have you a message?
We ... [indistinct]
If the word is 'well', say yes.
Yes ... Marianne.
Do you want us to look in the well – yes or no?
Yes.
Is the well in the cellar?
Yes.
Is there something you want us to find?
Yes.
Is anything in the well to do with a child?
Yes.
Was the child dead when it was born?
[indistinct]
Do you mean 'yes' or 'no'?
Yes.
Do you want us to find it?
Yes.
Shall we find it in the cellar?
Yes.[12]

After Helen's success, Glanville became convinced that the manifestations at the Rectory were strongest when there were women present. On 30 October, Glanville took the planchette back to Borley and held a sitting with Clifford Henning at 11.50 p.m. They now started using rolls of plain white wallpaper in order to record the many messages written with the planchette.

What happened to you?
I died.
How?
Murdered.
Who by?
Henry.
What is your name?
Mar ...
What is your surname?
Lairre.
Were you a nun?
Yes.
Were you buried here?
Yes.
Where?
In the garden.
How can we help you?
Light, Mass ...[indistinct][13]

On Halloween, Helen Glanville was joined in a sitting at Streatham by her father and brother as well as Mark Kerr-Pearse.

Who is there?
Mary Lairre.
How old were you when you passed over?
Nineteen.
Were you a novice?
Yes.
Were you murdered?
Yes.

When?
1667.
How?
Stran . . ..
Were you strangled?
Yes.[14]

There now began to emerge a dialogue with the spirits of two women, a nun, Marie Lairre, as well as a woman who had died on 13 June 1888 called Katie Boreham. There was no further communication with the nun Evangeline Westcott, who the Marks Tey Circle had contacted in 1932.[15]

On 3 November, Glanville wrote to Price that he had consulted the Essex Archaeological Society in an attempt to confirm the truth of the story of the doomed relationship of the monk and the nun. The secretary of the society had been very clear: 'There was certainly no religious house at Borley; nor is there any record of a chapel or ecclesiastical building other than the church having existed there.' Glanville was disappointed but resigned. 'So there goes the monastery and the nunnery legend,' he wrote to Price. 'Unfortunate, but there it is.'[16]

After the departure of Kerr-Pearse at the beginning of November, Price re-established his authority at Borley and took part in a BBC broadcast himself, without mentioning the Rectory by name. Having investigated 'so-called haunted houses' for thirty years, he had concluded that most of them were 'just nonsense'.[17] He used the talk to declare both his scepticism in general and his conviction in the particular case that he was currently engaged in, thus exciting the audience's curiosity and priming them for his investigation on Borley when it appeared in print.

I believe in ghosts! Sceptic as I am regarding the alleged supernormal, I have been forced to the conclusion that certain buildings and places are inhabited by invisible beings – call them spirits or entities, or what you will – which manifest themselves in various

ways, familiar to all readers of ghost stories. I have seen things
for myself.[18]

He went on to share some of the occurrences that had taken place
at the Rectory. His 'scientific' investigation had confirmed the existence of ghosts. 'As a scientist', he claimed, 'I can guarantee you
a ghost.'[19]

Price's radio talk was printed by Richard Lambert in *The
Listener* on 10 November, a copy of which Sidney Glanville sent to
the Smiths at Sevington. They were grateful, Smith wrote, 'to see
photos of those old familiar haunts again, and where we spent, well
let us say, some of the darkest hours of our lives'.[20] He suggested to
Glanville that after Christmas, he and Mrs Smith might meet him
at the Rectory and that they bring with them some of the objects
that had been involved in the phenomena when they lived there.
Corresponding with Glanville herself, Mabel Smith seemed less
than enthusiastic about the visit, though she was keen to bring an
end to the activity at Borley: 'We should like to hear that all this
mystery was cleared up and that all the poor restless "ghosts" were
at peace – we don't worry them, so why worry us?'[21]

On 29 November, Dodie Bull died in a nursing home in
Lowestoft at the age of 73. She had died of heart disease and dementia. The thirteen siblings who had filled the Rectory with youth and
energy were now facing old age and illness. Dodie's sister Mabel had
died the year before and Kathleen in 1934. Their remaining siblings,
Freda, Gerald, Constance, Alfred and Ethel – all unmarried – lived
together at Chilton Lodge. Dodie, the eldest sister, had chosen not
to be buried with her husband in Yorkshire, but to come home to
Borley. A funeral was held on the following Friday, officiated by
Clifford Henning and well attended by family, clergy and local dignitaries, including Florence Whitehouse and the Bulls' staff, Mr and
Mrs Cooper. As at her brother Harry's funeral, Dodie's coffin was
carried to the graveside as Henning intoned 'Nunc Dimittis' and
around the grave the mourners sang 'Abide with Me'. Among them
was Marianne Foyster, who had attended the service alone as her

husband was ill. Significantly absent were Ivy Bull and her daughter Constance, though they sent a wreath 'With Love'.[22]

By the autumn, Kenneth Potter had offered Price an advance of £75 for a book about Borley. Lambert wrote to Price, offering to make an immediate start on drafts of several chapters of the Borley book using material already in Price's possession. This would be used without acknowledgement as long as Price was willing to share the advance that had been offered by Longmans. However, despite his enthusiasm for the book, Lambert was advised by his wife to withdraw from the Borley project, leaving Price to write it alone.

With the contract for his book about Borley finally being prepared, on 21 December Price was disturbed to receive a worrying report from one of his observers, Joseph Burden, from Dartmouth.

We saw nothing and heard no sounds that could not have been explained by the wind or the natural shifting of boards and windows. I was most interested in the pencil marks and writing but was never certain that any of it was new because there is so much wall-space to inspect that we could never be absolutely sure that we had not overlooked marks here and there. Also, your rule that observers 'should make a point of taking meals at the same times each day' and should carry out their inspections at regular intervals may easily give some outsider an excellent opportunity to enter the building (either with Arbin's [sic] key – if no observations are going on – or perhaps with a key of his own) and to do all the 'spirit writing' he wishes. As duplicates are invariably made of all important house keys, it seems odd that Arbin should be the sole possessor of such a key. Lastly I would hesitate to place some of the 'manifestations' beyond Arbin because he might easily realise that 'Phenomena Appearing Strong' would mean more observers and consequently more tips, not forgetting the fact that you would be more inclined to rent or buy the house if the ghosts were active! The fact is, of course, greatly modified by the fact that the written messages would hardly be the type of messages which a man like Arbin might write under such circumstances.

I hope you will excuse these few remarks of mine. I am not entirely sceptical about the haunting, but I do feel that the wall writing is the most 'vulnerable' of all the phenomena, and I suggest that you put padlocks on the doors unless it is absolutely necessary for Arbin to enter the house when observers are absent.[23]

After Christmas, a defensive Price thanked Burden for his report and reiterated that 'of course, the evidence for the "haunting" of the house does not rest with the present observers; I have a great mass of evidence from the owners and rectors who have lived in the house, going back for nearly fifty years. You may be interested in an experiment we are about to try. One of the previous rectors, who experienced many manifestations, is about to live there again for a short while, in an effort to induce further phenomena.'[24]

On 12 January 1938, Sidney Glanville waved his newspaper out of the car window as he spotted the Smiths drawing near their rendezvous at Lewisham clock tower at 11 a.m., as they were to drive to Borley in convoy.[25] Price had sent his apologies and would not be attending, though they would be joined by Roger Glanville. Mabel Smith was keen to 'set the stage' for the Glanvilles and had brought the velvet curtains from the library, the mirror that had tapped during the seance that Price had attended on his first visit, as well as the jug that was hit by a bar of soap, the keys that had been thrown about when Lord Charles Hope had visited and the clock that would never keep time.[26] The Smiths hoped that these artefacts from their occupation of the Rectory might inspire a particularly revealing seance that evening.

The sitting comprised the Smiths and their chauffeur as well as Sidney and Roger Glanville. But despite their preparations, they were to be disappointed. At the seance, they had a communication from a Roman centurion who promised 'information', but told them nothing. They asked 'Harry Bull' where the skull that Mrs Smith had found in the library had come from. He told them the skull was that of a woman from Borley, but little else. Writing to Sidney

Glanville on their return to Sevington, Smith reflected that, 'it does one good to get out of the ordinary routine sometimes, but it was a pity the "spooks" did not show up.'[27]

Meanwhile, Price received another letter from one of his observers, BBC producer Gordon Glover, who, again, queried the veracity of the phenomena. 'It does strike one,' he suggested, tentatively, 'that the evidence in connection with this house is flimsy.'[28]

> I was interested in the Rev. Foyster's diary, but I would be more interested still to know something more about Marianne Foyster and her state of mind at the time these phenomena occurred. Most of them appear to have come to his notice by report from her ... and I do not think it impossible that a woman of highly-strung and nervous character could not only imagine things happening but even go so far as to reproduce them herself.[29]

As with Burden, Price high-handedly dismissed Glover's concerns. Contrary to his estimation of Marianne Foyster, on the two occasions Price had met her, she had struck him as being 'particularly self-possessed and normal'.[30] Certainly it was possible that she might have 'helped out' the phenomena if she had wanted to leave the Rectory. But Price had been in contact with the house for years before the Foysters had arrived and their testimony wasn't necessary to support the case for the phenomena to be genuine.

Despite claiming that the Foysters' testimony wasn't essential, Price now wrote to Lionel telling him about his investigations at the Rectory over the preceding months. The manifestations at Borley over the previous fifty years were so striking that they must be recorded. Price was keen to make use of Lionel's notes that he had read back in 1931, but had since lost the manuscript.[31] In a caustic reply, Lionel admitted to being extremely surprised to hear from Price, given that he had previously been convinced that his wife was responsible for the phenomena at the Rectory. He was curious to know if Price's planned study would be a 'popular account' that would be serialised in the newspapers or a 'scientific record of facts' aimed at psychical researchers. He had plans for a book of his own about their time at the Rectory and made clear that their former agreement meant that Price could not use any of the material that had been sent to him in 1931 without permission.[32]

Price was disingenuous about the possibility of success for *Fifteen Months in a Haunted House.* He doubted if any publisher would print it, given that it only covered the Foysters' time at the Rectory – 'the tale would be incomplete', he insisted.[33] He stressed that the motivating force behind *his* book about the Rectory was the 'extraordinary accounts of the <u>many</u> observers we have had there over the past few months'.[34] He assured Lionel that his report would not be 'a mere ghost story'.[35] He was imagining a 'readable account' that would be written in 'narrative form to appeal to potential readers' as well as providing plans and illustrations. It would be 'neither too scientific nor too popular'.[36] He aimed to follow the success of *An Adventure,* a bestseller when it was published in 1911, which outlined the experiences of Charlotte Anne Moberly and Eleanor Jourdain, who had visited Versailles together in 1901.[37] Exploring the gardens of the Petit Trianon, a small neoclassical chateau built by Loüis XV, they claimed to have experienced the gardens as they had been in the eighteenth century and to have seen several figures of the period, including the ill-fated queen, Marie Antoinette.

The story of this 'time slip' was at the forefront of Price's mind. Following the death of Miss Moberly in 1937, he had been sent an unpublished study of the case written by J. R. Sturge-Whiting that claimed that the women had not had any paranormal experience at all. Price had agreed to try to interest a publisher in it and had sent the manuscript to Kenneth Potter at Longmans who wasn't keen on the idea. 'We think that there is always a much bigger market,' he told Price, 'for the "bunk" than the "debunk".'[38] *The Mystery of Versailles: A Complete Solution* was published later that year with a foreword by Price that almost directly quoted Potter's commercial instinct. 'The more credulous will not accept Mr Sturge-Whiting's answer to the

Versailles legend,' Price wrote, 'and shouts of "Iconoclast!" will be raised. So *many* people prefer the "bunk" to the "debunk!".'[39]

Lionel indicated that his health had broken down over the past couple of years and he could no longer walk. He was confined to bed and at a loose end, so he told Price he would write a summary of events for him that had taken place during their time at the Rectory, leaving Lionel the possibility of publishing *Fifteen Months in a Haunted House* in the future.[40]

On 12 March 1938, despite vehement protests from Britain and France, the Wehrmacht marched across the border as Hitler annexed Austria. In Vienna huge crowds greeted the declaration that the country was entering a new era of 'one great German Reich'. In the Ballhausplatz, thousands filed past a huge portrait of Hitler flanked by the swastika flag. At 11.45 a.m., the Vienna radio station paused its broadcast of gramophone records to relay the sounds of the activity in the streets, with marching crowds shouting 'Sieg Heil! Sieg Heil!' in chorus. The excitement, the *Daily Mirror* reported, was terrific. The Austrian Nazi leader, Hubert Klausner, announced the *Anschluss* on national radio, shouting into the microphone, 'One people, one nation, one Fuehrer. Heil Hitler!' From the back benches, Churchill worried that Britain was 'lamentably unprepared' for the war that by now was clearly coming. The *Sunday Times* journalist Virginia Cowles later recalled despairing that 'peace was dying. Everyone in their hearts knew it, but the actual fact was so appalling they clung desperately to every hope.'[41]

In Britain, poltergeists seemed to be an expression of the anxious political times. *The Christian Guardian* noted 'extraordinarily significant points of resemblance between the records of *Poltergeist* hauntings and the Nazi movement. Both are manifested in a subconscious uprush of desire for power. Both suck, like vampires, the energies of adolescents, both issue in noise, destruction, fire and terror. Hitler speaks best in a state of semi trance. Whether the uprush of subconscious energy generated through him and sucking into itself the psycho-physical forces of German youth is merely the outcome of an unformulated group-desire for power, or whether, like some Poltergeist hauntings it would seem to have another source, is open to question.'[42] The British press announced that 'the poltergeists are here again'[43] as strange psychic manifestations were being reported 'from all parts of the country'.[44] They quoted Price, who said, 'I have never had such a time. I am getting letters from all over the British Isles asking me to investigate strange occurrences.' The 'spook haunting a Suffolk rectory is extraordinarily virile', it was reported, referring to the activity at Borley; 'in fact it has all the tricks and is learning more.'[45]

On 27 March, the Glanvilles held another planchette seance at their home in Streatham. This revealed the most threatening message that the investigators would receive.

Does anyone want to speak to us?
Yes.
Who are you?
Sunex Amures and one of the men [indistinct] mean to burn the rectory tonight at 9 o'clock end of the haunting go to the rectory and you will be able to see us enter into our own and under the ruins you will find bone of murdered [indistinct] wardens [not clear] under the ruins mean you to have proof of haunting of the rectory at Borley [indistinct] the understanding of which gamenl [large full stop written] game tells the story of murder which happened there.
In which room will the fire start?
Over the hall. Yes, yes, you must go if you want proof.
Why cannot you give us proof here?
We will.[46]

Over the year of Price's tenancy of the Rectory, Sidney Glanville had gathered a large body of correspondence, drawings and notes, including transcripts of the seances and planchette readings as well as tracings of the wall-writings. As the tenancy came to an end, he collated the material into a dossier entitled *The Haunting of Borley Rectory – Private and Confidential Report*.[47] Glanville presented the typescript to the bibliophile Price, who duly had the document bound in three-quarter calf leather. It contained, Price later explained, 'the names and alleged doings of several living persons who might be pained if the very intimate details of their – alleged – acts were made public'.[48] As the contents were so sensitive, it was fitted with a Bramah lock and became known as the 'Locked Book'.

On 9 May, Price was driven to Borley by Geoffrey Motion, a former wine-seller and near neighbour of his from Chanctonbury who owned a conveniently large car, which they planned to fill with Price's belongings.[49] They surveyed the house several times with a powerful lamp and a torch. Their task complete, at midnight they made a last inspection of the Blue Room and saw something shining on the floor. Motion ran to pick it up. It was a woman's 22-carat gold wedding ring dating from 1864, the year that construction of the Rectory was completed.

Price handed the keys back to Clifford Henning; on 19 May, his tenancy was over. Though he had considered buying it himself, he felt the Rectory was too big to run and too far away from Pulborough to use as a weekend retreat. Besides, things had been very quiet at the Rectory for the previous few months.[50] Henning had it valued by a local estate agent. The agent was not at all optimistic of a future for the Rectory but a 'For Sale' sign board was placed outside the house.

On 11 August 1938, Price wrote to Kenneth Potter at Longmans that he was ready to start work on his book about Borley; 'I venture to prophesy that, when published, it will be the finest example (so far as real evidence is concerned) of a haunted house ever recorded.'[51] He was particularly pleased that he had secured permission from Lionel Foyster to use his diary as this was to be a 'very valuable part of the book.'[52] On 18 August, he signed a contract with Longmans and immediately started taking interviews prior to the publication of his 'exhaustive' study, which was planned for publication in the spring of 1939. On 1 November, Price was a guest on the wireless, once again talking about an anonymous haunted house, in a regional programme called *The Under Twenty Club*. The next day he received a letter redirected to him by Broadcasting House from a Captain William Hart Gregson, an estate manager and development consultant from Maldon in Essex. He introduced himself as the new owner of Borley Rectory.[53]

Fifty-nine-year-old Gregson had been born in Lancashire. His mother was a musician and his father had been the vicar of St Paul's in Rusland, Cumbria, for seventeen years. As a young man, Gregson had been apprenticed to an architectural firm in Lancaster – Walker, Carter and Walker – before moving to Essex to advance in his profession. In 1902, he had settled on Canvey Island and over the next twenty-five years was responsible for the design and building of many of the properties there.

During the First World War, Gregson, an army reservist, had served with the Royal Engineers as a lieutenant. He had a distinguished and traumatic war record, taking part in the Battle of the Somme. On 2 July, the second day of the campaign, the then 37-year-old Gregson had led a group of engineers who were tasked with supplying water to British frontline trenches. This was carried out over three weeks under heavy shell-fire by day and night. Gregson and his men completed the task, but two thirds of them were killed doing so.

In August, Gregson's company experienced a severe gas attack. Though Gregson managed to rouse his men, he had been unable to wear his own gas mask as he was calling out instructions to get them to safety. He inhaled a large quantity of gas and was ordered to go to hospital, but as there was no officer to relieve him, he carried on with his duties. Of soldiers that survived a gas attack without protection but who managed to reach a clearing station, 5 per cent would die within 48 hours. Gregson survived and was returned to the front after sixty days' convalescence.

During leave on the Channel Islands, Gregson met Rita Pattard, the daughter of a Guernsey farmer. They married in 1920 and lived on Canvey Island, where he continued to work as a developer and landlord, accumulating a large portfolio of private homes and commercial properties. By the mid-1920s, he was the largest single landowner on the island. As a homage to his wife, many of Gregson's bungalows were given French names such as Jethou, Sailly Laurette and Herm. Gregson and Rita had two sons, Alan in 1921 and Anthony in 1925, though the marriage didn't last and they divorced in 1934.

Gregson seemed to be a pillar of the establishment and had been promoted to captain in 1922, but while he was never known to use violence or bad language, he was not averse to nefarious dealings. In November 1923, he had appeared at the Essex assizes charged with fraudulently attempting to procure an entry in the Land Registry and with forging some title deeds. It was, the director of public prosecutions claimed, the first case of its kind among the 300,000 that had arisen since the Land Registry was inaugurated in 1875. Gregson had claimed the ownership of a triangular plot on the Starbrock Park Estate on Canvey Island, which was adjacent to some land that he had bought in 1916. Due to its potential for development, the plot had increased in value since the war. When the company who believed they owned the land began to develop it as an entertainment complex, they were challenged by Gregson, who submitted title deeds that showed the plot of land coloured in pink and belonging to him. The prosecution claimed that Gregson had fraudulently coloured in the plot on the title deeds. Gregson's defence referenced his war record and the fact that he had never been accused of such a crime before. The jury found him 'guilty of uttering' but without intent to defraud. Though he was released, the judge warned him that he had been 'pretty lucky'.[54]

Active in local politics, by 1935 Gregson had become an associate of Alexander Raven Thomson, who was policy director for Oswald Mosley's British Union of Fascists. Subsequently Gregson was appointed as the Union's political agent for the Maldon Division. On 15 May, engaging with the beleaguered farmers and angry rural workers who felt neglected by Westminster, Thomson held a two-hour meeting at the Institute Hall in Braintree, in an attempt to promote Fascism. Fascism, he promised, would restore British agriculture, with secure markets, higher wages and better conditions for farmworkers. Dealing 'very capably with interrupters', he explained that Fascism 'stood for Britain'.

On hearing Price's radio broadcast, Gregson wrote to him via the BBC. He was very interested in the rumours regarding the hauntings at the house, 'though without', he admitted, 'any particular degree of nervousness with regard to them'.[55] On visiting the Rectory, he had been most amused at the sightseers who had come in their cars to see the 'Haunted House'.[56] One man had been so persistent that Gregson had shown him around. By the time he got to the library he began to collapse 'because of the malevolent influence which he said existed just there'.[57] Gregson admitted that he didn't feel any such thing, but he liked to think that there was 'really something eerie. It adds a charm to the place.'[58] He informed Price that as it was no longer a church property, he had agreed with the ecclesiastical authorities to change the name of the Rectory to 'Borley Priory'.

Price wrote to Gregson immediately outlining the book he was working on and requesting his cooperation. He was particularly keen to establish if there was any truth in the persistent legend of the nunnery or monastery in the vicinity. 'I note that you are not nervous about living at the rectory. This is important. As a matter of fact, there is nothing to be nervous about. But the place is intensely interesting and, if I did not happen to live in the heart of Sussex, I would have purchased Borley myself as a sort of weekend place.'[59]

After the sale of the Rectory, the Arbons moved out of the Rectory Cottage to a house in Brook Hall Lane. As they waited for the dilapidated Rectory to be refurbished and redecorated, Gregson, his two sons and their dog moved into the cottage just in time for Christmas. Their furniture and most of their possessions were to be stored in boxes and packing cases in the Rectory hall until the work was completed and the property could be lived in again.

The February of 1939 proved to be the sunniest on record, with twenty-three days of sunshine. The prospects for March, though, looked to end the sunny spell as the weather was to be 'cold and unsettled'.[60] Around midnight on 27 February, his sons in bed in the cottage, Captain Gregson was alone in the hall at the Rectory, sorting through piles of books. Some of them were damp, so he had spread them out to air. About a hundred volumes were piled on a large board, supported by a small chest of drawers and a two-tier medicine cupboard. Perched just next to the books was a paraffin lamp.

Noticing an odd copy of *Chambers's Encyclopaedia* in one of the piles, Gregson went to extract it, but in doing so the stack of books collapsed, knocking over the lamp, which smashed on the floor, releasing the oil in its reservoir. Immediately there was a blaze. The burning oil quickly spread among the piles of books that were stored in the hall. Gregson rushed into the courtyard to get some water from the wheel pump, but with the hall already a mass of flames, he 'lost his head'. Rather than seek help from the neighbours, he raced into the cottage to rouse his sons, before getting into his car and dashing to the nearest fire station. From their bedroom across the road in Place Farm Cottage, the Pearsons shouted to draw attention to the fire, but nobody seemed to be about. Lionel Arbon said that the fire 'got a good hold before it was noticed'.[61] Pearson ran over to Borley Place to raise Basil Payne, who had a telephone and called Sudbury fire brigade at about 12.15 a.m.[62]

The intense flames rapidly taking hold of the building were as fierce as a blast furnace. The rooms overlooking the lawn burned ferociously, with tongues of fire streaming out of the windows as a column of flames and sparks shot up into the dark night air. The burning Rectory made a red glow in the winter sky visible for miles around. When the fire brigade arrived at 12.30 a.m., they found the vicinity around the Rectory 'as light as day' with the glare of the fire.[63] The ground-floor rooms and the bedrooms were alight, the staircase having also started to burn intensely. The firemen sourced water in the pond 50 yards from the house and began to pump it towards the building. But before they could take control of the fire, the roof collapsed and the inferno continued to devastate the house.[64]

Borley Rectory, March 1939

CHAPTER SIXTEEN

'THE MOST HAUNTED HOUSE IN ENGLAND'

28 February 1939–29 March 1948

I saw a blackened ruin. The lawn, the grounds were trodden
and waste: the portal yawned void. The front was, as I had
once seen it in a dream, but a well-like wall, very high and very
fragile-looking, perforated with paneless windows: no roof, no
battlements, no chimneys – all had crashed in. And there was
the silence of death about it.

Charlotte Brontë, *Jane Eyre*[1]

After about an hour and a quarter, the fire brigade managed to take
control of the flames. Having secured the site and cleared the debris,
they left at a quarter past eight the next morning. In the dawn light,
the Rectory stood a skeletal, singed and charred ruin.

Following its destruction, the press were swift to report the
demise of the notorious Borley Rectory: 'Most Haunted House on
Fire', 'Ghosts Burnt Out' and 'Rectory Ghost Goes West'. When
Harry Price was contacted by the *Telegraph* and the *Evening
Standard* for comment, he realised that the fire had taken place
eleven months to the day of the prediction that the Glanvilles had
been given at the seance in Streatham. 'Thus,' he observed gravely,
'was the prophecy, threat or promise of "Sunex Amures" ...
fulfilled!'[2]

Lionel Arbon wrote to Price from his new lodgings in Brook Hall Lane informing him that there was 'nothing left of it only brick walls and chimneys, the inside is burnt clean out'.[3] Clifford Henning also contacted Price, advising him that the Gregsons had experienced many odd things since they'd moved into the Rectory.[4]

One night, when going to use the water pump, Captain Gregson had heard footsteps in the courtyard. His cocker spaniel had gone mad and ran away; they hadn't seen the dog since.[5] He'd also placed a heavy board over the well in the cellar, only to find one morning that it had been inexplicably thrown aside. A glass of water left by his son in the hall overnight was found the next day smashed in pieces, but with no water surrounding it.[6] It was all very strange. A 'curious ending,' Price observed, 'to a curious tale.'[7]

The fire offered Price a fine dramatic climax to his book about the rectory. It was like the denouement of *Jane Eyre* or Daphne du Maurier's homage to Charlotte Brontë's Gothic classic *Rebecca*, which had been a bestseller the previous year. 'From start to finish,' Price enthused, 'it is an amazing story.'[8] Writing a letter of commiseration to Captain Gregson, Price hoped that he was fully insured. He also requested that he send a detailed account of how the fire had started and asked him to share any unusual incidents he had experienced at the Rectory – 'for inclusion in the final chapter of my book'.[9] He was extremely keen to have a photograph of the ruins, 'showing the most damaged portions',[10] and was willing to pay for it: 'no history of the Rectory would be complete without a picture of the damage'.[11] Gregson responded that 'all our stuff was in the Rectory and has been destroyed'.[12] He confirmed the strange occurrences since he and his sons had taken up residence: 'we have had family arguments as to who had been "messing about", but generally without coming to any satisfactory conclusion'.[13]

Gregson confided in Price that on the night of the fire, at 4 o'clock in the morning, a police constable had asked him who the cloaked lady and gentleman were who had just preceded him, passing through the courtyard. But there had been no such couple on the premises. Raised from their beds by the fire, some startled villagers claimed to have seen ghostly figures through the window of the Blue Room, now smashed and alight. It was the ghosts, some said, who had brought an end to the Rectory. Crowds of sightseers once again descended on the burned-out shell. The whole upper portion of the house now unsafe, Gregson had 'KEEP OUT' notices erected, warning visitors that they entered the building at their own risk. But Price was relieved to hear that Gregson's long-term plan was to rebuild the Rectory, with a few minor adjustments. 'I like the place,' Price admitted, 'and as now it has become historical, it would be a pity not to restore it.'[14]

As the drama of the fire subsided, the incident was investigated by three insurance companies. It appeared that Captain Gregson had raised a mortgage of £600 to buy the house and the garden surrounding it, paying £500 to the ecclesiastical authorities. He had subsequently insured the property for £10,000. He now submitted a claim for 'accidental loss by fire' of £7,356. His insurers, having investigated 20,000 similar claims, were immediately suspicious.

A chest of drawers, which Gregson claimed had been full of his expensive underwear, had survived the fire. Though the exterior had been carbonised by the flames, tightly packed, the underwear inside was only lightly singed. When inspected by the loss adjuster Colonel Cuthbert Buckle, the underwear was found to be of the poorest quality – 'darned, worn-out and fit only for the rag-bag'.[15] Gregson also claimed to have lost a prized collection of ancient coins in the fire. Suspecting that he had started the fire himself, the salvage team passed all the relevant debris through quarter-inch metal sieves. All they recovered was a single Victorian farthing. Updating Price about Gregson's insurance claim that was now in dispute, Clifford Henning reluctantly concluded that the apparently upstanding captain had been revealed to be 'rather a bad egg'.[16] In a sad humiliation, the Rectory that had been built with all the confident bombast of imperial Britain had been destroyed, not by malevolent ghosts or destructive poltergeists, but at the hands of a fascist chancing his luck.

A compelling ending to *The Most Haunted House in England* now secure, Price set about assembling the testimony of the key witnesses. On 28 March, he travelled to Borley with Sidney Glanville. Calling at Arthur Hall, they interviewed Florence Whitehouse, who was now widowed, Sir George having died the previous year. She told Price that she had known the Rectory and the various rectors – and their families who had lived there – for many years and had not the slightest doubt that it was haunted. She had witnessed the 'most astonishing happenings – happenings that could only have been produced by supernatural means'.[17] Bottles had flown across the room, stones were thrown, pencilled messages were scribbled on scraps of paper, bells rang – and then there was the occasion they found the skirting board of a locked and empty room on fire. She considered the Foysters 'quite the bravest couple' she had ever known and readily agreed to write up her testimony for Price.

On the trip to Borley, Price and Glanville interviewed the Bulls at Chilton Lodge. While at Great Cornard, accompanied by Clifford Henning, Price visited the Coopers to take notes about their experiences in the Rectory Cottage. Henning also advised Price to speak to Herbert Mayes, his chauffeur-cum-gardener, who'd had a strange experience very recently – since the Rectory had burned down.

A fortnight or so before, Mayes was cycling up the hill in the dark towards the church, about 9 p.m. He had reached the Rectory gate when he suddenly heard horses' hooves coming towards him. At first he thought it was a loose horse from one of the farmers' fields nearby. As the lane was so narrow, he leaned with his bicycle into the hedge. He could hear the horses approaching – about four of them, he imagined – from the direction of Borley Green, but he couldn't see anything. He swung his bike round into the road, to get a better look, but nothing passed him. All he could hear was the noise of the hooves as they gradually faded away down the hill. Though the Rectory was gone, it seemed that the ghosts continued to haunt the village.

Lady Whitehouse had given Price her nephew's address in order for him to request that Edwin write a contribution to the book.

Since leaving Sudbury, in 1931, Edwin had suffered a severe nervous breakdown before finally taking holy orders, and was now living at St Augustine's Abbey in Ramsgate. Having adopted a new Christian name, he was now a Benedictine monk, Dom Richard Whitehouse. He'd had some correspondence with Marianne Foyster in Ipswich, who, he felt, was aggrieved with Price as his comments in the press about the Rectory had given her a 'great deal of unneeded pain and annoyance'.[18] He was happy to offer an account of his time at Borley with the condition that it was not altered or edited without his permission. He would send a copy of his version of events to Marianne to verify and to cut anything that she felt should be omitted.

The demise of the Rectory had also given it fresh currency in the media, so Captain Gregson began to consider how he might turn this to his advantage as he was planning to develop the place into a tourist attraction, running guided coach trips from Sudbury in the summer. When he appeared on the BBC's radio programme *In Town Tonight* on 15 April, he used the broadcast as an opportunity to set the spooky scene and to suggest to listeners – and potential customers – that there were still strange happenings to be experienced at Borley: 'It's so dark and cold, and the oppressive atmosphere everywhere never fails to make your flesh creep.'[19] He told the story of his dog – terrified of strange footsteps at the Rectory and then running away, never to be seen again. He recounted the discovery of some imprints he had come across one morning in the snow on the lawn – almost formless, yet quite distinct. He had wondered if there had been a trespasser during the night until he realised that the prints could not have been made by a human foot – nor by any animal known to him.[20] He went on to mention the strange ghostly figures seen on the night the house was burned to the ground. Despite the scepticism of the locals, Gregson was convinced that 'all of them believe there is something queer about the old place'.[21]

The next week, Price gave a lecture about Borley to the Ghost Club, of which he was chairman, at a dinner held at the Overseas Club. In 'Ten Years Investigation of Borley Rectory', clearly a teaser for the book he was writing, he recounted the story of his own relationship with the house – the phantom nun, her escape in the coach and her tragic fate, bricked up alive in the convent.[22] He illustrated his talk with thirty-five slides showing the Rectory before and after the fire, the latter courtesy of Captain Gregson. As well as the Borley legend, he discussed more recent phenomena such as Marianne's black eye and bricks being thrown through the air. Finally, he outlined the inferno that had left the Rectory a shattered ruin. The affair of the Suffolk Rectory, Price concluded, was remarkable, being 'the best authenticated and documented record in my case book. Most ghost stories usually stand or fall upon the evidence of a very few people – often only one or two. But I could produce fifty persons who would swear to having seen or heard, at the Rectory, things which, in our ignorance, we are pleased to call "supernormal". And that is why the place has been called, very appropriately, "the most haunted house in England".'[23]

Price used his talk as an opportunity to invite Ghost Club members to a 'Psychic Fete' which was to take place in the grounds of the Rectory in the summer. Like Captain Gregson, Clifford Henning was also keen to exploit the renewed interest in the Rectory to raise funds for the church. There would even be, he hoped, a tantalising procession of 'historical ghosts'.[24]

Reported in *The Times*, Price's lecture instigated a wry correspondence with the barrister Letitia Fairchild, who had been one of the first qualified female doctors in Britain. She feared that the 'unscrupulous phantoms' had been pulling Price's leg – it being unthinkable, she protested, that Price 'has been pulling ours'. The presence of a convent – and the nun – indicated that the story must have taken place *before* the Reformation. Yet coaches were unknown in England until after 1550. The bricking-up of individuals as punishment had long been proved to be mythical. The doomed monk and the nun, she concluded, 'seem to have been singularly ill-fitted for the religious life'.[25] Price tartly responded that *he* did not believe in spirits, *nor* did he believe in the legend. On the contrary, he protested, his address to the Ghost Club had opened with the remarks that the Borley Mystery was the 'most remarkable *alleged* "haunting" in the annals of psychical research'.[26] He could not resist another plug for his forthcoming book.

In May, Price wrote to Eric Smith at Sevington informing him that at long last he was writing about Borley and was collecting the testimony of those involved. Even since the recent arrival of the new owner, Captain Gregson, 'some extraordinary things have been happening'.[27] He asked if Smith and his wife would write a long enough statement with 'as many details as possible'[28] of what had transpired during their time at the Rectory – 'enough to form a chapter in a book'.[29] Price suggested that he should send the notes that Glanville had made from his visit to the Smiths for their approval. Reverend Smith replied that the experiences that he and his wife had shared with Glanville had not been for publication but were strictly confidential. Borley was now a 'distasteful memory' to them. He insisted that they had deserted the Rectory because of the poor sanitation, not because it was haunted. Despite their previous correspondence, Smith now claimed that 'we really did not believe there were any such things as ghosts!'[30] He insisted that Price omit any reference to them whatsoever in his book. Price was bemused by the Smiths' change of heart – he had letters from them clearly stating that they had believed in the ghosts – but was also peeved at how this new attitude might affect his book. He insisted that it would be impossible not to mention them. It was, after all, Smith and his wife who had alerted both the press and Price himself to the phenomena at the Rectory in the first place. It was their testimony that had caused the furore at Borley, which was now established as a matter of public record. Also, had not Smith *repeatedly* suggested that Price produce such a report? He did agree, however, that he'd be careful not to say that the Smiths believed in ghosts.

Posters and flyers announced that the 'Psychic Fete' was to open at 2.30 p.m. on 21 June, with the traditional sideshows and teas. But the focus of the event would be the Rectory, advertised as the 'Most Haunted House in England', which would be available for conducted tours. The appellation of the house was now established,

with Price's encouragement, as a brand. The fete was to be opened
by the wife of Rab Butler, the Under-Secretary of State for Foreign
Affairs. Ahead of the event, the *Daily Herald* interviewed some of
the villagers: 'everybody I speak to in Borley,' journalist A. B. Austin
wrote, 'says it is all along of a "black man", an Indian parson who
came to the Rectory a good many years ago and spread tales'.[31]

On the afternoon of the fete, the longest day of the year, members
of the Ghost Club drove through 'miles of Britain's spookiest countryside' to see the places that Price had described in his lecture. Price
attended with his secretary, now known by her married name, Ethel
English.[32] This was the first time she'd visited the house. 'The village people and their friends came out in full force to their modest
fete and enjoyed the music from the loud speaker van, the coconut
shy, the haunted rooms, the tea and the sideshows, including the
visit of the Ghost Club.'[33] Captain Gregson and his two sons conducted tours of the building. The visitors, the Ghost Club and the
press were disappointed as Price's promised 'procession of ghosts'
was aborted after Henning advised that it wouldn't be particularly
spooky in broad daylight.[34] *The Times* lamented that 'no ghosts
were seen. No bricks were hurled at visitors, and no one received
a black eye'.[35] Captain Gregson's seventeen-year-old son, Alan,
insisted that 'you just cannot explain these things ... but if you wish
to get in touch with the spirits you must go about the business with
understanding. Idle curiosity displeases them.'[36] Also attending the
fete was the Foysters' former daily woman, Mrs Pearson, who dismissed the notion of the Rectory being haunted: 'I have lived in my
cottage for eighteen years and never a ghost have I seen yet. I don't
believe a word of it.'[37]

Henning was pleased with the £24 that the fete had raised,
though half of that would cover expenses. Price felt that it had been
a very pleasant day out. But with the loss of the Rectory and the
declining international situation, he could not help wondering, as
he stood in the shelter of the summer house and watched the festivities – English eccentrics in pursuit of ghosts – if this might be his

last visit to the sleepy Essex hamlet. For England itself was under threat, poised for attack.

In 1937, British experts had estimated that a war with Germany would start with immediate bombing raids that would last for sixty days. With no real idea of what a modern air war between two major European powers would be like, beyond reports from Spain and China, experts based their predictions on misleading figures from 1917–18. It was assumed that each ton of high explosive dropped would result in fifty casualties. 'The bomber will always get through,'[38] Stanley Baldwin had warned darkly in 1932. 'I think it is well for the man in the street to realise that there is no power on earth that can protect him from being bombed.'[39] Forecasts predicted that 1,000,000 people would be killed and twice as many wounded; 1,000,000 coffins were ordered. The prospects of the coming war – and the scale of death – were terrifying. With the invasion of Poland on 1 September 1939, the blackout was initiated across the country. When war was finally declared, two days later, the prime minister addressed the nation: 'It is the evil things we shall be fighting against – brute force, bad faith, injustice, oppression, and persecution – and against them I am certain that right will prevail.'[40] In America, *Life* magazine stated that the 'Second Armageddon' was on.[41]

Throughout September, there were mass movements across the country that affected a quarter to a third of the population, with children and the vulnerable evacuated to rural areas. Refugees continued to arrive from the Continent. As poison gas aimed at civilians was thought to be a very real threat – 44 million gas masks were issued. Public shelters and mass-produced Anderson shelters for gardens and backyards had been erected since 1938. On 8 September *The Times* reported that millions of pets had been put down over the previous two weeks. In London alone, 400,000 pets were euthanised in the first four days of war. This mass extermination of domestic animals would prove to be misguided. Many areas became infested with mice and by Christmas, kittens were exchanging hands for extraordinary sums. By the New Year, 1.5 million air raid wardens had been enrolled and 1.5 million men had been conscripted. As German bombers now targeted Britain, and the nation primed itself for apocalyptic devastation, in rural West Sussex, Harry Price edited his story of the uncertain and the unknown, of fear and ghosts in a Victorian rectory situated at the heart of an ancient English village.

Having submitted the manuscript to Longmans, Green and Co., Price was impatient for his book to reach the public. Because of the wartime paper shortage, the income from his day job as a paper salesman had been badly affected. With Norway occupied by the Germans, wood pulp for making paper was in short supply. Paper was rationed from 1939, with newspapers restricted to 50 per cent of their pre-war size.[42] Wrapping for most goods, the core of Price's business, was prohibited. The wartime shortage of labour and materials affected publishing, too. As well as the scarcity of paper, binding books became particularly challenging, making the publication of new titles a protracted process. Following a direct hit at Longmans's new office and warehouse in the city, the company also had to find new premises, further delaying the publication of the book until the summer of 1940.

'The Most Haunted House in England': Ten Years' Investigation of Borley Rectory was published in August, priced at ten shillings and six pence, with a distinctive black-and-blue dust jacket depicting the shell of the Rectory after the fire. Ever the conjuror, with the subtlest sleight of hand, on the first page Price had added quotation marks to his title, suggesting that the story was true – it was indeed the most haunted house in England – but that he, assuming the role of the 'dispassionate narrator', remained sceptical.[43] As in his attitude to supernatural phenomena throughout his long career, Price seemed to declare that his position on Borley Rectory was ambivalent.

From the first line of the preface, he was at pains to stress that he had 'done little more than edit the remarkable records that constitute the major portion of this monograph'.[44] He had reproduced 'verbatim the oral and written testimony which, in nearly every case, is first hand'.[45] He was a mere recorder of the evidence. The integrity of his contributors seemed to be exemplary: the diary of an Anglican clergyman contemporary with the phenomena,[46] the first-hand reports of a journalist from a national newspaper, the experiences of a knight of the realm and his wife, the testimony of a Benedictine monk. At the same time, he had presented the reports of the various (male and middle-class) soldiers, doctors, Cambridge undergraduates, BBC producers and enthusiastic amateurs who had taken part in his year-long investigation of the Rectory. The book certainly appeared to be a scientific – perhaps bordering on exhaustive – study of the evidence, with footnotes, photographs, appendices and a chronology of events. He even included architectural ground plans of the house so that the reader could pinpoint exactly where particular events took place, just like the contemporary whodunnits of Agatha Christie and Dorothy L. Sayers. From the credibility of the contributors to the graphics, the bibliophile Price had created a book the very appearance of which seemed to exude authority.

Having presented the evidence, at the end of *The Most Haunted House in England*, Price steps back, as if in a courtroom, addressing the readers as a jury. 'Readers of this monograph are now in possession of all the evidence I have accumulated for the alleged haunting of Borley Rectory, and it is for them to decide – as the jury – whether in fact the place *is* haunted or not. It is all a question of evidence.'[47] He wonders if all the witnesses he has consulted could be mad, lying or hallucinating? 'Is Borley haunted, or is it not?'[48] he asks. 'My answer to my own question is "Yes, decidedly!"'[49] The 'dispassionate narrator' that Price had appeared to be at the start, was, in the end, no sceptic at all.

The book was reviewed enthusiastically as exciting, thrilling and creepy. Despite the competition, *Time & Tide* thought it 'among the events of the year 1940'.[50] *The Tatler* announced that it was 'just about the most convincing account of a Poltergeist' the reviewer had ever read and was 'one of the most extraordinary stories imaginable'.[51] 'A title like *The Most Haunted House in England*', the

Aberdeen Press said, 'suggests a thriller. That it certainly is, but it has the advantage over most thrillers that it is no work of fiction. It deals with facts, with actual happenings, and the most weird happenings at that.'[52] One reviewer thought the remains of the Rectory should be saved 'as a national monument – a tribute to a spirit of scientific enquiry which can brave the most eerie terrors of the supernatural in order to arrive at a particle of truth.' *Notes and Queries* declared that it was 'a model of what such a record should be'. However, a minority voice, V. S. Pritchett in *The Bystander,* was unconvinced:

> Trickery? Mystery? Projections from the unconscious mind of someone in the house or of some collective unconscious? Science inclines to the psychological theory nowadays. The amount of data is large. One can only note a dissatisfaction with some of the checks on observation, the unfortunate influence of wishful thinking ... Looking at the timetable one notes that the more investigation, the more phenomena. For the credulous and the curious this book provides a thrill; for the detached, there is sometimes an unconscious humour.[53]

For some reviewers, Price's study was the perfect distraction from the stresses of the bombing raids. The *Daily Telegraph* described the book as an 'Antidote to Blitzkrieg':[54] 'Mr Price, his official observers and various rectors and their wives showed a coolness and intrepidity which must impress even a bomb-conscious reader.'[55] None of the reviews appeared to consider that the book might also be an expression of the time it was written in, preoccupied as it was with mortality and a yearning for a confirmation of life beyond the grave as the nation faced invasion. The book sold out quickly, but soon became additionally scarce as Longmans's warehouse was destroyed – a second time – by enemy action. As it couldn't be reprinted because of paper rationing, the book went out of print. High prices were soon being offered for second-hand copies in the personals columns of *The Times*.

On 14 August, a broken Mabel Smith wrote to Price on black-edged mourning paper informing him that after months suffering with lung trouble, her husband had died of tuberculosis. They had been corresponding since she and her husband had retired to Sheringham in Norfolk. She reminded Price of the novel she had written, based on their experiences at Borley, *Murder at the Parsonage*, a title she continued to delight in 'because [she'd] found the head in the cupboard'. But she dismissed her book as 'sheer fiction', as 'a deeper kind of literature' appealed to her.[56] Had she really believed in ghosts, she declared, she could never have remained in the house. But worried, as ever, about money, she did wonder if a successful novel might earn her sufficient funds to buy her husband a 'nice [head]stone'.[57] She wondered if, with Price's help, it might be published one day as an 'entertaining novel conjured up by a resi-dent of Borley'.[58] One of the characters, a doctor, was even based on Price. She wondered if it were ever filmed, whether he might play himself.[59]

Price replied that he would be happy to read her novel, so she sent him fifteen pages, hoping that he might think it could be a bestseller in the wake of the success of his own book. Despite her experience in self-publishing, she exhibited a certain naivety in her expectations of a swift publication and even suggested that it might be advertised as a sequel to *The Most Haunted House in England*: 'If [you think it's] any good we could discuss something very mys-tifying for a picture on the cover.'[60] By the end of September, Price had sent her copies of his book, which she congratulated him on as 'wonderful ... how you pieced it all together puzzles me'.[61] She continued to work in earnest on *Murder at the Parsonage* and was keen for him to read a further draft and give her notes. After the death of her husband she had become depressed and anxious about her finances and the process of probate, which had been protracted due to wartime conditions and the fact that some of his affairs were being dealt with in India. Her writing was very much a distraction from her gnawing sense of loss. 'I miss Eric so much,' she wrote, 'that I do not think I shall ever be happy again.'[62]

On 18 October, Cyril Joad, head of philosophy at Birkbeck College, a member of the Ghost Club and regular panellist of the BBC's programme *The Brains Trust*, reviewed Price's book in *The Spectator*.

> Thank God, I say, for ghosts! I do not mean merely that the intangible terrors of haunting are a welcome change after the all-too-tangible terrors of bombing, or even that the craziest poltergeist comes to one with a refreshing appearance of sanity after the craziness of war. I mean also, what a mercy that there should still be a little mystery! The world has never been so trite. All the legends are exploded, nobody even claims to see fairies, while Father Christmas, the presents distributed, visibly doffs his beard and takes his seat at the dinner table. Hence a generation grows up with nothing to revere and precious little to wonder at. It travels 'over the hills and far away' only to find a Woolworth's store on the other side.[63]

Joad was an associate of Price and had actually visited the Rectory as one of his official observers, so was hardly an objective reviewer. He noted that Price hadn't attempted to explain the happenings at Borley, merely to record them. He praised him for telling a fantastic story to distract the anxious reader from the privation of rationing, the absence of loved ones and the threat from the skies. 'Thank God for ghosts and thank God also for Mr Price. Granted that you want to forget the war, I do not know a better book; granted that an account of Borley was worth doing, I do not see how it could have been better done.[64]

It was not only reviewers who were impressed by the book, but also some of the most experienced legal minds of the day. In the *Law Times* on 9 August, Sir Ernest Jelf, Senior Master of the Supreme Court, wrote that *The Most Haunted House in England* was 'one of the most remarkable books of marvels, put forward as being literally true, which has ever been published'.[65] Sir Albion Richardson, Recorder for Nottingham, concurred: Borley stood 'by itself in the literature of psychical manifestation'.[66] Richardson's legal colleagues, previously sceptical as regards paranormal activity, were now completely convinced that Price had proved the authenticity of the phenomena at Borley 'to the point of moral certainty'.[67]

Price started to receive many communications from readers who had been beguiled by the Borley story. In October, he had a letter from a Mrs Cecil Ryan Baines of Oxford, who had a great interest in Roman Catholic history and suggested that the seance in which 'Marie Lairre' communicated had the 'ring of truth'. After the Restoration of the monarchy in 1660, she explained, Charles II had relaxed the laws against Catholics, which might account for the presence of a nun in Borley in 1667. A devout Catholic herself, Mrs Baines wondered, like many other correspondents, why a Mass had not been said for the tragic nun?

In the New Year of 1941, Price had a letter from William John Phythian-Adams, Canon of Carlisle Cathedral and Chaplain to the King, who had also become fascinated by the story. Over Christmas, he had been in bed with flu. As he was recuperating, he'd read Price's book, which his wife, Adela, had borrowed from the library. Using his unexpected time off, he began to examine the wall-writings that appeared in the text, as well as the transcripts of the seances, in an effort to 'diagnose the trouble at Borley Rectory'.[68] He was convinced that the focus of the haunt 'would seem to be a crime of a peculiarly distressing nature, which has "impregnated" the spot with the thoughts (and some of the actions) of the victims; and the stirring up of the ground by the building of the new Rectory [in 1863] and the presence in it of its living occupants [had] combined to release a new and powerful outpouring of this inexplicable psychic energy'.[69]

Piecing together the clues, Phythian-Adams argued that the inspiration for the haunt was the 'peculiarly atrocious murder' of a young novice from a French convent.[70] This was the reason for the Roman Catholic flavour of much of the phenomena and the appeals for a requiem Mass to be held. The nineteen-year-old Marie Lairre from Le Havre had been tricked into marriage by a member of the ancient Waldegrave family and brought to Borley as his wife. But he had subsequently deserted, then strangled her on 17 May 1667, dumping her body in the well, these details being revealed in the planchette seances. The young novice's skull may have been that which had been discovered by Mabel Smith in the library when they first took possession of the house. Phythian-Adams concluded that Marianne Foyster, herself a French-speaking Canadian, 'was a strong "Poltergeist-focus" and that she was responsible (of course, unconsciously) for the violence of the phenomena during her residence at the Rectory'.[71]

Inspired by this startling solution, Price resolved to investigate the cellars at the Rectory in order to establish Marie Lairre's resting place. Had not 'Sunex Amures' prophesised that they would find the nun's bones 'under the ruins' of the Rectory? This would require excavating a fairly large area, including two filled-in wells, which would necessitate an expensive well-draining engine and suction plant from London to remove the debris. Price contacted Clifford Henning with a view to gaining permission from Captain Gregson to investigate the Rectory cellars.

But Henning advised him that because of conscription and the needs of the Home Guard, there were no labourers currently available to work on the excavations. He couldn't even secure somebody to cut the grass in the churchyard. Consequently, Price temporarily shelved his plan to work on the cellars and focused on completing his autobiography, *Search for Truth*, which would include his personal history as well as his most famous cases.

While the war was raging, numerous visitors claimed to experience phenomena in the ruins of the Rectory. Dr Andrew J. B. Robertson was a young chemist from Cambridge University with an interest in psychic phenomena. He'd first visited the Rectory shortly after the fire in 1939. In 1941, he organised a rota of observers, mostly undergraduates from St John's College, Cambridge, to observe activity at the Rectory site in a scientific manner. Known as the Cambridge Commission, a total of fifty-eight students would make twenty-five visits between 1941 and 1944, monitoring changes in temperature and documenting unusual noises, which included the sound of footsteps, knocking, ticking and whistling sounds. They also observed white shapes and strange lights.

In 1942, a woman who lived in a cottage near the Rectory, Mrs Savage, claimed to hear 'queer sounds that couldn't be made by man or beast, nor wind nor decay'.[72] The Air Raid Precautions warden had seen lights in the area and accused Mrs Savage of breaking the blackout until she explained to him that the Rectory was rumoured to be haunted. 'I never did believe in ghosts until I came here,' she told an American journalist, 'but there is certainly something strange about the Rectory. The only thing that surprises me is that they do no harm to people. They want to be left alone, poor lonely things. Each and every one of them seems to tell us humans to mind our own business.'[73] But such was the appetite for stories about the Rectory that, even in wartime, the ghosts were not allowed to rest in peace. In August 1943, Price wrote another article about the Rectory in *Everybody's Weekly*. Shortly afterwards, he received a letter from a Lieutenant G. B. Nawrocki, a doctor attached to the Polish Army Medical Corps who had a keen interest in psychical research. Nawrocki told Price that between 28–29 June and 28–29 July, he had stayed in the Rectory grounds with three other Polish officers and two Englishmen. They investigated the whole ruin, from the cellar to the roof. They claimed to have seen a black shadow in the garden as well as the shadow of a man in the house. 'I am quite sure,' Nawrocki told Price, 'that I twice saw the shadow on the nun's walk, and once a shadow of a man in Room No. 3.'[74] They also noted scratching noises, dull thumps and doors slamming, and witnessed as many as thirty stones being thrown in the Blue Room. Price noted that 28 July was also the anniversary of the appearance of the nun to the Bull sisters in the summer of 1900.

Captain Gregson asked Price if he'd be interested in buying the Rectory ruins as a memorial to psychical research, as he was planning to move to British Columbia with his sons when the war was over. Gregson was asking £1,100 for it, but he hastily added that

he'd consider a 'reasonable offer'. Price didn't feel able to buy it himself as he lived too far away and wouldn't be able to look after it.
But he agreed that it should not be lost to posterity. Gregson assured
Price that if he could help him find a suitable buyer, he'd agree to a
'rattling good [commission]' – as much as £50.[75] Perhaps some 'real
keen Yank psychist' might be interested? But the war had put paid
to any such interest from American buyers.

In 1942, Longmans had asked Price to write a sequel to *The
Most Haunted House in England*, and he had begun to plan a new
book to appear when the war was over. As well as an update of the
original text, inspired by Phythian-Adams's theories, the core of the
new book would be the investigation of the murder of the 'Borley
nun'. So, in 1943, Price decided to proceed with his investigation of
the cellars, which would provide fresh material for his new book.
Henning offered the services of his elderly gardener, Jackson, to
do the digging ('rather old but very active with his spade').[76] He
even volunteered to assist with the physical work himself. Price
protested that he, unfortunately, would not be able to help because
of a 'long-standing strained heart'. With wartime accommodation
prioritised for military personnel, The Bull at Long Melford was
full, so the Hennings invited Price and his secretary, Ethel English,
to lodge with them at Liston Rectory and to make it their headquarters. Henning thought Price ought to be able to hire a car in Long
Melford, so long as there was no change in the petrol ration.[77]

Before the excavation of the cellars at the Rectory, Price planned
to locate the entrance to the crypt of Borley Church to investigate
the Waldegrave tombs within it. These, it was said, were known
to move paranormally. So, at 9 a.m. on the morning of 17 August,
Price and Ethel English, Reverend and Mrs Henning, and Captain
Gregson met a team of masons from Sudbury inside the church.
Having surveyed the building, the head mason suggested that the
opening to the crypt must lie under a slab of stone in the central
aisle. At 5 feet long, 3 feet wide and 6 inches thick, the slab weighed
nearly a ton. The masons erected a tripod and pulleys, and gradually raised the heavy stone from the floor. Though it didn't reveal

the entrance to the crypt, or access to the Waldegrave tomb, it did reveal the ancient history of the church. As the slab was raised from its bed of sand, it became clear that it had been buried with its ornamentation face down. This was the base of the pre-Reformation altar that had been secreted away for the past 400 years.

Proceeding across the road to the Rectory with a team led by Jackson, and Ethel English to take notes, Price was dismayed by the state of the building that had once confronted him with such power. Time and storms had devastated the shell of the house. The brick gables at the front and rear had fallen to the ground. What remained of the glass-and-iron veranda had been stolen and the place where the glasshouse once stood had been overtaken by vigorous under-growth, already climbing up the walls. The pinnacle tower to the front of the building, so distinctive in its day when topped with once-fashionable ironwork, had collapsed. Shrubs had opportunistically taken over the exposed, windowless ground-floor rooms. The cellars were jammed with burned flooring, rafters and the remains of the staircases from the floors above. Once dark, the cellars now were exposed to the full heat of the summer sun. The only parts of the building to survive the gales were the chimney stacks.

With Price supervising, 'slow but steady' Jackson spent two and a half hours emptying the debris from one of the wells in the cellar, which was full of broken glass, tiles, bricks and empty wine bottles. Among the rubbish was a brass preserving pan and a silver Victorian milk jug. Jackson then started to break up the cellar floor with a pickaxe. At 1.45 p.m, he uncovered some bones, which he presumed belonged to a pig. But these were immediately identified by Dr Eric Bailey, who had been invited by Price to attend the dig, as the left jawbone of a woman and the left side of a skull.

That night, over dinner at Liston Rectory, the Hennings, Price and Mrs English discussed the day's discoveries. Price felt that it was almost certain that at one point a complete skeleton had been buried on the site and that, when digging the foundations of the Rectory in 1862, Thomas Farrow's builders had disturbed and scattered the remains. Perhaps other parts of the skeleton were still to be found. Further digging the next day revealed a Catholic medallion with an image of the Virgin Mary crushing the head of a serpent under her feet. With the excavations successful, before Price left Borley, Captain Gregson presented him with a souvenir of his fourteen-year association with the Rectory: the bronze bell that had stood high above the courtyard. 'No question,' he assured Price, of making it a commercial transaction.'

Returning to London the following day, Price took the bones they had unearthed to be investigated by Leslie Godden, a 'West End dental surgeon of repute'[78] and fellow member of the Ghost Club. Dr Godden X-rayed the remains and deduced that they were over 100 years old. He could not be sure of the sex of the owner of the fragment of skull, but suggested that the jawbone belonged to a woman of about thirty who had suffered from a deep-seated abscess in the jaw. Being near the mandibular nerve, this would have caused a great deal of pain. Finally returning home to Pulborough, Price hung the bell from the Rectory courtyard above his studio in the garden at Arun Bank. He would see this last surviving relic of the Rectory every day for the rest of his life. Bringing the story of 'Marie Lairre' to a close, on 29 October, Father Wright of St Philip Neri's Roman Catholic church in Arundel[79] wrote to Price to say that he was holding a Requiem Mass for the soul of the Borley nun the next day.

Once the pride of Henry Dawson Bull, a High Victorian, up-to-the-minute modern building echoing with the busy sounds of many servants and a large, high-spirited family, the Rectory had proved too isolated, too large and too awkward for sleek, compact twentieth-century life. In 1943, the Rectory ruins were bought from Captain Gregson by a contractor called Woods for a bargain £560. Early in the New Year of 1944, Woods began to demolish it. As wartime conditions had made building materials scarce, he salvaged anything that might have value; the rest would be sold as building rubble.

On 5 April, Price drove to Borley with the photographer David Scherman and researcher Cynthia Ledsham from *Life* magazine, who were keen to take some photographs of the last days of the Rectory as part of a feature about haunted England. When they arrived, they were shocked to find the building in the process of being razed to the ground. Only the back portion of the house was still standing. 'The wreckage of this large – if ugly – Rectory was,' Price lamented, 'pathetic to behold.'[80]

In order to take a picture encompassing all the ruins, Price suggested that the journalists stand by his side, at least 100 feet from the house. A workman was throwing bricks as Scherman released the shutter from his American camera. When a brick suddenly shot up about 4 feet in front of what remained of the kitchen passage, Cynthia Ledsham laughed, 'Look, poltergeists!' Price walked over and picked up the brick and said, with a large smile, 'Yes, indeed; look; no strings, no wires attached!'[81]

The slates from the roof of the Rectory, and the distinctive red bricks with which Thomas Farrow had constructed the walls just eighty-two years earlier, were salvaged. But much of the material from the site was crushed into hardcore and used to build concrete runways at American airbases nearby that had been established as part of the air war against Nazi Germany. Mr Woods divided the cleared grounds into two building lots, a 5-acre site comprising the orchard and the lower part of the garden, and an upper lot that included the site of the building itself. The summer house would be demolished and the Nun's Walk built over. Few relics of the Rectory survived. The inlaid Italian marble mantelpiece with the monks' heads, sourced by John Johnson from the Great Exhibition of 1851, had been carefully removed and put to one side. But the next day it was found smashed to pieces, more likely the result of mischievous local lads than poltergeists. Now empty, the site was exposed to the winds from the Stour Valley, haunted by fragments of the past from a lost, pre-war world: Price's first journey to Borley with Lucie Kaye, their lunch with Eric and Mabel Smith, the seance with the Bull sisters, his association with the Foysters, his accusation of Marianne, and his volunteer investigators – particularly Sidney Glanville and Mark Kerr-Pearse. With nothing now remaining of the most haunted house in England, the sad demise of Borley Rectory marked the end of one of the most significant relationships in Harry Price's life. 'Well,' he sighed, 'I have lost an old friend.'[82]

Price was disappointed with how few copies of *The Most Haunted House in England* had been produced and how quickly it had gone out of print. He complained to the publisher R. G. Longman, that he didn't expect to make money out of his books, but he did hope to cover his expenses; he'd received less than £200 to date. 'It seems a pity,' he complained, 'that a book on the most important case I have ever handled, and the most important case in the annals of psychical research, should have reimbursed me so inadequately.'[83] Consequently, in September he met J. H. H. Gaute, a commissioning editor with publisher George Harrap, to discuss a second Borley book. Gaute enthused that 'the full story is going to make a fascinating book which will take everyone's mind completely away from the war'.[84] Price was offered an advance of £500, substantially more than the £75 he'd been paid by Longmans for *The Most Haunted House in England*.

After the news of Hitler's suicide in Berlin on 30 April 1945, the war in Europe came to an exhausted end. The *Daily News* reported of 'Ghost Walks', a parade of the defeated, the homeless and the liberated as a mass of humanity moved west across Europe, including skeletal figures 'from the horror camps ... unmistakable in [their] weird, striped prison garb'.[85] After the celebrations for VE Day, Price was once again welcomed by the Hennings as a guest at Liston Rectory in order to lay to rest the remains of 'Marie Lairre', the Borley nun.

While Price was staying at Liston, Annette Henning told him about a successful talk that she'd given about Borley at the Cambridge Women's Luncheon Club the month before. The talk had been attended by Alfred Bull, who informed her after the lecture that, coincidentally, his cousin Lionel had died earlier that day at Rendlesham, a few miles from Woodbridge in Suffolk. Price was saddened. With Eric Smith and Lionel Foyster now both gone, only their wives remained as witnesses to the extraordinary events at Borley.

The evening of 29 May was glorious, with the sun pouring into Liston churchyard. Earlier that day, the sexton had dug a small hole to bury the casket made of cedar wood that held the remains that had been discovered in the Rectory cellar. The simple ceremony was led by Clifford Henning and attended by his wife and Price, a photographer – of course – recording the historic moment for inclusion in Price's new book. As some puzzled village children watched the burial, 'Marie Lairre' was laid to rest as another chapter in the strange saga of Borley came to an end.

On 28 September the *Church Times* dedicated its editorial column to a review of Price's *Poltergeist Over England*, a study of historical poltergeist cases that included a chapter about Borley. In the next issue of the newspaper, a letter appeared from a Reverend Sinclair, who, in 1940, had moved into Chale Rectory on the Isle of Wight with his wife. At the time, they were warned by local people that extraordinary things happened at the rectory, including the appearance of a carriage and horses that was frequently to be heard, though not seen, driving into the yard. The Sinclairs soon heard clangings, creaks and grinding for themselves, as well as a 'rather stagey horses-hooves noise' of a somewhat 'coconutty' quality. Then objects were found to be knocked off shelves, footsteps were heard on the landing, 'cold spots' were felt and the family pets would maintain mysterious vigils outside closed and empty rooms.[86] Even pencil scribblings were discovered, but these were established as the work of a child. The Sinclairs called in pest-control men, who left poison all over the house. After three days, the curious noises stopped. Reverend Sinclair deduced that the poltergeist activity was not supernatural at all; it was just rats.

Some weeks later, Clifford Henning drew Price's attention to another letter that had appeared in the 19 October issue of the *Church Times*, in response to the Sinclairs' story.

Sir, I have read with interest your articles and letters on 'Thump Ghosts', and as I was in residence for some time at Borley

Rectory, Sussex ('the most haunted house in England'), I would
like to state definitely that neither my husband nor myself
believed the house haunted by anything else but rats and local
superstition. We left the Rectory because of its broken down condition, but certainly found nothing to fear there.

(Mrs) G. Eric Smith[87]

Henning was astonished by Mrs Smith's volte-face. Why had she
changed her mind? And why had she decided to make this public
now? There were several people living in Borley who still remembered her showing them the mysterious light at the Rectory and
then taking them into the house only to find no light in the room.
Though it might have been true that they didn't leave the Rectory
specifically because of the hauntings, Henning didn't believe that the
Smiths left because of vermin and poor sanitation. Price wrote to
him, enclosing the correspondence between himself and the Smiths
that clearly outlined that they definitely *had* believed the place to
be haunted. Henning wondered if Mrs Smith might be upset that
Price hadn't succeeded in helping her get *Murder at the Parsonage*
published. He mused that 'It looks very much as if the Smiths were
desperately anxious to have their names in print!'[88] Feeling perhaps
that the *Church Times* had a limited circulation and would not have
much impact on his new Borley book, Price didn't engage in further
dialogue with Mrs Smith, publicly or privately.

The End of Borley Rectory was published by George Harrap on 10
October 1946, in time for Christmas. The striking black-and-red
dust jacket depicted the Rectory engulfed in flames, the shadow of a
nun haunting the inferno. A fragmented work, as well as a precis of
the material outlined in the first book, it was heavily reliant on the
theories of Phythian-Adams, with the Watson-like Price assembling
the history and evidence regarding the murder of 'Marie Lairre'. The
narrative included material from Sidney Glanville's 'Locked Book',
with several transcriptions from the planchette seances, together
with reports from the investigation of the Cambridge Commission,

the story of the burial of the bones discovered at the Rectory and the tale of a mysterious 'flying brick' that was photographed during its demolition. Curiously, Price also included a detailed comparison of the phenomena at Borley with those at Ballechin House. The Ballechin mystery, the disingenuous Price concluded – well knowing its questionable authenticity – 'was never solved'.[89]

Borley, he believed, presented 'a better argument for "survival" than that of any similar case'.[90] But he continued to waver: 'I personally, still feel that I want something more. I want scientific proof that the ephemeral and intangible figures which flit hither and thither across the ill-lit stage of the Borley drama were once living men and women. Whether such scientific proof is possible is another matter.'[91] His one regret was that the phenomena at Borley had not been studied 'officially' by a university department (he favoured Cambridge).[92] If the Borley affair had gained notoriety at the end of the twentieth century, instead of its beginning, he imagined that the very best physicists, psychologists and physiologists would be able to explain *everything*. 'I *do* believe,' he wrote, 'that in fifty years' time we shall know a great deal more about these matters.'[93]

The *Sunday Mirror* welcomed *The End of Borley Rectory* as the 'best documented and most astonishing ghost story of our time'.[94] James Agate in the *Express* simply enjoyed it as a piece of spooky entertainment, though not recommending it to 'the nervous'. 'Nothing,' he wrote, would induce him to 'take it up after midnight'.[95] The *Church Times*, though, found Price and Phythian-Adams's theories unconvincing: 'ingenious as they are, [they] fall a long way short of proof'.[96] As Price listed over 100 books and articles that had already been written about the Rectory in his bibliography, *Psychic News* wryly speculated whether the Rectory ought to be known as 'the most *publicised* haunted house in England'. Recommending the book as 'very great fun', *The Times Literary Supplement* thought that perhaps the reader 'will wonder whether there may not be something in the human mind which, in certain circumstances, compels one to see and hear or, it may be, to write things that belong to another world altogether than that of common daylight.'[97] With wartime economy standards now less strict, *The End of Borley Rectory* was quickly reprinted and became a bestseller.

The story continued to fire the public's imagination. At 9.30 p.m. on 29 June 1947, the BBC broadcast 'The Haunted Rectory' on the Home Service: an 'impartial investigation by Peter Eton and Alan Burgess into the strange "goings on" at a lonely Essex Rectory'.[98] Part documentary investigation, part dramatisation, it included interviews with Price, the Hennings, the Coopers, Florence Whitehouse, Ethel Bull, Sidney Glanville and Captain Gregson. Mabel Smith, who was approached to appear in the programme, declined to take part. Marianne Foyster could not be traced and was rumoured to have moved abroad during the war. Also taking part was the writer and broadcaster James Turner, who had bought the Rectory Cottage and the site of the Rectory from a Captain Russell in May of that year, with the intention of growing fruit trees. He and his wife Catherine had never seen any of the marvels recorded in Harry Price's books. 'I don't think that the poltergeists will continue,' he told Peter Eton; 'their influence, I think has died and gone, and so here we're left with a lovely spot surrounded by trees with peace and quiet. And the atmosphere – except perhaps for a large number of people who come up here, sober and not sober – is one of utter peace and quiet and happiness.'[99] Just as the BBC broadcast ended, Turner turned to his wife and said, 'I bet you the first car will be here in twenty minutes. I'm going to shut the gate and to stand guard.' Even before he'd closed the gate, he heard a car coming up the hill. Within seconds the Rectory site was invaded by curious visitors. Turner found it impossible to keep them out: 'people were everywhere.'[100]

Perhaps inevitably, in the summer of 1947 plans emerged for a feature film dramatising the story. Price signed an agreement with the Pulitzer Prize-winning American writer Upton Sinclair, giving him exclusive rights to both his Borley books for eighteen months. Sinclair was keen to avoid Hollywood's default treatment of ghosts as farce or melodrama and depict a 'serious presentation of psychical research'. In cinemas, the story of Borley Rectory and the science of the paranormal would reach an even wider international audience, as indeed would the name of Harry Price. For the lower-middle-class boy from south-east London who had once dreamed of his name appearing in *Who's Who* (it had since 1935) and owning a Rolls-Royce (he had since 1936), Price may have allowed himself some sense of self-satisfaction.[101]

Easter fell exceptionally early in 1948. The weather was unusually fine over the holiday weekend, with millions heading for the country or the coast. On Easter Saturday, 200,000 people watched Cambridge win the boat race in record time. Many motorists ignored petrol rationing restrictions on unnecessary journeys and made the most of the good weather, though their licence plates were noted by the police. Their numbers would be sent to the Ministry of Fuel and they'd be asked to justify why they'd used petrol for leisure journeys.

Price had not been feeling well for the previous week, but had continued to work on a projected third book about the Rectory, with the working title *Borley III*.[102] This would include further contributions from Phythian-Adams and a detailed examination of the Roman Catholic background to the Borley story by Mrs Ryan Baines. He also intended to include a detailed riposte to Mabel Smith's letter to the *Church Times*. He'd drafted a plan for the book and had even completed drafts of some chapters. After lunch on Easter Monday, 29 March, he went out to post a letter to Mollie Goldney about a forthcoming lecture at the Ghost Club. On his way to the post box, he saw Sidney Glanville drive past and wave to him from the car.[103] When he returned to his study at Arun Bank, Mrs Price suggested that she'd make them both a cup of tea and left him sitting in his favourite armchair next to the fireplace. When she returned with the tea tray, Constance was shocked to find Price dead in the chair, his freshly lit pipe still smoking in his hand.

The obituaries were warm and considered. The *Daily Telegraph* announced the death of 'Britain's best-known ghost-hunter' from a heart attack, just like his father, at the age of sixty-seven.[104] *The*

Times noted that Price's books had summed up 'the conclusions of a singularly honest and clear mind on a subject that by its very nature [lent] itself to all manner of trickery and chicanery'.[105] Mourning his passing, the young psychical researcher Peter Underwood wrote that Price's place in the 'annals of the great in Psychical Research' was assured.[106]

PART THREE

THE HUNTED

Harry Price, 'psychic detective'

CHAPTER SEVENTEEN

SEARCH FOR TRUTH

30 March 1948–21 August 1952

I wonder how many of my readers are aware of the number of squabbles, petty jealousies and open feuds that are taking place amongst those investigating psychic phenomena. Quarrels, backbiting, lawsuits, sharp-practice, scandal mongering, the gratification of personal spite, these things are rampant, to the detriment of the science of psychical research and a paralysing drag on the wheel of progress.

Harry Price, 'A Plea for a Better Understanding', *British Journal of Psychical Research,* January–February 1929[1]

Price's own ghost would not rest peacefully. Even before he was buried, his methods, his objectives and his integrity were called into question. At the heart of the battle for his posthumous reputation were competing perceptions of his character. Was he a sceptic or a hypocrite? A scientist or a showman? More widely, was psychical research a serious subject for academic study or merely a diverting popular entertainment? In the months and years that followed, the controversy would prove to be both ugly and bloody.

Within twenty-four hours of Price's death, now protected by the laws of libel, Douglas Craggs, the vice president of the Magic Circle, bruised by Price's rejection of Magic Circle members during his tenancy of the Rectory, made an extraordinarily contentious claim:

Price had 'bamboozled the public into believing things in which he placed no credence whatsoever'.[2]

Price's colleague Clarice Richards told the press that though Price had *seemed* a sceptic, he did believe in an afterlife. Mrs Richards was convinced that the deceased Price would try to establish contact from the other world. 'If he does,' she declared, 'he will use a Russian test phrase, so that there will be no possible doubt of his identity or the genuineness of the message.'[3] The press descended on Arun Bank to interview Price's widow, keen to know if the gamekeeper might turn poacher and make a return from the dead. Mrs Price told reporters that her husband 'never said he believed he would be able to "come back" in any form after he died.'[4]

As Price had left only a modest amount,[5] the chairman of the trustees of Price's estate, J. Eldon Walker of the Midland Bank in Brighton, looked to recruit one of Price's colleagues as his literary executor to further exploit his work and bring in royalties to alleviate the financial strain on his widow. Having first canvassed Sidney Glanville, who felt unable to accept, they approached Mrs Ryan Baines, who had been collaborating with Price on *Borley III*. She had known nothing of Borley until 1939, when she had read in the press of the destruction of the Rectory. She'd subsequently visited the site and corresponded with Price after reading *The End of Borley Rectory*, though they had met only twice.[6] About a year before his death, though, Mrs Baines had begun to doubt his integrity, feeling that they had differing views about psychical research in general and Borley in particular. She felt that he had neither the experience nor the patience for checking the facts in order to establish the truth.

Mrs Baines was charged by Mr Walker with editing the third Borley book, using the chapters that Price had already written. But consulting the material held in his files, she was 'horrified':[7] Price had wilfully misrepresented the facts, including 'rubbish' simply because it had a 'sensational value'.[8] Mrs Baines withdrew from the project. 'It was perhaps,' she felt, 'the best thing for him to have died when he did.'[9]

Price's trustees then secured another writer, Paul Tabori, as literary executor. Tabori was a Jewish Hungarian academic who had fled the Continent with his mother in 1937; his father died in Auschwitz in 1944. Settling in London during the Blitz, he had worked as a critic and broadcaster, and as a contract writer for Sir Alexander Korda's production company, London Films. Tabori claimed he had an open mind as far as psychic phenomena was concerned and was 'neither a spiritualist nor a die-hard sceptic'.[10] He now planned a biography of Price as well as the completion of *Borley III*. But just as Tabori set about consolidating Price's legacy, the Society for Psychical Research began to cast doubt over his achievements and to question his reputation.

K. M. Goldney – known as Mollie – had been raised in India, where her father had been a judge in the civil service. A qualified midwife, she had been fascinated by psychical research since she began a correspondence with the physicist Sir Oliver Lodge, who had served as the president of the Society for Psychical Research and had written a bestseller about the death of his son Raymond in 1915, charting his attempts to contact his son beyond the grave in a series of seances. In 1927, on returning to England with her husband, Mollie had joined the Society for Psychical Research and was elected a full member of its council in 1945. She had extensive experience in psychical investigation, having also worked closely with Price at his Laboratory of Psychical Research. But she felt she never really understood him and had become sceptical of his methods. She now worried that the general public seemed to regard Price's books about Borley as a 'cast iron case and almost proving the paranormal'.[11]

On hearing of the plans by Price's estate to commission a biography and to continue with the publication of *Borley III*, as well as the possibility of Upton Sinclair's Hollywood film version of the Borley story, a concerned Mollie wrote to William Salter, who had been nursing his antipathy towards Price over many years. He had concluded at the time of his visit to the Rectory in 1931 that with the help of her daughter, Marianne Foyster was 'the villain' behind the activity.[12] But he was convinced that Price had also faked phenomena. It had always seemed odd to him that what had been a 'subjective hallucinatory haunt, probably pathological to start with', had developed noisy, destructive poltergeist characteristics as soon as Price arrived on the scene in 1929.[13] Significantly for Salter, Price had deliberately excluded experienced researchers from his year-long tenancy of the Rectory. Why would he do so if he were serious about establishing a genuinely scientific investigation? Had his ultimate objective been not to record phenomena at the Rectory, but to collect material to include in a bestselling book?

Mollie and Clarice Richards had accompanied Price to the Rectory during the occupancy of the Foysters. At the time, Price had dismissed the phenomena as fraudulent and accused Mrs Foyster of cheating. None of this had appeared in his two books about the Rectory. Mollie worried to Salter that the public had clearly taken Price's word at face value. She suggested that she provide Salter with her own version of events for comparison with Price's published account. He agreed that if the version given in Price's books could be accepted, Borley was a truly exceptional case. But if it could be proved to be fraudulent, that was another matter altogether. He suggested that the Society for Psychical Research should put together 'a connected narrative of Borley from the beginning with as much first hand statement and as little hearsay as possible'.[14] At first Mollie was ambivalent, but encouraged by the disingenuous Salter, and impelled by her fiercely single-minded desire for the 'TRUTH' (she favoured capitals even when writing the word), she volunteered to start on an investigation of the Borley material. Immediately she sought permission from Tabori to study Price's extensive archive that was now held at the University of London.

Meanwhile, more troubling stories began to reach the Society for Psychical Research. Cynthia Ledsham, the *Life* journalist who had accompanied Price to Borley in 1944 to record the demolition of the Rectory, had been astounded by Price's 'bare-faced hocus pocus' in the way he had misrepresented a photograph in *The End of Borley Rectory*. When the image had been developed, a brick thrown by one of the demolition men was visible as a white dot. At Price's request, the photographer, David Scherman, had enlarged it, show-ing the brick in close-up; it appeared to be hovering or levitating in mid-air. 'If this was a genuine paranormal phenomenon,' Price had written augustly, 'then we have the first photograph ever taken of a Poltergeist projectile in flight.' But Cynthia Ledsham now insisted that, contrary to what he had written in *The End of Borley Rectory*, she, Scherman and Price had all seen a workman as they passed the house and who was throwing bricks at regular intervals as part of the demolition work. Yes, she had said to Price, 'Look, poltergeists!' But it had been a joke.

The most damaging revelation came before Christmas 1948. The *Inky Way Annual* was published in aid of journalist charities, full of cartoons and light-hearted articles. There were contributions from over fifty journalists, including that of the veteran *Daily Mail* reporter Charles Sutton, who reflected on his early days on the *Bristol Evening Times and Echo* during the First World War. He'd learned from the night editor of the *Daily Mirror* 'how to tell a 1000 word story in 10,000 words, but to write it in 200'.[15] He also recalled his dealings with Price in a brief aside:

> Many things happened the night I spent in the famous Borley Rectory with Harry Price and one of his colleagues, including one uncomfortable moment when a large pebble hit me on the head.
>
> After much noisy 'phenomena' I seized Harry and found his pockets full of bricks and pebbles. This was one 'phenomena' he could not explain, so I rushed to the nearest village to phone the Daily Mail with my story, but after a conference with the lawyer, my story was killed. The News Editor said; 'Bad luck old man, but there were two of them [Price and his secretary] and only one of you.'[16]

Harry Price, the world's most celebrated ghost hunter, was a fraud. A shocked Mollie Goldney wrote to Lord Charles Hope and sug-gested that they interview Sutton.[17]

Hosting lunch with Sutton and Goldney on 21 January 1949,

Lord Charles talked about his own visit to the Rectory on 5 July 1929, before the Smiths had moved to Long Melford, and his growing suspicions of Price. Sutton then outlined his history with Price, including his reporting of the Rudi Schneider sittings. He had collaborated with Price on many press stories and felt that there was a tacit understanding between them that the various mediums they had investigated were fraudulent. It was a mutually beneficial relationship – Price provided Sutton with great stories and Sutton provided the publicity that Price wanted.

After the Smiths had abandoned the house, Sutton told them, he had been keen to spend a night in it before he left for America. On Friday 25 July, Lucie drove Price and Sutton out to Essex, with Price priming the journalist on the journey with legends of the phantom coach, the lascivious monk and the walled-up nun – all enticing copy.[18]

Upon arrival at Long Melford, they had first visited Westgate Terrace to interview Mr and Mrs Smith, who told Sutton tales of bell-ringing, noises at night and moving furniture. By the time Lucie had driven the car to Borley, it was dusk. Almost as soon as they'd arrived, Price absented himself, taking, Sutton noted, an 'ostentatious' stroll around the grounds. As they walked onto the lawn, they looked up at the eerie façade of the house with its dismal windows. By then it was almost dark and Price was standing behind Sutton. Price pointed out a window on the first floor. The week before, he said, he had been standing on the same spot with his fellow investigators when the glass of the window on the upper storey had suddenly shattered. Before Price had even finished his story – as if on cue – another window broke and glass cascaded dramatically to the ground. Just before the glass had smashed – Sutton wasn't sure, but he believed that he'd heard a swishing noise. He was already suspicious of Price, who he felt was more interested in headlines than in rigorous research. Going into the house, Sutton requested that they should check all the rooms – Lucie should open the doors, Sutton would follow her with a paraffin lamp and Price would lock the doors behind them.

Entering the pitch-dark Rectory, Sutton locked the front door and prepared to light the lamp. Immediately, the house was stifling and he felt distinctly uncomfortable. He became aware of an 'atmosphere of evil'. But he was also convinced that he was in for a battle of wills that night with Price. Starting their tour of the house, Lucie opened the door of the first room on the ground floor. Sutton followed her in and examined it. All seemed in order. But as Price was closing the door behind them, suddenly there was a considerable noise – made, so it seemed, by a pebble or stone thrown violently across the room. The same phenomena happened in all the rooms on the ground floor.

As they mounted the staircase to examine the first floor, Sutton was convinced that the stones thrown in the rooms, the breaking of the window and the disappearance of Price immediately upon their arrival were all connected. For whatever reason, Price was faking the phenomena. Thinking on his feet, Sutton formulated a plan to catch Price out.

While in the Blue Room, the party looked out of the window hoping to see the nun or a headless horseman careering around the garden. Though there was no physical phenomena to be seen, Sutton did hear strange noises, like the sounds of a man trying to speak. Price explained that a former occupant of the Rectory had been murdered in that very room – his earthbound spirit must be attempting to communicate with them. Sutton was unconvinced and suspected that Price had been trying to throw his voice like a ventriloquist. He then proposed that they reverse their positions so that Price should walk in front of him. Price argued against this, and they continued in the same order. Just as they locked the Blue Room behind them, Sutton sensed the swish of an arm, and almost simultaneously heard a series of echoing crashes caused by a large stone rolling down the stairs. He was sure that the stone had been thrown by Price. Quickly putting the lamp on the floor and swinging round, he grasped Price by the hand. 'Now I have got you!' Sutton plunged his hands into Price's coat pockets: they were full of stones and pebbles. A winded Price asked, 'What are you going to do? What are you going to do?' Lucie, who was present throughout, was silent. Sutton told Price that he would not stay in the house another minute and asked to be taken to The Bull in Long Melford. From there he would be telephoning the *Daily Mail*. He needed to phone in his story before midnight in order to make the early editions.

Arriving at The Bull, Sutton went off to telephone his news editor with his exclusive: the world's greatest ghost hunter was a fraud. But when he was passed on to the *Mail*'s libel lawyer, he was advised that it would be impossible to print an exposure of Price. Clearly, he and his secretary would deny everything and Sutton had no other witnesses. Returning to the pub lounge, frustrated and disappointed, he told Price that he was *very* lucky. Unphased and unrepentant, Price simply shrugged his shoulders.

Sutton, though, was confused by the motive for Price's trickery. The Rectory was evidently evil. It would be impossible to produce anything more eerie than the malign atmosphere that already pervaded the house. There had clearly been activity there – well before Price had arrived on the scene – that should be properly investigated. Price's tricks occluded anything of real value to the examination of genuine paranormal activity at the Rectory.

When Price had died, Sutton had considered writing an exposé in the *Mail*, but decided against it in order to spare Mrs Price's feelings. Sutton remained aggrieved with Price and there was still no love lost between the two men. 'I consider Price one of the biggest crooks going,' Sutton declared, 'and I know no other crook who has got away with it for so long unmasked.'[19]

Mollie was perturbed by what she'd heard, though Lord Charles advised caution. Sutton had always been 'somewhat prejudiced against Price and the whole subject [of psychical research]'.[20]

The only other witness to the incident with Sutton was Lucie Kaye. So Mollie invited her to dinner with Lord Charles. Mollie had met Lucie only briefly, a couple of times before. Now known as Mrs Meeker, Lucie had two sons, one of twenty by her first husband and one of thirteen by her second.

When they got onto the subject of Price, Mollie admitted that she was very uncomfortable making accusations against the dead, but felt that they needed a critical appraisal of the Borley material. Lord Charles told her that they specifically wanted to discuss Sutton's accusation in the *Inky Way Annual*. What did Lucie have to say?

She was astonished. 'Well, really, you know, I just don't remember the occasion at all.'[21] She didn't think it could possibly have happened while she was there. She said she *did* recall that Sutton had wanted to get some swift copy for his newspaper before he went to New York. Lord Charles and Mollie asked Lucie very bluntly if, in her long association with Price, she had any occasion to doubt his integrity. Lucie agreed that Price *could* be difficult and he certainly courted publicity, but in her opinion he was 'absolutely and completely straight'.[22] To Mollie, Lucie seemed very genuine and Lord Charles agreed that there was nothing in her manner that should make them question the truth of her testimony.

Soon after the dinner, Lucie wrote to Lord Charles. Could Sutton be sure of his memory after all this time? And might he have a personal agenda in exposing Price in this way?[23] She also wondered why the society was taking Sutton at his word to such an extent: 'is there something else going on of which I am quite unaware?'[24]

Now that Price's principles were being questioned in print, Lucie wrote to the Society for Psychical Research indicating that she had been alerted to Sutton's 'foul remarks'.[25] She enclosed a light-hearted article that she had written, 'The Ghost Kept Price Awake', about the first visit to Borley she had made with her employer, twenty years earlier. She vehemently believed Sutton's allegation to be 'a falsehood from beginning to end'. As far as she was concerned, Harry Price was a man of 'unimpeachable integrity'.[26]

Meanwhile, at Borley, unexplained phenomena seemed to continue. The Hennings heard footsteps in and around the church as well as organ music and bell-ringing when the building was empty. Since they had moved into the Rectory Cottage, James and Catherine Turner had also heard strange noises – pistol shots, the breaking of crockery and warm patches where cats might have slept when there was no cat in the house. But they believed that such things weren't peculiar to Borley and occurred in many old houses. As far as they were concerned, most of the stories concerning the Rectory had no basis in fact and few were first-hand.

On 23 May, a light-hearted – and perhaps tongue-in-cheek – article appeared in the *Daily Mail* entitled, 'Whiff of Evil at Borley'. Two naval officers and their girlfriends had reported an overpowering 'wall of perfume' they had experienced within the ruins of the Rectory. 'The "wall" was of some sickly sweet perfume so powerful as to be absolutely revolting,' said Susanna Dudley, one of the young women. 'It was an evil smell.'[27] Three days later, a letter appeared in the *Mail* from Mabel Smith in Sheringham, who had not publicly commented on the Rectory since her little-regarded letter to the *Church Times* in 1945. This time, writing to a national newspaper, she was determined to be heard:

As the wife of a previous rector of Borley, I would like to state that we lived in the Rectory for over three years and did not think it was haunted (except by rats). It was an old house and very creaky and broken down. The "wall of perfume" can well be explained, as pigsties are adjacent.

It was because of local superstition that we called the Research Society in, hoping to show the people that there was nothing supernatural, and to our lasting regret the place was made a centre for sightseers. Surely, now that fire has demolished the place, all this absurdity should drop.[28]

Almost immediately, William Salter wrote to the editor of the *Mail* protesting that 'the Society was never called in to investigate the Rectory', implying that the fault lay firmly with Price's National Laboratory.[29] He insisted that the Society for Psychical Research was 'in no way responsible for the excessive publicity the place has received'.[30] Salter then decided to contact Mrs Smith himself. He was very interested to hear that she thought the Rectory was haunted by nothing but rats. She quickly responded, promising that she could enlighten him 'upon several things', inviting him to visit her in Sheringham and wishing that Borley could just 'be left in peace'.[31]

By now Mollie Goldney had studied the Borley material in Price's archive and was extremely troubled by what she'd read. 'As an investigation,' she wrote to Salter, 'it couldn't be worse and is not worth the paper it is written on.' She worried that 'a legend will undoubtedly grow up – it is already in existence – unless we issue a critical appraisal of the whole matter.'[32]

By now, Goldney and Eric Dingwall had submitted their contributions to Tabori's biography of Price. Mollie wrote that Price had certainly put psychical research on the map, 'but was it,' she wondered, 'the right map?'[33] Dingwall's piece was equally negative. 'It is only by realizing Harry Price's excusable love of the limelight and of personal adulation that we can understand his work in psychical research,' he wrote, adding 'he never, in my opinion advanced our real knowledge of the supernatural in any way whatsoever'.[34] As Price's executors considered their pieces would hurt Constance Price, both contributions were withdrawn.[35]

Meanwhile, having heard of Salter's intention of visiting Mabel Smith, Mollie suggested that she might go with him. As he was committed to a holiday abroad when the visit was set, he suggested that Eric Dingwall should accompany her to Sheringham.

On Friday 1 July, Mollie and Dingwall took the train to Sheringham, arriving just after 9 p.m. The town was small and 'only country and sea'.[36] They speculated if Mrs Smith would be a half-mad old woman, but when she met them at the railway station she seemed an eminently practical, sensible lady,[37] though she'd had a trying time since the death of her husband, probate having been delayed for eight years due to the war. At her bomb-scarred house she told her tale consistently, without contradicting herself, for more than three hours. Though she was open to the possibility of spirit communication, Mrs Smith was absolutely emphatic that there had been no ghosts at Borley Rectory.[38]

When they were first offered the living, she and her husband had no reason to think the house was possessed by ghosts or spirits and no reason to be frightened, either, as they were devout Christians. Occasionally things happened and they'd think, 'That's funny ...', but surely, Mabel argued, such things happened in all houses?[39] They would often find that doors and windows had been opened or shut in a way that puzzled them, but she was sure this was just the locals playing tricks on them, climbing in and out of the house. There were undoubtedly villagers who didn't want a new rector occupying the Rectory. At the same time, the place was in a deplorable condition, infested with bats and rats that would scratch through the floorboards and gnaw at the bell wires, causing the house bells to ring at all hours of the day and night.

With so much local gossip about ghostly legends, both the young maid and her boyfriend would join in the fun, with Fred Tatum walking about with his coat over his head, which, in the dark, might seem like a headless figure – or even a nun. Mrs Smith thought young Mary a mischievous girl who would often produce 'phenomena', but these were just jokes and harmless pranks. She was certainly confused by the vehicle she had once seen in the driveway, but didn't think it was supernormal or uncanny. And though her husband had heard a voice once, when they had vacated the rectory, saying, 'Don't Carlos, don't,' this may well have been passers-by in the lane or even the sound of a wireless. The effect of a light in a window worried them for a long time until they realised that it was caused by the reflection of trains passing on the line from Sudbury to Long Melford. Nothing, to this point, occurred that they considered couldn't be explained. But as the reputation of the house was putting the villagers off from coming to meetings, they decided to ask their daily newspaper to approach a psychical research organisation on their behalf.

As soon as Price arrived, Mr and Mrs Smith were astonished by the bangs and clatterings that he seemed to bring with him. They were immediately suspicious that he might be producing some of the effects himself. Once, when he was in a room with her, Mabel was astonished when little pebbles suddenly whizzed past her head.

Nothing like this had ever happened before. She couldn't help think-ing that Price must have thrown them. The Smiths knew Price was an expert conjuror, but they never actually saw him throw anything himself. He was too clever for that. When he left the morning after the seance they held on his first visit, Mabel sat chatting with Lucie Kaye for hours and no phenomena occurred at all. She observed to Lucie at the time that it was extraordinary that all this activity should suddenly have started when Price arrived. Lucie had agreed that he *did* seem to attract the spirits wherever he went.

Mabel admitted that they had a terrible time at Borley, not because of ghosts or poltergeists, but because of the hordes of sightseers.

Mollie and Dingwall wondered why she hadn't protested about Price's exaggerations in *The Most Haunted House in England*? She told them that it wasn't published until shortly after her husband's death, and she was too devastated by grief to worry about it. But later, she had been appalled when friends had sent her copies of the book and told her that their names had been used in it. She claimed that she hadn't read the books but burned them on the fire.[40] It ought to have been called, she added, tartly, '*The Most* Maligned *House in England*'.[41]

Returning to London from Sheringham, a troubled Mollie updated William Salter about their visit, worrying that it showed Price in an extremely bad light. It was now clear to her, Dingwall and Salter that a rat-infested old house, superstition, practical jokes and local legend had been opportunistically distorted by Price in order to conjure a potent ghost story.

As Mrs Smith had burned her copies, Mollie now sent her another copy of *The Most Haunted House in England* and asked her to make notes. Mabel was stunned. 'My first impression on reading the volume was utter astonishment at the clever mixture of legend, truth, phantasy, and disregard of the intellects of intelligent people; the facts are so twisted that they lend an idea of reality to them. Everything appears distorted and borders on the ridicu-lous.'[42] If Mollie and Dingwall could only trace Mary Pearson, she would be able to confirm that the majority of the phenomena at the Rectory were simply tricks, pranks and tall tales.

Much of Mabel's testimony, though, was contradictory. It was recorded in Price's archives that she had written to him, thanking him for sending her *The Most Haunted House in England* and congratulating him on it. Now she claimed she had never read it. She had also told Mollie and Dingwall that she didn't remember ever meeting Edwin Whitehouse – though he had visited them at Sheringham before Christmas of 1931. As well as these and other inconsistencies, Mollie continued to puzzle why Mrs Smith had changed her mind about the genuineness of the haunting. The letters from the time they lived at the Rectory indicated that she and her husband both believed that the house was haunted. Lord Charles Hope had spent time there, when it was clear that she had been upset and apprehensive about ghosts. Either she *hadn't* believed the house was haunted, but, for whatever reason, had claimed that she did at the time; or she *had* believed it was haunted, but had since changed her mind.

Mollie was confused and concerned. Could Mrs Smith's memory be relied on after twenty years? And was she emotionally stable after all that she had suffered? She was very religious and had a keen sense of sin. She also admitted to Mollie that it had troubled her that she'd used the Borley haunt to urge the Bishop of Chelmsford for a transfer to another living because they were desperate to leave the house. She had deliberately exaggerated the phenomena. For a God-fearing woman, it must have played on her conscience over the intervening years that the only reason that Borley had become so notorious was because *she* had invited the press – and Price – in the first place.

In August, Mollie met Ethel English, who had succeeded Lucie Kaye as Price's secretary. She'd been saddened by his unexpected death but shocked to hear about Sutton's accusation and Mabel Smith's letters to the press. As far as she was aware, neither had said anything at the time about Price's trustworthiness. As far as the accusations of Price's duplicity were concerned, she didn't think it made any sense. He was spending hundreds of pounds a year on rent, gas, lighting, expenses and her salary. Why would he do all this just to fool people?[43]

Mollie's instinct was that after Price had alienated himself from the psychical research community due to his controversial treatment of Rudi Schneider in 1932, nobody of any significance would work with him. His National Laboratory was effectively over, so she surmised that he had focused on Borley as a way of bringing himself back into the public eye, even if that meant doing so by fraudulent means.

Salter decided that Mollie and Eric Dingwall should prepare a dossier on Borley and that the Society for Psychical Research should publish a book based on it. This would become the *Borley Report*. But Dingwall had had a fractious relationship with Price for decades, and was unconvinced of the validity of psychical research. Meanwhile, Mollie had been sceptical of Price's methods for years – and Salter knew it. As there seemed to be such abundant and damning evidence, he was clear that Price's intention to deceive should be 'prominently stated'. Guided by him, the objective of the *Report* seemed not to investigate the truth of the haunting of Borley Rectory, but to discredit Harry Price.

Over the next two years, Mollie and Dingwall interviewed the key Borley witnesses. In the summer of 1950, they travelled to Fittleworth in West Sussex to meet Sidney Glanville. He made it clear that he would resent any attack on Price very strongly. Though he felt that Price's egotism was pathological and, at times, shocking, Glanville had never had any cause to doubt his honesty.

He wondered if the motivation for Mabel Smith's new attitude to Price might be more complicated than she'd cared to admit. He recalled Price had the manuscript of her novel, *Murder at the Parsonage*, and he had said it was 'absolute rubbish'. Knowing Price to be capable of extreme rudeness, Glanville imagined that he'd perhaps sent Mrs Smith an insulting letter. Unconsciously or not, did she resent disparaging comments he might have made about her novel? And had she also been disappointed having nursed hopes that the publication of the book might alleviate her distressed financial position following her husband's death?

Visiting Ethel and Alfred Bull at Great Cornard, Mollie and Salter found them now frail, though not senile. Alfred Bull continued to insist that he had never experienced anything paranormal at the Rectory, but Miss Bull recounted the story of the nun she and her sisters had seen half a century earlier. She had clearly told the tale hundreds of times before and was regarded as something of a local celebrity because of it. She was mildly annoyed with Price as he never gave her the opportunity to approve the section of *The Most Haunted House in England* that her testimony appeared in. She insisted that he was incorrect on a number of small points. She was quite certain that there had been no poltergeist phenomena at the Rectory before the arrival of the Smiths. And whatever Mrs Smith said in the press now, she was sure that she was 'scared stiff'[44] when she lived at the Rectory and had abandoned it because of the ghosts.[45]

Miss Bull was surprisingly arch, Mollie felt, about Marianne Foyster, who was, she thought, 'mad as a hatter' and 'a little beast.'[46] She'd heard Marianne was a widow once again and probably on the lookout for another man to marry. Miss Bull's brother agreed that she was an 'unusual woman'.[47] They had no idea where she was now. She seemed to have disappeared during the war.

They then called on Lady Whitehouse at Arthur Hall. She told them that she had very much liked Lionel Foyster, but she thought that Marianne was 'man mad'. As far as the phenomena at the Rectory were concerned, she was absolutely convinced that they were real. She didn't think Marianne was responsible for it, but she did believe that she was psychic and that her fainting fits were actually trances. She admitted to having felt hurt when Marianne had left Borley in 1935 without even saying goodbye. She had thought they were friends.

Mollie and Dingwall then visited Annie Pearson, who continued to live at Place Farm Cottage, opposite the Rectory site. She took a very dim view of the whole Borley story. In all the years they had lived there, neither she nor her husband had ever seen or experienced anything at all. She insisted that the Smiths left the house because it was far too big and too expensive for them to run. Regarding the ghosts, she thought that Mrs Foyster had been desperate to get away from Borley, so produced much of the 'phenomena' herself. She had been often absent from the Rectory, having opened a flower shop with Francois D'Arles, who had rented the Rectory Cottage. They had grown quantities of flowers in the garden and sold them in London. Mrs Foyster would be away for weeks at a time, neglecting the children and her husband, whose arthritis was by then very bad. The image of Marianne that was beginning to emerge was completely at odds with the tortured rector's wife who appeared in the pages of Price's books. Mollie then asked Mrs Pearson if she would put them in touch with her niece Mary, who also had intimate knowledge of the house during the Smiths' time.[48]

Mary and Fred Tatum were still married – with ten children – and living in an overcrowded house in Sudbury. Mary was delighted to meet Mollie and Dingwall but if the investigators were hoping to have Mabel Smith's story confirmed by her former maid, they were to be disappointed.

Contrary to what Mrs Smith had said, Mary believed that the Rectory was *definitely* haunted. She never saw the nun, but she was convinced that she had seen the phantom coach. Despite the fact that she now lived so close to it, she avoided going near the Rectory – she had only been past it three times in the past twenty years. There were, Mary told them, 'forces at work' there.[49]

By this point, Mollie and Dingwall had interviewed many of the surviving witnesses relating to the alleged haunting. Some were convinced that the phenomena were genuine, others dismissed them as a hoax. At the same time, though many doubted Price's integrity, some vehemently defended him. He may well have been an egotist and self-publicist, but he was not, they insisted, a cheat.

Marianne Foyster with John Emery, 1932

CHAPTER EIGHTEEN

THE WIDOW OF BORLEY

23 January 1932–8 June 1954

Events undoubtedly happened [at Borley] which one does not
associate with a normal home, and still less, in a Rectory.

Letter from Sidney Glanville to Mollie Goldney,
12 May 1952[1]

In 1950, Paul Tabori's *Harry Price: The Biography of a Ghost-Hunter* was published, acknowledging that Price was a controversial figure who had been accused of saying one thing in his letters and another in his published writings. By now, Upton Sinclair's movie had stalled,[2] and Goldney and Dingwall's reinvestigation of the Borley material had already been drawn out for two years. It had been mooted by William Salter that they should perhaps contribute their report as part of *Borley III*, now called the *Borley Symposium*.[3] But what they needed was an injection of energy, a fresh perspective and a clear focus.

In 1949, Eric Dingwall had been to a lecture at the Magic Circle about conjuring and the psychology of deception, given by the 39-year-old Trevor H. Hall. Hall's interests in the esoteric and paranormal had been ignited when he'd been introduced as a boy to Sir Arthur Conan Doyle by his father in Doyle's psychic bookshop in Westminster. After being demobbed from the army, Hall had read *The End of Borley Rectory* and found 'the combination of ghosts and poltergeists, sex and murder, religion and a sense of the past which Borley offered quite irresistible'.[4]

After Hall's Magic Circle lecture, Dingwall introduced himself and invited Hall to his flat in Cambridge, where they had a long discussion about Borley, with Dingwall expressing scepticism about the case. Encouraged by Hall's insights, Dingwall invited him to accompany Mollie Goldney and him on a weekend in Borley.

Hall drove the three to the village, where they took photographs and called on Lady Whitehouse. On returning to Cambridge, Mollie and Dingwall asked Hall to join the Society for Psychical Research and to collaborate with them in writing the *Borley Report*.

Goldney and Dingwall had no idea to whom they'd allied themselves in the conceited and ambitious Trevor Hall. He was 'a supreme egotist, inflated to the breaking point with self-importance and a determination to get his name and exploits at all costs before the public'.[5] With the *Report* already skewed against Price, rather than the objective, scientific investigation that Mollie Goldney had first imagined, it now began to take on an agenda of outright hostility.

In January 1932, with the Marks Tey Circle having successfully cleared it of poltergeists, Borley Rectory was calm once more. But the district surrounding the house was far from settled, with increasing distress and agitation among agricultural workers. Farmers who were unable to meet tithe payments to the Church of England were losing their livelihoods and being made homeless, their stock and possessions confiscated by bailiffs and sold at public auction.

But the British Union of Fascists (BUF) now mobilised in support of the beleaguered farmers. 'Fascism stands for the revival of agriculture,' Oswald Mosley proclaimed, 'therefore we join in the tithe war.'[6] As bailiffs attempted to remove livestock and equipment in lieu of tithe debts, BUF Blackshirts now turned up in support, posting notices on farm gates, chalking anti-tithe slogans along the road, digging trenches and building barricades to obstruct the bailiffs' work. This culminated in an eighteen-day siege at Doreen Wallace's farms at Wortham Manor when nineteen Blackshirts were arrested and sent to Norwich Prison, watched by an angry crowd of 1,000 locals. The farmer and future founder of the Soil Association, Lady Eve Balfour, had worried that Westminster was so out of touch with life in the countryside that 'the whole of rural England will go Blackshirt'.[7]

With Price already firmly targeted, Trevor Hall now set his sights on the key surviving witness in the Borley story, Marianne Foyster. Among those who had worked at Borley Rectory after the house had been 'cleansed' by the Marks Tey Circle, was Edith Dytor (as she was then), who was now a nurse at Derbyshire Royal Infirmary. She was happy to be interviewed by Hall, so he travelled up to Derby to meet her.[8]

The 21-year-old Edith had been in training when she answered an advertisement in the *Nursing Mirror* – the rector's wife, Mrs Foyster, had been looking for a nurse–companion from April to November of 1932 to help with her new baby. When Edith arrived at the Rectory, the little boy, John, was just two weeks old. She found Mrs Foyster very attractive and well educated. She told Edith that she had originally been engaged to a man of her own age in Canada, but when this had fallen through, on the rebound she had married Mr Foyster, which she now regretted. She was a Roman Catholic – unusual and perhaps uncomfortable for the wife of an Anglican minister. She slept with a rosary under her pillow and was fluent in French. Edith liked Mrs Foyster but also felt sorry for her. She had been used to a vibrant, colourful life and had come to loathe the gloomy and isolated Borley. Edith observed that she was extremely anxious much of the time and took small white pills three times a day. This was a barbiturate, Luminal, prescribed for anxiety and sleep disorders. Side effects of taking this drug include restlessness, delirium and, significantly, in view of the situation at the Rectory, confusion and hallucinations.

Mr Foyster, Edith told Hall, was much older than his wife,

crippled with arthritis, swollen hands and a pronounced limp. As his investments had dwindled after the Wall Street Crash, he worried that when he retired, the family would have to survive on his Church pension of £125 a year. They'd also need to secure and pay for their own accommodation when he gave up the living as they would need to vacate the Rectory. In an attempt to live on a budget, he had become very tight with money and meals were austere, such as rice and macaroni cooked in water. He particularly couldn't abide waste. But he was a good, kind man and adored the children.

Other than Mrs Pearson, who came to help out every day, the third adult in the household was Francois D'Arles, a short, tubby, dark Frenchman of around thirty. Though he rented the Rectory Cottage, he spent much of his time in the house and took most of his meals there. He worked in a mundane job at the film studios at Elstree but spent a lot of time in the garden and decorating the Rectory Cottage. With Lionel concerned about money, it seems to have been D'Arles who suggested Marianne open a flower shop in London that he would run with her, stocked with flowers that they'd grow in the garden.

Edith heard about the haunting on her first day. Mrs Foyster didn't like talking about it and, worried that she might leave, assured Edith that there was nothing to fear. She also saw the wall-writings as soon as she arrived and wondered what they were. Marianne dismissed them as of no importance. Edith presumed they could only have been done by Mrs Foyster, as Adelaide was too young to write. That first night she heard limping footsteps outside her room and, in view of the stories she'd heard, it had frightened her. Later, Edith heard the same footsteps and realised that it was simply Lionel Foyster's limping gait due to his arthritis.

The young nurse quickly became aware of a strained atmosphere in the house and of a peculiar and complex web of relationships. It was clear that D'Arles completely dominated the household. Mrs Foyster was afraid of him and her husband was jealous of him. Mr Foyster would shut himself off in the library writing his book, which he allowed Edith to read. Studying it, Edith thought it must be Lionel who was behind most of the odd things that happened at the Rectory.

Edith neither liked nor trusted Francois D'Arles. He was manipulative and sly, sometimes cruel, belittling Mrs Foyster. When she claimed that the pills she took were prescribed by her doctor, D'Arles insisted they weren't; she'd bought them herself. He would often ask Edith to go into Marianne's room and remove them. Lionel was also taking medication and had been prescribed synthetic digitalin for a heart condition. Sometimes he'd take too much and would be violently sick, but when the dose was reduced, his stomach problems would settle. D'Arles, only half joking, claimed that Marianne was trying to poison him.

On 20 September, at only four and a half months old, Mrs Foyster's baby died of convulsions and protein malnutrition. He was buried in an unmarked grave in the churchyard across the road. The parish register records that the child had been officially adopted by the Foysters, just as they had adopted Adelaide. John Emery had been born to an unmarried mother on 25 April 1932. Though she was from Kent, he had been born in the home of a midwife in Southend-on-Sea.

By the early 1930s, 29,000 illegitimate babies were born to unmarried mothers in Britain every year. Adoption legislation had been formalised in 1926, but in reality the process remained casual and haphazard, with even reputable agencies rarely interviewing prospective parents and making only rudimentary checks with referees. Many of these unregulated transactions were carried out in a matter of hours. This could lead to tragic circumstances. One woman in Glamorganshire was jailed after it was revealed that two dozen children had passed through her hands. Six had been removed by their parents and three by the NSPCC because of the way they had been neglected. A further six had died in her care.

After the death of the baby, Marianne asked Edith to stay on and take care of Adelaide and Francois. She agreed to stay until January 1933, when she returned to Derby to start work at the Royal Infirmary. During her time at the Rectory, little untoward happened, but she did find the atmosphere of the house overpowering. Only once, she told Hall, did she experience something really strange. She was in one of the bedrooms with Mrs Foyster when Adelaide came upstairs and told them that there was a lady she didn't recognise on the doorstep. When Edith and Marianne reached the front door, there was nobody there. When asked to describe the visitor, Adelaide told them it was a woman wearing black with something white around her face. Like a nun.

Having completed his schooling in Canada, in January 1933, at the age of sixteen, Marianne's own son, Ian Shaw, had arrived to stay at the Rectory. Relations between mother and son were fraught, as he resented her, as he saw it, for abandoning him as a baby. As they were both French speakers, he and Francois D'Arles became good friends. The nature of the relationship between D'Arles and Marianne was clear to Shaw. He later claimed that D'Arles had told him that Marianne was 'a sexual maniac',[9] though this might be an indication of just how toxic relations stood between mother and son. Relations between the high-spirited Shaw and Lionel were no better.

As Lionel was increasingly ill, he had been encouraging Marianne to earn money. In February, she and D'Arles took over a florist's shop in Wimbledon, Jonquille et Cie ('Daffodil & Co'), which Lionel financed. Marianne would stay in Wimbledon during the week, living above the shop as D'Arles's wife, returning to Borley at weekends. She and D'Arles made friends with Mr and Mrs Fenton, a Jewish couple who ran a chemist's in the same parade of shops.

Trevor Hall traced and interviewed Mrs 'Billy' Fenton.[10] Marianne had enjoyed feeding the credulous Billy with a series of tall stories about her life and background; she was the daughter of Count and Countess von Kiergraff of Schleswig-Holstein and a graduate of Cambridge University. Marianne later admitted that these were 'flights of fancy; kind of a soap opera. It seems too horribly silly, but it seemed a lot of fun at the time to tell a continuous story.'[11] Keen to be nearer to London than to sleepy Borley, Ian Shaw had moved to Wimbledon to help Marianne and D'Arles in the shop.

Hall then began a correspondence with Evelyn Gordon in Bournemouth, who, during the tenancy of the Foysters, had run a childrens' playgroup at Borley Lodge, a fifteenth-century manor house situated in the nearby settlement of Borley Green.[12] By 1933 Lionel was very slow, in terrible pain and used two sticks to get about the house. Marianne blamed this on the harsh life he'd experienced in Canada. As she was now spending much of the week in London, Miss Gordon was concerned about Lionel, but particularly about Adelaide. She had become a very nervous, excitable child who had been raised very strictly and pressed hard by Lionel with her lessons. As Marianne was unable to keep staff at the Rectory, and was now infrequently at home, Adelaide had started to cook herself – simple dishes such as rice and potatoes. This pressure on the young girl (she was five years old), along with the unconventional living arrangements in the house, began to affect her behaviour. She had started to draw on the walls. Mrs Pearson had sighed that she had 'a horror for scribbling'.[13] Several times Adelaide had been discovered building small fires out of pillows in one of the bedrooms, though the smell would alert somebody in the house and the fire would be extinguished. She would talk incessantly of 'having to burn down the Rectory'.[14] An experienced nursery nurse, Miss Gordon did not think this the normal psychology and behaviour of a five-year-old.

There was only the ailing Lionel in the house to look after Adelaide when she fell dangerously ill with mastoiditis. This was a common infection in children, of the mastoid bone just behind and below the ear. Before the advent of antibiotics, the condition could be life-threatening. The only effective treatment was surgery, which would drain the pus from the mastoid before the infected tissue was removed. With her ear badly discharging, Adelaide was taken to the Hospital for Sick Children at Great Ormond Street. The surgeons sent for Marianne and told her that Adelaide had already had two operations. She now had an extremely high temperature and there was little hope of recovery – Marianne must prepare for the worst. Having already lost baby John, this was unspeakable anguish. One Sunday, Lionel led the congregation at Borley in prayers for Adelaide. All day he expected to hear bad news from London and told young Francois that he might never see his playmate again. The next day, Marianne felt impelled to take the St John Vianney relic to the hospital and asked one of the nurses to slip it into Adelaide's bandages. A few days later the crisis was over and Marianne wrote to Lionel that the doctors were astonished; Adelaide's ear had healed. Lionel was convinced that they had been blessed by divine forces – 'And God wrought special miracles by the hands of Paul,' he quoted from the Acts of the Apostles, 'so that from his body were brought unto the sick handkerchiefs or aprons, and the diseases departed from them, and the evil spirits went out of them.'[15]

Given the girl's behavioural issues and the lack of care she seemed to be getting, Evelyn Gordon approached the NSPCC and informed them that she thought Adelaide might be suffering from neglect. Miss Gordon was informed that she was not the first to approach the society about the welfare of the child. But on investigating the case, though conditions at the Rectory were far from satisfactory, there had been no technical cruelty. There was nothing they could do.

In 1940, some weeks after the appearance of Cyril Joad's glowing review of *The Most Haunted House in England* and his unstinting praise of its author in *The Spectator*, a response had appeared in the letters page from Henry Lawton, the vicar of St Luke's, Rochdale. He had stayed at Borley in 1933 as *locum tenens* while Lionel Foyster was away. His experience was very much at odds with that which Price described in his book. As far as Lawton was concerned, there were no ghosts at Borley. He had hoped that his letter might draw some attention, but it had gone unanswered and unnoticed, quickly forgotten with the intensification of the Blitz. But in January 1942, Eric Dingwall had met him at Tavistock Square in order to discuss his experiences at the Rectory. Trevor Hall now followed this up and went to meet Lawton near his current parish in Manchester. Hall found him highly intelligent, shrewd, level-headed and with a first-rate memory.[16]

Lawton had been forty years old when he, his Welsh wife Irene and their two children – a boy of nine and a girl of seven – had moved into the Rectory for the month of August. Lionel Foyster was at Long Melford hospital with heart trouble, while Marianne was busy with the flower shop.

On his first day at the Rectory he came across the manuscript of *Fifteen Months in a Haunted House*. Irene being heavily pregnant at the time, Lawton was alarmed by the title and, with some trepidation, read the document. In view of his wife's condition, he decided not to tell her or the children and, knowing that the neighbours were aware of the reputation of the house, asked them not to discuss it with his family.

Throughout the time they were in residence, Lawton and his wife slept in the Blue Room, apparently the most haunted room in the house, but their sleep was undisturbed. He would often go down to the kitchen at the far end of the house in the middle of the night when the children wanted drinks, lighting his way with a candle. He felt that this would have seemed an 'irresistible temptation to the bottle-throwing poltergeister allegedly infesting the Rectory to demonstrate their presence'.[17] But he neither saw nor heard anything. He did note that the almost entirely enclosed courtyard within the building did produce a peculiar acoustic, so that sounds in the yard echoed throughout the house, particularly if any of the windows facing it were open. At the same time, he never saw any evidence of mice or rats, though he admitted that the weather that summer was particularly warm, so the rodents could feed and sleep outside in the plentiful fields, rather than finding shelter within the house as they would in the winter.

During their stay, Irene Lawton spent much of her time indoors. As it was a hot, dry August, she was particularly fond of sitting in the drawing room that looked out over the Nun's Walk. Lawton would often find her happily sitting there well into twilight when he returned from the many tennis tournaments that he took part in. There was no suggestion that she was ever troubled by anything untoward, despite the hypersensitivity of her condition and what appeared to be ideal circumstances in which the nun was supposed to haunt the garden.

Over the summer, Lawton acquainted himself with many of the locals, especially Ethel Bull, who would become godmother to his daughter Esme when she was born that September. He felt that the Bull family were mildly proud of the ghostly legend of the Rectory but didn't take it very seriously. Alfred Bull repeatedly told him that he had never seen or heard anything abnormal at all.[18] During their stay, Lawton also became friendly with Mr and Mrs Bigg across the road at Borley Place. William Bigg was a former church warden and had known the Smiths very well, though they had not got on. Over several conversations with Lawton, he had revealed his view that the 'haunt' during the Smiths' time had been engineered by Eric Smith.

A friend of Smith's was keen to buy the Rectory and the land surrounding it, on the condition it could be secured for a bargain price. Presumably this would lead to a healthy commission for Smith for arranging the sale, so he had tried to convince the Bishop of Chelmsford and the Bulls that the house was not fit to live in and should be sold. By inviting the press to inflate the notoriety of the house, he had deliberately attempted to depreciate its market value. This ruse may also have inspired the Smiths' persistent requests for Harry Price to submit a professional report about the paranormal activity in the house. Lawton became convinced that the Smiths had lied about the phenomena to the Bishop, Price and the press in order to tarnish the Rectory's reputation. This would easily explain, so Lawton thought, Mabel Smith's later change of heart. The Smiths had *never* believed the house was haunted, but only pretended to do so. Once Eric Smith had died, Mrs Smith's fervent religious conscience had weighed heavily on her and inspired her letters to the press, contradicting their former statements.

Henry Lawton had met the Foysters, but only once. He had

heard a story in the village that Marianne had admired some jew-
ellery in a London shop that later appeared on the mantelpiece at
Borley. This was clearly an attempt to conceal from her husband a
trinket that had been bought for her by an admirer. Lawton believed
that the Rectory's ghostly reputation was inspired by the legend of
the nun, which had given Eric Smith a convenient focus with which
to embroider his petitions to the Bishop. This was further inflated
when Marianne Foyster used the phenomena as a smokescreen to
conceal her illicit behaviour from her husband.

As their investigations continued, Eric Dingwall received a suggestion to contact Gay Taylor, a reporter for the Mass-Observation
Archive that had begun recording everyday life in Britain since
1937. Mollie and Dingwall arranged to meet Mrs Taylor at the
Society for Psychical Research in Tavistock Square.

Mrs Taylor had corresponded with Price since 1942, discussing
the Waldegrave and Catholic backgrounds to the story. She had visited the village herself and become acquainted with Ethel Bull and
the Turners, who now lived at the Rectory Cottage. She'd had what
she believed to be 'a variety of small experiences', though she had
been disappointed to be met with little but scepticism in the village,
being advised by the locals that 'there waunt no ghosts till Harry
Price brought 'um'.[19]

She told them that during Christmas 1949, a friend of hers,
Wanda Haines,[20] had taken part in a seance in Gloucestershire
where Borley had also been mentioned. Another of the sitters, Edith
Shaw, had flared up at the mention of Marianne Foyster's name.
She was, Mrs Shaw declared, a liar, an adulteress and a bigamist.[21]

As a commercial traveller living in lodgings in Ipswich, in the
autumn of 1934 Mrs Shaw's brother, Johnny Fisher, had met
Marianne on the station platform at Marks Tey as she was changing
trains.[22] A vulnerable man, he'd had a motorcycle accident in his
youth and had suffered head injuries leading to permanent mental-
health problems. He had become, his sister admitted, particularly
susceptible to the charms of women. He asked her when the train

would be going in the opposite direction. She wasn't sure. He asked where she was going. Telling him she was going to London, where she worked, she introduced herself as Marianne Voyster, the daughter of Leon Alphonse Voyster, the rector of Borley. There was an instant attraction and they arranged to correspond. Soon afterwards they spent the night together in a London hotel.[23]

Meanwhile, as her son Ian Shaw had returned to Belfast, Marianne had taken on a sixteen-year-old girl to help out in Jonquille et Cie. When she discovered that D'Arles was sleeping with the girl, Marianne ended her own relationship with him. At this point, money still a concern, the Foysters had rented out part of the Rectory to a Mr Viall, his daughter Ursula and their housekeeper, Mrs Warren, but their financial problems were now exacerbated as they closed the shop. D'Arles subsequently set up his own business with his new girlfriend elsewhere in Wimbledon, taking his young son with him.

With no money coming in from the shop, Marianne got a job in Ipswich selling Jiffy washing machines so took a room locally on Gippeswyk Road, where she would also carry on her affair with Johnny Fisher. This was actively encouraged by Lionel, who was keen to see Marianne happy and, aware of his declining health, worried for her future. Fisher seemed to come from a good family and the Foysters assumed that he was financially comfortable and able to offer Marianne security. Marianne invited him to the Rectory and introduced Lionel as her father and Adelaide as her sister. To the smitten Fisher, it all seemed above board. Meanwhile, Lionel began to have fainting fits, he developed problems with his speech and his memory started to fail. Marianne accompanied him to St Luke's Hospital in London, where he was diagnosed with a further decline in his heart condition. Once again, he was taken into Long Melford hospital. Marianne worried that he might never leave it. This may have precipitated her next decision; she told Johnny Fisher that she was pregnant, predicting that he would do the decent thing and marry her.

Having persuaded Fisher to convert to Catholicism, the pair

married on 23 February 1935 and thereafter they lived at both Gippeswyk Road in Ipswich and Borley, where she continued to act as the rector's wife whenever Fisher was on the road. Lionel's health had unexpectedly improved and he was allowed to return home, where she explained the bigamous arrangement she'd made, which he seemed to condone. In August, while Fisher was away for several weeks visiting his family, Marianne surreptitiously adopted another baby boy, from the Church of England Adoption Society.

Timothy Eaves had been born in Birmingham on 14 July to an unmarried shorthand typist. Taking the child home, she sent a telegram to Fisher in Michaelchurch: 'It's a boy!' When he returned to Borley, Fisher was thrilled to meet his son, now named John Fisher. Though adopting him had been a way of securing and validating the marriage, the child gave Marianne the opportunity to fulfil the maternal role that she craved. She could, perhaps, correct the mistakes of the past.

One Sunday in October, Marianne had to push Lionel across the road to the church in a wheelchair. Since her marriage to Fisher, Lionel had become very preoccupied with the notion of sin. In the pulpit he was 'hollering'[24] about it in his sermon, when he suddenly collapsed. The doctor insisted that there must be no more preaching. His life as a priest was over and he must relinquish the living at Borley.

Marianne, her two husbands and two adopted children left the Rectory and moved into a modest, much more manageable bungalow they had built with some money from an insurance policy of Lionel's, in Woodbridge Road East, Ipswich. But after the remoteness and peace of Borley, Lionel didn't enjoy living in the suburban bungalow. The road outside was busy, the house unsuitable for a wheelchair and the garden overlooked by the neighbours. When she had visited, Fisher's sister, Mrs Shaw, had been discomforted when Lionel sometimes referred to Marianne as his wife, before quickly correcting himself. Marianne would explain that this was simply age; his mind was wandering. But Mrs Shaw began to suspect that all was not right between the aged rector and his daughter.

When Marianne had visited her at her home, Edith also became concerned about the baby, who she thought was being neglected. His nappy was a dirty piece of rag. When Marianne took it off to check his nappy, his bottom was one vast red sore. She replaced the dirty rag – excrement and all – back on the child. She told Mrs Shaw that she 'loathed children and had no patience for them'.[25] When the two women had arranged to go out, Edith said that Marianne hadn't started to change the child's nappy and she'd told her that they couldn't leave him on his own unless they had somebody to babysit. Marianne told her that she never bothered with a babysitter and always left the baby on his own.

As the bungalow ultimately proved to be impractical, the Fishers were glad to move to a large redbrick farmhouse at Chillesford, which everybody liked. They now had land to grow vegetables, raise poultry and keep goats.[26] Once settled there, in order to tighten her hold on Fisher, Marianne pretended to be pregnant again and adopted another illegitimate child, Mary Lex, also passing her off as Fisher's daughter. She was baptised Astrid Fisher at St Mary's, a Roman Catholic church in Ipswich. John and Astrid would be brought up as brother and sister with Marianne dressing them and styling their hair as if they were twins. But Fisher had doubts that the baby girl was his, which he shared with his mother and sister.

When war broke out, medically unfit for service, Fisher was conscripted to work in a munitions factory in Saxmundham. The farmhouse had been perfect for peace time but was not suitable for wartime life, so, in 1941, the family moved again, to Dairy Cottages in Rendlesham. Meanwhile, Fisher had been hospitalised with a duodenal condition at the hospital in Saxmundham, leaving Marianne to manage Lionel and the children alone while living with the anxieties of rationing and bombing raids.

Increasingly suspicious of her sister-in-law and concerned about her brother's well-being, Edith Shaw now wrote to Ethel Bull in Great Cornard. Miss Bull told her that, whatever Marianne had said, she and Lionel Foyster were husband and wife, not father and daughter. An appalled Mrs Shaw wrote to Marianne accusing her of entrapping her brother into a bigamous marriage. Marianne begged Mrs Shaw not to expose her, for the sake of the children. Dairy Cottages, she claimed, had been bombed and she was penniless. Eventually Mrs Shaw and her family prevailed on Fisher and managed to remove him from Marianne's influence, to live 'in seclusion'.[27] Marianne had left him completely broke and suffering from a nervous breakdown. Edith Shaw felt that Marianne's cruelty and self-interest knew no bounds. Lionel Foyster had died in 1945, but if his body were to be exhumed and examined, she was sure that traces of poison would be found; she was absolutely convinced that Marianne had murdered him.

Johnny Fisher was not the only vulnerable man that Marianne had apparently manipulated and exploited. Trevor Hall now traced Dr John Russell Davies, who had become entangled in a relationship with Marianne through his acquaintance with Harry Price.[28]

Davies was a GP who had studied at Cambridge University before joining a general practice in Leamington Spa. When his wife Mabel had died of cancer, in 1941, he had been floored with grief. They had no children and he had no remaining blood relatives. He couldn't bear the idea of living alone, so sold his practice and moved to London. At the height of the Blitz, he was living in the Grosvenor Hotel at Victoria Station, wandering aimlessly around London during the day and frequently contemplating suicide. At the time, the railway lines from Victoria were a target for German bombers and several bombs hit the terminus as well as the hotel.

The focus of Davies's life had become making contact with his dead wife, who he called 'Tweatie'. He knew very little about spiritualism other than what he'd learned in popular books by writers such as Harry Price. So, he wrote to Price and was pleased to receive a reply, inviting him to visit Price's Laboratory and to his home in Pulborough. Price recommended various mediums who he thought might be able to help, but none were successful. Having read *The Most Haunted House in England*, Davies became convinced that Marianne Foyster was an extraordinarily powerful medium. He thought that she could offer him the best chance of communicating with his wife, so he asked Price if he could be put in touch with her.

In September 1941, a letter arrived at the Grosvenor from Dairy Cottages in Rendlesham. Marianne wrote that she would be willing to travel to London to help Davies, if he sent her the train fare. When they met at the hotel, he thought Marianne exceedingly attractive, with her raven-black hair and dark, shining eyes. Davies told her that she looked very similar to Tweatie. She expressed great sympathy for his loss and assured him that she would use her powers to communicate with his dead wife.

At first their relationship had been very much that of medium and client. On one occasion Marianne had gone into a trance in a quiet corner of the hotel lounge. During this trance, she embraced him, which he admitted he found sexually arousing. Over the next six months, during further trances, Marianne started to embrace him more intimately. As Davies talked about his wife, Marianne told Davies of her invalid husband, whom she called 'Lion', who had, she lamented, no growl left. He was old and ill-tempered, and didn't like visitors. Her life in Rendlesham was dull and she much preferred the pleasure and excitement of London. The lonely widower quickly became infatuated with the lonely rector's wife.

Davies took Marianne to restaurants and the theatre in the midst of wartime. She apologised that she had little suitable to wear on these outings as her financial situation was so dire. So, Davies offered her all of his dead wife's clothes, which Marianne gratefully accepted. She was very keen to know of his financial position and was particularly eager to learn how much he had sold his practice for. But by 1942, he admitted that his reserves of money were running low. This seemed to immediately chill Marianne's ardour. At the end of March, she wrote to him saying that the relationship was over and demanded the return of the love letters that she had sent him. He asked her to do the same and to return his wife's clothing. When the clothes arrived at the Grosvenor Hotel, he was deeply disturbed. The dresses had been tied into the shape of dolls with strange cabalistic shapes cut out of cardboard. Pinned to the garments were scraps of paper with insulting messages written on them, and silk stockings had been knotted through coloured circles of cardboard. He suspected that Marianne was trying to put a curse on him. He never received his letters, nor did he hear from her again. Though he had fallen in love with her, Davies felt there was something ' rather Satanic' about Marianne.[29]

By 1952, Mabel Smith's health had declined and her concerns about any renewed interest in the Rectory were making her paranoid. 'Borley seems to have been a curse,' she lamented, 'and it has got to stop.'[30] She wrote to Mollie Goldney, wondering what was happening with the *Borley Report*. Mollie replied that she didn't know when, but they were determined to expose Price. This horrified Mrs Smith and made her even more anxious, as she worried about being involved in a litigation case with Price's estate, which she could ill afford. She had therefore decided that she did not want the letters that her husband had exchanged with Price to appear in print. Mollie reassured her that the focus of the *Report* would be Price, not her.

But by 1953, Sidney Glanville had died and Paul Tabori had gone to work in America, leaving the *Borley Symposium,* Price's projected final volume of the Borley story, without an editor. When they read a draft of it, Mollie felt it was incomplete. Trevor Hall was 'too bored' to finish it and regarded it 'as of no value'. Dingwall dismissed it altogether. But William Salter wasn't concerned. As far as he could see, the *Borley Report* would be a bestseller and a credit to all. He didn't agree that a thorough exposure of Price would discredit either psychical research or the Society for Psychical Research in any way. In the end, the society would focus on their own report and the *Borley Symposium* would never be published.

When Trevor Hall travelled up to Carlisle to interview him, William Phythian-Adams declared that his contributions to *The End of Borley Rectory* were made very much with his tongue in his cheek. As far as he was concerned, it was just a bit of fun that he'd conjured while ill in bed that Christmas. Nobody was more surprised than him when Price appeared to take his theories seriously and then decided to publish them. But he was very critical about Hall's investigation of Price's work on Borley. There was no justification for the Society for Psychical Research to publish an attack on Price after his death. The investigators would upset Price's widow and damage their own reputations as well.

Despite his warning, Hall continued his investigations – if anything, with more vigour and determination. Casting Marianne Foyster as the seductive enchantress, he attempted to track her down, ostensibly to establish if she had any psychic powers. He was assisted in this by Herbert Pratt, Honorary Librarian of the Magic Circle, whom he employed, effectively, as a private detective. Both Hall and Pratt were fascinated, even obsessed, with their femme fatale. 'Quite frankly,' Pratt admitted to Hall, 'I am about twice as interested in Marianne as I am in Borley Rectory.'[31]

Pratt travelled from Liverpool Street to Suffolk with a map of the area, making precise notes of his bus and train fares, as well as his lunches. Marianne's last known address was Dairy Cottages in Rendlesham, 4½ miles from Woodbridge. The house was one of a pair of two-storey red-brick houses that had originally been used to accommodate workers from the Rendlesham Hall estate. Pratt was struck by how very remote and rudimentary the cottage was, with no running water and served by a single outside lavatory. Talking to Marianne's former neighbour, he was advised to talk to a Mrs Knights at a house called 'Kantara' on Kingston Road in Woodbridge, within sight of the Debden Estuary.

A grey-haired lady with glasses in her mid-fifties came to answer the door. Pratt wondered if she knew the whereabouts of Mrs Fisher? Her face blanched. She only wished she did. She invited him into the house to talk in private.[32]

Letty Knights had first got to know Mrs Fisher at St Thomas's, the Roman Catholic church in Woodbridge. As far as Mrs Knights knew, Marianne Fisher was a cultured and well-bred woman who lived in Rendlesham with her husband and father, a retired Anglican clergyman. Marianne's mother, so Letty believed, had been Danish and had died when Marianne was very young. She was an only child and had been brought up in her mother's Roman Catholic faith. Mr Foyster had married again, and they had a child, Marianne's half-sister, Adelaide, who boarded at a covent in Braintree run by the Sisters of the Immaculate Conception. But Foyster's second wife had left him, leaving Marianne to look after him in his later years. Mrs Knights thought Marianne's husband, Johnny Fisher, was 'slightly mental' but had been a great help looking after his father-in-law during his long illness.[33] The war had been difficult for the Fishers. Marianne had worked as a full-time carer for her bedridden father, lifting and carrying him when he lost the strength to move himself, and cleaning him when he lost control of his bodily functions. Fisher was unable to help as he had been conscripted to work in a munitions factory in Saxmundham and could seldom return home because of the blackout. Young John was at school during the week, but returned home at weekends. Astrid, a sickly child, rarely left the convent that she boarded at. As if the situation wasn't demanding enough, Marianne had also taken in two evacuees from Bromley, David and Stewart Dowding. It was compulsory for homes to host assigned evacuees, with host families like the Fishers being paid 10 shillings and sixpence for the first unaccompanied child and eight shillings and sixpence for any subsequent children. Marianne wouldn't have made a profit from housing the evacuees, but larger families could make rations go further.

One day, Lionel had collapsed, so Marianne had sought help from an army doctor at a nearby American airbase. Following the incident, a couple of GIs from the base had come to Marianne's cottage to see how he was. One of these was a member of the ground crew for the 390th Heavy Bombardment Group, a young Irish farmer's son from Wisconsin called Robert O'Neil. He began to call at the house bringing alcohol for Marianne and sweets for the children. In comparison to the rationed and beleaguered British, Americans like O'Neil were awash with luxury goods and money.

With the end of the war in sight, on 18 April Lionel Foyster died from exhaustion, bedsores and arthritis. This was both a blow and a relief to the exhausted Marianne. However unconventional their marriage, they had stayed together, across continents – though more in sickness than health – for twenty-three years. It was the longest and closest relationship of her life. Two days later she took out a death notice in *The Times*'s personals, listing Lionel's appointments in Canada. There was no mention of Borley. It ended with a brief quotation from a popular American poem: 'There is no death.'

Finding the facilities at Dairy Cottages too rudimentary, as soon as another house became available, Marianne moved once again – to Deben Avenue in Martlesham, where O'Neil became a lodger. At the new house, Marianne became acquainted with a woman from Framlingham called Kate Howlett who had come to collect her insurance premiums. Mrs Howlett confessed to Marianne that she had been having an affair with an American serviceman, who had now returned home. When her husband was demobbed, he found she was pregnant with the American's child. He was prepared to reconcile with her, but only on the condition that she had the baby aborted. She didn't know what to do. Marianne undertook to take the baby when it was born. She was delighted when Mrs Howlett gave birth to a little boy called Peter on 8 October.

After Easter 1946, Marianne had called at Letty Knight's house to ask her a favour. She needed to go to Ireland for a few days over the Whit weekend to deal with her father's affairs. She wondered if Letty would look after John, who was now ten. Adelaide and Astrid were at school and, now the war was over, the two Dowding boys had been sent back home to their father. Marianne would take with her baby Peter, who was only six months old at the time. Letty said she'd happily take care of John for a couple of days over the half term. The next week Marianne arrived with the boy and, after a few minutes, she said goodbye and left, 'just as if she was going to post a letter'.[34] That had been eight years ago. Letty Knights told Pratt that she had never seen or heard from Marianne since. She had completely vanished, leaving John with only the clothes he stood up in.

Letty had taken care of John as agreed for two days, but when another couple of days went by, she had begun to worry. She went to Deben Avenue, taking John with her, but when they arrived, the house was empty. Talking to the neighbours, she was told that the Fishers had vanished a few days before. Nobody had seen them move out. Mrs Knights immediately went to the police. The next day, a letter arrived from Marianne that had apparently been posted from a ship, enclosing John's ration book, but no explanation. Letty then consulted a solicitor in an attempt to trace her. He discovered that Marianne had gone to Canada and was living near the US border. She had deliberately abandoned her own children. Mrs Knights consulted the police about the possibility of extradition, but had been told that the abandonment of the children was 'a misdemeanour to which extradition is not applicable'.[35] Realising that Marianne had disappeared and didn't want to be traced, Letty had written to Somerset House, the records office, for John's birth certificate and had then legally adopted the boy herself.

John then began to confide in Mrs Knights about the life they'd led at Rendlesham. He'd enjoyed his time with old Mr Foyster, who, though confined to his bed, had a lively, inquisitive mind. The boy would often feed him with an invalid cup or write letters for him. His room, he confessed, became a refuge from the fierce temper and abusive behaviour of Marianne. They were never to call her 'Mother' or 'Mummy'; she insisted on being called 'Morny'. John revealed that Morny would have 'strange soldiers' billeted on her every night. Owing to lack of beds, they 'always slept with mother'. Letty Knights was clear on this point: Marianne was a prostitute.[36] She had treated all the children with sadistic cruelty, beating them continually and making their lives miserable. If they misbehaved, she would punish them by holding their heads in buckets of cold water.[37] Letty was in tears as she told Pratt of her worries for the baby 'that cruel woman' had taken with her. What sort of mother – what sort of woman – would collect vulnerable children, offer them a home, but treat them with such cruelty, then discard them like unwanted pets?[38]

Dust-jacket, *The Haunting of Borley Rectory*. First edition, 1956

CHAPTER NINETEEN

THE BORLEY REPORT

January 1956–1 October 1978

> The Legend was already there. It had only to be clothed,
> embellished and supported by the testimony of others to come
> alive again.
>
> Eric Dingwall, Mollie Goldney, Trevor Hall,
> the *Borley Report*[1]

Following fraught relations between the three writers of the *Report*, fractious negotiations with Mabel Smith about quoting from her husband's letters, and anxiety from the publisher and the Society for Psychical Research about a potential libel suit from Marianne Foyster, the *Borley Report* was finally published in a stand-alone volume of the society's *Proceedings* in January 1956. Having heard of the combustive nature of the material, Mervyn Horder, the director of the publisher Gerald Duckworth, was excited that it felt like a 'real life detective story of a unique type'.[2] He persuaded the society to publish a simultaneous commercial edition, *The Haunting of Borley Rectory*.

In the 180-page report, Dingwall, Goldney and Hall cast themselves as valiant truth-seekers in the campaign to expose Price and rid psychical research of deception, trickery and fraud. They argued that Price realised that at Borley, there was a framework around which he could build a dramatic and complex ghost story with the veneer of 'scientific' authority. Anything that weakened or challenged this flimsy structure, however, was dismissed or simply ignored. 'Normal causes were discounted, critics silenced or their objections overruled, and commonplace happenings were magnified into mysterious and incredible phenomena.'[3]

If Price had believed in the genuineness of the phenomena, he'd had an extraordinary opportunity to investigate it scientifically when he took on the tenancy of the house. But instead of securing experienced observers, he invited amateurs, blocking the attendance, for instance, of members of the Magic Circle. By the time of Price's tenancy, the forbidding house was dank, dark and draughty, a maze-like rabbit warren with heaps of rubbish in the courtyard, which had peculiar acoustics. He then provided the observers with the *Blue Book*, which tantalised them with what they might see and experience at the Rectory. No record or logbook was kept.

Curiously, many of the careful distortions, deletions and exaggerations that Price made in his books about Borley were easy to check against his archive held in the University of London, or even in the press.

Sidney Glanville's 'Locked Book', held in the University of London, revealed that Price had shown him an account that he was going to include in *The Most Haunted House in England* from an observer who claimed to have experienced some remarkable phenomena. Glanville pointed out that the report was fanciful as the phenomena couldn't have taken place as suggested because of the actual layout of the Rectory. Glanville was much more familiar with it than Price, as he had drawn up the ground plans. He advised Price to consign the report to the bin. But Price didn't agree. 'No,' he said, 'I will alter it. It makes a chapter.' The facts, he felt, shouldn't get in the way of a good story.

Despite being situated next door to a noisy and smelly working farm – which is barely mentioned throughout *The Most Haunted House in England* – Price consistently denied the presence of mice or rats at the Rectory. Price also chose to ignore the testimony of anybody who questioned the notion of paranormal activity at the

Rectory, such as Annie Pearson, who had worked there every day for years and continued to live opposite the Rectory site but was never interviewed by Price; and Henry Lawton, who had stayed at the Rectory in 1933 and experienced nothing untoward. Yet he did include an interview with Fred Cartwright, a carpenter he had apparently met in 1930 'over a pint of ale at the White Horse' in Sudbury.[4] Cartwright claimed to have seen the nun on four separate occasions in 1927, but had subsequently disappeared, his story impossible to verify. The *Report* presumed that Cartwright had exaggerated his story to encourage the willing Price to pay for another round, though it also hinted that he had made up the meeting altogether.

Focusing on Charles Sutton's testimony, the *Report* accused Price of actively faking phenomena and planting evidence. He had form for this, and had been suspected of malpractice during his investigation of the Battersea poltergeist. Two members of the Robinson family had complained that 'things always seemed to happen' when Price was around, and that 'there was some power about Mr Price that attracted things'.[5]

Mollie Goldney spent seventeen pages of the *Report* attempting to reconcile the contradictory statements made by Mrs Smith, but the longest chapter, focusing on the Foysters, was written by Trevor Hall. Despite repeatedly saying in private that she was the conscious source of all the phenomena during her period at the Rectory, in *The Most Haunted House in England*, Price accepted the phenomena as continuations of the haunting. Hall hinted that he had been unable to tell the full story, and didn't directly accuse Marianne of adultery, bigamy, child abuse or murder. Using the established legends surrounding the Rectory, he argued, she had played tricks on her gullible and infatuated husband in an attempt to prove that the house was haunted and impossible to live in, so that they could leave it. Of the 103 paranormal incidents during the Foyster tenancy, 99 were dependent on Marianne's good faith, though the *Report* hinted that she may have had accomplices. Edwin Whitehouse had longstanding mental-health issues and Francois D'Arles, who wasn't mentioned in either of Price's books, may have had his own motivations for colluding with Marianne in the production of trickery.

In his attempt to write a bestselling sequel to *The Most Haunted House in England*, Price realised that he needed a strong story at the heart of the book. Having been contacted by Phythian-Adams, he developed the 'cold case' murder story of the nun, Marie Lairre. Her bones had been discovered not at the bottom of a well, as the planchette seances had foretold, but conveniently near the surface of the cellar floor. Sidney Glanville was Price's best friend and near neighbour. He was one of the most regular and loyal of his observers as well as a man of absolute integrity and rectitude – and yet he had not been invited to the excavation of the cellars at the Rectory. Price had, the *Report* implied, surreptitiously planted the bones during the excavation in order to provide a dramatic and touching denouement to the story. He even had a photographer on hand to record the burial, which would provide an illustration in the book.

The 'final accusation of flagrant misrepresentation'[6] by Price was his inclusion of the 'flying brick' in *The End of Borley Rectory,* which he had written about as 'The Last Phenomenon'.[7] Yet it was clear from Cynthia Ledsham's testimony that she, Scherman and Price had all been aware of the builder throwing the bricks as part of his job, just outside the frame of the photograph. There was nothing supernatural about the 'flying brick' at all.

The *Report* concluded that Price was a brilliant if cynical journalist who used the material he'd gathered in the laboratory or in the field to provoke the greatest publicity. If the material lacked the sensational elements that he thought necessary, he was prepared to provide these himself. Goldney, Dingwall and Hall were aware that the case did not rest on Price's testimony alone; there had been hundreds of witnesses over many years. But their distorted memories and guesses, partly derived from notes and partly from recollections of what they thought they saw, felt and heard, had been coloured by a barrage of suggestion conjured by Price.

*

As perhaps William Salter had intended, demolishing both the Borley legend and Price's reputation in one savage blow, the *Borley Report* proved to be a controversial sensation. Godfrey Smith in the *Sunday Times* wondered if Price had 'deceive[d] the world cynically from the beginning, or was there some point at which his genuine and passionate interest in psychic matters overbalanced into fraud so that he might win more converts?'[8] Reviewing the *Report* in *The Spectator*, Anthony Flew thought it a 'shattering and fascinating document: offering satisfaction at last to all who have been curious to know what really was the truth about Borley. Harry Price was able to erect and maintain for years the house of cards which he built out of little more than a pack of lies.'[9]

But the defence of Price was equally vigorous. In a lacerating review in *Tomorrow*, Nandor Fodor, no friend or ally of Price, admitted that he had been a difficult man, 'easy to resent' and could be a dangerous enemy.[10] But he was disgusted with the *Report*, and the people who had written it, two of them – Goldney and Dingwall – claiming to be Price's friends. It was not only the damning of Price that offended Fodor, but the damage the book would do to the study and investigation of the paranormal.

Following the controversy created by the publication of the *Report*, the BBC recorded a programme based on it, *The Haunted Rectory*.[11] In the programme, Eric Dingwall confessed that he had always been astonished that anyone had ever taken Price seriously. First and foremost, he had been a journalist – a storyteller, not a scientist. The programme was scheduled to be broadcast at 5.30 p.m. on 10 September. But after the BBC legal department expressed concerns about a potential libel suit from Marianne Foyster's lawyers, it was cancelled. To this day, it has never been broadcast.

Over the Christmas of 1956, having read the *Report* alongside *The Most Haunted House in England* and *The End of Borley Rectory,* a Welshman curious about psychical research, called Robert J. Hastings, wrote to William Salter. In the course of his study, he had noticed several inaccuracies and mistakes. 'It was disquieting and very puzzling to discover,' he wrote, 'that every one of the mistakes I had noticed, tended in a direction unfavourable to Price.'[12] An unsettled Salter wrote to Mollie Goldney that he regarded Hastings 'with some suspicion'.[13]

After repeatedly refusing his requests, in 1965 the Society for Psychical Research finally funded a re-examination of the *Report* by Hastings, even paying his £50 expenses. This eventually appeared as 'An Examination of the "Borley Report"' in March 1969.[14] Hastings's primary argument was that much of the case directed against Price rested on his own writings. But since he himself had deposited his archive at the University of London, where anybody could consult it during his lifetime, he clearly hadn't regarded the material as incriminating, or even compromising. Fundamentally, the *Report* was a prosecutor's case and no attempt had been made to find arguments in Price's defence. Hastings felt it was so biased, it should never have been published. The three authors of the *Report* responded at length to Hastings's findings but in doing so sought to firmly draw a line under the matter: 'we do not propose to continue the controversy any further'.[15]

Trevor Hall imagined that he and his collaborators had had the last word on Borley and Harry Price, but Hall became increasingly aggrieved that the story of the Rectory had been completely revised by its depiction in television programmes that had prompted sensational accounts of the haunting in illustrated books and tabloid newspapers. In 1973, Peter Underwood and Paul Tabori (Price's 'disciples', Hall sneered)[16] published *The Ghosts of Borley: Annals of the Haunted Rectory,* dedicated to 'the memory of Harry Price the man who put Borley on the map'.[17]

Hall's hostility to Price culminated in 1978 with a biography, *Search for Harry Price*, in which he derided Price's background, highlighted his pretensions and repeatedly questioned his integrity. Much to Hall's chagrin, Price's understanding of the public had been astute; they preferred the 'bunk' to the 'debunk'. 'Borley's reputation as the most haunted place in the world,' Hall seethed, 'seems to be completely restored.'[18]

Reviewing *Search for Harry Price*, *The Times* wryly observed that its author had 'left no stone unturned or un-thrown', leaving Price 'without a rag of integrity and utterly nothing to his credit'.[19] The Society for Psychical Research's John Randall had 'never read anything so infused with unmitigated malice'.[20] Fermented and sustained over many decades, Hall's near-fanatical hatred of Price is difficult to fathom – they had never even met. They had similar interests – the esoteric, book-collecting – and shared similar insecurities about their backgrounds, a penchant for self-aggrandisement, a snobbishness about academic qualifications and a curious fetishisation of their appearance in *Who's Who*. Perhaps the similarities didn't end there. The review of Hall's book in *The Times* concluded that the real truth of Harry Price may have been that he just wanted 'to be somebody, to be significant and famous'.[21]

In the autumn of 1967, Peter Underwood had been to visit Price's widow at Arun Bank. A short, deaf, rather dumpy lady with tinted spectacles opened the door and introduced herself as Constance Price. Underwood explained that he was a friend of Paul Tabori and had been friends with Sidney Glanville. He wondered if he might photograph the bell that had been salvaged from the Rectory, which he knew was fitted above her husband's workshop. At the rear of the house, Mrs Price showed Underwood the bell, which hung over some green doors marked 'Workshop'. It was larger and heavier than he had imagined. She told him that she often used it to summon her brother and sister-in-law, who lived next door.

Underwood found Mrs Price warm and kind. He commiserated with her about her husband's death. It had come as a great shock to everyone, he told her. She agreed it had been unexpected, though he had occasionally complained of a pain above his heart, but they hadn't thought it was anything serious. It was a shame, she thought, as he had just started another book about Borley. He had, she said, overworked himself; 'he never stopped,' she sighed; 'He was a clever man, really.' She wondered if Underwood would like a glass of sherry and invited him onto the white painted balcony that looked out over the garden and the octagonal pond where Price used to keep his golden carp. She brought out a silver tray on a bamboo table, with some sherry, glasses and plain biscuits. Talking of Borley, she said she knew nothing about it but had been advised by Mr Walker at the Midland Bank not to read the *Borley Report*. She was disappointed that Mollie Goldney had turned out to be so two-faced and that Eric Dingwall was no better. They had often visited and she had looked on them as friends.

At the end of the visit, Underwood wondered what would eventually happen to the Borley bell. Mrs Price said that was in the gift of Price's executors and the University of London. As he prepared to leave, she led him through the hallway and pointed out the portrait of Price painted by John Dumayne; handsome, arrogant, young. On reaching the front door they passed the hall stand. Here were several of Price's hats and coats, still hanging up after twenty years, his walking sticks standing in the corner. It was almost as if, Underwood felt, Price had just stepped out but very shortly would return home.[22]

Marianne Foyster in the backyard at Jonquille et Cie,
Worple Road, Wimbledon, 1933

CHAPTER TWENTY

MOST HAUNTED

11 August 1945–18 December 1992

'I was in the wrong place, at the wrong time.'

Letter from Marianne O'Neil to Peter Underwood, 1986[1]

In the autumn of 1945, as peace descended across Europe, American servicemen were sent home and demobilised.

Despite the difference in their ages when they had first become acquainted at Dairy Cottages – he was twenty-five and she forty-six – Lionel had observed how well Robert O'Neil and Marianne got on. They had quickly begun sleeping together, which Lionel had condoned. He had frequently suggested that she should return to North America after he died. They had always been so happy in Canada. The warmth and openness of the people suited them, compared to the rigid conventions they had experienced in England. Marianne could only agree. Now bedridden and worried about the prospects for her and Adelaide without him, he suggested that she should marry O'Neil and go back home. When she protested that she was already married to Johnny Fisher, Lionel countered that she could have that marriage annulled. After all, neither of their children were his. Marianne resolved to leave England and start a new life in America, at all costs.

When the war ended, O'Neil's unit was to be sent to Europe before returning to the United States. If he went back to America, she might never see him again and her opportunity would be lost. Marianne had to think and act quickly. Just as she had done with Johnny Fisher, she told O'Neil that she was having his child. A young, naive and decent Catholic, he asked her to marry him. As she expected he would.

On 11 August, Marianne arrived at the register office in Ipswich for a wedding that had been arranged by special licence with one day's notice. The application had been signed by her only, though much of the information she provided was bogus. This was necessary as US servicemen were not authorised to marry foreigners without permission. The witnesses were two cleaners who worked in the building. One of them, Mrs Benneworth, remembered that Marianne had looked downcast and seemed to be about three and a half months pregnant ('I have always had a high stomach,'[2] Marianne later explained). The office closed at 3 p.m. on Saturdays and the groom had arrived, out of uniform, with only three minutes to spare. Once they were married, O'Neil was sent to France.

In October, when Marianne had taken in Kate Howlett's baby as arranged, she had written to tell her husband that he was now a father to a baby boy named after him, Robert Vincent. He was thrilled and proud: 'I guess the baby is like me in his ways, too Hon.'[3] Taking a photograph of 'Junior', she sent it O'Neil's mother, Esther, in Wisconsin, who wrote back advising her on the details of her entry into America. It would be essential for the child to submit a birth certificate. Soon, Marianne's acquaintances began to notice that she had started to cultivate an American accent.

Like all GI brides, she was faced with a complex transatlantic bureaucracy of visas, immigration laws and transport quotas, before having to submit the correct documentation and provide proof that she had sufficient funds to cover her train fare when she arrived in America. She was informed by the American embassy that she wouldn't need a visa to enter the country but would have to register her child's birth at the American consulate. Having done so – fraudulently – on 20 May, she and Vincent were processed through the

ex-military base at Tidworth near Southampton, which had become
a holding camp for such women. Marianne was obliged to strip and
queue to have a torch shone between her legs to check for venereal
disease. The brides were required to give up their British ration
books and were now fully taken care of by the American state.

Marianne and the baby stayed at Tidworth for four months as
they waited for passages to America. In June, having sold all the
furniture from Deben Avenue, Marianne quit the house and abandoned all three of her adopted children. John was adopted by Letty
Knights. Astrid was told that as she was often ill, Marianne couldn't
cope with her at home, so she would remain at the convent. Adelaide
had started training as a nurse in a hospital in Manchester. In July,
Marianne had Vincent baptised as a Roman Catholic at St Mary's
Church in Axminster, Devon. In August, she carefully packed
Lionel's sixteenth-century family Bible before sailing for New York.

Unlike the well-travelled Marianne, most of the women on board
had never left the country before and some had never seen the sea.
Many looked battered and older than they were, after years of sleepless nights and meagre rations. Marianne had endured six years of
anxiety with dwindling finances, caring for an ailing, bedridden
husband and surviving on potatoes, carrots, Spam and powdered
egg. In contrast, when they arrived in New York, it felt like a won-
derland of luxury, scale and opportunity. She had always thought of
America as the New World and all that that implied – a fresh start,
away from war, hardship, heartache and all the ghosts she hoped to
leave behind. If the thought of three abandoned children crossed her
mind, it didn't stop her.

Having arrived on the east coast, Marianne and her son travelled
over a thousand miles by train to the prairie town of La Crosse in
western Wisconsin, situated on the Mississippi River. In his letters
to her, O'Neil had projected a future for them in farming. They'd
buy 500 acres of land next to his uncle's farm and would eventually
build their own house on it. They'd need about $4,000 to buy the
land and to invest in tractors, ploughs and cultivators. As there
wasn't much time left for the spring planting, they'd need to start

as soon as Marianne arrived and O'Neil was hoping that she would finance it. But once probate was passed, she received only £850, about $3,500, from Lionel's estate.

When she first arrived at O'Neil's grandmother's farm, where they were to stay, Marianne found it to be up a very poor road, deep and isolated in the Minnesota hills. O'Neil's father had died when he was eleven and his mother and grandmother lived together in a large, welcoming house with the extended family. They were generous and devout Roman Catholics, but their living conditions were basic, with no electricity or indoor plumbing. They used kersosene lanterns and chamber pots, and though La Crosse enjoyed very hot summers, it suffered freezing winters, a memory of Marianne's harsh life in New Brunswick. Their dreams of a farm curtailed by their lack of funds, O'Neil decided to join a plumbing firm instead and bought a house in the small town of Hokah, some 13 miles away. As they settled into life in Minnesota, O'Neil acquired a new Hudson automobile. The summer of 1946 was bright, sunny and happy for the O'Neils and their little boy, who they now called 'Vinny'.[4]

In 1947, O'Neil had allowed one of his friends to take the driver's seat in the Hudson, but he'd been drinking, which resulted in the car being run off the road. O'Neil was hospitalised, his jaw and clavicle broken. The car was ruined. The accident signalled a change in his behaviour, as he began to recall his wartime experiences, though Marianne dismissed them as all talk. She was popular with the neighbours, but her new husband, at nearly half her age, soon revealed himself to be feckless, more fond of drink and women than work. A reckless driver, he was arrested several times. He would often not turn up for work and soon the money Marianne had inherited from Lionel ran out, forcing her to take a job in the office of the local newspaper, the *Hokah Chief*. She subsequently found employment at a prairie school near Bangor in Wisconsin, falsely claiming that she had teaching experience and a degree from the University of London. Struggling to pay the bills and the mortgage, soon creditors began to call constantly. When writing to Billy Fenton in Wimbledon, Marianne bitterly regretted that she hadn't stayed in England. 'I thought it would be fun to be back on the American continent,' she wrote sadly, 'but one can't go back in life, only forward.'⁵

The marriage continued to deteriorate as bailiffs repossessed their furniture and valuables for non-payment of bills. By early 1951, they had separated and five-year-old Vinny was placed in care at the La Crosse Home for Children. But despite promising to pay $35 a month towards his board, O'Neil paid nothing, and didn't provide any clothes for his son, either.

Meanwhile, having proved a failure as a teacher, Marianne was working as a cleaner, washing floors to make ends meet, until she could find a long-term position away from the alcoholic and increasingly violent O'Neil. She travelled 500 miles to Jamestown, a North Dakota prairie town where she was interviewed by the editor of the *Jamestown Sun*, Mr Hansen. When he asked her if she had any experience as an assistant editor, she was honest and told him that she hadn't, but was willing to learn. Marianne charmed Hansen and he intuited that she was in dire need of a job. He offered her $45 a week.

Marianne having now secured a regular income, the La Crosse probation department agreed to send Vinny from the children's home and they moved into a modest apartment together. Marianne would start very early at the office in the morning and occasionally she'd take Vinny to work with her. To earn extra money, in her spare time Marianne would teach dancing and write freelance articles, stories and poems for other publications. Soon they were able to move to a larger apartment and to buy back the china, silver and furniture that had been pawned or sold when they left Hokah. Marianne juggled the demands of her new life in America, effectively as a single mother, though the jobless O'Neil soon moved back in with her. She found it hard to be alone and felt that he was a good man – when he wasn't drinking.

She continued to correspond with family and friends in England, including Lionel's sister Hilda and Billy Fenton, to whom she'd

send pairs of nylon stockings. Letty Knights wrote to her from
Woodbridge, signing her letters, 'with fondest love'.[6] They would
continue to correspond, exchanging their news and sharing photographs of John and Vinny. Marianne was thrilled when Letty told
her that John wanted to train for the priesthood. Despite her small
income, she managed to send money in order to help with his education at a seminary. Though she had lost touch with Adelaide, who
had moved to Manchester, for a while she continued to send letters
and gifts to Astrid, who replied from the convent in Braintree, her
correspondence supervised by the nuns. When Astrid was about
nine years old, Marianne sent her a parcel containing two dolls,
a bride and groom. When Astrid wrote to thank her, addressing
her as 'Dear Mum', Marianne wrote back and insisted that Astrid
wasn't to call her 'Mum' anymore, only 'Mama' or 'Morny'.[7] She
would never hear from Astrid again.

In February 1954, Marianne had an unexpected letter from Peter
Underwood in England. He explained that he was working on a
new book about the Rectory, the projected *Borley Symposium*. He
had read a draft manuscript of the Society for Psychical Research's
Report that he felt was 'devastating and mischievous'.[8] Underwood
felt that the only way to balance the damage of this report would
be to publish Lionel's *Fifteen Months in a Haunted House* in its
entirety. Loath to cause any more trouble or court more publicity,
Marianne refused permission for him to print it. Despite her best
efforts to contain the past in England, it would not lie.

On the publication of the *Borley Report* in 1956, Marianne had
a letter from her brother Geoffrey, informing her that in some of the
footnotes, it had revealed her true age, her whereabouts during the
war and her bigamous marriage to Johnny Fisher. The interest in the
paranormal events at Borley was now threatening to expose intimate
details of her past and to destabilise the life that she was trying to
construct for herself and her young son in America. At the same
time, her older son, the now forty-year-old Ian Shaw, had also read
about the *Borley Report*. He wrote to Trevor Hall via the University

of London, telling him that he knew a great deal about his mother and the alleged phenomena at Borley. 'The whole business,' he wrote, 'was founded on a mass of falsehoods and deception.'[9] He informed Hall of various aspects of her character, and particularly her sexual history, in England and in Canada – little of which was verifiable. He was driven, it seemed, by anger and resentment. Hall was an all-too-willing listener and thrilled when Shaw told him that he could also offer Marianne's address in America. Finally, he had his quarry.

Though they had not corresponded for some years, Ian then wrote to warn his mother that Hall, Dingwall and Goldney were in pursuit of her. They were confident that she was responsible for the haunting and that she had sold Lionel's diary to Harry Price. They also knew about her affair with Dr Davies, that she was a bigamist and that she had made her escape from England pretending her adopted child was that of an American serviceman.

When she read Ian's letter, in Jamestown, a shocked Marianne was left trembling. As the possibility of her being tracked by the Society for Psychical Research seemed inevitable, she started to panic. The past that she thought she'd escaped was coming back to haunt her. She admitted to Ian that she *had* told grand stories, but only to 'offset the pain and hunger and misery' she'd suffered.[10] But since she had come to the United States she insisted, 'I have not gone around telling lies, and I don't do soap opera anymore.'[11] But she now worried that if her lies and duplicity were exposed, the American authorities would take Vinny away and send her to prison. All she had ever wanted, she protested, was a baby of her own. 'I was not allowed to bring up my own child and longed above all things in life for a little boy. Do you understand that?' This was a bitter pill for her natural son to swallow. She went on to tell him that she'd had a letter from Edwin Whitehouse warning her that Mollie Goldney, who she couldn't abide, also had her address and was threatening to visit. She was adamant that she was not responsible for the activity in the house: 'I didn't do it but I think every kid and youth in and around Borley for the past 75 years has had a hand in it.'[12]

She asked Ian – hardly an ally but the only person she could turn to – for advice: 'Do you think if I wrote to [Hall, Dingwall and Goldney] and told them I didn't do it and that all this about my so called love affairs is nothing to do with ghosts and that Harry Price didn't buy the diary they would stop persecuting me?'[13] She just wanted the investigation to stop and begged Ian to steer her pursuers away from Vinny. Her desperation was evident: 'Shall I commit suicide? I have contemplated it so often.'[14]

Hall and Dingwall both wrote to calm her. 'Do not distress yourself,' Dingwall assured, 'your private affairs have nothing to do with the haunting.'[15] She was insistent that she was not responsible for the phenomena at the Rectory. Again, she threatened to kill herself: 'If I have to go through any more I will shoot myself. I cannot go on. Life isn't worth it.' A distressed Marianne feared that she lived 'in the shadow of a volcano'.[16]

In the depths of a snowy February in 1958, Marianne returned home from work at the *Jamestown Sun* offices, to be told by O'Neil that she had a visitor. Startled and immediately suspicious, she was introduced to a good-looking young man, Robert Swanson. He had told O'Neil that he wanted to talk to Marianne about 'some facts for a book', but he was more direct with her and admitted that he was a private detective.[17] Immediately, she knew: he was here about Borley, wasn't he?

Marianne protested that all she wanted was to be left alone. But the charming Swanson persisted and eventually persuaded her to meet him later that evening at the Gladstone Hotel, the largest hotel in Jamestown. As he prepared for their meeting, Swanson talked to several of Marianne's friends and neighbours in the small town of 7,000 inhabitants. It seemed that she was regarded as a very pleasant woman who'd had a difficult time in England during the Blitz. She worked hard to make ends meet and to make sure that her son was cared for. There was no indication that she had relations with other men, though it was rumoured that her husband 'liked his women as well as his liquor'. Marianne patiently supported him in his drinking habit and what she called his 'wildness'.[18] Despite her long-standing devotion to Roman Catholicism, in 1955 she had been baptised as a member of the Mormon Church of the Latter-day Saints. She did so, she told friends, because following the death of her baby daughter, the Catholic Church had not allowed the child to be buried in a cemetery because she hadn't been baptised before her death.

Swanson was employed by the Irish medium Eileen Garrett, who had founded the Parapsychology Foundation of New York, but his arrival in Jamestown had been instigated by Marianne's nemesis, Trevor Hall. Having decided not to disturb her mental health further by corresponding with her, he had approached Mrs Garrett. Hall justified his prurient interest in Marianne's private life by claiming that it was crucial to a study of the case. Mrs Garrett had insisted that a qualified investigator should question Marianne. Apprised of her apparent weakness for men, Garrett had deliberately chosen Bob Swanson, who was recommended by her lawyer for his masculine good looks.

The snow fell hard and settled deep in the freezing night air outside the Gladstone Hotel, where Swanson interviewed Marianne. Swanson observed that Marianne's slim figure had filled out. Her hair was neat though 'in need of work by a beautician'[19] and her clothes decent but inexpensive. He thought her a 'strange woman' and felt that the only reason she had agreed to be interviewed was because the psychical investigators knew too much about her past. She had lied in official records, which could lead to her being turned over to the federal authorities and deported.

The questions Swanson asked had all been prepared by Hall in advance and the whole interview was recorded on a tape recorder. Marianne adamantly denied that she had anything to do with the phenomena at Borley. She thought that the whole situation had started years before, in the time of the Bulls. But there had always been 'something there'.[20] She believed that the Smiths had been intimidated by the size and condition of the house and by naturally occurring noises such as rats and starlings caught in the roof. Much of the alleged haunting during their stay at the Rectory was due to pranks by mischievous local boys, who carried on during her time there. She suggested that Lionel may have been responsible for some of the phenomena and Edwin Whitehouse certainly had something to do with the wall-writings.

She stressed to Swanson that when Lionel wrote the manuscript recording the activity in the house, he was a very sick man, 'always off his rocker', suggesting that he may have been suffering from dementia. And besides, the book was not intended for publication; it was 'more or less fiction'. The manuscript was not intended to fall into the hands of 'such an unscrupulous person' as Harry Price. As far as Price was concerned, she regarded him as a fake, a magician 'who might readily have produced the effects for his own purpose'.

At one point in the interview, she told him that she wanted to start a new life and wondered if she would be able to find work in New York. If she could get away, she would leave her husband and take her son with her. But she was now terrified of being deported. Breaking down, she wept on Swanson's manly shoulder. An awkward Swanson felt that if he had stayed around much longer, Marianne 'most certainly would have made a pitch for him'.[21]

Marianne had been very upset by the meeting. But when Swanson sent the tapes and his report to Garrett and Hall, they were dissatisfied. Her answers were evasive and sometimes contradictory. So, Eileen Garrett suggested that they bring her to New York, where she could be interviewed more rigorously over more time. Hall came up with a dozen lengthy questions that he was anxious to have clarified. Mrs Garrett invited him to join the next interview in New York but as he felt that he might inhibit Marianne, he preferred to remain in the background.

In April, the charming Swanson invited Marianne to New York, offering to pay for her air fare and accommodation as well as expenses. When she received the letter – and the money – she was overjoyed, flattered by the attentive and alluring detective. She was looking forward to the trip as an adventure away from her ordinary life. 'I have never had a proper holiday which included airplane trips and a stay in a hotel. I have only passed through New York. Among your many kindnesses,' she asked, 'will you arrange that I am allowed to look at the Statue of Liberty?'[22]

Marianne flew to New York and was interviewed by Swanson from 9 to 13 May at the Governor Clinton Hotel on Seventh Avenue. She was cheerful when she arrived, bolstered by the adventure of her plane trip east. She told Swanson that she wanted to get the entire Borley Rectory affair finished and out of her life. She intended to be truthful but pleaded with him not to focus on her private life. But many of Hall's questions were intrusive and personal. Whenever Swanson tried to pose such questions, she would ask, 'What has that to do with Borley Rectory?'[23]

Again she denied all responsibility for any activity at the Rectory. She did feel that certain rooms in the house were unhappy – it wasn't only her who had felt this. The same was true of the church. There were incidents at the Rectory that she couldn't explain, such as a light in the schoolroom that would mysteriously appear. 'I don't know that could have been produced by fraud,' Marianne said, 'and I don't think it was. It was ... there are phenomena like that often experienced in Ireland around people going crazy. It's just one of the things you have to accept. I think people have forgotten that there are other things inhabiting the house beside human beings.'[24]

However, she had suspected that some of the phenomena might have been down to Lionel: 'he had opportunity there to do it if he wanted to'.[25] Marianne insisted that Lionel had started writing his book as 'something to do, something to while away many tedious hours, and if it ever had been published, it would have been as a book of fiction'.[26] She hadn't read it, but Lionel had read her excerpts and they had both laughed. It was ludicrous and unfair of Price to have used it in a scientific way, as if what Lionel was writing was true.

After the interview, Eileen Garrett took Marianne out to dinner to her favourite restaurant, accompanied by Swanson. Though she found her wilful and mischievous, Garrett was charmed by Marianne. The flirtatious Marianne admitted that she had every

intention of lying to Swanson – for lying, Garrett felt, was a game
to her. It was evident that she adored Vince, as she now called him,
who was twelve, and she was delighted when Mrs Garrett proposed
that she might be able to help him out with a scholarship in the
future. Marianne then agreed to write up an outline of her experiences at Borley. Finally, Garrett, Hall and the investigators were to
have the testimony of *the* key witness to the most infamous haunting in the world, in her own words.[27]

Garrett wrote to Trevor Hall that they hadn't gained very
much from the interviews and weren't sure what more it would
add to Hall's investigations. What was most elusive was the motivation for her actions and repeated patterns of behaviour. Why
had she adopted the children simply to abandon them? Why the
restless moving from one address to another? Why the stories and
contradictions?

Hall had now completed the five volumes and 600 pages of
Marianne Foyster of Borley Rectory. But so sensational and libellous was the material that it stood little hope of being published
until after Marianne's death. He sent Mrs Garrett a copy and suggested that the material be made available to students of psychic
studies at her discretion. He insisted that no other copies were to
be made or notes made on any part of it 'for a few years at least'.[28]
Hall would die in 1991, never having seen the results of his long,
obsessive pursuit of Marianne in print.

When she returned from New York, Marianne's marriage disin-
tegrated further as O'Neil became more violent towards her and
Vince. The drunken O'Neil would abuse his son, then tearfully
apologise: 'Why do you make me do this? I don't want to hit you.
Why do you make me do it?'[29] After he broke both of Marianne's
wrists, she refused to press charges but divorced him and moved
away to Fargo in North Dakota. Being a much larger town than
Jamestown, in Fargo Marianne could be anonymous, away from
O'Neil and far from the vengeful furies who seemed insistent on
drawing her back to the past.

She got a job with the town's branch of the Lutheran Welfare Society, counselling unmarried mothers. With no intention of ever returning to England, she became an American citizen in 1959. As Vince grew to be a teenager, Marianne struggled with his temper and relations between them were fraught. She seemed so secretive about the past and would never explain what the boy's own background was. When he got into trouble for stealing a car, the court threatened time at a correctional centre. He was sent to live on a farm with some of Marianne's Mormon friends in Utah. Immediately, she missed him and would send him cards and letters every week, though he rarely replied. Her letters express an overwhelming, even suffocating love for Vince as she feels him grow up and grow away from her ('You are my whole world and the meaning of it')[30], as well as the constant anxiety of being haunted by past sins and the fear of being hunted because of them.

In 1963, when Vince was finishing high school in Utah, Marianne moved back to La Crosse to work as a social worker with families, rather than dealing solely with pregnant teens. By 1966 she was working as coordinator for the La Crosse Committee of Aging, though she herself was already sixty-seven years old. Though her career had progressed, she was disappointed. 'All I ever wanted in life has been a home and children; a garden, a pet and church work,' she wrote to Vince. 'I have never attained it. I know now that I never will.'[31]

When Vince married and started his own family, she told him several times that she would find a job and move to Utah to be near him. But she never did.

In 1981, following a car crash, O'Neil had a routine X-ray that revealed an inoperable tumour. He was given six months to live. When he died, despite their unstable marriage, Marianne was hit hard. 'It's my turn next,' she told Vince. Her hair now grey, she started to wear a wig. Due to a hernia, she was unable to wash in the bathtub and began to lose interest in personal hygiene. After she suffered a stroke at work in 1990, Vince went to visit her and was shocked to find the house stashed full of empty whisky bottles – he was able to fill two large bags with them.

In order finally to be closer to her son, she moved to a retirement home in Utah in 1992. 'I do love you Vinny,' she told him, 'I
always have.' But after she broke her hip in August that year, an
X-ray revealed a lump in her lungs and death began to stalk her
by degrees.

On 18 December, Marianne, the femme fatale at the heart of
the drama of the most haunted house in England, died, unnoticed
by many and mourned by few, in a hospital in Utah at the age of
ninety-three.

In the first of the bequests in her will, Marianne had stipulated that
the sixteenth-century Foyster family Bible should be offered to the
Smithsonian Institution in Washington. If they declined, it should
be passed to Vince, and when he died, it should be shared between
his children. But on 30 June 1994, he received a letter from a Mrs
Cartwright in Eccles in the north of England, asking for the return
of the Bible. It had 'no historical interest in the USA and should
never have left England with M. O'Neil'. She signed herself 'formerly Adelaide Foyster'.[32]

Vince had never heard of Adelaide Cartwright – or Adelaide
Foyster – but the two began a correspondence. She explained that
she was the Foysters' adopted daughter – which was news to Vince,
who had no idea about his secretive mother's past life in England.
Adelaide wrote that she had been in Manchester since 1944, where
she had worked as a nurse. In 1950, she had met and married her
husband Gordon, a diesel engineer. She had some good memories
of Marianne, but hadn't had contact with her since she had left for
America. She was able to offer him several names and dates to piece
together his own history. Vince relinquished ownership of the Bible
and it was returned to Adelaide.

On 8 September, Vince posted a public notice on the internet
asking for help with his genealogy. Very quickly he was contacted
by Nick Rowland, a local history enthusiast in Suffolk, who offered
to help him investigate his background. Soon Nick had turned up a
huge amount of information relating not only to *The Most Haunted*

House in England but also to the recently published *Widow of Borley.* This had been commissioned by Gerald Duckworth after Marianne had died and was based on Trevor Hall's research. 'Your "Mother",' Nick wrote, 'was one of the most amazing women of her time and also became one of the most notorious. This part may not be pleasant for you.'[33] Vince began to order, from libraries and book dealers, as many books about Borley as he could find. He learned that only two copies of Trevor Hall's account of Marianne's life existed – one in Hall's own archive and another in Eileen Garrett's Paraspsychology Foundation in New York. When he contacted them to trace the book, the Foundation sent him some photocopies of it, but also put him in contact with the psychical researcher Iris Owen, a British immigrant to Canada, who had also investigated Borley. She had actually interviewed Marianne in 1979, but had promised not to publish the contents of the interview until after Marianne's death.

In 1976, Iris had received a call from Paulene Mitchell, a book reviewer from Toronto who was looking for an experienced psychical researcher, such as Iris, to collaborate with. She had read about Borley and had become intrigued by the whereabouts of Adelaide Foyster. She decided to write to the local newspaper in New Brunswick, who published her letter. Within a couple of weeks she was in touch with Adelaide's sister, Edna Tower, who told Paulene that Adelaide had very unhappy memories of her life at Borley and didn't want to talk about it. There were very bad feelings between the Tower family and Marianne, who had told Adelaide that she was an only child and had never revealed that she had a family of blood relatives in North America.[34]

Two years earlier, in November 1974, Adelaide had received a phone call that had left her speechless. On the line was a man called Wallace Tower from Chepachet, Rhode Island, who told her that she was his long-lost sister, Barbara. He had last seen her when she was eleven months old. As far as she'd known, she was an only child and had no brothers or sisters. Edna had written to her regularly, but she had been told by Marianne that she must refer to her only as a cousin, not a sister. But when Lionel Foyster had died, in 1945, the letters had stopped. The last letter Edna had sent had been returned, marked 'Addressee Unknown'. For the next twenty-nine years, the Tower siblings had heard nothing about their youngest sister. 'It really bothered us,' said her brother Fred, 'but what could we do? We didn't have the time to do anything else.'[35]

In 1973, Wallace, who was the oldest brother, felt it was his responsibility to try to track Adelaide. He had travelled to England, placing advertisements in local newspapers in Suffolk. On his last day there, he was contacted by John Knights in Woodbridge, who told him that Marianne had remarried and was living in Wisconsin. Wallace had duly visited Marianne in La Crosse, who at first said she had no knowledge of Adelaide. But after some persuasion she finally gave him two pictures of her and reluctantly provided Adelaide's last known address in England. But when Wallace wrote to the house, he found that it had been demolished.

He had then been contacted by the writer Alan Roper, who had been investigating the Borley case and had finally tracked the Cartwrights down in Manchester. He gave Wallace their address and phone number. When Adelaide received the phone call in November 1974, Wallace invited her to Rhode Island for Christmas. 'It was not until we set foot at Kennedy Airport ... that we knew it was not a fairy story,' she said.[36] When Adelaide walked out of the airport gate, her family were there to greet their youngest sister 'magically returned from the dead'.[37] They recognised her immediately. Finally, after forty-six years, the Tower children were reunited. It was, Adelaide said, 'the most marvellous reunion of a lifetime'.[38]

Having spoken to Adelaide's sister, and now intrigued by Marianne's story, Paulene wrote to Marianne in La Crosse. Marianne was shocked to have been traced. She was now extremely reluctant to discuss Borley as she had been badly treated by earlier investigators and was very wary of them altogether. It was only when Paulene pointed out that by giving her version of the story she would finally stop the continual speculation about it, that

Marianne began to consider giving her point of view. She said that she was happy to discuss her life, but only with somebody who had not written about her before. In particular, she did not want Trevor Hall involved, though she was happy for Paulene to refer to the recordings that Swanson had made in Jamestown and New York.

Marianne agreed to a meeting with Paulene and Iris at the Stoddard Hotel in La Crosse. Though seventy-nine at the time, she was very youthful-looking and well turned out. Iris felt she could pass for a woman some fifteen years younger than she was. After the initial meeting, they continued to talk on the telephone or by letter. Marianne wrote full accounts of her life and answered questions quite freely. She did insist, though, that her son Vince should never be contacted and that Iris and Paulene should do everything in their power to prevent him from knowing that she was part of the Borley story. He knew nothing about her past and she wanted it to stay that way. She also made them promise not to publish anything until after she had died. Over the next few months, as they discussed her life with her, Iris and Paulene found her a delightful person – witty, charming and clever. But she was a woman to whom life had dealt a hard, challenging hand. Half a century on, as the key surviving witness to the haunting at Borley Rectory, Marianne offered what *she* felt should be the final story.

On returning from Canada, the major issue that had faced the Foysters at Borley was not ghosts, but Lionel's health. They were aware that their tenancy at Borley could only be temporary. He had lost most of his investments and securities in the Wall Street Crash, so he had become very anxious about money. Marianne had no income of her own and no qualifications.

Knowing the history of the Rectory from his visits there as a child and hearing the experiences of the Smiths from his cousins, the Bulls, Lionel conceived the idea of writing a real-life ghost story. If this became a bestseller like Walter Hubbell's book about Amherst, which had sold 55,000 copies, it would solve their immediate financial problems and secure a future for Marianne and Adelaide. Lionel's initial *Diary of Occurrences* was the basic plot that he began to flesh out in the form of a book (with all the names fictionalised) that was to be called *Fifteen Months in a Haunted House*. Marianne said that everyone in the household knew that Lionel was writing the book, and they all knew that it was a novel.

She was sure that they were regularly troubled by local boys throwing things and creating mischief, and the house was open at all times of the day and night with people coming for parish business or to use the lavatory. But she thought that Lionel produced some of the phenomena himself in order to see how people would react. He didn't intend to frighten or deceive, but he did want to test people's reactions to apparently paranormal phenomena so that he could record it in his book. Always drawn to the theatrical, he would often relate stories of the phenomena to visitors to gauge their response. Significantly, the phenomena stopped completely when Lionel was finally confined to a wheelchair.

She thought it possible that Edwin was also a confederate of Lionel's. They were very close, and had developed a romantic, and possibly sexual, relationship. He was an emotionally disturbed young man, obsessed with religion and unsure whether he wanted to be a spiritualist or a Roman Catholic. The wall-writing, Marianne felt, was certainly down to him. Again, when Edwin had left the district to become a priest, around the time of the Marks Tey Circle seance, the phenomena had suddenly stopped.

When Lionel sent Harry Price the *Diary of Occurrences* prior to his first visit, it suited Price's purposes to pretend to believe that it was true. When he failed to send back the manuscript months later, Marianne telephoned him to request its return but Price claimed that he had lost it. After Lionel had died, Marianne wanted no part of Lionel's Borley writings, so she gave everything she had to his sister Hilda. When Marianne left for the USA, she presumed that Price then acquired the manuscript of *Fifteen Months in a Haunted House* directly from Hilda.

Iris felt that Trevor Hall had 'put together a picture of Marianne as an adventuress, a bigamist, a baby farmer and obviously someone who would take part in frauds to suit her own ends'. But Iris and

Paulene didn't recognise this picture from the woman they had met. Badly taken in by her first husband at a young age, she then had only a couple of years of happiness with Lionel before his illness overshadowed their lives. 'She did the best she could with the life she had and the circumstances she had to deal with,' Iris felt. It was only Harry Price and Lionel Foyster who had claimed that there had been paranormal activity at the Rectory. Marianne herself had never made any such claims. Iris told Vince O'Neil that she was sure that what Marianne had told them was true. At eighty years old, with the end of her life in sight, why would she lie?

In October 1994, Nick Rowland emailed Vince from Suffolk, informing him that a documentary, 'Haunted', was about to be broadcast the following week on BBC2 as the first in a series called *Picture This*. Vince contacted the BBC and they sent him a copy of the programme, which he was able to watch in November. It would dramatise, once again, the long and painful influence over many years that Marianne had had over the children that she had drawn to her.

Kevin Taylor, a young police officer from Essex, had been trying over fourteen years to trace his birth mother. She'd had him out of wedlock in 1958 and given him up to the Catholic Children's Society. She'd originally named him Michael John, but had subsequently emigrated to Australia, where all traces of her went dead. Her name was Astrid Fisher.

The documentary followed Kevin and his wife as they visited the convent where Astrid had been raised. Then they discovered that she had been abandoned when her 'mother' left for America after the war. Having placed an advertisement in the *East Anglian Daily Times* asking for any information about Astrid, the Taylors were contacted by John Knights, who was still living in the area.

When they met, John told Kevin that he had only found out that he and Astrid were adopted when Marianne had abandoned him to the care of Letty Knights in 1946. After they were small children, he had met Astrid only once, as the rest of the time she was at the convent in Braintree. But they had corresponded and she would send him holy pictures that he would keep in his missal. Despite Marianne's casual relationship with Catholic doctrine, which she would at times embrace or ignore, the two children were brought up strictly as Roman Catholics, which was to profoundly affect their lives, and their relationship as brother and sister.

Funded by Marianne, John had been trained for the priesthood. But after discovering that he and Astrid were not blood relations, he was advised at the seminary that it would not be appropriate for him to have a relationship with a young woman who was not his 'real sister'.[39] After much agonising, John had written a letter to Astrid telling her that they could no longer communicate. Now, decades later, a haunted John confessed to the TV camera that he had thought, '"She's got nobody now – even I've disowned her." That lived with me for years and years. I still keep the photographs and the holy pictures she sent me.' John didn't finish his training and went on to marry and have a family of his own. He was able to give Kevin an address in Western Australia and it was arranged for Astrid to come to the UK and be reunited with her son and her brother. 'I just hope she forgives me for what I did to her,' John worried. 'I won't know I'm forgiven until I actually can hug her and say "sorry" for writing that letter.'[40]

The documentary crew recorded the emotional moment when Kevin was reunited with his mother Astrid at the airport. He then drove her to John Knights's house to be reunited with him. As the two met in the kitchen, they didn't speak; they hugged each other tightly as Astrid, a middle-aged woman, all of a sudden a girl again, broke down in his arms. She wept as she tried to get the words out, to express the inexpressible: 'I never forgot you.'

Reunited with his sister, John revealed that in 1992 he'd had a letter out of the blue from America telling him that Marianne was in a Utah hospital, very ill and in a coma. So he'd written a short message to be read to her: '*To Morny. From all over here, love and forgiveness.*' John recalled, 'We were told that when that message was read to her by a nun, a sort of look of relief and happiness came over her face. Of course addressing it as "Morny", she knew it could come from only one or two people just because no one else knew her as Morny. I just feel she felt that, "John has forgiven me for what I've done to him – I can die at peace." '[41]

Late in her long life, a red wig covering her greying hair and maxims ready for every occasion ('You start alone and you end alone'), increasingly Marianne felt like a remnant from another world, a pre-war curiosity from a forgotten tabloid tale. Trapped as a character in a story she couldn't control, she was haunted, too, by the woman she used to be. Once settled in the United States, a great teller of tales and stories since childhood, she had fantasised about putting her imagination to use by writing the great American novel;[42] she even bought herself a typewriter. But in its extremity and length, her life was more soap opera than fiction – by turns absurd, intense, sentimental, occasionally comic. Though she tried desperately to forge a second act 'of quiet dignity in the serenity of the American way of life',[43] Borley Rectory came to define her, so powerful was its draw. However far or fast the running, one can never really escape the ghosts that haunt the dark corners of the past or the shadows of one's own nature. 'I hoped that I had heard the last of that other life, in another country, in another world,' she said resignedly. 'I am not the person I was. You may not believe me, but it is true.'[44]

The Hamlyn
Book of
Ghosts
in fact and fiction

Daniel Farson

AFTERWORD

No other story based in the years between the wars so
illuminates the spirit of the times. It is not just the importance
of examining the best evidence so far produced for the
persistence of the spirit after death, but also the strange ways
in which the story becomes an allegory for the age, telling us
about the pains and strivings of a generation. No author could
have ever had the temerity to construct such a potent myth.

Andrew Clarke, *The Bones of Borley*[1]

During the severe winter of 1978, when the economic climate was
as dark and forbidding as the weather, I was given a book for
Christmas by my father, the *Hamlyn Book of Ghosts* by Daniel
Farson.[2] It was a colourful illustrated history of classic hauntings and paranormal happenings, from the time-slip incident at
Versailles to the curse of Lord Carnarvon following the opening of
the tomb of Tutankhamen. On the cover was a striking depiction of
the night of the fire that had consumed Borley Rectory, with strange
figures at the window of the Blue Room, a bewildered lady in a
nightdress commanding the centre of the image. In his introduction, Farson wrote that 'we are moving towards an understanding
of ghosts rapidly. I believe they will soon be easy to explain as
radio, television, tape recordings or photographs – and will prove
remarkably similar'.[3] As a ten-year-old, the story of Borley seemed
to me fascinating, dramatic and, indeed, plausible. What particularly intrigued me was the deft sketches that Farson had drawn of

the protagonists: the bewildered Eric Smith and his wife; Marianne Foyster, the focus of so much of the drama; and Harry Price, a sort of 'psychic detective'.

In 1990, I was working as a young assistant director at the Theatre Royal in Plymouth. One Friday night, a colleague asked if I'd like to join him and his old friend Dan for a drink. Dan had a patrician manner, with the waistline of a man who enjoyed his food and the ruddy face of one who enjoyed his drink more. He was a brilliant conversationalist and I was fascinated when he told me that, as a child, he'd been introduced to Adolf Hitler. He was, Hitler had said as he'd patted Dan's head, a 'good Aryan boy'. I realised this was Daniel Farson, whom I knew, among many other accreditations, was the great nephew of Bram Stoker. So, we talked of *Dracula* and Stoker's day job and mine, the theatre. But his eyes lit up when I mentioned Borley Rectory and we discussed the case into the night. Was Harry Price a scientist or a rogue? Was Marianne Foyster an innocent housewife or a calculating vixen?

Some years later, I had been invited to a wedding in the country. I booked a B&B nearby and made the journey from London out to Essex by train, then through the narrow, winding roads by taxi – for the wedding was to take place at Borley Church. I was excited to arrive there on that bright morning, having read so much about the place. As I looked out over the Stour Valley, I felt a sense of isolation. The towns and villages around – Long Melford and Sudbury – seemed distant from the top of the hill and I wondered what must it have been like for a woman such as Marianne in the years before the war, with no telephone, no electricity and no public transport.

Spring 2022: travelling to Sudbury from Liverpool Street is arduous now, since Dr Beeching closed many rural stations in 1967. You change at Marks Tey, where, years ago, Marianne met Johnny Fisher on the station platform. Just up the road from the station, Mr and Mrs Warren ran their post office and conducted seances in a sitting room behind the shop. The loss of the Stour Valley Railway has had a dramatic effect on the area's current fortunes. There is no train to Long Melford anymore, and no route to Cambridge as there had been before the war. Sudbury is the end of the line.

A busy little English county town, Sudbury has been hit hard first by Brexit and then the pandemic. Though it's only 60 miles from London, it feels like the town that Westminster forgot, 'levelling up' just a phrase here, not a reality.

I hire a car, and on the way to Long Melford I stop at Arthur Hall, which for some years was an Italian restaurant but, after being gutted by fire, had become a local eyesore. Now it has been renovated and developed into flats. At the end of the garden you can walk the footpath that Marianne and Edwin Whitehouse took in June 1931 when they visited the Rectory over nine days to say a novena.

Long Melford is now home to a strip of gift shops, art galleries, estate agents and the odd tea shop. The ironworks and the coconut-matting factory that flourished here in the nineteenth century are long gone, and Stafford Allen, the chemical factory which blew a variety of scents up the hill to the Rectory, finally closed in 2004. Like Harry Price and Lucie Kaye, I stay at The Bull, which stands opposite the Braithwaites' Brook House. The pub is welcoming, if shabby.

The villagers at Borley are very reluctant to speak to anyone about the Rectory, but I had discovered that the former rector, Margaret King, is an avid fan of *The Archers*, which I used to run for BBC Radio, so she agreed to put me in touch with some of them. The village isn't far from Long Melford, but as I drive further into the countryside, the signal becomes poor, the satnav doesn't work and I quickly get lost down the narrow, muddy lanes. I don't meet anybody on the road until I'm bumper to bumper with a surly farm-worker, who refuses to reverse, arms folded, face sullen. I'm amused more than frustrated; the area has never been keen on strangers. A few minutes later, I'm at the top of the hill and park the car by the church. Though it's cold, the day is sunny and the expanse of the Stour Valley lies before me, Long Melford and Sudbury clear in the distance. But it is as isolated as I remember from my previous visit. On the site where the Rectory once stood, there are some smart bungalows, though the red-brick Rectory Cottage still stands opposite the church.

I've arranged to meet Michael Stebbing, who now lives in Borley Place Cottage, Mrs Pearson's former home. He is the stepson of Patrick Payne, one of the five Payne brothers, whose family owned Borley Hall. His Uncle Basil had lived at Borley Place during Price's tenancy. Mr Stebbing has seen many changes since he arrived in the village at the age of two in 1948. Before the war, he tells me, there was a post office, a sweet shop and off-licence in the village. More recently there had been two buses a week. Now there are none. The village is smaller than it has been at any time in its history.

Topiary yew trees still edge the pathway to the church door and Mr Stebbing opens it up for me. Inside it is cool and peaceful, dominated by the Waldegrave tomb. On the walls are memorials to the Herringham sisters and a plaque to commemorate the losses of the Great War, including Basil Bull. On a wall in the bell tower, there's a formal photograph of Harry Bull with the church choir and the organist Ernest Ambrose, which had been presented to the rector for his wedding in 1911.

Michael Stebbing wonders how long the church can remain open, as it costs £50,000 a year to keep going. At Borley, twenty or so parishioners attend the Sunday service that's held only once every two months. Gill Morgan, who took over as rector in 2020, now serves fourteen parishes over a district of 80 square miles. There are few weddings these days as many locals are retired, though, like their forebears, they still choose to be buried in the churchyard.

Mr Stebbing tells me that for decades now, the people of the village have been haunted not by ghosts, but by would-be ghost hunters. Much of the time the little church is locked, a barred gate at the entrance. Outside, there is now CCTV to discourage the visitors who plague the area, not just on Halloween and New Year's Eve but throughout the year. People come up the hill late at night, drunk, and have sex on the tombstones. Canny dealers sell drugs outside the church and, when stopped by the police, simply say they are 'looking for ghosts'. Whenever a television programme is broadcast or a book is published about the Rectory, the behaviour gets worse. This has only been exacerbated by the internet. The rector continues to have two or three requests a month from 'out-and-out cranks' to spend a night in the church. Colonel Dorey, I'm told, who occupied the Rectory Cottage for many years, became so exasperated by ghost hunters that he took to chasing them away with a gun. Vince O'Neil, who had collated a fascinating and detailed website about the Rectory, has taken it down at the request of the long-suffering locals.

Outside in the churchyard on a bright spring day, it's touching to find that Dodie is buried next to Harry Bull. She chose to come home to Borley to rest next to her older brother, rather than with her husband in Yorkshire. None of the other siblings are buried here, just the two of them, positioned behind the graves of their parents, looking out over the Stour Valley. A sad sight: all of the Bull family graves have been vandalised, the stone crosses knocked over or stolen by ghost hunters eager to acquire a souvenir of all that remains of the most haunted house in England.

We're all too familiar today with the warning that prefaces television programmes inspired by real events, eager to dodge accusations of libel or to add a frisson of authenticity: 'What follows is true – apart from some of it.' History is a point of view, an interpretation. In a post-truth world, suffused with fake news, facts are by degrees questionable, malleable, unpalatable. Unverified stories are shared and retweeted. The gospel truth we believed inviolable is revealed, ultimately, to be brittle. But what might be the truth at the heart of the mystery of Borley Rectory?

The natural topography of Essex and Suffolk had made these counties vulnerable to invasion, giving rise to a deep sense of distrust of strangers among the local people. Though there is no evidence of a ghost story specifically relating to Borley until the nineteenth century, the surrounding villages all had their tales of the supernatural. The area clung to ancient superstition. As an old man, Ernest Ambrose recalled that 'People believed explicitly in evil spirits and in apparitions and most certainly in the Devil. Children were often threatened with the Devil: "You marn't do that do the Dev'l get ya." Spirits of good and evil were considered a natural part of everyday life, and heaven and hell were very real places in the minds of ordinary people.'[4]

The development of sensational anti-Catholic literature in the nineteenth century, particularly relating to nuns, may also have influenced the Borley legend in an area that was hostile to Roman Catholic belief. At the same time, the fictional ghost story had become a popular entertainment for the new mass reading public and spiritualism emerged as a new science as well as a parlour entertainment. Ghosts and the paranormal were the currency of the new technological age in which the Rectory was built, where electricity and photography were still regarded by many as contemporary magic.

With the drowning of John Whyard in a nearby river and the storm that destroyed one of the trees in the garden, the construction of the new Rectory seemed to be cursed from the start. When the house was completed, it was beset with various issues that affected the structure of the building, such as the north-east winds, subsidence and even the occasional earthquake, as was the case with the 'Most Haunted House in Scotland', Ballechin House. The Rectory's timber skeleton would creak and the windows would rattle in their frames. There were rumours, too – all unsubstantiated – that there had been a monastery on the site and a plague pit in the garden, with old bones frequently unearthed in the churchyard.[5] These factors all contributed to enrich the legend.

By the last quarter of the nineteenth century, the Rectory was full of young people, including the imaginative and frustrated Dodie Bull, who told ghost stories to her siblings and cousins, and experimented with spiritualism. In her diary she wrote of her 'strong imagination' and the 'rather good stories' she wrote. She longed 'to do something wicked even for the sake of change. I have an intensely wicked heart I fear'.[6] She and her brother Harry encouraged the notion of the Rectory being haunted by the tragic nun and it soon became part of family lore.

In its heyday, the Rectory was served by a large staff, many of whom lived on the premises, most of them women. Female servants were known to be the source of many alleged hauntings, with young women removed from their families at a formative age and forced to live and work with strangers. As a girl, Martha Byford was one of a succession of nursemaids to the thirteen Bull children. Like many young women in service, she was the victim of practical jokes by the other servants who, armed with the spooky tale evolved by Harry and Dodie Bull, set out to frighten newcomers.

Harry's college friend Shaw Jeffrey was known to have an interest in the esoteric, which was probably the reason he was asked to stay at the Rectory in the first place, but he also became the object of affection of two of the Bull sisters. His French dictionary vanishing, and then mysteriously reappearing in his room, seems more likely to be the result of a prank between jealous teenage girls than the action of a poltergeist.

The most significant sighting at the Rectory took place in 1900, when four of the Bull sisters apparently saw a figure in the garden at the same time. The Bulls regarded this very much as a family joke and told the same story over fifty years. But looking at their testimonies, they did not all agree to have seen a nun, only a dark figure. Though Price wrote that the incident had taken place during the day, the sun had set at eight o'clock that evening and by 9 p.m. it would have been dark. The Rectory garden was frequently used by local people as a short cut from Bound's Meadow, through the churchyard to Belchamp Walter. Like Harry Price's record of the man's legs seen among the fruit trees by Harry Bull, in all probability a surreptitious poacher, the Bull sisters may simply have witnessed a villager hurrying through the garden at night.

In the period following the First World War, the neurotic Harry Bull had become more interested – even obsessed – with the supernatural and was happy to talk to the locals about his beliefs and experiences. At the same time, his relationship with his wife had deteriorated and the atmosphere at the Rectory was heavy with discontent. When Harry's sisters were banished from their childhood home by his wife, exacerbated by her Catholicism, they began to nurse a deep resentment towards her. When he died, they broadcast the story around the district that Ivy had poisoned him, thus adding suspicion and murderous intrigue to the Borley story.[7] By then, the house was deemed to be overly large for the post-war age – servants had become expensive and hard to come by. In a generation, it had morphed from a busy family home into a mausoleum. Cold, ugly, unlucky, expensive *and* haunted, the house had developed a toxic reputation and no rector was prepared to live in it. Seemingly uninhabitable, the Rectory was abandoned to the locals, who colonised the empty house as a place for unmarried couples to have sex in and for children to play.

It's into this unpromising atmosphere that the Smiths had taken the house sight unseen. Having arrived from India, where they were able to employ many servants cheaply, they were dismayed by the size of the Rectory and the condition in which they found it. It was vast, cold and damp, and they could ill afford to live there. When Eric Smith arrived, the villagers were dismayed to find that he was Anglo-Catholic. The surrounding district had been anti-Catholic for hundreds of years, and distrusted and disliked Anglo-Catholics. He was colonial, a foreigner, and what's more, he was Black. In the English countryside in the 1920s, a non-white parson would have been not just unusual, but alien to the vast majority of the villagers. They were also in the midst of an economic depression that was affecting farmers and agricultural workers alike, and it would have inflamed their ire – and perhaps their prejudices – to watch the newly arrived rector refurbish his home when many could not afford to make their tithe payments or feed their children. The villagers expressed their dissatisfaction by intimidating the Smiths, attempting to frighten them out of the house and out of the village.

Given the condition of the Rectory and the rumours they had

heard, when the Smiths' appeals to the Bishop for an alternative living were dismissed, they deliberately inflated the stories of ghosts so that they could be moved to another parish. But they needed some sort of official investigation to support their plea, so wrote to their daily newspaper for assistance.

The Society for Psychical Research was the senior paranormal institution in Britain, but given that he was keen on running a newspaper story, not a serious investigation, the editor of the *Daily Mirror* put them in touch with an organisation that he knew would offer good copy, Harry Price's National Laboratory of Psychical Research. Recently arrived from India, the Smiths had no idea that the investigators they had been introduced to weren't the Society for Psychical Research and had no way of knowing what they had let themselves in for.[8] They were unaware of the bitter professional and personal rivalry between the two organisations. Instead of hosting a scientific investigation, they were to find themselves unwitting players in a media story.

Price was smug that he had been invited to investigate the Rectory, instead of the Society for Psychical Research. For William Salter, this rankled for years and may have motivated his insistence that Price's investigation – and his reputation – be questioned in the subsequent *Borley Report*.

When he first arrived at the Rectory, Price wasn't aware that he was confronting the case that would be his focus for the next twenty years and would define his career. Just as he had done at Battersea, he 'helped' the phenomena at the Rectory by throwing a stone at the glass roof above the veranda and then throwing stones and mothballs down the stairs. He was, after all, an expert conjuror. All of this made a good feature for the *Daily Mirror*. But when the Bull sisters attended the seance that night in the Blue Room, Price was soon compelled by the potency – and the potential – of the story. Here was an ancient legend, a haunted house, a terrorised clergyman and his wife, and, like the ghost of Hamlet's father, the former rector making accusations of murder most foul from beyond the grave.

When the Foysters moved into the Rectory, though Lionel was a member of the Bull family, he too was Anglo-Catholic and, like Eric Smith, considered colonial. And just as the suspicious locals were disinclined to welcome a rector of mixed race, they were equally unhappy with the new rector's wife, who was young, attractive and forthright in her opinions as well as her sexuality. She wore fashionable clothes and lipstick, and expressed anti-establishment sentiments – pro-Irish, anti-British and left wing. This was at a time when the agricultural depression was seeing rural areas such as Borley becoming fiercely right wing, targeted as they were by the British Union of Fascists. Having successfully 'haunted' the Smiths from the Rectory, the local people were determined to make the Foysters feel equally uncomfortable.

Marianne insisted over many years that she was not responsible for the phenomena at the Rectory, either consciously or unconsciously. Among others, Lionel Foyster, Florence Whitehouse and Harry Price all considered her psychic and that she may have been a focus for paranormal forces, though Marianne did not consider herself so. There was a history of mental illness in her family and her physical health was poor, necessitating medication that could provoke anxiety and hallucinations. Despite the fact that, by the end of her life, she had formulated the story that Lionel was writing fiction, it seems clear from his writing that Lionel was recording what he genuinely believed to be true. Much of it was also corroborated by contemporary witnesses, including Florence and Edwin Whitehouse.

Marianne had no money of her own and was frustrated by Lionel's tight-fistedness, his income having diminished after the Wall Street Crash. She admitted that she saw an opportunity to use the apparent phenomena at the Rectory to acquire trinkets and clothing that she wanted but that Lionel said they couldn't afford, a harmless enough deceit. But she also admitted to an urgent desire for sex that would occasionally overwhelm her. As she had certainly used the phenomena at the Rectory to disguise her relationship with Francois D'Arles, she may well have done so to disguise more casual flings. Marianne continued to exchange passionate love letters with a man in Canada twenty years after she had left the country.

Marianne had a vivid imagination and had helped Lionel put on plays in Canada. Living in the isolated Rectory with few friends and no money for trips or hobbies, a frustrated and bored housewife, she used the Rectory as a playground, utilising the help, when needed, of Adelaide, D'Arles and the local boys.[9] Some of the phenomena, including the writing on the walls, was inspired by Marianne's stay in Amherst in 1927, when she had heard the story of Esther Cox.[10] Marianne's stories would fuel Lionel with incidents to fill his circular letters. 'What set out as a bit of fun,' she later admitted, 'can surely get one into trouble.'[11]

Convinced – by the reputation of the house, and by the pranks and tricks initiated by Marianne – that the Rectory was haunted, Lionel began to accept supernatural causes for the most mundane phenomena. Things disappearing, he assumed, was due to the 'goblins' rather than his increasing forgetfulness. Mysterious knocking suggested communications from spirits rather than bushes tapping at the window panes in the breeze. Peculiar scents around the house indicated a paranormal presence, rather than the north wind carrying fragrances up the hill from the pharmaceutical factory in Long Melford.

When Harry Price was invited back to the Rectory by Ethel Bull, he assumed that either there was paranormal activity there or that somebody in the household was cheating. It didn't take him long to identify Marianne as the culprit. When he revealed his suspicions to the Foysters, he was banished from the house. As Lionel's health declined and he started to use a wheelchair, Marianne tired of the accusations of the local people. Once she had adopted the baby John Emery and was busy opening the flower shop in Wimbledon with her lover, she was occupied and, perhaps, content. The phenomena stopped. The play-acting was over. The Foysters continued to live at the Rectory for another three years untroubled, it appeared, by ghosts.

Marianne focused her attention on earning money and on the

adoption of the children. She regretted that she had been denied
a meaningful relationship with her biological son and sought a
second chance at motherhood. But perhaps this was play-acting,
too. Self-interest and self-preservation ultimately overrode any
maternal instincts that she may have had. For her, life was a solitary, brutalising experience dominated by fear. 'It's a terrible thing
to live in fear,' she wrote to Vince. 'Moral fear. Fear that every
time the phone rang it could mean trouble ... I sometimes wonder
though how it is possible for someone like me to live through what
I have.'[12] Her marriages transactions, her relationships parasitic,
what haunted Marianne was an awareness that, in a long life, she
had never experienced reciprocal, mutual love.

Once Harry Price had alienated most of his colleagues in the psychical research community, due to his exposure of Rudi Schneider,
he became fully focused on writing books, most of them based
on his former investigations. He began to reconsider the potential
of Borley as a bestseller that he imagined becoming a paranormal classic.

In the years leading to the outbreak of the Second World War,
familiar with the response to the losses of the First World War and
the public's renewed interest in the paranormal at that time, Price
saw an opportunity to construct a popular legend, a modern myth
that suited the times by exploring ancient fears. Though many of
the reviewers of *The Most Haunted House in England* saw it as an
antidote to, or distraction from, the pressures and anxiety of the
war, with hindsight it seems very much a product – and an expression – of its time. The rural village with a church at its heart was the
vision of England that Churchill felt Britain should be defending:
history, tradition, essential Albion. But like Ada Goodrich Freer's
study of Ballechin House, it was entertainment masquerading as
a scientific report. Even the illustrations were a nod to the escapist
crime novels of the period, complete with floorplans. Price manipulated and edited the 'facts' in order to offer the reader a compelling
story. Some things he'd leave out, others he'd exaggerate if he felt it
would 'make a chapter'. But *The Most Haunted House in England*

succeeded in deftly articulating the darkest fears of the war years: death, loss, grief. What he offered to the wartime reader staring into the abyss was the reassurance that ghosts did exist and that human life survived after death. Like all ghost stories, *The Most Haunted House in England* suggested the comforting possibility that 'We'll Meet Again'.

The story of Borley Rectory closely follows the archetypal structure of many celebrated hauntings, such as Ballechin, Amherst, Battersea, Amityville and Enfield. Some low-key activity is experienced by a family, which is, in turn, reported by the press. A professional psychical body is then invited to investigate, at which point the phenomena increases in intensity. This inspires a bestselling book and the story becomes a valuable commercial commodity. Then a myth. The fact that the stories behind these famous hauntings have been proved to be grossly exaggerated and distorted hasn't prevented them from being presented as being at least based on real events, nor has it affected their commercial value. As Iris Owen observed, 'the general buying public does not seem to care very much whether the stories are true or not; they are prepared to believe them.' If Harry Price had been alive in the 1970s, she felt that 'he might very well have made a fortune out of the film rights of his Borley books'[13] as Jay Anson had done with the worldwide bestseller *The Amityville Horror*.[14] Even the cynical Eric Dingwall had grudgingly admitted that Borley Rectory was 'one of the best of all ghost stories and few people could have told it more convincingly than Harry Price'.[15]

Though the Smiths, Price and Marianne were all guilty of exaggerating the phenomena at the Rectory for their own purposes, several of the witnesses were adamant that there *was* something strange about the house and that at least some of the phenomena were real. The Rectory – or rather the story that possessed it – seemed to infect successive residents and investigators like a contagious disease that could be caught and transmitted. The first time they encountered it, the Glanvilles both agreed that 'if ever there was a house that should be haunted, this was it'. Charles

Sutton was convinced that there was 'something evil, something definitely abnormal' about Borley.[16] Mary Pearson also believed that there were dark 'forces at work' at the Rectory.[17] Marianne told Robert Swanson that she thought some of the phenomena *couldn't* have been produced by fraud – 'there are other things inhabiting the house,' she told him, 'beside human beings'.[18]

The haunting of Borley Rectory may be interpreted as a curious parable from history demonstrating the commanding power of the story over the facts in uncertain times, the *real* ghosts perhaps manifestations of deeply held prejudices of a small, isolated and insular community towards anything – anyone – that it regards as 'other': strangers, foreigners, autonomous women or believers in an old religion long dismissed as superstition. Perhaps, in the darker corners of England, those ghosts continue to haunt us. Now, that *is* frightening.

ACKNOWLEDGEMENTS

I began to research this story about ghosts and the relentless pressures of the past in 2019. For many reasons, that now seems not just a foreign country, but a different world.

The staff of the London Library, as ever, have provided excellent support and advice but also offered a lifeline during the pandemic by sending books by post. This enabled many writers to continue with their work at a time of great isolation. Alea Baker, Emily Chu, Jon Morrison and the archive team at Senate House Library have provided enormous help in accessing the vast archive of Harry Price, for which I'm most grateful. Frank Bowles, Michelle Barnes and their colleagues at Cambridge University Library were also extremely helpful in letting me examine the archives of the Society for Psychical Research. The Essex Record Office in Chelmsford offered invaluable insight into the deep history of Essex. Andrew Clarke, who has been researching Borley since the 1960s and met Trevor Hall at the Dorothy L. Sayers Society, has been very generous in sharing his research and his long study of the history of the Rectory and its inhabitants. His excellent website, the Bones of Borley at foxearth. org.uk is a great place to further investigate the history of the Rectory and the ancient and fascinating area of England that surrounds it.

At Borley, I'm indebted to Corinna Brown for opening many doors in the district for me. Former Rector Margaret King and current church warden, Kath Just, met me at the church and showed me round. Fiona Binks welcomed me to the former Liston Rectory as did Paul and Cara Fen at Pentlow Rectory where the Tower still stands in the garden. I'm particularly indebted to Michael Stebbing for sharing his memories of Borley after the war and for his insight into the lives of the current residents and how the story of the Rectory continues to haunt the village. The staff at The Bull in Long Melford were very kind in letting me stay in one of the rooms that Price and Lucie Kaye may have occupied all those years ago. Justin Gollan valiantly negotiated the winding lanes in the area without a satnav, while retaining his good humour.

I'm very thankful to the late David Meeker for sharing his memories of his mother, Lucie Kaye. David went on to have a successful career as an archivist and researcher at the British Film Institute. He told me that when he was managing the National Film Library in the 1960s, he discovered that the first films that had been donated to the collection were shorts featuring Harry Price. He was stunned to find that they had been registered by his own mother on Price's behalf when she was working in the film industry in the 1930s. I'm also very grateful to Alan Rhodes for his recollections of Harry Price. Possibly one of the last people alive to have had significant dealings with him, whatever Price's reputation, Mr Rhodes remembers Price as a good, decent man. Richard Morris also shared his research and thoughts about Price. I'm very grateful too to Captain Gregson's grand-daughter, Leonie Gregson, for sharing her family history with me. Kevin Taylor kindly told me about the painful circumstances of meeting his birth mother, Astrid, and her brother John. Adam Underwood has been extremely helpful and most generous with his father's archive and letters.

Ghost expert Roger Clarke was very generous with his thoughts about the case. David Tibet has been very helpful with his ideas about all things Borley. Both Roger and David kindly looked over the manuscript for me. Vivienne Roberts at the College of Psychic Studies has been most helpful with my enquiries. Roy Tricker gave me valuable background information about the sectarian tensions in the area surrounding Borley and Professor Liam Kennedy gave me an insight into Marianne's life in Ireland before independence. Dr Francis Young offered excellent guidance about the history of exorcism in the Church of England. Professor Dominic Janes of Keele University gave me a fascinating insight into Anglo-Catholic culture in the twentieth century and its attraction for gay men, as well as the importance of the shrine at Walsingham. Mark Yates Hopper kindly gave me access to Alan Roper's Borley research and archive material, which enabled me to discover what happened to Adelaide Foyster after she left the Rectory.

Paul Adams is a mine of information about Harry Price and Borley. He has been extraordinarily generous with his archive, his insight and his time. On our first phone call, which seems so long ago now, the hairs on the back of my neck stood up when he went to ring the Borley bell which now hangs outside his kitchen door. This was bequeathed to him by Peter Underwood, who in turn had been left it by Harry Price; the Borley mantle passed on. Nothing has been too much trouble for Paul and I'm indebted to him for his encouragement and his enthusiasm for this project.

Lizzie Francke-Daniels has been very generous with her insights into English Gothic and she and her husband Tim have kindly taken me on distracting away days. Belinda Wright and Laura Scott have also provided very good dinners when I most needed them. I'd like to thank Paul Marquess and Martin Ridgwell who read early drafts of the book and were encouraging and helpful with their thoughts. For their support, I'd also like to thank Paul Baker, Marina Caldarone, Buffy Davis, Matt Evans, Andy and Laura Frame, Mark Gatiss, Emma Hoyle, Alan Ivory, Pete and Jackie John, Natasha Kerr, Gillian McCafferty, John Michie, Charlie Milnes, Neil Mullarkey (not that one), John and Nicola Moxham, Nigel Norman, David Taylor, Angus Towler, Donna Wiffen and Darren Winstone. Simon Williams has been a dear and granite support. I'd also like to express my gratitude to my family – my parents, Anne and Alan O'Connor, my mother-in-law Rene Johnson, Elspeth Haywood, Ben Haywood, Liz McClean and her family.

My agent Judith Murray enthused about the idea of a book about Borley from the start and Jane Villiers has also been a constant support. At Simon & Schuster, Suzanne Baboneau has been an extraordinary champion of this book since we first discussed it over lunch. In the challenges I've faced while writing it, she has not only been patient, but always encouraging, understanding and extremely kind. Once again, Mike Jones has been an instinctive and creative editor, helping me to shape the text and clarify the story with real sensitivity. Kaiya Shang and Alexandra Newby have been hugely diligent and supportive in helping me refine the text. Sophia Akhtar has been an enormous help in sourcing the photographs that illustrate the text.

I am indebted to Dr Mark Harries in the Oncology Department and to the staff in Critical Care at Guy's Hospital. They know why.

The biggest debt I owe is impossible to repay now, but at least can be acknowledged. Since I started to research this book, as the world around us has been in flux, my own life has changed profoundly. My husband Rob and I had been together for twenty years when he died in the summer of 2021. It was an aggressive melanoma, a fairly rare disease. After an unexpected and swift illness, he was taken to the Critical Care Unit at Guy's Hospital where we were told, in the kindest way possible, that he might only have 24 hours to live. There was no fear, no regret and there were no tears, at least not then. We hadn't expected that death was so close, but in reality, it had been haunting us for months.

He died surrounded by his loving family with extraordinary courage. Just after the tube that was feeding him oxygen and keeping him alive was removed, I asked him how he felt. Even in that moment, knowing what he was facing, he squeezed my hand, beamed a familiar smile and said, 'I'm so relieved.' It took five minutes for him to die, with me talking to him all the time and holding his hand. In the midst of the pandemic, when we were surrounded by stories of families, just like us, obliged to say goodbye by Zoom or on iPads, despite the terrible circumstances, we considered ourselves fortunate.

Shortly after Rob died, finding myself a recent widower, I went to Borley to carry on with my research, as he would have wanted. After visiting the destroyed Bull graves in the churchyard, I went into Sudbury to discuss a new memorial of my own. I'd commissioned a headstone for Rob's grave from Neil Luxton, a stonemason who has a workshop there. In those early months, it felt at times that I was surrounded by death and that the ghosts were inescapable. But I was. They are. We just choose to look away. 'We are never finished with grief,' V. S. Naipaul says. 'It is part of the fabric of living. It is always waiting to happen. Love makes memories and life precious; the grief that comes to us is proportionate to that love and is inescapable.' This book is dedicated to Rob with the fondest love and deepest thanks. For everything.

Sean O'Connor
London, 10 May 2022

NOTES

1. Joe Burroughs, *The Haunted Rectory*, unpublished script for BBC radio programme, 1956 – 'Cancelled (on legal grounds).' Society for Psychical Research (SPR) archive, Cambridge University Library, SPR/6/13/36, p. 24
2. Edward Marshall, '"No Immortality of the Soul" says Thomas A. Edison', *New York Times*, 2 October 1910

Foreword

1. Audrey Niffenegger, *Ghostly: A Collection of Ghost Stories* (London: Vintage Classics, 2015), p. ix
2. Owen Davies, *The Haunted: A Social History of Ghosts* (London: Palgrave Macmillan, 2007), p. 241
3. Harry Price, *Poltergeist Over England: Three Centuries of Mischievous Ghosts* (London: Country Life Ltd, 1945), p. 279
4. Lucie Meeker (née Kaye), *The Lighter Side of Ghost-Hunting*, unpublished manuscript, Senate House Library, HPA/5/1, p. 5
5. Upton Sinclair, *Most Haunted House*, unpublished screenplay, c.1946, Senate House Library, HPD/2/6
6. David Cannadine, 'War and Death, Grief and Mourning in Modern Britain', in Joachim Whaley (ed.), *Mirrors of Mortality: Studies in the Social History of Death* (London: Europa, 1981)
7. Ibid, p. 194
8. Ibid, p. 193
9. Sigmund Freud, 'Reflections on War and Death', 1918, in *The Standard Edition of the Complete Psychological Works of Sigmund Freud* (trans. James Strachey), Vol. 14, (London: The Hogarth Press, 1957), p. 291
10. Charles G. Harper, *Haunted Houses: Tales of the Supernatural, with Some Account of Hereditary Curses and Family Legends* (London: Chapman & Hall Ltd, 1907), p. 2
11. Elliott O'Donnell, *More Haunted Houses of London* (London: Everleigh Nash Company Limited, 1920), p. 127
12. Joanna Timms, 'Ghost-Hunters and Psychical Research in Interwar England', *History Workshop Journal*, 74 (2012): pp. 88–104
13. Price, *Poltergeist Over England*, op. cit., p. 303

Prologue: Death of a Rector

1. H. E. Pratt's account of his visit to Ipswich on 22–23 June 1953, Society for Psychical Research (SPR) archive, Cambridge University Library, SPR/6/14/32, p.1 2. Pratt recounts an interview with a second-hand bookseller whom he quotes here.

2. Harry Bull's funeral is described in the *Suffolk and Essex Free Press*, 16 June 1927, p. 5, and in the *Chelmsford Chronicle*, 17 June 1927, p. 5

3. Ibid.

1. A First-Class Ghost Story

1. Charles Mackay, *Memoirs of Extraordinary Popular Delusions and the Madness of Crowds* (London: Richard Bentley, 1841), quoted in John Henry Ingram, *The Haunted Homes and Family Traditions of Great Britain* (London: W.H. Allen & Company, 1886), p. iv

2. 'Ghost Visits to a Rectory', *Daily Mirror*, 10 June 1929, p. 4

3. Letter from Mabel Smith to K. M. Goldney, on her annotations of reading *'The Most Haunted House in England'*, 4 August 1949. Contrary to Vernon Wall's claim in the *Daily Mirror*, Mabel Smith insisted that they were 'complete strangers' and had no warnings from Dr Warman that the house was allegedly haunted.

4. Ibid. Mabel later suggested that her husband had used the hockey stick to frighten away mice or rats.

5. Harry Price, *'The Most Haunted House in England': Ten Years' Investigation of Borley Rectory* (London: Longmans, Green and Co., 1940), p. 1

6. Telegram from Rev. Guy Eric Smith to Harry Price, Senate House Library, HPC/4B/237

7. Harry Price, 'My Adventures with Ghosts in Haunted Houses', *Sunday Sentinel,* 19 May 1929, p. 11

8. Ibid.

9. 'Haunted Room in a Rectory', *Daily Mirror*, 12 June 1929, p. 4. The letter that appeared in the *Daily Mirror* was much edited from the version that Mrs Byford had sent, which was received by the *Mirror* on 11 June 1929 (Society for Psychical Research archive, Cambridge University Library, SPR/6/11/66). The original letter hints at a conspiracy among the other maids to frighten the newcomer.

10. Lucie Meeker (née Kaye), *The Ghost Kept Price Awake*, unpublished manuscript, Society for Psychical Research (SPR) archive, Cambridge University Library, SPR/6/3/9, p. 5

11. Harry Price, *Stella C.: An Account of Some Original Experiments in Psychical Research* (Gateshead: Souvenir Press, 1973), p. 8

12. Sidney Glanville's memories of Price, quoted in Paul Tabori and Peter Underwood, *The Ghosts of Borley Rectory: Annals of the Haunted Rectory* (Dawlish: W. J. Holman Ltd, 1973)

13. Lucie Meeker's memories of Price, op. cit., pp. 300–4

14. Price, *'The Most Haunted House in England'*, op. cit., pp. 5–6

15. A. Clifton Kelway (ed.), *Memorials of Old Essex* (London: Benrose & Sons Ltd, 1908), p. 1

16. C. Henry Warren, *Essex* (London: C. Robert Hale, 1950), p. 140

17. *Daily Mirror*, 30 May 1929, p. 3

18. *Sunday Pictorial*, 19 May 1929, p. 8

19. Poster, 1929 Conservative General Election campaign

20. *Daily Mirror*, 12 June 1929, p. 3

21. William Alfred Dutt, *Highways and Byways in East Anglia* (London: Macmillan, 1901), p. 216

22. Jennifer Westwood and Jaqueline Simpson, *The Penguin Book of Ghosts* (London: Penguin Books, 2008), pp. 130–141

23. Indictment, 1 March 1578, Essex Records Office, Q/SR 68/34

24. Kelway, *Memorials of Old Essex*, op. cit, p. 255

25. Ibid., p. 17

26. Wesley H. Downes, *The Ghosts of Borley* (Clacton-on-Sea: Wesley's Publications, 1993), p. 36

27. Harry Price, *Confessions of a Ghost-Hunter* (London: Putnam & Co Ltd, 1936), p. 25

28. Price, 'The Most Haunted House in England', op. cit., p. 15. Price suggests that he first heard the Rectory referred to thus on his initial trip to Borley on 12 June 1929. However, Ballechin House had been known as 'The Most Haunted House in Scotland' for many years. Price recognised a good, commercial title and understood its potential as a brand for Borley Rectory.

29. Lucie Meeker (née Kaye), 'Journey London to Borley', in unpublished play script, Senate House Library, HPA/5/1

30. James Turner, *My Life with Borley Rectory* (London: The Bodley Head, 1950), p. 1

31. Lucie Meeker (née Kaye), *The Ghost Kept Price Awake*, op. cit., p. 1

32. Ibid.

33. A. C. Henning, *Haunted Borley* (Colchester: E. N. Mason & Sons, 1949), p. 6

34. Harry Price, *The End of Borley Rectory: 'The Most Haunted House in England'* (London: George G. Harrap and Co. Ltd, 1946), p. 110

35. Lucie Meeker (née Kaye), 'Scene IV: Arrival at the Rectory' in unpublished play script, op. cit. As well as attempting a play, Lucie also wrote a detective novel inspired by the Borley story, with herself and Price as central characters.

36. Ibid.

37. Lucie Meeker (née Kaye), *The Ghost Kept Price Awake*, p. 1

38. Ibid.

39. Mabel Smith interviewed by K. M. Goldney and E. J. Dingwall 1–2 July 1949, SPR archive, Cambridge University Library, SPR/6/12/84

40. Lucie Meeker (née Kaye), 'Scene IV: Lunch at the Rectory', in unpublished play script, op. cit. In Lucie's play, Mrs Smith is depicted as tearful and hysterical throughout the lunch: 'Mr Price, we are at the end of our tether – most of my china is broken, I'm ashamed that some

of these plates have to be odd – we can only just serve five people at a time – *(becomes hysterical)* my lovely dinner service'.

2. The Thirteenth Man

1. Shirley Jackson, *The Haunting of Hill House, The Masterpieces of Shirley Jackson* (London: Raven Books, 1996), p. 248

2. Virginia Nicolson, *Singled Out: How Two Million Woman Survived Without Men After the First World War* (Oxford: Oxford University Press, 2008), p. 29

3. Mabel Smith interviewed by K. M. Goldney 18–19 August 1952, Society for Psychical Research (SPR) archive, Cambridge University Library, SPR/6/12/137. See also Clive Dewey, *Anglo-Indian Attitudes: The Mind of the Indian Civil Service* (London: Hambledon Continuum, 1993), p. 5

4. Timothy Jones, 'The Stained Glass Closet: Celibacy and Homosexuality in the Church of England to 1955', *Journal of the History of Sexuality*, Vol. 20, No. 1 (2011), p. 149

5. D. F. Karaka, *I Go West* (London: Michael Joseph, 1938), p. 192

6. 'Race Prejudice in England', from *The Negro Worker*, March 1932, in Nancy Cunard (ed.), *The Negro: An Anthology* (London: Wishart & Co., 1934), p. 554

7. Anthony Jennings, *The Old Rectory: The Story of the English Parsonage* (London: Continuum, 2009), p. 44

8. Deborah Alun-Jones, *The Wry Romance of the Literary Rectory* (London: Thames and Hudson Ltd, 2013), p. 10

9. Mr and Mrs Smith interviewed by Sidney Glanville 6 October 1937, SPR archive, Cambridge University Library, SPR/6/1/75

10. Mabel Smith interviewed by K. M. Goldney and E. J. Dingwall 1–2 July 1949, SPR archive, Cambridge University Library, SPR/6/12/84

11. Ethel Bull interviewed by Harry Price and Lucie Kaye 12 June 1929, SPR archive, Cambridge University Library, SPR/6/13/4

12. Letter from Mabel Smith to K. M. Goldney, 21 July 1949, SPR archive, Cambridge University Library, SPR/6/12/85

13. Mabel Smith interviewed by K. M. Goldney and E. J. Dingwall 1–2 July 1949, SPR archive, Cambridge University Library, SPR/6/12/84

14. Jennings, op. cit., pp. 13–19

15. H. E. Pratt's account of his visit to Ipswich on 22–23 June 1953, SPR archive, Cambridge University Library, SPR/6/14/32, p. 12. He observes even in the 1950s how inaccessible Borley was, with no public transport to the village.

16. *Daily Mirror*, 21 January 1928, p. 3

17. *Daily Mirror*, 3 October 1928, p. 3

18. *Daily Mirror*, 4 October 1928, p. 2

19. *Daily Mirror*, 5 October 1929, p. 2

20. *Daily Mirror*, 1 October 1928, p.2

21. Ibid.
22. Ethel Bull interviewed by Harry Price and Lucie Kaye 12 June 1929, SPR archive, Cambridge University Library, SPR/6/13/4
23. Letter from Mabel Smith to K. M. Goldney, Cambridge University Library, SPR/6/12/114
24. Mr and Mrs Smith interviewed by Sidney Glanville 6 October 1937, SPR archive, Cambridge University Library, SPR/6/1/75. See also letter from Mabel Smith to K. M. Goldney on her annotations of *The End of Borley Rectory*, SPR archive, Cambridge University Library, SPR/6/1/85. This is confirmed by Ethel Bull in an interview with Harry Price and Lucie Kaye 12 June 1929, SPR archive, Cambridge University Library, SPR/6/13/4. The discovery of the skull in the library is a curious story in itself. When Harry Bull had taken ill, he had been asked by one of the gravediggers to reinter a skull that they had unearthed in the churchyard. This was a frequent occurrence as it contained many ancient unmarked graves and human remains were often turned up during the preparation for funerals. As the rector was too sick to bury and bless the skull as usual, it was put to one side in the house. Following his death in June 1927, when Ivy Bull and her daughter vacated the Rectory, the skull was left behind. When it was later found, it was forwarded by post to Ivy at her new home at 35 Regents Park Road, Primrose Hill, NW1. She duly posted it back with instructions that it be buried again in the churchyard. With the Rectory by then unoccupied, the skull was wrapped in newspaper and left in a cupboard in the library, where Mabel Smith would later find it.
25. Mr and Mrs Smith interviewed by Sidney Glanville 6 October 1937, SPR archive, Cambridge University Library, SPR/6/1/75
26. J. C. Cannell, *When Fleet Street Calls: Being the Experiences of a London Journalist* (London: Jarrolds, 1932), p. 166
27. Mr and Mrs Smith interviewed by Sidney Glanville 6 October 1937, SPR archive, Cambridge University Library, SPR/6/1/75
28. Letter from Mabel Smith to K. M. Goldney 21 July 1949, SPR archive, Cambridge University Library, SPR/6/12/85
29. Mabel Smith interviewed by K. M. Goldney and E. J. Dingwall 1–2 July 1949, SPR archive, Cambridge University Library, SPR/6/12/84
30. George Orwell, *Coming Up for Air* (London: Penguin Classics, 2020) pp. 151–2
31. Letter from Mabel Smith to K. M. Goldney, 3 August 1949, SPR archive, Cambridge University Library, SPR/6/12/116
32. Letter from Mabel Smith to William Salter, 8 July 1949, SPR archive, Cambridge University Library, SPR/6/12/107
33. Sidney Glanville, *The Haunting of Borley Rectory: Private and Confidential Report ('The Locked Book')*, p. 118. On 20 November 1937, a painter who had worked on the house, Mr Hardy, told Glanville that 'the house had the reputation of being "haunted" as long as he could remember. And that some years ago the villagers were afraid to pass it at night if they were alone.'

34. Letter from Mabel Smith to K. M. Goldney, 30 July 1949, Cambridge University Library, (SPR) MS 6/12/114

35. Letter from Mabel Smith to K. M. Goldney, 4 August 1949, (SPR) MS 6/12/86. Mary was sourced through Collins' Agency in King's Lynn. Notes given by Mrs Smith to K. M. Goldney 18–19 August 1952, SPR archive, Cambridge University Library, SPR/6/12/137

36. Mr and Mrs Smith interviewed by Sidney Glanville 6 October 1937, SPR archive, Cambridge University Library, 6/1/75

37. Letter from Mabel Smith to K. M. Goldney, SPR archive, Cambridge University Library, SPR/6/12/86

38. Op. cit. Mabel Smith contradicted Mary Pearson's testimony: 'We both used to laugh at ghosts, and I know [Mary] did not believe a word about the legend.'

39. Mr and Mrs Smith interviewed by Sidney Glanville 6 October 1937, SPR archive, Cambridge University Library, SPR/6/1/75

40. *Framlingham Weekly News*, 22 December 1928, p. 4

41. See example in the *Weekly News*, 23 December 1928, p. 8

42. *Radio Times*, 14 December 1928, Issue 272, Vol. 21, p. 762

43. Mr and Mrs Smith interviewed by Sidney Glanville 6 October 1937, SPR archive, Cambridge University Library, SPR/6/1/75

44. Letter from Mabel Smith to Harry Price, 15 May 1940, SPR archive, Cambridge University Library, SPR/6/1/16

45. Letter from Mabel Smith to K. M. Goldney, 3 August 1949, SPR archive, Cambridge University Library, SPR/6/12/116

46. Letter from Rev. Guy Eric Smith to Harry Price, 20 November 1929, SPR Archive, Cambridge University Library, SPR 6/12/30

47. Mabel Smith interviewed by K. M. Goldney and D. J. Dingwall 1–2 July 1949, SPR archive, Cambridge University Library, SPR/6/12/84

3. Sixteen Hours of Thrills!

1. 'Rectory "Spook": A Mystery of Walled-up Sounds,' *Midland Advertiser*, 21 November 1929, p. 7

2. Lucie Meeker (née Kaye), 'Scene IV: Arrival at the Rectory', in unpublished play script, Senate House Library, HPA/5/1

3. Inventory of the Rectory made in preparation for its sale on 26 May 1938 by the estate agent Stanley Moger of Halstead, Society for Psychical Research (SPR) archive, Cambridge University Library, MS 6/3/38

4. Harry Price, *'The Most Haunted House in England': Ten Years' Investigation of Borley Rectory* (London: Longmans, Green and Co., 1940), pp. 35–6

5. Alfred Bull interviewed by William Salter 12 August 1950, SPR archive, Cambridge University Library, SPR/6/6/26: 'Alfred, showing me a photo of the garden and summerhouse, said that it was nonsense to suggest that his father had built the summerhouse so as to commune with spirits. It was built so that they could have tea near the lawn at croquet or tennis parties.'

6. Ibid., pp. 24–26
7. Price, 'The Most Haunted House in England', op. cit., p. 38. See also Vernon Wall's testimony of the same events, Daily Mirror, 14 June 1929, p. 4
8. Lucie Meeker (née Kaye), The Ghost Kept Price Awake, unpublished manuscript, Society for Psychical Research archive, (SPR) MS 6/3/9, p. 3
9. Lucie Meeker, The Lighter Side of Ghost-Hunting, unpublished manuscript, Senate House Library, HPA/5/1, p. 3
10. This seance is recorded by several witnesses, who offer contradictory versions of the same events: Harry Price in 'The Most Haunted House in England', Lucie Kaye in The Ghost Kept Price Awake and The Lighter Side of Ghost-Hunting, and Vernon Wall, 'Weird Night in "Haunted" House', Daily Mirror, 14 June 1929, p. 4. Neither Wall nor Lucie Kaye record the presence of the Misses Bull, but they must have been present for Reverend Smith to call an end to the proceedings.
11. Lucie Meeker, The Ghost Kept Price Awake, op. cit., p. 2
12. Ibid., p. 4
13. 'Séance Held in Haunted House', Daily Mirror, 15 June 1929, p. 4
14. Letter from Mabel Smith to K. M. Goldney, 4 August 1949, SPR archive, Cambridge University Library, SPR/6/12/86. 'I think,' Mrs Smith told Mollie Goldney, 'that "tricks" were being played all around us, but if any evil communications did come across, it must have been from evil forces, and one never knows what may happen if we put ourselves outside the pale of God's protection.' Mrs Smith also thought it significant that Price had 'soft felt overshoes' in his ghost hunter's kit, as they could also be used 'for creeping about'.
15. The incident with the soap is not mentioned at all by Lucie Kaye in The Ghost Kept Price Awake or The Lighter Side of Ghost-Hunting. At Eland Road in Battersea, Price was also present when a bar of yellow soap 'as used for washing clothes' in the scullery mysteriously appeared on the upstairs landing of the house (see Harry Price, Poltergeist Over England, p. 236). Andrew Clarke suggests in The Bones of Borley (http://www.foxearth.org.uk/BorleyRectory) that the 'knocking' sounds from the wooden back of the mirror might have been the result of the changes in temperature when the paraffin lamps were lit and extinguished.
16. Letter from Mabel Smith to K. M. Goldney, 4 August 1949, SPR archive, Cambridge University Library, SPR/6/12/86
17. Mr and Mrs Smith interviewed by Sidney Glanville 6 October 1937, SPR archive, Cambridge University Library, SPR/6/1/75
18. Lucie Meeker, The Ghost Kept Price Awake, op. cit., p. 4
19. Mr and Mrs Smith interviewed by Sidney Glanville 6 October 1937, SPR archive, Cambridge University Library, SPR/6/1/75
20. Meeker, The Ghost Kept Price Awake, op. cit., p. 5
21. Meeker, The Lighter Side of Ghost-Hunting, op. cit., p. 4
22. Ibid, p. 2

23. Price, 'The Most Haunted House in England', op. cit., p. 43
24. Lord Charles Hope quoting Lucie Kaye, SPR archive, Cambridge University Library, SPR/6/3/33. See also Mabel Smith interviewed by K. M. Goldney and E. J. Dingwall 1–2 July 1949, SPR archive, Cambridge University Library, (SPR) MS 6/12/84
25. Meeker, The Lighter Side of Ghost-Hunting, op. cit., p. 5
26. 'Shy "Ghost" of Borley Rectory Declines to Reveal Itself to London Medium', Daily Mirror, 17 June 1929, p. 4
27. Letter from Mabel Smith to K. M. Goldney, 1 August 1949, SPR archive, Cambridge University Library, SPR/6/12/116
28. Meeker, The Lighter Side of Ghost-Hunting, op. cit., p. 5
29. Letter from Mabel Smith to K. M. Goldney, 4 August 1949, SPR archive, Cambridge University Library, SPR6/12/86
30. Ibid.
31. Meeker, The Lighter Side of Ghost-Hunting, p. 6
32. Ibid.

4. Ancient and Modern

1. T. S. Eliot, 'Little Gidding', Four Quartets (London: Faber & Faber, 1944), p. 43
2. Harry Price, 'The Most Haunted House in England': Ten Years' Investigation of Borley Rectory (London: Longmans, Green and Co., 1940), pp. 11–12
3. Essex Recusant, Essex Recusant Society, Vol. 3 (1961), p. 14
4. Sir Egerton Brydges, K. J., Collins's Peerage of England: Genealogical, Biographical and Historical, Vol. 4 (London: Collins, 1812), pp. 236–41
5. Calendar of State Papers, Domestic Series, of the Reigns of Edward VI, Mary, Elizabeth 1547–1580 (London: Longman, Brown, Green, Longmans & Roberts, 1856), p. 173
6. Translated in Paul Adams, Eddie Brazil and Peter Underwood, The Borley Rectory Companion: The Complete Guide to 'The Most Haunted House in England' (Stroud: The History Press, 2009), p. 304
7. B. Anthony Bax, The English Parsonage (London: John Murray, 1964), p. 155
8. Deborah Alun-Jones, The Wry Romance of the Literary Rectory, (London: Thames and Hudson Ltd, London, 2013), p. 20
9. 'The Late Suicide of a Clergyman', Bury and Norwich Post, 29 November 1848, p. 2
10. 'Suicide of a Clergyman', Nottingham Review and General Advertiser for the Midland Counties, 17 November 1848, p. 8
11. 'The Late Melancholy Suicide at Nottingham', The Globe, 18 November 1848, p. 4
12. 'Nuptial Festivity', Essex Herald, 19 September 1854, p. 2
13. Ibid.
14. Diary of the Reverend Henry Dawson Ellis Bull, Essex Record Office, D/DU 2062/2/1

15. Ibid.
16. Matthew Arnold, 'Dover Beach', 1867
17. James Knowles (ed.), *The Nineteenth Century: A Monthly Review*, Vol. 4 (July–December 1878), p. 674
18. 'Anti-Popery Lectures: Disturbances in Ipswich', *Ipswich Journal*, 7 November 1863, p. 8
19. Bridget Cherry and Nikolaus Pevsner, *The Buildings of England – London 4: North* (New Haven and London: Yale University Press, 2002), p. 388
20. 'To Builders', *Bury and Norwich Post*, 10 June 1862, p. 1
21. 'Melford', *Bury and Norwich Post*, 5 August 1982, p. 5

5: A Clergyman's Son, a Clergyman's Daughter

1. Daphne du Maurier, 'The House of Secrets' (1946), in *The Rebecca Notebook and Other Memories* (London: Victor Gollancz, 1981), p. 135
2. 'Thunderstorm', *Bury and Norwich Post*, 24 May 1864, p. 8
3. William Charles Crocker, *Far from Humdrum: A Lawyers' Life*, (Hutchinson, London, 1967), p. 200
4. Steve Roud, *The English Year: A Month-by-Month Guide to the Nation's Customs and Festivals from May Day to Mischief Night*, (Penguin Books, London, 2006), pp. 19–22
5. Ibid. pp. 243–7
6. Harry Price, *The End of Borley Rectory: 'The Most Haunted House in England'* (London, George G. Harrap, 1946), p. 99
7. Ibid.
8. *Diary of Caroline Sarah 'Dodie' Bull* (1885), unpublished manuscript, David Tibet archive, Hastings
9. Op. cit.
10. Ibid.
11. Ibid.
12. Ibid.
13. Ibid.
14. Catherine Crowe, *The Night Side of Nature: or, Ghosts and Ghost Seers* (London: G. Routledge & Co., 1852)
15. Michael Slater, *Charles Dickens* (London: Yale University Press, 2009), p. 274
16. Jennifer Westwood and Jaqueline Simpson, *The Penguin Book of Ghosts* (London: Penguin Books, 2008), p. 339
17. 'A Ghost Story', *Suffolk and Essex Free Press*, 17 December 1857, p. 2
18. *Diary of Caroline Sarah 'Dodie' Bull*, op. cit.
19. Ibid.
20. Ibid.
21. Ibid.
22. Harry Price, *The End of Borley Rectory*, op. cit., p. 99
23. Ibid., p. 100
24. *Diary of Caroline Sarah 'Dodie' Bull*, op. cit.

25. Ibid.
26. Harry Price, *The End of Borley Rectory*, op. cit., p. 100
27. Ibid.
28. Letter from Martha Byford to the Editor, *Daily Mirror*, 11 June 1929, HPC/4B/35
29. Ibid.
30. Peter Underwood, *Borley Postscript* (Haslemere: Whitehouse Publications, 2001), p. 113
31. *Diary of Caroline Sarah 'Dodie' Bull*, op. cit.
32. 'Borley: Marriage of the Rev. J. A. Hayden and Miss Bull', *Suffolk and Essex Free Press*, 3 July 1895, p. 8
33. 'Howden,' *Hull Daily News*, 15 June 1895, p. 8. Anna Mary Johnson had been thirteen years old when she had given birth to Hubert Bull's child, a daughter. Hubert went on to say, 'I never thought it would come to anything like this.'
34. Ethel and Alfred Bull interviewed by K. M. Goldney, 11 August 1950, Society of Psychical Research (SPR) archive, Cambridge University Library, SPR/6/4/10
35. Peter Underwood, op. cit., *The Haunted Rectory*, broadcast script, BBC, 1947, p. 41
36. Ibid. p. 42
37. Ernest Ambrose, Melford Memories (1972), p. 76
38. Ibid.
39. James C. Whisenant, *A Fragile Unity: Anti-ritualism and the Division of the Evangelical Party in the Nineteenth Century Church of England*, (Vanderbilt University, 1998), p 153
40. Eve Brackenbury interviewed by Mrs Coghill 8 December 1931, SPR archive, Cambridge University Library, SPR/6/6/8
41. Joachim Whaley (ed.), *Mirrors of Mortality: Studies in the Social History of Death* (London: Europa, 1981), p. 198
42. 'Ghosts, Cats and Mothballs', J. Osborne Harley, *East Anglia Daily Times*, 15 March 1956, p. 4
43. Ibid.
44. Ibid.
45. Ibid.
46. Ibid.
47. Ibid.

6. Murder at the Parsonage

1. Harry Price, *Poltergeist Over England: Three Centuries of Mischievous Ghosts* (London: Country Life Ltd, 1945)
2. 'The Borley Ghost', *Suffolk and Essex Free Press*, 13 June 1929, p. 5
3. *Psychic News*, 24 March 1956, Society for Psychical Resarch (SPR) archive, Cambridge University Library, SPR/6/9/117
4. 'Shy "Ghost" of Borley Rectory', *Daily Mirror*, 17 June 1929, p. 4
5. 'The Borley Ghost', *Suffolk and Essex Free Press*, 13 June 1929, p. 5

6. Lord Charles Hope, Testimony, SPR archive, Cambridge University Library, SPR/6/3/33. In these notes ('the Nun story as told to me by the Misses Bull') made after Lord Charles's second visit to Borley Rectory, on or around 28 July 1929, he is clear that the sisters did identify 'a figure of a nun with a hood and a white coif'.

7. Ethel Bull interviewed by Harry Price and Lucie Kaye 12 June 1929, SPR archive, Cambridge University Library, SPR/6/13/4

8. Sidney Glanville, *The Haunting of Borley Rectory: Private and Confidential Rupert ('The Locked Book')*, p. 118. On 20 November 1937, Mr Hardy, a painter who was working at the Rectory, told Glanville that the Bulls' marriage was 'most unhappy and that there was a great deal of quarrelling. [Hardy] had, in fact, seen Mr Bull's face badly marked as a result.'

9. Eve Brackenbury interviewed by Mrs Coghill 8 December 1931, SPR archive, Cambridge University Library, SPR/6/6/8. Mrs Coghill claimed that though there was no history of 'actual insanity in the [Bull] family ... they were all rather abnormal'.

10. Harry Price, *'The Most Haunted House in England': Ten Years' Investigation of Borley Rectory* (London: Longmans, Green and Co., 1940), pp. 53–4

11. Ibid., p. 59

12. Letter from Lucie Kaye to Mabel Smith, 25 June 1929, SPR archive, Cambridge University Library, SPR/6/12/23

13. Hope, op. cit., p. 9

14. Letter from Rev. Guy Eric Smith to Harry Price, 9 July 1929, SPR archive, Cambridge University Library, 6/12/19

15. Mr and Mrs Smith interviewed by Sidney Glanville 6 October 1937, SPR archive, Cambridge University Library, SPR/6/1/5

16. Letter from Rev. Guy Eric Smith to Harry Price, 7 August 1929, Cambridge University Library, SPR/6/1/16

17. Ernest Ambrose, 'That Ghost Again', *East Anglian Magazine*, Vol. 33, (March 1974), p. 274

18. Ibid.

19. Letter from Rev. Guy Eric Smith to Harry Price, 20 November 1929, SPR archive, Cambridge University Library, SPR/6/1/16

20. Letter from Rev. Guy Eric Smith to Harry Price, 14 March 1930, SPR archive, Cambridge University Library, SPR/6/12/32

21. Letter from Rev. Guy Eric Smith to Harry Price, 22 February 1930, SPR archive, Cambridge University Library, SPR/6/12/31

22. Letter from Rev. Guy Eric Smith to Harry Price, 18 March 1930, SPR archive, Cambridge University Library, SPR/6/12/19

23. Letter from Rev. Guy Eric Smith to Harry Price, 14 March 1930, SPR archive, Cambridge University Library, SPR/6/12/33

24. Harry Price, 'International Notes', *Journal of the American Society for Psychical Research*, Vol. 23 (1929), p. 455

7. Confessions of a Ghost Hunter

1. Harry Price, *Search for Truth: My Life for Psychical Research* (London: Collins, 1942), p. 260
2. Ibid., pp. 31–4
3. Ibid., pp. 13–14
4. Ibid., p. 13
5. Ibid., pp. 16–17
6. Ibid., p. 22
7. Ibid., p. 22
8. Ibid.
9. Reuben Briggs Davenport, *The Death-blow to Spiritualism: Being the True Story of the Fox Sisters, as Revealed by Authority of Margaret Fox Kane and Catherine Fox Jencken* (New York: G. W. Dillingham, 1888), p. 41
10. Herbert Thurston, 'Spiritualism and its Dangers III', *Studies: An Irish Quarterly Review*, Vol. 9, No. 34 (June 1920), p. 246
11. Paul Kurtz, 'Spiritualists, Mediums, and Psychics: Some Evidence of Fraud.' Paul Kurtz, ed., *The Skeptic's Handbook of Parapsychology* (Buffalo, New York: Prometheus Books, 1985), p. 182. Margaret Fox made a written confession in the *New York World*, 21 October 1888: 'The rappings are simply the result of a perfect control of the muscles of the leg below the knee which govern the tendons of the foot and allow action of the toe and ankle bones that are not commonly known. Such perfect control is only possible when a child is taken at an early age and carefully and continually taught to practice the muscles which grow still in later years.' Kurtz, op. cit., p. 229
12. Henry Sidgwick, *A Memoir* (London: Macmillan, 1906), p. 53
13. Susan Owens, *The Ghost: A Cultural History* (London: Tate Publishing, 2017), p. 213
14. Harry Price, *Fifty Years of Psychical Research: A Critical Survey*, (London: Longmans, Green and Co., 1939), p. 24
15. *Journal of the Society for Psychical Research*, Vol. 3, No. 145, (January 1898), p. 260
16. Email from Richard Morris to Sean O'Connor, 28 May 2023
17. Harry Price, *Search for Truth*, op. cit., p. 54. On p. 55 he adds: 'There has been a great deal of nonsense written about Rolls-Royce cars – or rather about the alleged opulent owners of them. One does not have to be rolling in riches to roll in a Rolls ... they never want repairing and they never wear out.'
18. With some self-knowledge, Price admitted of his younger self, 'I wished to experience the thrill of being "interviewed" and I wanted to collect press-cuttings about myself. I must have been very vain!' See Price, op. cit., *Search for Truth*, p. 54.
19. Price confided this to Sidney Glanville, who Constance Price regarded as her husband's best friend. After Price's death, Glanville relayed the information to the investigators of the *Borley Report*.
20. Richard Morris, *Harry Price: The Psychic Detective* (Stroud: Sutton Publishing Ltd, 2006), p. 43.

21. Harry Price, *Confessions of a Ghost-Hunter* (London: Putnam & Co. Ltd, 1936), p. 7
22. Price, *Search for Truth*, op. cit., p. 77
23. Ibid.
24. David Cannadine, 'War and Death, Grief and Mourning in Modern Britain', in Joachim Whaley, *Mirrors of Mortality: Studies in the Social History of Death* (London: Europa, 1981), p. 228
25. Arthur Conan Doyle, *The History of Spiritualism*, Vol. 2 (London: Cassell, 1926), p. 225
26. 'Sir Arthur Conan Doyle's Message to Aberdeen: Challenge to the Church by "Religion of the Future"', *Aberdeen Press and Journal*, 13 November 1919, p. 5
27. Price, *Search for Truth*, op. cit., p. 263
28. Harry Price, *Fifty Years of Psychical Research*, op. cit., p. 218
29. Price, *Search for Truth*, op. cit., p. 263
30. Ibid.
31. Harry Price, *Fifty Years of Psychical Research*, op. cit., p. 309
32. Eric J. Dingwall and Trevor H. Hall, *Four Modern Ghosts* (London: Gerald Duckworth & Co. Ltd, 1958), p. 58
33. Harry Price, *Fifty Years of Psychical Research*, p. 96
34. Morris, op. cit., pp. 63–4
35. Harry Price, *Fifty Years of Psychical Research*, op. cit., p. 318
36. Ibid., pp. 111–2
37. Ibid, p. 119
38. Ibid., p. 51
39. Morris, op. cit., p. 66
40. Ibid.
41. Harry Price, *Fifty Years of Psychical Research*, op. cit., p. 121
42. Jenny Hazelgrove, *Spiritualism and British Society Between the Wars* (Manchester: Manchester University Press, 2000), p. 211
43. Ibid.
44. Morris, op. cit., p. 67
45. E.J. Dingwall on Harry Price, Trevor H. Hall, *Search for Harry Price* (London: Gerald Duckworth and Co. Ltd, 1978), p. 10. Dingwall's essay had originally been written for Paul Tabori's biography of Price in 1950, but was rejected by Price's estate lest it offend his widow.
46. Harry Price, *Search for Truth*, op. cit., p. 92
47. Morris, op. cit., p. 91
48. Ibid., pp. 91–2
49. Lucy Meeker on Harry Price, Paul Tabori, *Search for Harry Price*, p. 301
50. Ibid.
51. E.J. Dingwall on Harry Price, in Trevor H. Hall, *Search for Harry Price* (London: Gerald Duckworth and Co. Ltd, 1978), pp. 10–11
52. Ibid, p. 11
53. Harry Price, *Search for Truth*, op. cit., p. 9
54. Paul Tabori, *Harry Price: The Biography of a Ghost-Hunter* (London: Athenaeum Press, 1950), p. 144

55. K. M. Goldney on Harry Price, SPR archive, Cambridge University Library, SPR/6/13/30
56. Ibid.
57. Morris, op. cit., p. 90
58. Tabori, op. cit., p. 303
59. Morris, op. cit., p. 89
60. David Meeker interviewed by Sean O'Connor 3 February 2021
61. Letter from the National Children Adoption Association to Harry Price, 7 July 1930, Senate House Library HPC/1B/3. 'We would be grateful if you would tell us ... whether Miss Kaye, before the birth of her little boy had always borne a good reputation.'
62. Letter from Harry Price to National Children Adoption Association, Senate House Library , 8 July 1930, HPA/1A/2
63. David Meeker interviewed by Sean O'Connor, op. cit.
64. Letter from Lucie Kaye to Harry Price, 23 December 1937, Senate House Library, HPA/1B/2
65. Morris, op. cit., p. 111
66. David Meeker interviewed by Sean O'Connor, op. cit.
67. Tabori, op. cit, p. 303
68. Morris, op. cit., p. 88
69. Harry Price, *Poltergeist Over England: Three Centuries of Mischievous Ghosts* (London: Country Life Ltd, 1945), p. 238
70. Price, op. cit., p. 233
71. Letter from Harry Price to Arnold Lunn, 17 April 1936, Senate House Library, HPC/4A/149
72. Morris, op. cit., p. 107
73. 'Testing Medium', *Daily Mirror*, 9 April 1929, p. 4
74. Ibid.
75. 'Medium in Clouds of Electricity', *Daily Mail*, 20 November 1929, p. 13
76. 'Rudi's Certificate: Mr Price Gives him a "Clean Sheet"', *Daily Mail*, 21 January 1938, p. 6
77. 'Climax of Absurdity', letter from E. J. Dingwall to the Editor, *Daily Mail*, 22 November, p. 14
78. Andrew Lycett, *Conan Doyle: The Man Who Created Sherlock Holmes* (London: Weidenfeld & Nicolson, 2007), p. 431
79. Ibid., p. 432
80. Harry Price, *Leaves from a Psychist's Case-Book* (London: Victor Gollancz, 1936), p. 105
81. Ibid.
82. 'Bombshell by Hitler', *Daily Mirror*, 26 September 1930, p. 3
83. Harry Price, *The End of Borley Rectory: 'The Most Haunted House in England'*, (London: George G. Harrap and Co. Ltd), p. 64

8. The Rector's Wife

1. Trevor H. Hall, *Marianne Foyster of Borley Rectory: A Biographical, Psychological and Psychical Investigation*, Vol. 5, unpublished manuscript, 1958, Cambridge University Library, p. 14
2. 'The Manchester Ship Canal', *Preston Herald*, 31 March 1888, p. 3
3. Iris Owen and Paulene Mitchell, *Borley Rectory: 'The Most Haunted House in England': A Report by New Horizons Foundation of Some Investigations Made into This Alleged Haunting* (New Horizons Foundation, 1986: cpb-us-w2.wpmucdn.com), p.27
4. Vincent O'Neil, *The Most Haunted Woman in England: The Biography of Marianne Foyster of Borley Rectory*, unpublished manuscript, 1996, p. 44
5. Ibid.
6. Vincent O'Neil, *The Most Haunted Woman in England*, p. 138
7. Ibid.
8. Ibid., p. 28
9. Ibid.
10. Ibid.
11. Ibid.
12. Ibid., p. 29
13. Letter from Marianne O'Neil (née Shaw) to Ian Shaw, May 1956, in O'Neil, op. cit., p. 236
14. Owen and Mitchell, op. cit., p. 30
15. Ibid.
16. Vincent O'Neil, *The Most Haunted Woman in England*, p. 138
17. Owen and Mitchell, op. cit., p. 31
18. Ibid.
19. Ibid., p. 35
20. Ibid., p. 30
21. Hall, op. cit.
22. Price, *Poltergeist Over England: Three Centuries of Mischievous Ghosts* (London: Country Life Ltd, 1945), pp. 28–30 and pp. 376–7
23. Ibid.
24. Edward Rowe Snow, *Strange Tales from Novia Scotia to Cape Hatteras* (New York: Dodd, Mead & Company, 1949), p. 69
25. Peter Underwood, *The Ghost Hunter's Guide* (London: Blandford Press, 1986), p. 161
26. Hall, op. cit., p. 43
27. Juliet Gardiner, *The Thirties: An Intimate History of Britain*, (HarperPress, London, 2010), p. 18
28. George Orwell, 'The Lion and the Unicorn: Socialism and the English Genius', 19 February 1941, in *The Collected Essays, Journalism and Letters of George Orwell*, Vol. II: *My Country Right or Left 1940–1943* (London: Secker and Warburg, 1968), p. 87
29. Hall, op. cit., p. 91

9. They Settle in the House

1. Daphne du Maurier, *Rebecca* (London: Virago Press, 2003), p. 194
2. Martin Pugh, *'We Danced All Night': A Social History of Britain Between the Wars* (London: Vintage, 2009), p. 304
3. James Leasor, *The Millionth Chance: The Story of the R101* (London: Hamish Hamilton, 1957), p. 54
4. 'R100's Great Task', *Daily Mirror*, 29 July 1930, p. 3
5. 'New Wireless Miracle', *Daily Herald*, 29 July 1930, p. 2
6. Ibid.
7. 'Television', *Yorkshire Post and Leeds Intelligencer*, 29 July 1930, p. 8
8. Dr J. R. A. Davies interviewed by Trevor H. Hall 6 October 1953, Society for Psychical Research (SPR) archive, Cambridge University Library, SPR/6 /14/50
9. Trevor H. Hall, *Marianne Foyster of Borley Rectory: A Biographical, Psychological and Psychical Investigation*, Vol. 5, unpublished manuscript, 1958 Cambridge University Library, p. 100
10. Ibid., p. 94
11. Ibid., p. 96
12. Ibid., p. 63
13. Ibid., p. 17. Mary Yelloly was Henry Dawson Bull's sister who had inspired the suicide of William Brown, the curate at Sneinton in 1848.
14. Ibid., p.63
15. 'Spiritualist Left Dead a Week', *Daily Herald*, 20 September 1930, p. 1.
16. Ibid.
17. 'Farm Wage Fight Today,' Ibid.
18. 'Bishop and Dagenham; Says it Should Never have been Built', *Chelmsford Chronicle*, 19 September 1930, p. 8
19. Ibid.
20. Hall, op. cit., p. 97
21. Ibid., p. 98
22. Rev. Lionel Foyster, *Fifteen Months in a Haunted House: A Record of an Experiment*, Senate House Library, HPC/3G/4, pp. 11–12
23. Lionel wrote three versions of the incidents he and Marianne experienced at the Rectory. Initially he wrote circular letters to members of the family, letting them know what was happening in the house. These documents, known as the 'Diary of Occurrences', were written in three instalments. The first was completed on 23 March 1931, the second on 7 May and the third on 6 July. Lionel sent Harry Price a copy of the 'Diary of Occurrences' on 3 October 1931, before Price returned to the house. Lionel then began to expand the narrative into *Fifteen Months in a Haunted House*, a 182-page typescript in eight chapters, which he told Sidney Glanville he was keen to publish. This version disguised the location of the house as 'Cromley Hall' and the identity of the protagonists with pseudonyms. The Foysters were 'John and Emily Jane Fowler'. Francois D'Arles/Frank Peerless was named – perhaps significantly – 'Mr

Lawless'. Lionel also changed the gender of Edwin Whitehouse, who appears as 'Edith Greycastle'. Henry Lawton read a copy of *Fifteen Months in a Haunted House* when he stayed at the Rectory in August 1933. Once Lionel had left the house, between 21 January and 11 February 1938, at Harry Price's request he wrote a 'Summary of Experiences' for inclusion in *The Most Haunted House in England*.

24. A Member of the Aristocracy, *Manners and Rules of Good Society: Or Solecisms to be Avoided* (London Frederick Warne and Co. 1913), p. 20

25. Ibid., p. 35

26. Hall, op. cit., p.99

27. Peter Underwood, *Borley Postcript* (Haslemere: White House Publications, 2001) p. 118

28. J. B. Priestley, *English Journey* (London: William Heinemann in Association with Victor Gollancz, 1934), p. 248

29. Hall, op. cit., p. 99

30. Florence Whitehouse interviewed by E. J. Dingwall, K. M. Goldney and Trevor H. Hall 2–3 November 1951, SPR archive, Cambridge University Library, SPR/6/4/24, p. 11

31. Ibid.

32. Hall, op. cit., p. 15

33. Ibid., p. 9

34. Ibid., p. 102

35. 'Christmas, To-day and Yesterday', *Bury Free Press*, 27 December 1930, p. 2

36. Ibid.

37. Ibid.

38. Hall, op. cit., p. 103

39. 'Do You Like Christmas?' *Daily Mirror*, 24 December 1930, p. 7

40. Ibid., p. 8

41. Foyster, op. cit., p. 20

42. Ibid.

43. Ibid., p. 27

44. Ibid.

10. The Evil in the Dark Closet

1. Stephen King, *The Shining* (New York: Doubleday & Company Inc., 1977)

2. Rev. Lionel Foyster, *Fifteen Months in a Haunted House: A Record of an Experiment*, Senate House Library, HPC/3G/4, p. 30

3. Rev. Lionel Foyster, *Diary of Occurrences at Borley Rectory Between February 1931 and July 1931 (Memorandum of Our Experiences in Connexion with the Borley 'Ghost')*, unpublished manuscript, Senate House Library, HPC/3G/3, p. 6

4. Foyster, *Diary of Occurrences*, op. cit., p. 8

5. Foyster, *Fifteen Months in a Haunted House*, op. cit., p. 62

6. Ibid.
7. Ibid., p. 41
8. Foyster, *Diary of Occurrences*, op. cit., p. 9
9. Foyster, *Fifteen Months in a Haunted House,* op. cit., p. 45
10. Ibid., p. 48
11. Until 1969, exorcisms were technically illegal in the Church of England without a specific licence from the bishop. A revival of exorcism was begun by Rev. Gilbert Shaw in Lincolnshire in 1926, and in rural parishes the practice of 'ghost-laying' (exorcising haunted places) had never really gone away. This embarrassed bishops so much that they didn't want to prohibit it, for fear of drawing attention to 'superstitious' practices in the press. There was a great reluctance to discuss such things in the Church of England until the 1960s, even though it was an open secret that many of the clergy were themselves involved in spiritualism.
12. Foyster, *Fifteen Months in a Haunted House*, op. cit., p. 49
13. Ibid.
14. Francis Young, *A History of Exorcism in Catholic Christianity* (Switzerland: Palgrave Macmillan, 2018)
15. Foyster, *Diary of Occurrences*, op. cit., p. 1
16. 'Personal', *The Times*, 15 November 1930, p. 1

11. Things That Go Bump in the Night

1. Gustave Flaubert, *Madame Bovary* (Paris, Michel Lévy Frères, 1857)
2. Trevor H. Hall, *Marianne Foyster of Borley Rectory: A Biographical, Psychological and Psychical Investigation*, Vol. 5, unpublished manuscript, 1958, Cambridge University Library, p. 43
3. Vincent O'Neil, *The Most Haunted Woman in England: Marianne Foyster of Borley Rectory*, unpublished manuscript, 1996, p. 44, p. 149
4. Letter from Edwin Whitehouse to Rev. Guy Eric Smith, 22 December 1931, Society for Psychical Research (SPR) archive, Cambridge University Library, SPR/6/3/57
5. K. M. Goldney interviewed by Trevor H. Hall 2–3 November 1951, Society for Psychical Resarch (SPR) archive, Cambridge University Library, SPR/6/4/24
6. Hall, op. cit., p. 109
7. Rev. Lionel Foyster, *Fifteen Months in a Haunted House: A Record of an Experiment*, Senate House Library, HPC/3G/4 p. 95
8. 'Earthquake', *Bury Free Press,* 13 June 1931, p. 3
9. Ibid.
10. Ibid.
11. Harry Price, *'The Most Haunted House in England': Ten Years' Investigation of Borley Rectory* (London: Longmans, Green and Co., 1940), p. 8
12. Rev. Lionel Foyster, *Fifteen Months in a Haunted House: A Record of an Experiment*, Senate House Library, HPC/3G/4 p. 100

13. Price, 'The Most Haunted House in England', op. cit., p. 88
14. Ibid.
15. Ibid.
16. 'Earthquake', Bury Free Press, 13 June 1931, p. 3
17. Raphael Brown, Saints Who Saw Mary (Charlotte, North Carolina: Tan Books, 1955)
18. Foyster, Fifteen Months in a Haunted House, op. cit., p. 122
19. Hall, op. cit.
20. O'Neil, op. cit., p. 147
21. O'Neil, op. cit., p. 161

12. The Return of Harry Price

1. Jay Anson, The Amityville Horror: A True Story (London: W. H. Allen, 1978), p. 66
2. Paul Adams, Eddie Brazil and Peter Underwood, The Borley Rectory Companion: The Complete Guide to 'The Most Haunted House in England', (Stroud: The History Press, 2009), p. 264
3. Letter from Mary Braithwaite to William Salter, 15 August 1931, Society for Psychical Resarch (SPR) archive, Cambridge University Library, SPR/6/6/18
4. For the Church's ambivalent attitude towards spiritualism in the 1930s, see Georgina Byrne, Modern Spiritualism and the Church of England, 1850–1939 (Woodbridge: The Boydell Press, 2010), pp. 144–182
5. John Braithwaite, notes on a sitting at Borley Rectory, 13 August 1931, SPR archive, Cambridge University Library, SPR/6/6/17
6. Ibid.
7. Ibid.
8. Ibid.
9. Ibid.
10. Ibid.
11. Rev. Lionel Foyster, Fifteen Months in a Haunted House: A Record of an Experiment, Senate House Library, HPC/3G/4, p. 117
12. John Braithwaite notes, op. cit.
13. Foyster, op. cit., p. 117
14. Letter from Mary Braithwaite to William Salter, 21 August 1931, SPR archive, Cambridge University Library, SPR/6/6/21. See also a letter from Mrs Salter to Dr Schiller, 25 November 1931, 'I have an idea that these new people at the Rectory may be very hysterical and strange in themselves, or else they are under the influence of some very strong power, not so much evil as extremely unhappy.' SPR archive, Cambridge University Library, SPR/6/6/5
15. Letter from Eileen Garrett to Trevor H. Hall, 10 May 1958, Trevor H. Hall, Marianne Foyster, pp. 252–3: '[Marianne] denied emphatically any relationship with Whitehouse but rather intimated that the latter and Foyster were exceedingly intimate which suggested a spot of homosexuality in the relationship although she did not say so outright.'

16. Hall, op. cit., p. 30
17. Foyster, op. cit., p. 125
18. 'Eclipse of the Harvest Moon', *Dundee Courier*, 23 September 1931, p. 4. See also Foyster, op. cit., p. 126
19. Foyster, op. cit., p. 127
20. Letter from Rev. Lionel Foyster to Harry Price, 1 October 1931, SPR archive, Cambridge University Library, SPR/6/10/1
21. Letter from Harry Price to Rev. Lionel Foyster, 12 October 1931, SPR archive, Cambridge University Library, SPR/6/10/5
22. K. M. Goldney interviewed by Trevor H. Hall 2–3 November 1951, SPR archive, Cambridge University Library, SPR/MS 6/4/24, p. 2
23. Harry Price, '*The Most Haunted House in England*': Ten Years' Investigation of Borley Rectory (London: Longmans, Green and Co., 1940), p. 67
24. Hall, op. cit., p. 106
25. Ibid., p. 107
26. In the notes she later wrote of her life story for Eileen Garrett, Marianne claimed that though Price and Mollie Goldney were both married, when they visited the Rectory they were 'in the throes of an affair'. There's no evidence for this other than Marianne's statement. The two women disliked each other immediately: 'She was the vulgar type,' Marianne said, 'who not only believe in calling a spade a spade, but believe in knocking down women with the same instrument.' Hall, op. cit., p. 106
27. Ibid, p. 65
28. Price, '*The Most Haunted House in England*', op. cit., p. 70. There's a suggestion here that Ballantyne was simply telling Price and his cohort what he thought they wanted to hear; phantom hands do not appear anywhere else in the Borley story.
29. Foyster, op. cit., p. 132
30. K. M. Goldney interviewed by Trevor H. Hall 2–3 November 1951, SPR archive, Cambridge University Library, SPR/6/4/24, p. 3
31. Foyster, op. cit., p. 133
32. K. M. Goldney interviewed by Trevor H. Hall 2–3 November 1951, SPR archive, Cambridge University Library, SPR/6/4/24, p. 4
33. Hall, op. cit., p. 55
34. K. M. Goldney interviewed by Trevor H. Hall 2–3 November 1951, SPR archive, Cambridge University Library, SPR/6/4/24, p. 5
35. Ibid.
36. Foyster, op. cit., p. 136

13. The World's Best Ghost Story

1. Hereward Carrington and Nandor Fodor, *The Story of the Poltergeist Down the Centuries* (Rider and Company, London, 1953), p. 11
2. Florence Whitehouse interviewed by E. J. Dingwall, K. M. Goldney and Trevor H. Hall 2–3 November 1951, Society for Psychical Research (SPR) archive, Cambridge University Library, SPR/6/4/24, p. 11

3. Ibid.
4. Harry Price, 'The Most Haunted House in England': Ten Years' Investigation of Borley Rectory (London: Longmans, Green and Co., 1940), p. 98
5. Ibid., p. 99
6. Rev. Lionel Foyster, Fifteen Months in a Haunted House: A Record of an Experiment, Senate House Library, HPC/3G/4, p. 148
7. Letter from Kathleen Bull to Rev. Guy Eric Smith, 25 November 1931, SPR archive, Cambridge University Library, SPR/6/12/39
8. Letter from Rev. Lionel Foyster to Rev. Guy Eric Smith, 4 December 1931, SPR archive, Cambridge University Library, SPR/6/12/37
9. Letter from Rev. Lionel Foyster to Guy Eric Smith, 15 December 1931, SPR archive, Cambridge University Library, SPR/6/12/38
10. Foyster, op. cit., p. 155
11. Ibid.
12. Ibid., p. 158
13. Harry Price, Search for Truth: My Life for Psychical Research (London: Collins, 1942), p. 266
14. Guy L'Estrange, The Haunted Rectory, Senate House Library, HPD/2/9, p. 1. In a letter to Price on 6 December 1944, L'Estrange wrote, 'I was simply staggered to learn that I made so many mistakes in my article about Borley Rectory. It just shows what tricks one's memory can play' – SPR archive, Cambridge University Library, SPR/6/11/9
15. Foyster, op. cit., p. 168
16. L'Estrange, op. cit., p. 2
17. Ibid.
18. Ibid.
19. Foyster, op. cit., p. 167
20. Ibid., p. 171
21. Harry Price, The End of Borley Rectory, p. 237
22. Ibid., p. 170
23. Ibid., p. 273
24. Foyster, op. cit., p. 164
25. Trevor H. Hall, Marianne Foyster, p. 12
26. Rev. Lionel Foyster, Summary of Experiences at Borley Rectory, Senate House Library, HPC/3G/2, p. 6
27. J. C. Cannell, When Fleet Street Calls: Being the Experiences of a London Journalist (London: Jarrolds, 1932), p. 158
28. Ibid., p. 170
29. Ibid., p. 171
30. Ibid., p. 173
31. Rev. Lionel Foyster, Fifteen Months in a Haunted House, Senate House Library pp. 171–2

14. The Alleged Haunting at B—— Rectory

1. Letter from Harry Price to D. F. Fraser-Harris, 15 October 1931, Society for Psychical Research (SPR) archive, Cambridge University Library, SPR/6/11/37

2. Postcard, SPR archive, Cambridge University Library, SPR/6/8/1

3. Letter from Rev. Lionel Foyster to Harry Price, 26 March 1932, SPR archive, Cambridge University Library, SPR/6/10/6

4. Letter from Lord Charles Hope to Harry Price, 1 April 1932, SPR archive, Cambridge University Library, SPR/6/3/40

5. Ethel English (née Beenham) interviewed by K. M. Goldney, 29 August 1949, SPR archive, Cambridge University Library, SPR/6/4/8

6. Letter from Harry Price to Lucie Meeker, 4 November 1935, Senate House Library, HPA/1A/1. Many of the letters from Lucie to Price after she stopped working for him were appeals for loans.

7. 'Mediums On Trial', *Yorkshire Post and Leeds Intelligencer*, p. 6

8. Harry Price, *Confessions of a Ghost-Hunter*, (London: Putnam 1936) pp. 7–8

9. Trevor H. Hall, *The Strange Story of Ada Goodrich Freer* (London: Duckworth, 1980), p. 94

10. Harry Price, op. cit., p. 35

11. 'Haunted House', *Radio Times,* Issue 649, 6–14 March 1939, p. 40

12. 'Haunted House Broadcast: Strange Sounds But No Ghost', *The Times*, 11 March 1936, p. 14

13. Letter from Harry Price to Arnold Lunn, 17 April 1936, Senate House Library, HPC/4A/149. In this letter Price assures Lunn that 'during the period of my first visits, the phenomena were absolutely genuine'.

14. Letter from Harry Price to Everard Fielding, 19 August 1935, SPR archive, Cambridge University Library, SPR/6/11/39

15. Harry Price, 'The Most Haunted House in England', *The Listener*, 14 August 1935, Vol XIV, No. 344, p. 282

16. Harry Price, 'A Really Haunted House', *The Listener*, 10 November 1937, Vol XVIII, No. 18, p. 1012

17. Letter from Rev A. C. Henning to Harry Price, 11 May 1937, Senate House Library, HPC/4B/103. Henning met Price at the station on the Liverpool Street train that arrived at 11.48 a.m.

18. A. C. Henning, *Haunted Borley* (Colchester: E. N. Mason & Sons, 1949), p. 7

19. Op. cit., p. 6

20. Ibid.

21. Harry Price, *'The Most Haunted House in England': Ten Years' Investigation of Borley Rectory* (London: Longmans, Green and Co., 1940), p. 104

22. Ibid., p. 106

23. Ibid., p. 107

24. Ibid., p. 108

25. Ibid.

26. Obituary, *Guardian*, 8 October 1991
27. Obituary, *The Times*, 8 October 1991
28. In 1934, Price dissolved the National Laboratory of Psychical Research and on 6 June that year the University of London Council for Psychical Investigation was formed, with Price as Honorary Secretary. Despite the title, there was no official connection with the university, though it benefited from the permanent loan of Price's extensive library of 13,000 items that remains at the University of London: the Harry Price Library of Magical Literature. The 'Blue Book' is reproduced in Harry Price, *'The Most Haunted House in England'*, pp. 194–7
29. Harry Price, *'The Most Haunted House in England'*, p. 195
30. Ibid., p. 196
31. Ibid., p. 197
32. Letter from Sidney Glanville to Harry Price, 25 May 1937, Senate House Library, HPC/4B/80
33. Ibid.
34. Sidney Glanville, Manuscript for *Borley III*, Cambridge University Library, SPR/6/2/2
35. Ibid.
36. Letter from Rev. Lionel Foyster to Sidney Glanville, 31 August 1937, SPR archive, Cambridge University Library, SPR/6/10/7
37. Ibid.
38. Sidney H. Glanville, *The Haunting of Borley Rectory ('The Locked Book')*, Senate House Library, HPC/3G/5, p. 56
39. Letter from Rev. Lionel Foyster to Sidney Glanville, 2 September 1937, SPR archive, Cambridge University Library, SPR/6/10/8
40. Letter from Mark Kerr-Pearse to Harry Price, 25 May 1937, Senate House Library, HPC/4B/194. It's clear from Kerr-Pearse's reports that there was no attempt to formally record the evidence. Various observers report 'new' wall-writing when this was actually added by Kerr-Pearse himself (eg. 'I STILL CANNOT UNDERSTAND. PLEASE TELL ME MORE.') Kerr-Pearse also notes scribbles and hand prints on the walls that have been made by Clifford Henning's son. This was further complicated when Sidney Glanville drew over the wall-writings in order to make them clearer to photograph.
41. Andrew Clarke, 'Dramatis Personae', *The Bones of Borley*: http://www.foxearth.org.uk/ BorleyRectory
42. Letter from Mark Kerr-Pearse to Harry Price, 9 June 1937, Paul Adams, Eddie Brazil and Peter Underwood, *The Borley Rectory Companion: The Complete Guide to 'The Most Haunted House in England'*, (Stroud: The History Press, 2009), p. 200
43. Report from Mark Kerr-Pearse, 19 July 1937, Senate House Library, HPC/3G/7
44. Ibid.
45. Glanville, *The Haunting of Borley Rectory*, op. cit., p. 28
46. Report from Mark Kerr-Pearse, 7 August 1937, Senate House Library, HPC/3G/8. Several observers noted the presence of a 'friendly black

cat' who wandered in and out of the house and was not mentioned in Price's writings about the Rectory. See Letter from Sidney Glanville to Harry Price 15 August 1937, Senate House Library HPC/3G/8

47. Letter from Mark Kerr-Pearse to Harry Price, 30 August 1937, Senate House Library, HPC/3G/8

48. Report from Sidney Glanville, 10 September 1937, Senate House Library, HPC/3G/8. Glanville records the movement of the tobacco tin, but suggests that its significance was void as the window had clearly been opened by somebody 'with nailed boots'.

49. Letter from Mark Kerr-Pearse to Harry Price, 28 September 1937, Senate House Library, HPC/6/10/49

50. 15 degrees Celsius

51. Letter from Rupert Haigh to Mark Kerr-Pearse, 2 October 1937, Sidney H. Glanville, *The Haunting of Borley Rectory*, p. 71

52. Ibid.

53. Letter from Mark Kerr-Pearse to the director, BBC Talks Department, 21 September 1937, Senate House Library, HPC/4B/194

54. Letter from Harry Price to Mark Kerr-Pearse, 23 September 1937, Paul Adams, Eddie Brazil and Peter Underwood, op. cit. p. 202

55. Letter from Sidney Glanville to Rev. Lionel Foyster, 8 October 1937, *Glanville, The Haunting of Borley Rectory,* Senate House Library, HPC/3G/5, p. 79

56. Rev. Lionel Foyster, *Fifteen Months in a Haunted House*, Senate House Library, HPC/3G/4, p. 1

57. Letter from Sidney Glanville to Rev. Lionel Foyster, 8 October 1937, op. cit.

15. The End of Borley Rectory

1. J. R. Sturge-Whiting, *The Mystery of Versailles: A Complete Solution*, (London: Rider & Co., 1938), p. vii

2. Letter from Harry Price to A.P. Drinkwater, Longmans, Green & Co,. Ltd, 24 September, 1937, Senate House Library, HPC/4A/25

3. Mr and Mrs Smith interviewed by Sidney Glanville, 7 October 1937, Society for Psychical Research (SPR) archive, Cambridge University Library, SPR/ 6/1/75

4. Letter from Rev. Guy Eric Smith to Sidney Glanville, 19 November 1937, SPR archive, Cambridge University Library, SPR/6/1/79. In his article, 'The Strange Happenings at Borley Rectory – Full Account of England's Most Famous Modern Ghost', Sidney Glanville observed that Eric Smith told him that the Rectory was 'evil from top to bottom and should have been burned to the ground years ago.' *Fate*, October 1951, p. 107

5. Letter from Sidney Glanville to Harry Price, 29 September 1937, Senate House Library HPC/4B/80

6. Report from Mark Kerr-Pearse, 11 October 1937, Senate House Library, HPC/3G/8

7. Ibid.

8. Sidney Glanville, *The Haunting of Borley Rectory: Private and Confidential Report ('The Locked Book')*, HPC/3G/5, p. 135: seance at Borley Rectory, 23 October 1937, Roger Glanville, Mark Kerr-Pearse, Alan Cuthbert.

9. Glanville, op. cit., p. 139: seance at Borley Rectory, 24 October 1937, Sidney Glanville, Roger Glanville, Mark Kerr-Pearse.

10. Letter from Sidney Glanville to Harry Price, 13 October 1938, Senate House Library, HPC/4B/81. Glanville writes to Price: 'I looked up the planchette writing and find that, we had the story of the maidservant who it is alleged, died in the kitchen at the Rectory; then we looked up the burial registers in the church and found the name of Kate Boreham of Sudbury. Immediately after that the table persistently tapped out "Katie" and the planchette repeatedly wrote "Katie Boreham". So I am afraid it was not a confirmation'.

11. Ibid., p. 141: seance at Borley Rectory, 24 October 1937: Sidney Glanville, Roger Glanville, Mark Kerr-Pearse and Alan Cuthbert.

12. Sidney Glanville, op. cit., p.152: seance at 125 Lewin Road, Streatham, 28 October 1937: Helen Glanville.

13. Ibid., p. 154: seance at Borley Rectory, 30 October 1937: Sidney Glanville and Rev. A. C Henning.

14. Ibid, p. 155: seance at 125 Lewin Road, Streatham, 31 October 1937: Sidney Glanville, Roger Glanville, Helen Glanville and Mark Kerr-Pearse.

15. Sidney Glanville interviewed by Trevor H. Hall, 20 June–4 July 1953: 'Mr Glanville said that he was completely sceptical as to [the planchette messages] and he had no belief that at all that they came from the spirit world. He regarded automatic writing as coming entirely from the subconscious mind of the operators and he said that had the words "Marie Lairre" not been written by his daughter during her solo planchette séance we should probably never have heard of her at all.' Cambridge University Library, SPR 6/1/71

16. Letter from Sidney Glanville to Harry Price, 3 November, 1938, Senate House Library, HPC/4B/81

17. Harry Price, 'A Really Haunted House', *The Listener*, 10 November 1937, p. 1012

18. Ibid.

19. Op. cit., p. 1014

20. Letter from Rev. Guy Eric Smith to Sidney Glanville, 19 November 1937, SPR archive, Cambridge University Library, (SPR) MS 6/1/79

21. Letter from Mabel Smith to Sidney Glanville, 23 November 1937, Cambridge University Library, SPR/6/1/80

22. 'Borley: The Late Mrs Hayden,' *Suffolk and Essex Free Press*, 9 December 1937, p. 14

23. Letter from Joseph W. Burden to Harry Price, 21 December 1937, SPR archive, Cambridge University Library, SPR/6/10/56

24. Letter from Harry Price to Joseph W. Burden, 29 December 1937, SPR archive, Cambridge University Library, SPR/6/10/57

25. Letter from Rev. Guy Eric Smith to Sidney Glanville, 6 January 1938, SPR archive, Cambridge University Library, SPR/6/1/87. Here Smith writes that his wife 'doesn't believe in ghosts, and nothing would scare her away'.

26. Letter from Rev. Guy Eric Smith to Sidney Glanville, 1 December 1937, SPR archive, Cambridge University Library, SPR/6/1/82

27. Letter from Rev. Guy Eric Smith to Sidney Glanville, 23 January 1938, SPR archive, Cambridge University Library, SPR/6/1/93

28. Letter from C. Gordon Glover to Harry Price, 26 February 1938, SPR archive, Cambridge University Library, SPR/6/11/16

29. Ibid. The BBC engineer, Mr M. Savage, was also an observer at the Rectory and informed Price that 'frankly the house gave me the impression of being far from haunted, but from the experiences and data given by Mr Glanville I certainly think that the house has been haunted very recently, and may be so again' – letter from Mr M. Savage to Harry Price, 19 March 1938, Senate House Library, HPC/3G/10

30. Letter from Harry Price to C. Gordon Glover, 28 February 1938, SPR archive, Cambridge University Library, SPR/6/11/4

31. Letter from Harry Price to Rev. Lionel Foyster, 5 January 1938, SPR archive, Cambridge University Library, SPR/6/10/9

32. Letter from Rev. Lionel Foyster to Harry Price, 7 January 1938, SPR archive, Cambridge University Library, SPR/6/10/10

33. Letter from Harry Price to Rev. Lionel Foyster, 18 January 1938, SPR archive, Cambridge University Library, SPR/6/10/13

34. Ibid.

35. Ibid.

36. Letter from Harry Price to Rev. Lionel Foyster, 10 January 1938, SPR archive, Cambridge University Library, SPR/6/10/11

37. J. R. Sturge-Whiting, *The Mystery of Versailles: A Complete Solution*, (London: Rider & Co, 1938)

38. Letter from Kenneth Potter to Harry Price, 13 January 1938, Senate House Library, HPD/4B/22

39. J. R. Sturge-Whiting, op. cit, p. vii

40. Letter from Rev. Lionel Foyster to Harry Price, 16 January 1938, SPR archive, Cambridge University Library, SPR/6/10/12

41. Juliet Gardiner, *Wartime: Britain 1939–1945* (London: Headline, 2004), p. xiii

42. *Christian Guardian*, 25 July 1941, in Harry Price, *Poltergeist Over England* (London: Country Life Ltd, 1945), pp. 5–6

43. 'The Poltergeists Are Here Again', *Yorkshire Evening Post*, 22 August 1938, p. 11

44. Ibid.

45. Ibid.

46. Glanville, *The Haunting of Borley Rectory*, op. cit., p. 156: seance at 125 Lewin Road, Streatham, 27 March 1938, Helen and Roger Glanville.

47. Glanville, *The Haunting of Borley Rectory*, op. cit.

48. Harry Price, *The End of Borley Rectory: 'The Most Haunted House in England'* (London: George G. Harrap and Co. Ltd, 1946), p. 118
49. Harry Price, *'The Most Haunted House in England': Ten Years' Investigation of Borley Rectory* (London: Longmans, Green and Co., 1940), p. 140. See also *1939 England and Wales Register*: Geoffrey H. Motion, Skeyne House, Chanctonbury, Sussex.
50. Letter from Harry Price to Rev. A. C. Henning, 30 March 1938, Senate House Library, HPC/4A/51. Price wrote to Henning: 'We appear to have frightened the ghosts away.'
51. Letter from Harry Price to Kenneth Potter, 11 August 1938, Senate House Library, HPD/4A/11
52. Ibid.
53. Letter from Capt. W. H. Gregson to Harry Price, 2 November 1938, Senate House Library, HPC/4B/89
54. Registering a Title', *Chelmsford Chronicle*, 12 July 1935, p. 12
55. Letter from Capt. W.H. Gregson to Harry Price, 14 November 1938, Senate House Library, PC/4B/89
56. Ibid.
57. Ibid.
58. Ibid.
59. Letter from Harry Price to Capt. W. H. Gregson, 10 November 1938, Senate House Library, HPC/4A/42
60. *Daily News*, 28 February 1939, p. 11
61. Letter from Lionel Arbon to Harry Price, 28 February 1939, HPC/4B/8
62. Letter from Lionel Arbon to Harry Price, 6 March 1939, HPC/4B/8
63. Letter from Capt. W. H. Gregson to Price, 2 November 1938, SPR archive, Cambridge University Library, SPR/6/11/22
64. 'Borley Rectory Fire,' *Suffolk and Essex Free Press*, 2 March 1939, p. 6

16. 'The Most Haunted House in England'

1. Charlotte Brontë, *Jane Eyre* (London: Smith, Elder & Co., 1847), pp. 272–3
2. Harry Price, *'The Most Haunted House in England': Ten Years' Investigation of Borley Rectory* (London: Longmans, Green and Co., 1940), p. 169
3. Letter from Lionel Arbon to Harry Price, 28 February 1939, Senate House Library, HPC/4B/8
4. Letter from Rev. A. C. Henning to Harry Price, 28 February 1939, Society for Psychical Research archive, Cambridge University Library, SPR/6/10/27
5. K. M. Goldney notes from lecture by Rev. A. C. Henning and Mrs Henning, Marylebone Spiritualist Society, 23 July 1953, SPR archive, Cambridge University Library, SPR/6/1/5: 'Referring to the dogs who "sensed" something paranormal, Mrs Henning said the dog shrieked and rushed off into the fields. It was shot the next day by the villagers. Gregson got another dog who behaved similarly and was never seen again.'

6. Letter from Capt. W. H. Gregson to Harry Price, 2 March 1939, SPR Archive, Cambridge University Library, SPR/6/11/24

7. Letter from Harry Price to Rev. A. C. Henning, 1 March 1939, Senate House Library, HPC/4A/51

8. Letter from Harry Price to Capt. W. H. Gregson, 3 March 1939, Senate House Library, HPC/4A/51

9. Letter from Harry Price to Rev. W. H. Gregson, 1 March 1939, Senate House Library, HPC/4A/51

10. Ibid.

11. Ibid.

12. Letter from Capt. W. H. Gregson to Harry Price, 2 March 1939, Senate House Library, HPC/4B/89

13. Ibid.

14. Letter from Harry Price to Capt. W. H. Gregson, 24 January 1940, Senate House Library, HPC/4A/42

15. William Charles Crocker, *Far from Humdrum: A Lawyer's Life*, (London: Hutchinson, 1967), p. 204

16. Letter from Rev. A. C. Henning to Harry Price, 29 November 1939, SPR archive, Cambridge University Library, SPR/6/10/29

17. Peter Underwood, *The Borley Postscript*, 'The Haunted Rectory', broadcast script, BBC, 1947, p. 53

18. Letter from Edwin Whitehouse to Harry Price, 6 July 1939, SPR archive, Cambridge University Library, SPR 6/3/61

19. Harry Price, *'The Most Haunted House in England': Ten Years' Investigation of Borley Rectory* (London: Longmans, Green and Co., 1940), p. 175. Price makes a connection between these mysterious prints in the snow and the 'Devil's Hoof Marks' that stretched 100 miles across a snowy Devonshire, from Totnes to Exmouth, in February 1855. The prints were seen even on the roofs of houses and on both sides of the River Exe. As Price noted, 'the mystery was never solved'. See *The Times*, 16 February 1855. Script for Capt. Gregson's talk on the BBC radio programme *In Town Tonight*, 15 April 1939, SPR archive, Cambridge University Library, SPR 6/11/27

20. Ibid.

21. Ibid.

22. Harry Price, 'Ten Years Investigation of Borley Rectory,' a Lantern Slide Lecture delivered before members of the Ghost Club, Overseas House, Park Place, St James's Street, 18 April 1939, Senate House Library, HPC/2/6, pp. 7–8

23. Ibid.

24. Letter from Harry Price to Rev. A. C. Henning, 21 April 1939, Senate House Library, HPC/4A/51. 'It would be nice,' Price wrote to Henning, 'if such an idea, on a modest scale, could be arranged.'

25. Letitia Fairchild, 'Strange Happenings at Rectory', *The Times*, 22 April 1939, p. 13

26. Harry Price, 'Strange Happenings at Rectory', *The Times*, 29 April 1939, p. 15

27. Letter from Harry Price to Rev. Guy Eric Smith, 5 May 1939, Senate House Library, HPC/4A/111

28. Ibid.

29. Letter from Rev. Guy Eric Smith to Harry Price, 16 May 1939, Senate House Library, HPC/4B/237

30. Ibid.

31. 'All Alone in Ghost House', *Daily Herald*, 16 June, 1939, p. 3

32. Ethel Beenham had married Alexander English in 1937.

33. 'A "Psychic Fete",' *The Times*, 22 June 1939, p. 14

34. Letter from Rev. A. C. Henning to Harry Price, 13 May 1939, Senate House Library, HPC/4B/103

35. 'A "Psychic Fete"', *The Times*, 22 June 1939, p. 14

36. 'Spook-Lovers' High Noon at Ruined Rectory', *Daily Herald*, 22 June 1939, p. 11

37. Ibid.

38. 'Mr Baldwin on Aerial Warfare', *Illustrated London News*, 19 November 1932, p. 4

39. Ibid.

40. 'Britain is Fighting Evil says Premier,' *News Chronicle*, 4 September 1939, p. 7

41. Nicholson Baker, *Human Smoke: The Beginnings of World War II – The End of Civilization* (New York, London, Toronto, Sydney: Simon & Schuster, 2008), p. 138

42. During the war, the reduction in the number of pages in newspapers had an impact on the stories that were printed. With war news the priority, there was no room for articles about ghosts or the paranormal, which had previously bolstered Price's celebrity – and his income.

43. Price, '*The Most Haunted House in England*', op. cit., p. 186

44. Ibid., p. v

45. Ibid.

46. This was actually the *Summary of Events* that Price had requested from Lionel Foyster, rather than the *Diary of Occurrences* that Price had read and claimed to have lost. Price was at pains to stress that the extracts of the 'diary' were verbatim and even reproduced a page of the handwritten diary as part of the text of '*The Most Haunted House in England*', giving the book an added veneer of authenticity.

47. Price, '*The Most Haunted House in England*', op. cit., p. 186

48. Op. cit., p. 192

49. Ibid.

50. Martin Tindal, 'Curious but True', *Time and Time*, 5 October 1940, p. 989

51. 'The Strange Case of Borley Rectory,' *Tatler*, 23 October 1940, p. 14

52. 'A Most Haunted House', *Aberdeen Press and Journal*, 2 October 1940, p. 2

53. V.S. Prichett, 'The Haunted Rectory,' *The Bystander*, 23 October 1940, p. 14

54. 'Antidote to Blitzkrieg', *Daily Telegraph*, 2 October, 1940, p. 3

55. Ibid.

56. Letter from Mabel Smith to Harry Price, 23 August 1940, SPR archive, Cambridge University Library, SPR/6/12/59

57. Ibid.

58. Letter from Mabel Smith to Harry Price, 16 May 1940, SPR archive, Cambridge University Library, SPR/6/12/56

59. Letter from Mabel Smith to Harry Price, 21 May 1940, SPR archive, Cambridge University Library, SPR/6/12/57: 'One day you shall see the mss. as a certain character mentioned happens to be you – if ever it was filmed, you should take it!! Who else could?'

60. Letter from Mabel Smith to Harry Price, 23 August 1940, SPR archive, Cambridge University Library, SPR/MS 6/12/59

61. Letter from Mabel Smith to Harry Price, 26 September 1940, SPR archive, Cambridge University Library, SPR/6/12/61

62. Letter from Mabel Smith to Harry Price, 29 November 1940, SPR archive, Cambridge University Library, SPR/6/12/65

63. C. M. Joad, 'The Ghosts of Borley,' *The Spectator*, 18 October 1940, p. 396

64. Ibid.

65. Sir Ernest Jelf, *Law Times*, 9 August 1941, SPR archive, Cambridge University Library, SPR/6/12/14

66. Letter from Albion Richardson to Harry Price, 22 May 1945, SPR archive, Cambridge University Library, SPR/6/11/76

67. Ibid.

68. Letter from Canon W. J. Phythian-Adams to Harry Price, 8 January 1941, Senate House Library, HPC/4B/3

69. Canon W. J. Phythian-Adams, 'On Borley Rectory', Senate House Library, HPD/2/5

70. Ibid.

71. Ibid.

72. Harry Price, *The End of Borley Rectory*, op. cit., pp. 77–8

73. Ibid.

74. Letter from Lt. G. B. Nawrocki to Harry Price, 8 August 1943, SPR archive, Cambridge University Library, SPR/6/11/46

75. Letter from Capt. W. H. Gregson to Harry Price, 14 September 1943, Senate House Library, HPC/4B/89

76. Letter from Rev. A. C. Henning to Harry Price, 5 November 1942, Senate House Library, HPC/4B/104

77. Ibid.

78. Price, *The End of Borley Rectory*, op. cit., p. 244

79. Now Arundel Cathedral.

80. Price, *The End of Borley Rectory*, op. cit., p. 283

81. Cynthia Thompson (née Ledsham) interviewed by M.K. Goldney, 17 October 1950, Society for Psychical Research Archive (SPR) 6/3/10-16

82. Price, op. cit., p. 283

83. Letter from Harry Price to R. G. Longman, 8 January 1945, Senate House Library, HPD/4A/8

84. Letter from J. H. H. Gaute to Harry Price, 27 October 1944, Senate House Library, HPD/4B/8

85. 'The Ghost Walks,' *Daily News*, 5 May 1945, p. 1
86. 'Thump Ghosts,' Letter from C. Sinclair to the Editor, *The Church Times*, 5 October 1945, p. 564
87. Letter from Mrs Smith to the *Church Times*, 19 October 1945, SPR archive, Cambridge University Library, SPR/6/8/10
88. Letter from Rev. A. C. Henning to Harry Price, 1 November 1945, SPR archive, Cambridge University Library, SPR/6/10/33
89. Price, *The End of Borley Rectory*, op. cit., p. 302
90. Ibid., p. 304
91. Ibid., pp. 304–5
92. Ibid., p. 334
93. Ibid.
94. 'The Astonishing Story of the Haunted Rectory of Borley,' *Sunday Mirror*, 13 October 1946, p. 4
95. 'Books by James Agate,' *Daily Express*, 12 October 1946, p. 2
96. 'Phantoms and Fire,' *The Church Times*,' 1 November 1946, p. 657
97. H.F. Carhill, 'Ghosts Troop Home,' The Times Literary Supplement, 16 November 1946 ,p. 566
98. 'The Haunted Rectory', *Radio Times*, 27 June 1947, Vol. XCV, No. 1237, p. 2
99. Peter Underwood, *The Borley Postscript*, 'The Haunted Rectory', broadcast script, BBC, 1947, pp. 63–64
100. James Turner, *Sometimes into England: A Second Volume of Autobiography*, (London: Cassell & Co. Ltd, 1970), p. 24
101. Price ended his book *Search for Truth* with a rhetorical, if needy, question: 'Is there a single reader of these memoirs who dares to assert that my life has been wasted?' Harry Price, *Search for Truth: My Life for Psychical Research* (London: Collins, 1942), p. 305
102. In the draft of a letter from Price to J. H. H. Gaute, Price claimed that *Borley III* 'will be the most important of the trilogy' and clearly saw the investigation of the Rectory as his legacy: 'As it is the classical case of all time, it will certainly have to be published.' Touchingly, Price's handwriting shows signs of significant decline. Undated (but probably 22 December 1947), Senate House Library, HPD/4A/4
103. Paul Tabori, *Search for Harry Price*, p. 292
104. 'Death of Man Who Exposed Fake Mediums', *Daily Telegraph*, 30 March 1948, p. 1
105. 'Mr Harry Price', *The Times*, 30 March 1948, p. 6
106. 'In Defence of Harry Price', *Suffolk and Essex Free Press*, 8 April 1948, p. 16

17. Search for Truth

1. Harry Price, *Search for Truth: My Life for Psychical Research*, (London: Collins, 1942), p. 260
2. 'Price a Fraud, Say Magicians', *Daily Mail*, 31 March 1948
3. 'He May Try to Return', *Daily Herald*, 31 March 1948

4. 'Price a Fraud' *Daily Mail*, op. cit.

5. Price left £17,000. Will of Harry Price, Society for Psychical Research (SPR) archive, Cambridge University Library, SPR/MS 6/12/11

6. Mrs Ryan Baines's contribution to *Borley III*, SPR archive, Cambridge University Library, SPR/6/2/4

7. Letter from Mrs Ryan Baines to K. M. Goldney, 12 June 1952, SPR archive, Cambridge University Library, SPR/6/2/25

8. Ibid.

9. Ibid.

10. Paul Tabori, 'These Ghosts Never Die', *Star Weekly*, 26 November 1949, p. 7, SPR archive, Cambridge University Library, SPR/6/9/45 CUL

11. Letter from K. M. Goldney to William Salter, 7 August 1948, SPR archive, Cambridge University Library, SPR/6/12/70

12. Letter from William Salter to K. M. Goldney, 3 October 1940, SPR archive, Cambridge University Library, 6/6/28

13. Ibid.

14. Letter from William Salter to M. K. Goldney, 6 August 1948, SPR archive, Cambridge University Library, SPR/6/12/69

15. 'The Meditations of Charles Sutton', *Inky Way Annual Book 2* (London: World's Press News Publishing Co. Ltd, 1948), p. 125

16. Ibid., p. 126

17. Sutton had been disabled during the war. 'Don't expect me to leap about the place – I wear a pair of tin legs as a result of the last fracas!' Letter from Charles Sutton to Lucie Meeker, 6 June 1949, Senate House Library, HPA /5/1

18. Report by Charles Sutton, 10 June 1949, SPR archive, Cambridge University Library, SPR/6/1/41

19. Charles Sutton interviewed by K. M. Goldney 1 February 1949, SPR archive, Cambridge University Library, SPR/6/1/30

20. Letter from Lord Charles Hope to K. M. Goldney, 24 January 1949, SPR archive, Cambridge University Library, SPR/6/3/17

21. Lucie Meeker (née Kaye) interviewed by K. M. Goldney, Clarice Richards and Lord Charles Hope 18 February 1949, SPR archive, Cambridge University Library, SPR/6/3/2

22. Ibid.

23. Lord Charles had fallen out with Price over the debacle surrounding Rudi Schneider (see Chapter 14). Lord Charles also questioned Henry Douglas-Home, who had been an observer at the Rectory during Price's tenancy. He thought Price 'as twisty as a corkscrew'. Letter from H. M. Douglas-Home to K. M. Goldney, 27 March 1953, SPR archive, Cambridge University Library, SPR/6/1/28: 'Old Harry was a rogue and the more people who realise it, the better for Truth's sake.'

24. Letter from Lucie Meeker (née Kaye) to Lord Charles Hope, 1 March 1949, SPR archive, Cambridge University Library, SPR/6/3/3. Writing to Mrs Ryan Baines, Lucie Meeker questioned the suitability of the Society for Psychical Research to write the *Borley Report* as it was all so personal: 'They always were as mad as tree cats. Should be called

the Society for Perpetual Retrogression', she wrote. 'They go round and round in circles. And don't forget, they hated Price!'

25. Letter from Lucie Meeker (née Kaye) to Clarice Richards, 28 February 1949, Cambridge University Library, SPR/6/3/4

26. Letter from Lucie Meeker (née Kaye) to the Society for Psychical Research, 21 March 1949, SPR archive, Cambridge University Library, SPR/6/3/8

27. 'Whiff of Evil at Borley', *Daily Mail*, 23 May 1939, SPR archive, Cambridge University Library, SPR/6/12/17

28. Letter from Mabel Smith to the Editor, *Daily Mail*, 26 May 1949, SPR archive, Cambridge University Library, 6/12/17

29. Letter from William Salter to the Editor, *Daily Mail*, 26 May 1949, SPR archive, Cambridge University Library, SPR/6/12/18

30. Ibid.

31. Letter from Mabel Smith to William Salter, 3 June 1949, SPR archive, Cambridge University Library, SPR/6/12/88

32. Letter from K.M. Goldney to William Salter, 18 July 1949, SPR archive, Cambridge University Library, SPR/6/12/76

33. K. M. Goldney on Harry Price, SPR archive, Cambridge University Library, SPR/6/13/3

34. Eric J. Dingwall and Trevor H. Hall, *Four Modern Ghosts* (London: Gerald Duckworth and Co. Ltd, 1958), p. 58

35. Letter from E. J. Dingwall to K. M. Goldney, 18 June 1949, SPR archive, Cambridge University Library, SPR/6/17/76. See also Mollie Goldney's withdrawal: K. M. Goldney to Paul Tabori, 20 June 1949, SPR archive, Cambridge University Library, SPR/6/17/77

36. Letter from Mabel Smith to K. M. Goldney, 27 June 1949, SPR archive, Cambridge University Library, SPR/6/12/103

37. Statement by K. M. Goldney and E. J. Dingwall regarding their visit to Mrs Smith 1–2 July 1949, SPR archive, Cambridge University Library, SPR/6/12/80

38. Mabel Smith interviewed by K. M. Goldney and E. J. Dingwall, 1–2 July 1949, SPR archive, Cambridge University Library, SPR/6/12/84

39. Ibid.

40. Statement by K. M. Goldney and E. J. Dingwall regarding their visit to Mrs Smith 1–2 July 1949, op. cit.

41. Letter from Mabel Smith to K. M. Goldney, 14 July 1949, SPR archive, Cambridge University Library, SPR/6/12/111

42. Letter from Mabel Smith to K. M. Goldney, 4 August 1949, SPR archive, Cambridge University Library, SPR/6/12/86

43. Letter from Ethel English (née Beenham) to K. M. Goldney, 20 August 1949, SPR archive, Cambridge University Library, SPR/6/4/4

44. Alfred and Ethel Bull interviewed by E. J. Dingwall, K. M. Goldney and Trevor H. Hall 4 April 1953, SPR archive, Cambridge University Library, SPR/6/4/34

45. Ethel and Alfred Bull interviewed by K. M. Goldney 11 August 1950, SPR archive, Cambridge University Library, SPR/6/4/10

46. Ethel Bull interviewed by Sidney Glanville 25 June 1938 in *Glanville, The Haunting of Borley Rectory*, op. cit., pp. 132–3

47. Ethel and Alfred Bull interviewed by K. M. Goldney 11 August 1950, SPR archive, Cambridge University Library, SPR/6/4/10. See also W. H. Salter's report of the same visit, SPR archive, Cambridge University Library, SPR/6/4/19

48. Letter from Mabel Smith to K. M. Goldney, 4 August 1949, SPR archive, Cambridge University Library, SPR/6/12/86: 'I finished the book,' Mrs Smith wrote, 'wishing I could meet Mr Cooper, and Mary; I am sure I could make the latter give her *real* views.'

49. Mary Tatum (née Pearson) interviewed by E. J. Dingwall and Trevor H. Hall 21 August 1952, SPR archive, Cambridge University Library, SPR/6/4/30

18. The Widow of Borley

1. Letter from Sidney Glanville to K.M. Goldney, 12 May 1952, SPR archive, Cambridge University Library, SPR/6/1/59

2. Letter from Paul Tabori to Lucie Meeker, 8 July 1949, Senate House Library, HPA/5/1. Tabori wrote: 'In the present state of the film industry here and in Hollywood I see little hope for a Borley film. Anything that isn't a "formula picture" frightens the money-bags.'

3. Minutes of the Society for Psychical Research council meeting, 17 November 1949, Society for Psychical Research (SPR) archive, Cambridge University Library, SPR/6/17/1

4. Trevor H. Hall, *New Light on Old Ghosts*, (London: Gerald Duckworth and Co. Ltd, 1965), p. xi

5. Letter from Alan Wesencraft to Vincent O'Neil, [undated] 2000, Paul Adams, Eddie Brazil and Peter Underwood, *The Borley Rectory Companion: The Complete Guide to 'The Most Haunted House in England'* (Stroud: The History Press, 2009), p. 186

6. *East Anglian Daily Times*, 9 August 1933, p. 5. For the story of the Fascist intervention in the Tithe War, see Andrew Martin Mitchell, *Fascism in East Anglia: The British Union of Fascists in Norfolk, Suffolk and Essex, 1933-1940*, Department of History, University of Sheffield, 1999

7. John Mead, 'Suffolk and the "Tithe War" of the 1930s', *East Anglian History Workshop Journal*, Vol .1 (n.d) p. 15

8. Edith Wildgoose interviewed by Trevor H. Hall 30 December 1953, SPR archive, Cambridge University Library, SPR 6/14/35

9. Vincent O'Neil, *The Most Haunted Woman in England: Marianne Foyster of Borley Rectory*, unpublished manuscript, 1996 p. 102

10. Mrs F. M. Fenton interviewed by Trevor H. Hall 16 May 1956, SPR archive, Cambridge University Library, SPR/6/14/57

11. Vincent O'Neil, *The Most Haunted Woman in England*, p. 231

12. Letter from Evelyn Gordon to Trevor H. Hall, 6 August 1954, SPR archive, Cambridge University Library, SPR/6/14/44

13. Letter from Lord Charles Hope to K. M. Goldney, 13 February 1949, SPR archive, Cambridge University Library, SPR/6/1/18: 'I asked [Mrs Pearson] if Adelaide was old enough to write *Marianne* and *she told me* that she was always writing as Mrs Foyster *told her to* and that she called her "Marianne", and that she wrote like Mrs Foyster taught her'.

14. Letter from Evelyn Gordon to Trevor H. Hall, 26 July 1954, SPR archive, Cambridge University Library, SPR/6/14/44

15. Rev. Lionel Foyster, *Fifteen Months in a Haunted House: A Record of an Experiment*, Senate House Library, HPC/3G/4, pp., 175–6

16. Canon Henry Lawton interviewed by Trevor H. Hall 8 April 1952, SPR archive, Cambridge University Library, SPR/6/3/76

17. 'The Ghost of Borley', *The Spectator*, 8 November, 1940, p. 477

18. Sidney Glanville, *The Haunting of Borley Rectory: Private and Confidential Report ('The Locked Book')*, Senate House Library, HPC/3G/5, p. 117. Glanville records a conversation with 'Mr Bull' at the Rectory on 20 November 1937. A handwritten insertion assumes this to be 'Walter' Bull, but it must refer to Gerald Bull, who was living at Chilton Lodge at the time. His brother Alfred frequently dismissed any suggestion of paranormal activity at the Rectory. But Glanville reports that '"When walking up the lane and approaching the house, [Gerald] fifty times heard footsteps following him, he always turned round but never saw anyone." He could not account for them.'

19. Letter from Gay Taylor to Harry Price, 26 January 1946, SPR archive, Cambridge University Library, SPR/6/14/1

20. Wanda Haines was the muse and, later, wife of the fashion photographer Norman Parkinson. Mrs Parkinson further discussed her knowledge of Marianne's relationship with Johnny Fisher with K. M. Goldney on 1 October 1954 – SPR archive, Cambridge University Library, SPR/6/14/27. Johnny Fisher's sister refused to cooperate with the Society for Psychical Research as she was 'afraid of publicity, and upsetting her brother's health as he [was] only [then] recovering from so severe a breakdown'.

21. Gay Taylor interviewed by K. M. Goldney and E. J. Dingwall 8 February 1950, SPR archive, Cambridge University Library, SPR/6/14/7. In this interview, Mrs Taylor suggested that there had been a rumour at the hospital in Long Melford that Lionel Foyster had been poisoned. But this may relate to the overdose of synthetic digitalin that Lionel had been taking for his heart condition.

22. Mary Edith Shaw interviewed by H. E. Pratt 15 October 1955, SPR archive, Cambridge University Library, SPR/6/14/53. Despite the fact that Mrs Shaw had been clear that she did not want to cooperate with the Society for Psychical Research investigation, Hall sent H. E. Pratt to visit her at her home in Bredon, where she made some of the more extreme charges against Marianne.

23. Vincent O'Neil, op. cit., p. 141. O'Neil quotes from sections of Trevor H. Hall's *Marianne Foyster* which are now no longer available for study. Swanson probes Marianne about her sex life. She admits that

she had a high sex drive but that Lionel was impotent. Swanson: 'The reason for having relations with D'Arles was because Lionel couldn't satisfy you sexually and later he agreed to your relations with other men, is that correct?' Marianne: 'Yes, well, not with other men, it wasn't as crude as that: it was just... (*sigh*).' O'Neil, op. cit, p. 148

24. Letter from Marianne Fisher (née Shaw) to Ian Shaw, May 1956, Vincent O'Neil, *The Most Haunted Woman in England*, p. 237

25. Mary Edith Shaw interviewed by H. E. Pratt 15 October 1955, SPR archive, Cambridge University Library, SPR/6/14/53

26. Letter from Ethel Bull to Harry Price, 16 January 1940, Senate House Library, HPC/4B

27. Ibid.

28. Dr J. R. A. Davies interviewed by Trevor H. Hall 6 October 1955, SPR archive, Cambridge University Library, SPR/6/14/50

29. Ibid.

30. Letter from Mabel Smith to K. M. Goldney, 1 July 1952, SPR archive, Cambridge University Library, SPR/6/12/126

31. Letter from H.E Pratt to Trevor H. Hall, 23 August 1953, SPR archive, Cambridge University Library, SPR 4/14/5

32. Letty Knights interviewed by H. E. Pratt 8 June 1954, SPR archive, Cambridge University Library, SPR/6/14/38

33. Ibid.

34. Ibid.

35. Ibid.

36. Ibid. Marianne was in dire financial straits and worried about the future. She may well have slept with soldiers for company, but according to Pratt, Mrs Knights was 'definite on this point' – that Marianne was paid for sex. When Pratt visited Johnny Fisher's sister, Edith Shaw, Mrs Shaw's husband insisted that Marianne was 'a prostitute, sir.' – SPR archive, Cambridge University Library, SPR/6/14/53

37. Pratt had been fascinated to investigate Marianne's life history until this revelation by Mrs Knights: 'This trait of sadistic cruelty is a common one in baby farmers, and it was these details that finally turned me against Marianne.' SPR archive, Cambridge University Library, SPR/6/14/38

38. Ibid.

19. The Borley Report

1. Eric J. Dingwall, Kathleen M. Goldney and Trevor H. Hall, *The Haunting of Borley Rectory* (London: Gerald Duckworth and Co. Ltd, 1956), p. 2

2. Op. cit., inside cover.

3. Dingwall, Goldney and Hall, op. cit., p. 3

4. Harry Price, *'The Most Haunted House in England': Ten Years' Investigation of Borley Rectory* (London: Longmans, Green and Co., 1940), pp. 56–58

5. Dingwall, Goldney and Hall, op. cit., p. 73

6. Ibid., p. 162

7. Harry Price, *The End of Borley Rectory: 'The Most Haunted House in England'* (London: George G. Harrap and Co. Ltd, 1946), p. 284

8. 'Rectory Ghosts', *Sunday Times*, 5 February 1956, p. 6

9. Anthony Flew, 'The End of Borley Rectory?', *The Spectator*, 27 January 1956, p. 107

10. Nandor Fodor, 'Was Harry Price a Fraud?', *Tomorrow*, Vol. 4, No. 2 (1956), pp. 53–61

11. Joe Burroughs, *The Haunted Rectory*, unpublished script for BBC radio programme 1956 – 'Cancelled (on legal grounds).' Society for Psychical Research archive, Cambridge University Library, SPR/6/13/36

12. Letter from Robert Hastings to W. H. Salter, 14 December 1956, SPR archive, Cambridge University Library, SPR/6/17/187

13. Letter from W. H. Salter to K. M. Goldney, 8 December 1956, SPR archive, Cambridge University Library, SPR6/17/184

14. Robert J. Hastings, *An Examination of the 'Borley Report,'*, Proceedings of the Society for Psychical Research, Vol. 55, Part 201 (March 1969)

15. 'Mr Hastings and the Borley Report,' E.J. Dingwall, K.M. Goldney and T. H. Hall, *Journal of the Society for Psychical Research*, Vol. 45, No. 741, (London: Society for Psychical Research, September 1969), p. 124

16. Trevor H. Hall, *Search for Harry Price* (London: Gerald Duckworth & Co., 1978), p. 5

17. Paul Tabori and Peter Underwood, *The Ghosts of Borley: Annals of the Haunted Rectory* (Newon Abbott: David & Charles (Holdings) Limited, 1973), dedication

18. Hall, op. cit., p. 3. Underlining his point that the public wanted to believe in a paranormal explanation of the Borley story despite the evidence of the *Borley Report*, Hall quotes an advertisement from the March 1975 edition of *Business Travel World*: 'DO YOU WANT TO TRY SOMETHING DIFFERENT? How about visiting the site of Borley Rectory – the most haunted spot in Britain? This is part of an eight-day Psychic Research Tour organised by Enjoy Britain and the World, Ltd., at a cost of £145 per person.'

19. John McCulloch, 'Ghost-haunting fraud,' *The Times*, 27 November 1978, p. 6

20. John J. Randall, 'Harry Price: The Case for the Defence', *Journal of the Society for Psychical Research*, Vol. 64, No. 860 (July 2000)

21. John McCulloch, op. cit., p. 6

22. Peter Underwood, *Borley Postscript*, (Haslemere: Whitehouse Publications, 2001), pp. 148–152

20. Most Haunted

1. Letter from Marianne O'Neil to Peter Underwood, 15 September 1986, Paul Adams Archive

2. Vincent O'Neil, *The Most Haunted Woman in England*, p. 117

3. Letter from Robert Vincent O'Neil to Marianne O'Neil, 30 January 1946, in Vincent O'Neil, *The Most Haunted Woman in England: Marianne Foyster of Borley Rectory*, unpublished manuscript, 1996, p. 162

4. Vincent O'Neil, op. cit., p. 4. Marianne's marriage to O'Neil and her journey from Tidworth to Wisconsin is told in O'Neil, op. cit., pp. 162–70

5. Letter from Marianne O'Neil to Mrs Fenton, 28 January 1947, in O'Neil, op. cit., p. 229

6. Letter from Letty Knights to Marianne O'Neil, 18 March 1947, in O'Neil, op. cit., pp. 131–2. The warmth of this letter ('My Dear Marianne …') is at odds with Mrs Knights's attitude towards Marianne in her interview with Pratt in 1953. Either they had overcome their differences surrounding Marianne's abandonment of John, or the arrangement between them was more complicated than Mrs Knights was prepared to admit. Marianne may have offered Letty a financial incentive to look after John. She may also have agreed to tell the story of Marianne's sudden disappearance in order to put anybody enquiring into her whereabouts off the scent.

7. Vincent O'Neil, *Who Am I: The Mysterious Search for My Identity*, p. 138

8. Letter from Peter Underwood to Marianne O'Neil, 15 September 1986, Paul Adams Archive

9. Vincent O'Neil, *The Most Haunted Woman in England*, p. 103

10. Letter from Marianne O'Neil to Ian Shaw, May 1956, in O'Neil, *The Most Haunted Woman in England*, op. cit., p. 235

11. Ibid., p. 231

12. Ibid., p. 235–7

13. Ibid., p. 237

14. Ibid., p. 236

15. Ibid., p. 239

16. Ibid., p. 238

17. O'Neil, *The Most Haunted Woman in England*, op. cit., pp. 241–2

18. Letter from Marianne O'Neil to Vincent O'Neil, 20 January 1963, in O'Neil, *Who Am I? The Mysterious Search for My Identity*, op. cit., p. 27

19. Robert Wood, *The Widow of Borley: A Psychical Investigation* (London: Gerald Duckworth and Co. Ltd 1992) p. 161

20. Trevor H. Hall, *Marianne Foyster of Borley Rectory: A Biographical, Psychological and Psychical Investigation, Vol. 5*, unpublished manuscript, 1958, Cambridge University Library, p. 62

21. O'Neil, *The Most Haunted Woman in England*, op. cit., p. 247

22. Ibid., p. 250

23. Trevor H. Hall, op. cit., p. 67

24. Ibid., p. 57

25. Ibid., p. 13

26. Ibid., p. 62

27. Marianne wrote what she called an 'imperfect outline' of her life story. Eileen Garrett returned it, asking her to rewrite it in a 'less superficial style' and to make less of an alleged affair between Harry Price and Mollie Goldney (See Trevor H. Hall, p. 72). No further draft was completed. The outline is contained in Trevor Hall's *Marianne Foyster*, op. cit

28. O'Neil, *The Most Haunted Woman in England*, op. cit., p. 256

29. O'Neil, *Who Am I? The Mysterious Search for my Identity*, op. cit., p. 7

30. Ibid., p. 27. Letter from Marianne Fisher (nee Shaw) to Vincent O'Neil, 20 January 1963

31. Ibid., p. 39. Letter from Marianne Fisher to Vincent O'Neil, 20 July 1966

32. Letter from Adelaide Cartwright (née Foyster), 'To Whom It May Concern', 30 June 1994, in O'Neil, *The Most Haunted Woman in England*, op. cit., p. 2

33. Email from Nick Rowland to Vincent O'Neil, 22 September 1992, in O'Neil, *The Most Haunted Woman in England*, op. cit., p. 5

34. Iris Owen and Paulene Mitchell, *Borley Rectory: 'The Most Haunted House in England': A Report by New Horizons Foundation of Some Investigations Made into This Alleged Haunting* (New Horizons Foundation, 1986: cpb-us-w2.wpmucdn.com, p. 25)

35. 'Sister "Found" After 45 Years', *Providence Journal Bulletin*, December 1974, Alan Roper Archive, care of Mark Hopper

36. *The Woonsocket Call and Evening Reporter*, 19 December 1974, p. 23

37. Ibid.

38. Letter from Adelaide Cartwright to Alan Roper, 11 January 1975, Alan Roper Archive, care of Mark Hopper

39. Vincent O'Neil, *Who am I?*, p. 139

40. Ibid.

41. Ibid.

42. Ibid., p. 291

43. Letter from Marianne O'Neil to Robert Swanson, 17 April 1958, in O'Neil, *The Most Haunted Woman in England*, op. cit., p. 249

44. Ibid.

Afterword

1. Andrew Clarke, *The Bones of Borley*: http://www.foxearth.org.uk/BorleyRectory

2. Daniel Farson, *The Hamlyn Book of Ghosts in Fact and Fiction* (London: Hamlyn, 1978)

3. Ibid., p. 9

4. Ernest Ambrose, *Melford Memories*, p. 77

5. Sidney Glanville, *The Haunting of Borley Rectory: Private and Confidential Report ('The Locked Book')*, p. 11

6. *Diary of Caroline Sarah 'Dodie' Bull*, (1885), unpublished manuscript, David Tibet archive, Hastings

7. Glanville, op. cit., p. 132. On 25 June 1938, Glanville interviewed Ethel Bull, who alleged that Harry had been poisoned by his wife. She told Glanville that after his death, they had found a bottle in the cellar half-filled with 'sugar of lead'.

8. Letter from Mabel Smith to William Salter, 8 July 1949, Society for Psychical Research (SPR) archive, Cambridge University Library, SPR/6/12/107: 'I only wish it had been your people [ie the SPR] that had come to us at Borley.'

9. Letter from H. M. Douglas-Home to Lord Charles Hope, 10 August 1949, SPR archive, Cambridge University Library, SPR/6/1/21: 'Mrs Foyster was determined to play up the previous history of the house. A very sane housekeeper saw her doing many things – removing keys, carrying empty bottles etc, etc.'

10. Letter from Mary Braithwaite to William Salter, 19 August 1931, SPR achive, Cambridge University Library, SPR/6/6/20. The wall-writing, Miss Braithwaite observed, was 'undoubtedly Mrs F[oyster]'s as she makes some letters in a funny way'.

11. Letter from Marianne O'Neil to Ian Shaw, May 1956, in Vincent O'Neil, *The Most Haunted Woman in England*, p. 235

12. Vincent O'Neil, *The Most Haunted Woman in England*, p. 266

13. Iris Owen and Paulene Mitchell, *Borley Rectory: 'The Most Haunted House in England': A Report by New Horizons Foundation of Some Investigations Made into This Alleged Haunting* (New Horizons Foundation, 1986: cpb-us-w2.wpmucdn.com, p. 52)

14. On 13 November 1974, Ronald DeFeo Jr shot his parents, two brothers and two sisters at 112 Ocean Drive, a Dutch colonial house in Amityville, Long Island. His lawyer, William Weber, offered a plea of insanity as DeFeo, a petty thief and drug addict, claimed to hear voices that had driven him to kill his family. DeFeo was found guilty of murder and sentenced to 150 years in prison. Weber was soon approached by publishers interested in turning the story into a book. Meanwhile, George and Kathy Lutz saw that the house was for sale for a bargain $80,000 and mortgaged themselves to the hilt to afford it. They moved in just before Christmas 1975. Twenty-eight days later, they 'fled in terror', claiming that the house was possessed by evil spirits. Lutz, who was interested in the occult, approached William Weber, suggesting that there may be some truth in the notion that voices had compelled DeFeo to commit the murders. Weber met the Lutzes as he felt that their story of a haunted house might increase interest in the book he was planning about the case as well as opening the possibility of a re-trial for his client. Weber insisted that he and the Lutzes 'created this horror story over many bottles of wine'. But the Lutzes weren't satisfied with the terms of the deal and didn't want to share the profits with DeFeo. Moving to California, they were introduced to an editor at the publisher Prentice Hall who suggested that they collaborate on a book about their experiences with the author Jay Anson. They would share the profits, fifty-fifty. The Lutzes didn't meet

Anson, but sent him forty-five hours of tape recordings, which were used as the basis for *The Amityville Horror: A True Story*. Inspired by Price's *Most Haunted House in England*, Anson outlined the story as a diary and provided ground plans of the house to illustrate the text. But Stephen Kaplan, the director of the Parapsychology Institute of America had been immediately suspicious of the Lutzes' story – and particularly their relationship with DeFeo's lawyer. After investigating the case, he concluded that he found no evidence to support any claims of a 'haunted house': 'What we did find is a couple who had purchased a house that they could not economically afford. It is our professional opinion that the story of its haunting is mostly fiction.' When Kaplan telephoned him, Jay Anson admitted that 'there are some inconsistencies, but it's too late to change them now.' Once *The Amityville Horror* was established as a best-seller, William Weber sued the Lutzes for reneging on their deal. At the same time, the new owners of Ocean Drive, Jim and Barbara Cromarty, sued Jay Anson and the publisher, maintaining that the fraudulent haunting claims had destroyed their privacy, as the house had been overrun by sightseers since the book was published: 'It is Long Island's equivalent to Watergate. None of us would be here today if a responsible publisher and author had not given credibility to two liars, and allowed them the privilege of putting the word "true" on a book in which in all actuality is a novel.' Despite these challenges to the authenticity of the story, by 1981 the book had made $6,500,000 and been reprinted thirty-seven times. In 1978, the film rights were sold for $6,000,000. To date, the story has spawned thirty films. DeFeo died in custody in March 2021, having confirmed that Amityville was 'a hoax that Weber and the Lutzes started. Yes, to make money.'

15. Joe Burroughs, *The Haunted Rectory*, unpublished script for BBC radio programme, 1956 – 'Cancelled (on legal grounds).' Society for Psychical Research archive, Cambridge University Library, SPR/6/13/36, p. 23

16. Report by Charles Sutton, 10 June 1949, SPR archive, Cambridge University Library, SPR/6/1/41. See also: Charles Sutton interviewed by K. M. Goldney 1 February 1949, SPR archive, Cambridge University Library, SPR/6/1/30

17. Mary Tatum (née Pearson) interviewed by E. J. Dingwall and Trevor H. Hall 21 August 1952, SPR archive, Cambridge University Library, SPR/6/4/30

18. Trevor H. Hall, *Marianne Foyster*, p. 57

BIBLIOGRAPHY

Archive Material:

The extensive Harry Price archive is held at Senate House Library in London. This includes a copy of Sidney Glanville's 'Locked Book' as well as the material that Price used to write *'The Most Haunted House in England'* and *The End of Borley Rectory*.

Three boxes of Borley-related material – including correspondence between Eric Dingwall, Trevor Hall, Mollie Goldney and William Salter – are held in the archives of the Society for Psychical Research at Cambridge University Library. This includes the interviews conducted during the investigation that became the *Borley Report*.

Borley Rectory:

Paul Adams, Eddie Brazil and Peter Underwood, *The Borley Rectory Companion: The Complete Guide to 'The Most Haunted House in England'*, The History Press, Stroud, 2009

Edward Babbs, *Borley Rectory: The Final Analysis*, Six Martlets Publishing, Sudbury, 2003

Ivan Banks, *The Enigma of Borley Rectory*, W. Foulsham & Co. Ltd, London, 2001

Caroline 'Dodie' Bull, *Diary*, unpublished manuscript, 1885–6

Michael Coleman, et al., 'The Borley Report: Some Criticisms and Comments', *Journal of the Society for Psychical Research*, Vol. 38, 1955–6

Eric J. Dingwall, Kathleen M. Goldney and Trevor H. Hall, 'The Haunting of Borley Rectory: A Critical Survey of the Evidence', *Proceedings of the Society for Psychical Research,* Vol. 51, University of Glasgow Press, Glasgow, 1955. This was also published in a commercial edition as *The Haunting of Borley Rectory,* Gerald Duckworth & Co. Ltd, London, 1956

Wesley H. Downes, *The Ghosts of Borley,* Wesley's Publications, Clacton-on-Sea, 1993

Sidney Glanville, *The Haunting of Borley Rectory – Private and Confidential Report* (known as the 'Locked Book'), unpublished manuscript

Sidney H. Glanville, 'The Strange Happenings at Borley Rectory – Full Account of England's Most Famous Modern Ghost', *Fate,* October 1951

R. J. Hastings, 'An Examination of the "Borley Report"', *Proceedings of the Society for Psychical Research,* Vol. 55, 201, 1969

A. C. Henning, *Haunted Borley,* E. N. Mason & Sons, Colchester, 1949

Louis Mayerling, *We Faked the Ghosts of Borley Rectory,* Pen Press Publishers, London, 2000

Iris Owen and Paulene Mitchell, 'The Alleged Haunting of Borley Rectory', *Journal of the Society for Psychical Research,* Vol. 50, London, 1979

Harry Price, *The End of Borley Rectory: 'The Most Haunted House in England',* George G. Harrap and Co. Ltd, London, 1946

Harry Price, *'The Most Haunted House in England': Ten Years' Investigation of Borley Rectory,* Longmans, Green and Co., London, 1940

Paul Tabori and Peter Underwood, *The Ghosts of Borley: Annals of the Haunted Rectory,* W. J. Holman Limited, Dawlish, 1973

Peter Underwood, *Borley Postscript,* Whitehouse Publications, Haslemere, 2001

Harry Price:

Trevor H. Hall, *Search for Harry Price,* Gerald Duckworth & Co. Ltd, London, 1978

Lucie Meeker, *The Ghost Kept Price Awake,* unpublished manuscript

Harry Price, *Christmas Ghosts*, St Hugh's Press, London, 1949

Harry Price, *Confessions of a Ghost-Hunter*, Putnam & Co. Ltd, London, 1936

Harry Price, *Fifty Years of Psychical Research: A Critical Survey*, Longmans, Green and Co., London, 1939

Harry Price, *Leaves from a Psychist's Case-Book*, Victor Gollancz, London, 1936

Harry Price, *Poltergeist Over England: Three Centuries of Mischievous Ghosts*, Country Life Ltd, London, 1945

Harry Price, *Search for Truth: My Life for Psychical Research*, Collins, London, 1942

Richard Morris, *Harry Price: The Psychic Detective*, Sutton Publishing, 2006

Paul Tabori, *Harry Price: The Biography of a Ghost-Hunter*, Athenaeum Press, London, 1950

Paul Adams and Eddie Brazil continue to add to their excellent website about Harry Price's life and work at harrypricewebsite.co.uk

Marianne Foyster:

Lionel Foyster, *Diary of Occurrences at Borley Rectory Between February 1931 and July 1931, (Memorandum of Our Experiences in Connexion with the Borley 'Ghost')*, unpublished manuscript

Lionel Foyster, *Fifteen Months in a Haunted House*, unpublished manuscript

Trevor H. Hall, *Marianne Foyster of Borley Rectory: A Biographical, Psychological and Psychical Investigation*, Vol. 5, unpublished manuscript, Leeds, 1958

Vincent O'Neil, *Borley Rectory, The Ghosts that will not Die*, unpublished manuscript, 1996

Vincent O'Neil, *Who Am I? The Mysterious Search for My Identity*, RVON Enterprises, Utah, 1994

Iris Owen and Paulene Mitchell, *Borley Rectory: 'The Most Haunted House in England': A Report by New Horizons Foundation of Some Investigations Made into This Alleged Haunting*, New Horizons Foundation, 1986: cpb-us-w2.wpmucdn.com

Robert Wood, *The Widow of Borley: A Psychical Investigation*, Duckworth, London, 1992

General:

William Addison, *Essex Heyday*, J. M. Dent and Sons Ltd, London, 1949

Deborah Alun-Jones, *The Wry Romance of the Literary Rectory*, Thames and Hudson Ltd, London, 2013

Ernest Ambrose, *Melford Memories*, Long Melford Historical and Archaeological Society, Lavenham, 1972

B. Anthony Bax, *The English Parsonage*, John Murray, London, 1964

Sir Ernest Bennett, *Apparitions and Haunted Houses: A Survey of Evidence*, Faber & Faber, London, 1939

E. F. Benson, 'The Confession of Charles Linkworth', *The Room in the Tower and Other Stories*, Alfred A. Knopf, London, 1929

G. F. A. Best, *Temporal Pillars: Queen Anne's Bounty, the Ecclesiastical Commissioners, and the Church of England*, Cambridge University Press, Cambridge, 1964

William Peter Blatty, *The Exorcist*, Blond & Briggs Ltd, London, 1972

Deborah Blum, *Ghost Hunters: William James and the Search for Scientific Proof of Life After Death,* Century, London, 2007

Ronald Blythe, *The Age of Illusion: England in the Twenties and Thirties 1919–1940*, Hamish Hamilton, London, 1963

Julia Briggs, *Night Visitors: The Rise and Fall of the English Ghost Story*, Faber & Faber, London, 1977

Kevin Brown, *The Pox: The Life and Near Death of a Very Social Disease*, Sutton Publishing Ltd, Stroud, 2006

Georgina Byrne, *Modern Spiritualism and the Church of England, 1850-1939*, The Boydell Press, Woodbridge, 2010

Angus Calder, *The People's War: Britain 1939–1945*, Jonathan Cape, London 1969

J. C. Cannell, *When Fleet Street Calls: Being the Experiences of a London Journalist,* Jarrolds, London 1932

Hereward Carrington and Nandor Fodor, *The Story of the Poltergeist Down the Centuries,* Rider and Company, London, 1953

Roger Clarke, *A Natural History of Ghosts: 500 years of Hunting for Proof*, Particular Books, London 2012

Helen Conrad-O'Briain and Julie Anne Stevens, *The Ghost Story from the Middle Ages to the Twentieth Century: A Ghostly Genre*, Four Courts Press, Dublin, 2010

William Charles Crocker, *Far from Humdrum: A Lawyer's Life*, Hutchinson, London, 1967

Catherine Crowe, *The Night Side of Nature or, Ghosts and Ghost Seers*, G. Routledge, London, 1852

Owen Davies, *The Haunted: A Social History of Ghosts*, Palgrave Macmillan, London, 2007

Anne de Courcy, *The Fishing Fleet: Husband-Hunting in the Raj*, Weidenfeld and Nicolson, London, 2012

Clive Dewey, *Anglo-Indian Attitudes: The Mind of the Indian Civil Service*, Hambledon Continuum, London, 1993

Eric J. Dingwall and Trevor H. Hall, *Four Modern Ghosts*, Gerald Duckworth & Co. Ltd, London, 1958

Arthur Conan Doyle, *The History of Spiritualism 1859–1930*, Cassell, London, 1926

Daphne du Maurier, *Rebecca*, Victor Gollancz Ltd, London, 1938

Daphne du Maurier, 'The House of Secrets' (1946), published in *The Rebecca Notebook and Other Memories*, Victor Gollancz, London, 1981

A. C. Edwards, *A History of Essex*, Phillimore and Co. Ltd, London, 1958

T. S. Eliot, *Four Quartets*, Faber & Faber, London, 1944

Daniel Farson, *The Hamlyn Book of Ghosts in Fact and Fiction*, Hamlyn, London 1978

V. R. Gaikwad, *The Anglo-Indians: A Study in the Problems and Progress Involved in Emotional and Cultural Integration*, Asia Publishing House, London, 1967

Juliet Gardiner, *The Thirties: An Intimate History*, Harper Press, London, 2010

Alan Gauld, *The Founders of Psychical Research*, Routledge & Kegan Paul, London, 1968

Rupert. T. Gould, *Enigmas: Another Book of Unexplained Facts*, Geoffrey Bles, London, 1946

Robert Graves and Alan Hodge, *The Long Week-End: A Social History of Great Britain 1918–1939*, Faber & Faber Ltd, London, 1940

Peter Haining, *Ghosts: The Illustrated History*, Sidgwick & Jackson Ltd, London, 1975

Trevor H. Hall, *New Light on Old Ghosts*, Gerald Duckworth & Co., London, 1965

Charles G. Harper, *Haunted Houses: Tales of the Supernatural, with Some Account of Hereditary Curses and Family Legends,* Chapman & Hall Ltd, London, 1907

Jenny Hazelgrove, *Spiritualism and British Society Between the Wars,* Manchester University Press, Manchester, 2000

Arthur J. Heighway (ed.), *Inky Way Annual Book 2,* World's Press News, London, 1948

Christina Hole, *Haunted England: A Survey of English Ghost-Lore,* B. T. Batsford Ltd, London, 1940

Chris Horrie, *Tabloid Nation: From the Birth of the Daily Mirror to the Death of the Tabloid,* Andre Deutsch Ltd, London, 2003

Catherine Horwood, *Keeping Up Appearances: Fashion and Class Between the Wars,* The History Press Ltd, Stroud, 2005

Frank E. Huggett, *Life Below Stairs: Domestic Servants in England from Victorian Times,* John Murray, London 1977

John H. Ingram, *The Haunted Homes and Family Traditions of Great Britain,* Gibbings and Company, London, 1901

Pat Jalland, *Death in the Victorian Family,* Oxford University Press, Oxford, 1996

Pat Jalland, *Death in War and Peace: A History of Loss and Grief in England 1914–1970,* Oxford University Press, Oxford, 2010

Henry James, 'The Turn of the Screw', *The Two Magics,* William Heinemann, London, 1898

M. R. James, *The Collected Ghost Stories of M.R. James,* Edward Arnold, London, 1942

Dominic Janes, *Visions of Queer Martyrdom from John Henry Newman to Derek Jarman,* University of Chicago Press, Chicago, 2015

Dominic Janes and Gary Waller, *Walsingham in Literature and Culture from the Middle Ages to Modernity,* Ashgate Publishing, Farnham, 2010

Alan Jenkins, *The Thirties,* William Heinemann, London, 1976

Anthony Jennings, *The Old Rectory: The Story of the English Parsonage,* Continuum, London, 2009

Allan Jobson, *A Suffolk Calendar,* Robert Hale Ltd, London, 1966

Anthea Jones, *A Thousand Years of the English Parish,* Windrush Press, Gloucestershire, 2000

D. F. Karaka, *I Go West,* Michael Joseph, London 1938

Shompa Lahiri, *Indians in Britain: Anglo–Indian Encounters, Race and Identity, 1880–1930*, Cassell, London, 2000

Christopher Lane, *The Age of Doubt: Tracing the Roots of Our Religious Uncertainty*, Yale University Press, London, 2011

June and Doris Langley Moore, *The Pleasure of Your Company: A Text-Book of Hospitality*, Gerald Howe Ltd, London, 1933

Andrew Lycett, *Conan Doyle: The Man Who Created Sherlock Holmes*, Weidenfeld & Nicolson, London, 2007

Theresa M. McBride, *The Domestic Revolution: the Modernisation of Household Service in England and France, 1820–1920*, Croom Helm, London, 1976

Joseph McCabe, *Spiritualism: A Popular History from 1847*, T. Fisher Unwin Ltd, London, 1920

William McElwee, *Britain's Locust Years, 1919–1940*, Faber & Faber, London, 1962

Charles Mackay, *Memoirs of Extraordinary Popular Delusions*, Richard Bentley, London, 1841

R. D. Macleod, *Impressions of an Indian Civil Servant*, H. F. and G. Witherby Ltd, London, 1938

Margaret MacMillan, *Women of the Raj*, Thames & Hudson, London, 1988

Hilary Mantel, *Giving up the Ghost: A Memoir*, Fourth Estate, London, 2003

F. M. Mayor, *The Rector's Daughter*, The Hogarth Press, London, 1924

P. G. Maxwell-Stuart, *Ghosts: A History of Phantoms, Ghouls, and Other Spirits of the Dead*, Tempus Publishing Ltd, Stroud, 2006

John Montgomery, *The Twenties: An Informal Social History*, Allen and Unwin, London, 1957

Maureen Moran, *Catholic Sensationalism and Victorian Literature*, Liverpool University Press, Liverpool, 2007

John Morley, *Death, Heaven and Victorians*, Studio Vista, London, 1971

Lisa Morton, *Calling the Spirits: A History of Seances*, Reaktion Books, London, 2020

Geoffrey K. Nelson, *Spiritualism and Society*, Routledge & Kegan Paul, London, 1969

Virginia Nicholson, *Millions Like Us: Women's Lives in War and Peace, 1939–1949*, Viking, London, 2011

Virginia Nicholson, *Singled Out: How Two Million Women Survived*

Without Men After the First World War, Oxford University Press, Oxford, 2008

Audrey Niffenegger, *Ghostly: A Collection of Ghost Stories,* Vintage Classics, London 2015

Elliott O'Donnell, *Byways of Ghost-land,* W. Rider, London, 1911

Elliott O'Donnell, *Haunted Britain,* Rider & Co., London, 1948

Janet Oppenheim, *The Other World: Spiritualism and Psychical Research in England, 1850–1914,* Cambridge University Press, Cambridge, 1985

George Orwell, *A Clergyman's Daughter,* Victor Gollancz, London, 1935

Alex Owen, *The Darkened Room: Women, Power and Spiritualism in Late Victorian England,* Virago Press, London, 1989

Susan Owens, *The Ghost: A Cultural History,* Tate Publishing, London, 2017

John T. Page (ed.), *Essex in the Days of Old,* William Andrews, London, 1892

Edward Parnell, *Ghostland: In Search of a Haunted Country,* William Collins, London 2019

Ronald Pearsall, *The Table-Rappers,* Michael Joseph, London 1972

J. B. Priestley, *English Journey,* William Heinemann, London, 1934

Martin Pugh, *Hurrah for the Blackshirts! Fascists and Fascism in Britain Between the Wars,* Pimlico, London, 2006

Martin Pugh, *We Danced All Night: A Social History of Britain Between the Wars,* The Bodley Head, London, 2008

J. Aelwyn Roberts, *Holy Ghostbuster: A Parson's Encounters with the Paranormal,* Robert Hale, London, 1990

Steve Roud, *The English Year: A Month-by-Month Guide to the Nation's Customs and Festivals from May Day to Mischief Night,* Penguin Books, London, 2006

John Salmon, *The Suffolk–Essex Border,* Boydell Press Ltd, Ipswich 1977

Pamela A. Sambrook, *The Country House Servant,* Sutton Publishing, Stroud, 1999

Esther H. Schor, *Bearing the Dead: The British Culture of Mourning from the Enlightenment to Victoria,* Princeton University Press, Princeton, 1994

L. C. B. Seaman, *Life in Britain Between the Wars,* B. T. Batsford Ltd, London, 1970

Brian Short (ed.), *The English Rural Community: Image and Analysis*, Cambridge University Press, Cambridge, 1992

Sacheverell Sitwell, *Poltergeists: An Introduction and Examination Followed by Chosen Instances*, Faber & Faber, London, 1940

Andrew Smith, *The Ghost Story, 1840–1920: A Cultural History*, Manchester University Press, Manchester, 2010

Mabel Seymour Smith, *The House of a Hundred and One Things*, Arthur H. Stockwell Ltd, London, 1931

William Oliver Stevens, *Unbidden Guests: A Book of Real Ghosts*, George Allen and Unwin, London, 1949

Roy Strong, *A Little History of the English Country Church*, Jonathan Cape, London, 2007

J. R. Sturge-Whiting, *The Mystery of Versailles: A Complete Solution*, Rider & Co., London, 1938

Roy Tricker, *Anglicans on High: The Anglo-Catholic Revival in Suffolk and the Surrounding Area*, Fitzwalter Press and Taverner Publications, Norfolk, 2014

E. S. Turner, *What the Butler Saw: Two Hundred and Fifty Years of the Servant Problem*, Michael Joseph, London, 1962

James Turner, *Sometimes into England: A Second Volume of Autobiography*, Cassell, London, 1970

Carol Twinch, *Tithe War 1918–1939: The Countryside in Revolt*, Media Associates, Norwich, 2001

Peter Underwood, *No Common Task: The Autobiography of a Ghost-hunter*, George G. Harrap and Co., London, 1983

Peter Underwood, *The Ghost Hunters: Who They Are and What They Do*, Robert Hale Ltd, London, 1985

Rozina Visram, *Asians in Britain: 400 Years of History*, Pluto Press, London, 2002

Doreen Wallace, *So Long to Learn*, Collins, London, 1936

C. Henry Warren, *Essex*, C. Robert Hale, London, 1950

Jennifer Westwood and Jacqueline Simpson, *The Penguin Book of Ghosts*, Penguin Books, London, 2008

Joachim Whaley (ed.), *Mirrors of Mortality: Studies in the Social History of Death*, Europa, London, 1981

Norman Wymer, *Village Life*, George G. Harrap & Co Ltd, London, 1951

Francis Young, *A History of Anglican Exorcism: Deliverance and Demonology in Church Ritual*, I. B. Tauris, London, 2018

Fiction and Drama Inspired by Borley:

Jay Anson, *The Amityville Horror: A True Story*, Prentice Hall, New Jersey, 1977

Pat Boyette, 'The Devil's in Borley', *Sorcery*, 1974

Terrance Dicks, *The Borley Rectory Incident*, Piccadilly Press, London, 1998

Trevor H. Hall, *The Last Case of Sherlock Holmes: Ivy Johnson Bull of Borley*, Paulette Greene, New York, 1986

Frank Harvey, *The Poltergeist: A Play in Three Acts,* H. F. W. Deane & Sons Ltd, London, 1947

Shirley Jackson, *The Haunting of Hill House,* Viking Press, New York, 1959

Stephen King, *The Shining,* Doubleday & Company Inc., New York, 1977

Eric Liberge, *Tonnere Rampant*, Soleil Productions, 2002

Richard Matheson, *Hell House,* Viking Press, New York, 1971

Gladys Mitchell, *When Last I Died,* Michael Joseph, London, 1941

Upton Sinclair, *Most Haunted House,* unpublished screenplay

Neil Spring, *The Ghost Hunters,* Quercus, London, 2013

James Turner, *My Life with Borley Rectory*, The Bodley Head, London, 1950

PICTURE CREDITS

INDEX